Tragedy, Philosophy, and Political
Education in Plato's Laws

Tragedy, Philosophy, and Political Education in Plato's *Laws*

RYAN K. BALOT

OXFORD
UNIVERSITY PRESS

OXFORD
UNIVERSITY PRESS

Oxford University Press is a department of the University of Oxford. It furthers
the University's objective of excellence in research, scholarship, and education
by publishing worldwide. Oxford is a registered trade mark of Oxford University
Press in the UK and certain other countries.

Published in the United States of America by Oxford University Press
198 Madison Avenue, New York, NY 10016, United States of America.

Library of Congress Cataloging-in-Publication Data
Names: Balot, Ryan K. (Ryan Krieger), 1969– author.
Title: Tragedy, philosophy, and political education in Plato's laws / Ryan K. Balot.
Description: New York, NY : Oxford University Press, [2024] |
Includes bibliographical references and index. |
Identifiers: LCCN 2023056713 (print) | LCCN 2023056714 (ebook) |
ISBN 9780197647226 (hardback) | ISBN 9780197647240 (epub) |
ISBN 9780197647257 | ISBN 9780197647233
Subjects: LCSH: Plato. Laws. | Political science—Philosophy. |
Political science—Study and teaching. | Plato—Political and social views.
Classification: LCC JC71.P264 B35 2024 (print) | LCC JC71.P264 (ebook) |
DDC 321/.07—dc23/eng/20240110
LC record available at https://lccn.loc.gov/2023056713
LC ebook record available at https://lccn.loc.gov/2023056714

DOI: 10.1093/oso/9780197647226.001.0001

Printed by Integrated Books International, United States of America

For my mother, Elizabeth K. Miranne

Contents

Preface and Acknowledgments

THIS BOOK SEEKS to advance a novel interpretation of Plato's *Laws*, by exploring the dialogue's presentation of the limits and possibilities of politics. Through a close, sequential investigation of the dialogue's drama and arguments, I argue that Plato's final work presents a tragic vision of politics, in a sense that I will explain. In making this argument, I aim to unsettle the new consensus according to which the dialogue describes, and even aims to bring about, a "community of the virtuous" (to use Bobonich's phrase). My own interpretive approach—which builds on, but also departs from, that of Strauss—is described in the Introduction.

I have in general used the Budé text of Diès and des Places 1951–1956, although in certain cases I follow the readings of Burnet (1907, repr. 2011) and the manuscripts. In doing so, I have found the commentaries of England and Schöpsdau instructive. Unless otherwise indicated, all translations are my own, usually informed by and adapted from published translations, including above all Pangle 1980 (whose clarity and proximity to the Greek text I admire), as well as Diès and des Places 1951–1956, Griffith 2016, and Bury 1967–1968. My goal has been nothing more than to provide an intelligible, reasonably literal, and serviceable translation in each case.

I have worked on Plato's *Laws* for a long time and have incurred many debts, above all to the successive cohorts of graduate students at the University of Toronto who have taken my seminars on the dialogue. Among those who were once graduate students and are now academic colleagues, I would thank in particular Larissa Atkison, Rob Ballingall, Kiran Banerjee, Zak Black, Nate Gilmore, Andrew Gross, Daniel Schillinger, Ella Street, Zhichao Tong, and Dorina Verli. My colleagues at Toronto have been supportive and challenging. For their comments on particular chapters, and for their instructive advice, I would single out Ronnie Beiner and Clifford Orwin. Many other colleagues have also been stimulating conversational partners and generous friends: Rebecca Kingston, Kanta Murali, Melissa Williams, Randall Hansen, Curie Virag, Ed Andrew, Joe Carens, Andy Sabl, and Steven Bernstein. I would also like to thank the Department's leaders, who have invariably supported my research: Rob Vipond, David Cameron, Louis Pauly, and Antoinette Handley. Farther afield, I am grateful to colleagues in ancient philosophy at the University of Bergen, especially Hallvard Fossheim, for their hospitality and warm reception of my ideas over a number of years. Among colleagues working on ancient Greek political thought in particular, I have benefited from the ideas, challenges, and advice of Arlene Saxonhouse, Brad Inwood, Stephen Salkever, Gene Garver, Thornton Lockwood, Josh Ober, Gerald Mara, Hayden Ausland, Olof Pettersson, Matthew Landauer, Sara Monoson, Victoria Wohl, Kurt Raaflaub, and Jill Frank, as well as colleagues who have participated over the years in the colloquium of Midwestern Greek Historians and Political Theorists. At an earlier stage of my career, I was taught and mentored by John Cooper, whose example remains inspirational. Despite my disagreements with them, I want to express my respect for the writings of Chris Bobonich, Malcolm Schofield, and André Laks, pioneers in the study of the *Laws*, all of whom have shown me kindness at different times; I regret that I have been able to engage with Laks 2022 only sparingly. My agent, Jill Marsal, has been an unwavering source of generosity and kindness. My editor at OUP, Stefan Vranka, has believed in the project from the beginning and offered his sound judgment throughout. At a late stage of the project, my student Max Morris provided invaluable research assistance. I also benefited from the careful copyediting of Ginny Faber. Finally, I am grateful to my family, above all, to Laura.

I

Introduction: Interpreting *Plato's* Laws

THIS BOOK OFFERS a new reading of Plato's last and longest dialogue, the *Laws*.[1] Widely regarded as Plato's most political text, the *Laws* dramatizes a conversation about the legislative scheme appropriate for the colonial foundation of "Magnesia."[2] In the course of this conversation, an itinerant philosopher known as the Athenian Stranger digs deeply into ethics and politics in the company of two elderly, nonphilosophical Dorians, Kleinias of Knossos and Megillus of Sparta. The three speakers consider the laws, customs, and rituals that will enable Magnesia's citizens to flourish. In observing this conversation, readers are invited to wonder about the possibility of establishing a healthy society among ordinary citizens, who are often overpowered by their passions and prove incapable of rational self-governance. The dialogue prompts us to inquire into the constraints, difficulties, and stubborn obstacles that may beset any idealistic projects of legislation or education.

From the beginning, readers will perceive that the elderly Dorians' political views are highly traditional, even procrustean. Upon examination, those views also emerge as manifestly incoherent and self-destructive. Recent studies have tended to focus on the Athenian's efforts to educate his interlocutors. Most scholars argue, in fact, that the *Laws* reveals Plato's newfound optimism

---

1. Fortunately, it is no longer necessary to answer the charges that the dialogue lacks authenticity or that Plato left it largely unfinished, to be completed by Philip of Opus. On the history of such readings, see Lisi 2001b: 11–13.

2. On the conventional name "Magnesia," derived from the name of its inhabitants, see e.g., 848d, 860e, 919d, 946b, and 969a, with Morrow 1960: 30–31; Schöpsdau 2011: 247; and Lewis 2010: 20n.5, who provide additional references and a fuller discussion.

Tragedy, Philosophy, and Political Education in Plato's Laws. Ryan K. Balot, Oxford University Press.
© Ryan K. Balot 2024. DOI: 10.1093/oso/9780197647226.003.0001

about the capacity of ordinary citizens to establish a virtuous polis.[3] At the heart of this approach is the view that the Athenian both appeals to and cultivates the rationality of ordinary citizens. Whereas Plato's *Republic* relegated nonphilosophers to a dreary, unenlightened "Cave," the *Laws* shows that ordinary people can achieve impressive ethical growth through education. Popular enlightenment leads citizens to flourish. In a landmark study, Bobonich (2002), building on earlier work (Bobonich 1991, 1996), argues that Magnesia is "a community of the virtuous" focused on the development of character and intellect. In his preludes, the lawgiver persuades the citizens rationally of the truth about the world and themselves: citizens are to "receive a true and reasoned account of what is good for human beings."[4] The utopian city thereby realizes what may be called "Platonic civic republicanism" of a highly demanding character.

In a further development of this approach, Schofield (2003, 2006) has argued that Magnesia's citizens are entitled to rational justification or persuasion because they have the potential for "rational freedom."[5] He discerns in the Athenian's persuasive preludes an approximation to the "Habermasian ideal" of deliberative rationality.[6] The "theory of legislative 'preludes' . . . presupposes a notion of fully rational freedom which would support the legitimacy of the consent the dialogue envisages."[7] Those who cannot rationally control their appetites "have no claim on the respect for other persons as minds which underlies the Platonic idea of rational freedom."[8] Likewise, Annas (2017)

---

3. Annas 2017; Bobonich 1991, 1996, 2002, 2010; Frede 2010; Gerson 2003; Irwin 2010; Mayhew 2008, 2010; Prauscello 2014; Sauvé-Meyer 2015; Schofield 2003, 2006, 2010, 2012, 2016; Scolnicov and Brisson 2003. In a different tradition, a different sort of optimism comes into view: Pradeau 1998 and Brisson 2019, both of which emphasize "order"; cf. also Brisson 2020.

4. Bobonich 2002: 97–119, at 104.

5. Schofield 2006: 87.

6. Schofield 2006: 56–57, 83–88. The preludes are "the most interesting . . . of all the ideas in the *Laws*": Schofield 2006: 84.

7. Schofield 2006: 83–84. Schofield 2006: 86–87 gives the preludes a Rawlsian twist: "Citizens are entitled to the opportunity to be persuaded" and "they *will* consent if they are reasonable" (86, emphasis original). For another treatment that emphasizes liberal notions such as consent, legitimacy, and autonomy, see Cohen 1993; for a helpful critique of the simplistic application of the notion of "consent," see Klosko 2006: 244–246; cf. 251 on "autonomy"; cf. Kraut 2010: 65–66 and Lane 2011.

8. Schofield 2006: 87. It is anachronistic to describe even the text's most idealistic moments by means of these Kantian, Habermasian, and Rawlsian categories. Such frameworks are explicitly based on Kantian ideals of autonomy, self-legislation, legitimacy, rationality, and consent. These concepts serve to obscure rather than to illuminate Plato's *Laws*. On the Kantian

maintains that the *Laws* reveals that law itself has a sufficiently rational character to cultivate virtue in ordinary citizens, by reorienting their priorities and establishing rational order in their souls.

By contrast with these readings, I argue that Plato's dialogue has important insights to offer, not only about education and reform, but also about the inevitable constraints on progress. Plato is a "realist" as well as an "idealist."[9] While the Athenian Stranger aspires to cultivate virtue in ordinary citizens, the dialogue emphasizes the entrenched obstacles to and constraints on his ambition. Like Kleinias in the dialogue itself, the future Magnesians are understood to be susceptible to overpowering anger, selfishness, greed, and erotic desire. They cannot rule themselves rationally. They are often tempted to disobey the law. They do not straightforwardly prioritize the common good over their own private interests. The Athenian's "realism" consists in his attention to these features of human nature, which powerfully counteract his own educational ambitions.

The underlying question is how to construct a polis that takes a clear-eyed view of the recalcitrance of the human passions. The Athenian responds with a mixture of constraint and religious ideology. Although his aspiration is that individual Magnesians should regulate themselves, the Athenian establishes a strict, punitive legal code. Education and daily life are rigidly controlled by law. Prizes of merit are awarded to those who best surveil their fellow citizens, inform on lawbreakers, and duly punish outlaws. The Athenian obviously anticipates that citizens will be too overwhelmed by their passions to make significant progress in virtue. In order to address these difficulties, instead of encouraging citizens to think clearly for themselves, the Athenian devises a compulsory civil religion. Magnesia's religion is designed to foster the belief that justice leads to happiness—a belief that citizens will not accept

foundations of Rawlsian and Habermasian ideals, see Salkever 2002. On the anachronism, see Brisson 2005: 116–19; for further criticism, see Lane 2011. More important than anachronism, though, is this approach's failure to take the *Laws* seriously on its own terms. Is Plato's *Laws* worthy of our attention only insofar as it anticipates the Kantian foundations of certain contemporary political theories?

9. For an illuminating discussion of the contemporary prospects of realist political theory, see Sagar and Sabl 2018. Geuss 2005 and 2008 outline political realism in ways that connect with my reading of the *Laws*; see especially, Geuss 2008: 2–3 for a pessimistic evaluation of most human beings' capacity to rule themselves rationally and 2008: 11 for a realist's view of religious belief, which is relevant to the interpretation of the *Laws*; see also Schlosser 2023 for an illuminating account of the different realisms that readers have discerned in Thucydides' *History*. Both Geuss and Schlosser emphasize the significance of "tragedy" for a more authentic grasp of politics. For connections between realist political theory and "realism" in International Relations theory, see Tong 2020. On Platonic realism, see especially L.S. Pangle 2014.

otherwise. In support of the civil religion, the Athenian establishes execution as the punishment for atheists. His punitive measures reveal that the standard approach is one-sided, because it pays inadequate attention to the dialogue's emphasis on inner conflict, the passions, and irrationality.

In doing justice to these "realist" elements of the dialogue, I build on a less familiar framework established by Strauss (1975) and Pangle (1980).[10] These "realist" readers begin with the premise that human nature is essentially irrational. As a result, politics itself, at its best, will make decent lives of moderation available for citizens, mostly through cultivating obedience to law and holding out the threat of punishment. Realists do not expect any significant degree of rational education or consent from citizens—much less a transformation of human nature itself.[11] There are strict natural limits on philosophy's capacity to guide political life to a condition of rational order or self-rule. Hence, realists do not shy away from Magnesia's civil religion, its constraints on individualism, or its regimented daily life (cf. Popper 2011).

Although I build on their work, my principal difference with these realists is their lack of attention to the Athenian's effort to promote "human flourishing" (*eudaimonia*). Despite the constraints imposed by human nature, the Athenian strives to foster *eudaimonia* through an education to virtue, to whatever extent possible. Realists view the Athenian Stranger's pursuit of *eudaimonia* as a "noble lie," an illusion designed to promote obedience based on fear. Despite his own sensitivity to human limitation, however, the Athenian Stranger is dedicated to the political project of cultivating virtue among Magnesia's citizens. By paying attention to the Athenian's ethical ambitions within the realist framework, my interpretation brings out the genuine conflicts and ambiguities characteristic of political life, as it is represented in Plato's *Laws*.

My contention is that, in juxtaposing realism with idealism, Plato cultivates in readers a compelling vision of politics as "the truest tragedy" (to use the Athenian's pregnant formulation). While political progress is possible,

---

10. The following description is based on my own reconstruction of the thrust of this approach, as found chiefly in Strauss 1975, 1987, 1988 and Thomas Pangle 1976, 1980; cf. also Balot 2014b, 2020a, and 2020b; Benardete 2000, Clark 2003, Ferrari 1997; Friedland 2020; Lewis 1998, 2009a, 2009b, 2010, 2012; Lutz 2012; L.S. Pangle 2014; Parens 1995; Recco and Sanday 2013; Zuckert 2009. This approach has become increasingly influential, despite the unusual "Straussophobia" that still grips many interpreters: on this subject, see Ferrari 1997; Minowitz 2009; Melzer 2014. For a first-rate interpretation of Strauss 1975 within the context of the "theological-political problem," see Lutz 2015.

11. Strauss 1964b: 22 provides an illuminating summary of these ideas.

the work emphasizes the ineradicable conflicts and tragic ambiguities of politics. The idea of "tragedy," in itself, requires substantial elaboration (see chapter 12). In brief, the tragedy of politics in Plato's *Laws* consists in the failure of Magnesia's citizens to become virtuous, independent, and rationally self-governing, despite the Athenian's wise legislation and remarkable ethical and political ambitions. Unlike many contemporary readers, the Athenian himself acknowledges the unavoidable frustrations of his own educational project. Whereas others have dismissed these difficulties in a rush to discern an optimistic message, our interpretation is richer—and more adequate to the text's apparent contradictions or loose ends—if we focus on the tension between the promises and limitations of human nature within a political framework.

The dialogue explores this tension by dramatizing the Athenian's thoughtful and diplomatic, though fraught and largely unsuccessful, effort to educate Kleinias. While the Athenian is a sophisticated philosopher, Kleinias and Megillus are conventional and passionate citizens, who have inherited their firm convictions directly from their respective cities. Hailing from paradigmatically "closed" societies, they are far from independent or enlightened thinkers. The question is how educable such citizens might be—a question that assumes special importance because, as I argue, Kleinias stands in for the future citizens of Magnesia. By attempting to educate Kleinias, the Athenian reveals the difficulties of educating ordinary citizens altogether. Over the course of their long discussion, it emerges that the Athenian's admirable project meets with hard limits. Human nature, as embodied dramatically in Kleinias, can fulfill few of its promises, and only defectively at that. Kleinias is exemplary of the ordinary citizen's inability to rule himself with reason.[12] As a result, neither Kleinias nor the ordinary Magnesians will significantly develop the ethical virtues. They will never understand and prize what is good (such as ethical virtue) for its own sake.[13] They will always require the support of a powerful, well-developed civil religion to grasp the happiness that may be found in living a just life. These limitations are central to the text's tragic vision of politics.

---

12. Contrast, for example, the interpretations of Flores 2022 and Folch 2015: 27–31.

13. Kraut 2010 offers a measured assessment of ordinary citizens' capacities, showing that in both *Republic* and *Laws* ordinary citizens' understanding and virtue are matters of degree, neither perfect nor non-existent.

The Athenian's Ambitions and Ambivalence

In line with this tragic outlook, the Athenian himself offers a highly ambivalent presentation of Magnesia. On the one hand, the regime of *nomos* (law) is characterized by constraint, surveillance, information-giving, punishment, and an all-pervasive civil religion—all measures of social control that indicate the Athenian's belief that Magnesian citizens cannot rule themselves successfully. The entire society is predicated on the Athenian's belief that its citizens will not internalize norms and cultural ideals without constant supervision or surveillance. If given the power to do so, they will always trample the laws in order to satisfy their desires.

Consider just a few of the practical measures proposed by the Athenian. The Athenian devises a compulsory civil religion, establishing execution as the punishment for atheists.[14] Socratic philosophical inquiry is prohibited, except within a tiny elite. Education and daily life are rigidly controlled by law. Travel abroad is rarely allowed and closely regulated; foreign currency must be forfeited to public officials. The penal code is dyed in blood. Although they vote in elections and serve on juries, citizens do not make major decisions on questions of public policy. The law-code (which Magnesians have adopted wholesale from a philosophical legislator) is almost entirely unchangeable.[15] Plato's Magnesia is, in Popper's language, the "closed society" par excellence.

On the other hand, the Athenian aspires to elevate Magnesia by imitating the example of Callipolis, the highest and best regime imagined in Plato's *Republic* (739e).[16] Noticeably, in founding Magnesia, he recalls Socrates' "three waves": the equality of men and women in the guardian class, the abolition of the nuclear family for guardians (in other words: community of property and family), and philosophical rule of the city. In Magnesia, the Athenian cultivates a rough equality between men and women, requiring that women serve in the military, participate politically, and share in a common life with men (805d).[17] He also develops a private property regime that hews as closely as possible to Callipolis' own communism of family and property: for

---

14. To say the least, this measure goes well beyond anything found in the classical Greek city: see Brunt 1993: 252–53.

15. On legislative change and fixity in the dialogue, see Balot 2020a.

16. Brisson 2005: 99 correctly compares the works based on the "three waves." I agree with Brisson 2005, Kraut 2010, and Kahn 2004, against Bobonich 2002, that the political theory of the *Laws* is not different in essentials from that of Plato's *Republic*.

17. Brisson 2005: 99–100 offers helpful qualifications.

example, each shareholder will consider his plot to belong in common to the city (740a); the plot will be inalienable (741b–c); and children are turned over to the city at dawn each day to be educated (808d). Finally, although the idea of philosophical rulers is explicitly suppressed when the regime of law is founded (711e–712a, 713d–e), it is reinstated when the Nocturnal Council is established. The Athenian's imitation of Callipolis' three waves makes it impossible to view his project as lacking in ambition, however limited the human nature that he confronts as a lawgiver.

More generally, the Athenian praises Magnesia's regime of *nomos* for its superiority to the chaotic, dangerous world of war that had always defined human history. Magnesia is secure, moderate, and decent—attributes that could hardly be ascribed to the savage and self-destructive regimes sketched in Book 3. As a Socratically educated realist, the Athenian uncovers a variety of creative strategies, and indeed "workarounds," for developing civic virtue among the Magnesians. The Magnesians' virtues embody, admittedly, a diminished shadow of fully realized virtue, but they are worth possessing, nonetheless. They lead to a marked improvement upon the lives these citizens might otherwise have lived. An awareness of these different scales of measurement helps us to locate the Athenian's political project and to assess it more accurately.

To be more specific, the Athenian emphasizes that the Magnesians make ethical progress through their habitual practices of citizenship—above all, through participating in elections and serving on juries. To the extent that the Athenian recognized the Magnesians' potential to make ethical progress, he saw that such progress comes through developing their prudence in the choice of magistrates, discussing questions of law and criminality with other citizens, and rendering judgment in courts, chiefly in local jurisdictions. In these ways, I argue, the Athenian cultivated the Magnesians' spirit (*thumos*)—a concept he borrowed from Socrates' tripartition of the soul in Plato's *Republic*.[18] He also cultivated the citizens' desire (*epithumia*), the lowest element of the tripartite soul, by establishing particular property arrangements, and by repeatedly emphasizing the restriction of desire. The citizens therefore tend to behave moderately. Notably, however, the Athenian restricted the philosophical education of reason (the highest element of the tripartite soul) to a narrow elite, in the belief that ordinary citizens were not adequate to the

---

18. A number of scholars find it essential to focus on "Plato's conception of the structure of the soul in the *Laws*" (Sassi 2008: 128): see, for example, the essays in Bobonich 2010, with the apt critique of Brisson 2011 and my discussion in Chapter 2n.13.

tasks of philosophical rationality. As a result, although the Athenian believed that progress in virtue was possible in Magnesia, he also showed that the ordinary citizens' ethical achievements, however worthwhile, were not meant to be highly impressive.

The mainstream, liberal-idealist account tends, therefore, to mischaracterize the Athenian's ambitions, by arguing that his goal is offer citizens a quasi-philosophical education. Trying to assimilate Magnesia's ordinary citizens to philosophical virtue, however, would amount to aiming too high, in ways that are unrealistic and perhaps even self-destructive.[19] The Athenian himself is far too sensitively attuned to the difficulties involved in his project to make that mistake. The scholarly effort to interpret this text along those lines has, however, been less moderate. An overemphasis on Magnesia as a "community of the virtuous" has had the disadvantage not only of creating an inaccurate impression of the Athenian's ambitions, but also of obscuring the goods realized by the activities of a peaceful political life in this hypothetical regime. It is critical to weigh the Athenian's ambitions appropriately, by acknowledging that Magnesia is superior to ordinary cities even if it falls far short of an ideal regime.

Scholarly Approaches and Methods

My substantive differences from the mainstream interpretation are also reflected in three significant differences of approach. First, I begin from the premise that the dialogue must be read as a unified whole, whatever its apparent conflicts and ambiguities. Conflict and ambiguity are central to the work's meaning. It is essential to do justice both to the text's aspirational features and to its emphasis on conflict, limitation, and frustration.

Because of its preoccupation with political optimism, by contrast, the mainstream view takes a different perspective on the dialogue's less appealing elements. How, one may reasonably wonder, do liberal-idealistic scholars integrate into their optimistic framework the Athenian's punitive, highly restrictive, and even manipulative measures of social control? How to address the city's compulsory civic religion, where execution is the punishment for atheists?[20] Or the prohibition on Socratic philosophical inquiry, except

---

19. Ballingall 2017.

20. On this provision, see Brunt 1993: 252–53.

within a tiny elite? Or the citizens' lack of decision-making power, however often they may vote in elections or serve on juries? Or the barriers to and strict regulations concerning travel abroad?[21]

On the basis of such concerns, liberal and idealistic readers should be appalled by Plato's *Laws*. Their most honest, intransigent representatives have reacted with hostility. Most famously in our time, Karl Popper condemned the dialogue's startling depiction of the "closed society." Popper's Plato was a "totalitarian party-politician," an anti-individualist, anti-humanitarian, and anti-Christian thinker.[22] Resistant to change and under the spell of his eternal Forms, Plato put his faith in authoritarian philosophical demigods. He subordinated the individual to the state's collectivist aims. Popper was keenly hostile to Plato as a "Utopian engineer," invested in a political project of "uncompromising radicalism," "dreaming of an apocalyptic revolution which would radically transfigure the entire social world."[23] No doubt hyperbolic, this critique is understandable for a reader who interprets Plato's *Republic* and *Laws* as visionary blueprints for political action, a là Marx's *Communist Manifesto*. How could a liberal or progressive possibly tolerate the repressiveness of Magnesia—the civil religion, the execution of atheists, the immutable legal code, the sacrifice of individual freedom, the constant surveillance and threat of punishment, and the power of the Nocturnal Council?[24]

Unaccountably, certain readers have ignored or simply dismissed the work's "unappealing" elements, such as its pervasive religious ideology, its unforgiving provisions for surveillance and punishment, and its suppression of individual freedom—as though it were necessary, and possible, to insulate Plato from his anti-liberal "lapses."[25] As Annas writes, for example, "Plato could not foresee the dangers of vigilantism"; he had a "blind spot here about what is lost when an individual is made the object of social pressure,

---

21. One further and considerable difficulty, for all accounts of the dialogue that focus on the citizen body, is that the leisure time available to citizens depends heavily on the existence of slave labor: Bobonich 2002: 390; Kahn 2004: 344–45; on slavery in the dialogue in general, see Morrow 1939.

22. Popper 2011: 162, 95–100.

23. Popper 2011: 153–54. Stalley 1983: 179–82 offers a helpful account of Popper's critique; Stalley argues that "Plato is an enemy of the open society, and a reading of the *Laws* may even strengthen Popper's case" (180).

24. Cf. Berlin 1990: 177 on de Maistre, fascism, and Plato's Nocturnal Council.

25. Bobonich 1991, 1996, 2002; Cohen 1993; Morrow 1960; Schofield 2003, 2006; Stalley 1983; Annas 2017.

including—and perhaps especially—ethical pressure."[26] I contend, by contrast, that Plato's so-called blind spots are keys to a more adequate interpretation of the dialogue as a whole.

The clearest example of the potential for "schizophrenia" in the liberal and idealist view is the proposal that the *Laws* involves two entirely different projects: the first, a subordinate and realist one, is intended as a "blueprint" with "general applicability," which is "realisable in communities consisting mostly of unregenerate humanity"; the other project, an idealist one, is primary and consists of "realising a community of the virtuous."[27] My view, by contrast, is that the work must be read as a unity: scholars are not justified in excising central elements in order to conjure up a sanguine interpretation that suits our own sensibilities. Readers can hardly do justice to the *Laws* as a philosophical text if they cordon off key sections or ideas on the grounds that they represent "darkness."[28] A sounder (and highly traditional) interpretive principle is to seek a coherent interpretation of the whole, to make all sections visible—even "the dark."[29]

Second, in displaying a philosophical legislator in conversation with nonphilosophers, the text draws attention to the interplay of characterization, action, and argument. Whereas mainstream scholars tend to view the dialogue in exclusively logical, argumentative terms, I interpret it as a complex literary and dramatic creation.[30] In order to understand the Athenian's focus on the passions, it is essential to grapple with the dialogue's presentation of character and dramatic action, as well as to explore its nondeductive forms of reasoning, e.g., allegory, analogy, symbol, and allusion.[31] Along the same

26. Quotations from Annas 2017: 103–4.

27. Schofield 2010: 27–28.

28. I am alluding to Richard Rorty's use of the phrase "the dark"—the universe of anti-liberal ideas and practices, which, as Rorty explained, Rawlsian liberals should consign to the dustbin: see Mara 2008: 198 for this idea and for discussion.

29. To its credit, Schofield 2010 grapples with the relation of idealism to realism. Ultimately, however, Schofield's interpretation yields simply another way of cordoning off the dialogue's realist elements. As I argue, by contrast, the two separate projects identified by Schofield are actually two textual "moments" that must be read together and seen as commenting on one another. The text is a unified, if paradoxical, whole.

30. I take the mainstream to be represented by the following, a nonexhaustive list: Bobonich 2002; Cleary 2001; Frede 2010; Gerson 2003; Irwin 2010; Klosko 2006, 2008; Landauer 2022; Lane 2011; Lisi 1998, 2001b; Mayhew 2008, 2010; Menn 1995; essays in Bobonich 2010; Sauvé Meyer 2015. Overlapping with my own approach is Bartels 2017, despite our significant substantive differences.

31. Kahn 2004; Brisson 2005; Pangle 1976; Halper 2003; Strauss 1975; Zuckert 2009.

lines, it is also essential to distinguish between Plato, the author, who does not appear in the dialogue; and his characters, such as the Athenian Stranger, who make different arguments and speak to different audiences within and outside the dialogue.[32] Plato's *Laws* is not a treatise. It presents a philosopher creating a system of public education for a healthy regime, among individuals who cannot rule themselves with reason.[33]

Because of my focus on character, action, and drama, I read the dialogue sequentially, instead of cherry-picking ideas that seem to us to form self-sufficient arguments.[34] By observing the Athenian's own way of unfolding the argument, we become truer than ever to his own presentation of substantial ideas in their particular contexts. Less captivated by our standards of organization or significance, we become freer to dedicate ourselves to the Athenian's own view of what makes sense, why, and when. Only by allowing the dialogue to unfold organically will we arrive at a satisfying interpretation—one that does justice to the dialogue as an artistic and philosophical whole.

Third, building on the "realist" interpretive tradition, I hold that the Athenian typically speaks to readers and his dramatic interlocutors in different ways, creating multiple layers of interpretation. The Athenian offers his interlocutors myths, rhetoric, and poetry in order to educate them for civic purposes alone. By contrast, he uses a variety of literary strategies to indicate his underlying purposes to readers: philosophical allusion, irony, paradox, and linguistic juxtaposition and variation. The dialogue is designed to illustrate, for readers, how a philosophical legislator speaks to and constructs

---

32. Contrast scholars who frequently assert that "Plato argues X or Y": Bobonich 2002, and essays in 2010; essays in Scolnicov and Brisson 2003; Stalley 1983, and many others. Scholars still speak of the Athenian—or even Kleinias—as Plato's "mouthpiece": cf. Laks 2000: 291 and Laks 2022. This problem has also found its way into literary interpretations of the dialogue, e.g., Folch 2015).

33. Along the same lines, see the introductory remarks of Catherine Zuckert 2013, with an apt critique of Saunders 1991.

34. By contrast with, e.g., Annas 2017; Bobonich 2002, 2010; Hobbs 2000; Kamtekar 1997; Mayhew 2008; Menn 1995; Saunders 2001; Sauvé Meyer 2015; Schofield 1999; Scolnicov 2003; Scolnicov and Brisson 2003; Stalley 1983, 1994. Kahn 2004: 343–53 offers a useful critique of the lack of attention to literary or historical context in Bobonich (2002), which might be applied in general to those working within this framework. Perhaps surprisingly in light of its narrow view of what counts in Plato's *Laws*, Kahn 2004: 338 says that Bobonich 2002 "covers an extremely wide range of topics"; but, as Kahn himself goes on to show, he means not an extremely wide range of topics within the *Laws* itself, but rather a range of special topics in Platonic "moral psychology" as discussed in *Laws, Phaedo, Republic, Statesman, Timaeus, Philebus, Phaedrus,* and other dialogues. For readings that, in my view, overemphasize context, see Morrow 1960; Nightingale 1999b; and Atack 2020; a more supple attempt at historical contextualization is Laks 2013.

laws for ordinary, non-philosophical citizens.[35] Although a few mainstream figures have begun to see the merits of this approach,[36] most interpreters fail to recognize the importance of different levels of communication in the dialogue; they therefore misrepresent the Athenian Stranger as unproblematically working to embody his enlightened philosophical ideas in the political world, by instituting a regime of law and by offering the Magnesian citizens a quasi-philosophical education.[37]

What is at stake is the place of philosophy both in Magnesia and in relation to politics altogether. As we discuss in chapter 11, the differences of approach lead, most importantly, to contrasting interpretations of the Nocturnal Council. Nowadays, most scholars hold that the *Laws* presents a "mixed regime" of law presided over (as we eventually learn) by a tiny elite of philosophers, in a body known as the "Nocturnal Council."[38] Mainstream scholarship domesticates this philosophical council by presenting it as a body of jurists who provide informal guidance to the city's judges and magistrates.[39] Implicit in this view, moreover, is the idea that Magnesia represents an ideal

---

35. This idea is at the heart of Strauss 1975, Pangle 1980, and others in this tradition: cf. the clear statement at Clark 2003: 2–3, who argues that Plato communicates different lessons to different readerships by exploiting the ambiguities of the art of medicine. The underlying idea is that Plato, the author, both conveys a rational discourse and illustrates its limits in political life.

36. For example: Schofield 2003; Rowe 2007, 2010. Schofield 2003: 3n5 understates its reliance on Strauss, to be compared with the dismissal of Strauss at Schofield 1978: 10. With Schofield 2003, compare, for example, Strauss 1975: e.g., 1–3, on the Dorian characterization of the interlocutors and on the setting in Crete; 27 (for example; cf. also 31) on the "sub-Socratic character of the conversations that take place in the *Laws*," and throughout for the theme of the work's religious ideology, which is also emphasized throughout by Schofield 2006. A reader of Strauss 1975 and Pangle 1980 will already be acquainted with much that is to be found in Schofield's interpretation. Even more strikingly, Rowe 2010, without any acknowledgment of Strauss, "rediscovers" the esoteric practice of interpretation, a Straussian hallmark; explores communication on different levels (cf. Strauss 1975: 5, 7, 17, 22–23, 27, 31, 44, 75, and throughout); and discusses the Athenian's own role in legislating, as opposed to the god's (cf. Strauss 1975: 58). Meilaender 2008 has similarly illustrated the surprising similarities of Rowe 2007 to Straussian interpretations of Plato.

37. Bobonich 1991, 1996, 2002; Morrow 1960; Klosko 2006, 2008; Schofield 2006, 2010; Wilburn 2013.

38. Schöpsdau 2011; Laks 2000, 2005; Morrow 1960; Samaras 2002; Piérart 1974.

39. Morrow 1960; Schöpsdau 2011; Laks 2000; Bobonich 2002; Schofield 2006; Annas 2017. To his credit, Bobonich (2002: 439–441) recognizes the problems for political equality created by the advanced knowledge and virtue of the Nocturnal Council, but, following Morrow 1960: 500–515, he manages to accommodate the Nocturnal Council to the rule of law, on the grounds that unaccountable power will lead inevitably to corruption (Bobonich 2002: 394). My discussion of the Nocturnal Council will illustrate the problems with this approach.

toward which philosophers and political agents should aspire; the text is even a blueprint for action.[40]

By contrast, my reading supports the interpretations of scholars from a previous generation, who found that the latter half of Book 12, with its description of the Nocturnal Council, represents a radical departure from the Athenian's law-based description of Magnesia. As I explain in chapter 11, this departure is intentional: the resurfacing of philosopher rulers in the dialogue's final exchanges is designed to offer a critique of the rule of law.[41] In those exchanges, the Athenian presents the Nocturnal Council in a dramatic way that is at odds with the regime defined by the rule of law.[42] At a minimum, the implication is that the regime of law needs to be rethought. For that reason, the dialogue ends aporetically; it resists closure. Hence, Magnesia does not represent a political ideal or a blueprint meant to be politically achievable. Instead, the text as a whole, with its internal conflicts, ambiguities, and persistent questions, is designed to provoke its readers to reflect deeply on the limitations of what is possible in political life.[43] Ultimately, the dialogue guides philosophical readers toward a tragic vision of politics—not for practical purposes, but purely for the sake of their own understanding.

---

40. Brisson 2020; Adomenas 2001: 31 ("a blueprint for a political project which would control its own conditions of possibility"); Rowe 2003: 96; Schofield 1999: 44; Annas 2017: 65 (an ideal sketch, though not blueprint); cf. Morrow 1960; Bobonich 2002; Schofield 2006, 2010; and many others. For the purposes of the present discussion, the distinction between ideal sketch and blueprint are insignificant.

41. "Resurfacing," because, at the foundation of Magnesia in Book 4, philosophical rule is suppressed in favor of the mixed regime of law. Notably, in fact, in the course of constructing Magnesia's law-code, the Athenian obscures philosophy itself, referring to it by name only twice (857d, 967b). Aptly Strauss 1975: 75 refers to Plato's own self-imposed law against the mention of philosophy in this text—"which he only rarely and, as it were, surreptitiously transgresses."

42. In making this point, I build on Cherniss 1953 and restore valuable older scholarship such as Barker 1918/2010. This point, above all, illustrates the continuity between the political philosophy of the *Laws* and that of the *Republic*. Compare the similar conclusions of Brisson 2019: 140–141; 2020: 403, 412. Differences between these dialogues result mostly, if not entirely, from their different purposes. The traditional view is that, having drawn up an excessively ambitious utopian ideal in Callipolis, Plato came in his old age to propose a more realistic, practicable ideal in Magnesia: see, for example, Klosko 2006 (e.g., 217: "The *Laws* is an old man's work"). On the history of such interpretations, see Lisi 1998, 2001b, 2004; Papadis 1998. For other understandings of this relationship, see Laks 1990, 2000; Schofield 1999; Bobonich 2002; Samaras 2002.

43. Cf. Waldron 1995.

Who Is the Athenian Stranger?

Since the Athenian Stranger is the dialogue's protagonist, and since his identity remains obscure throughout, it will be useful to offer preliminary guidance about his character and possible motivations. Who is he meant to be? Why does he decide to speak with these elderly Dorians in the first place? Why was he interested in, of all things, a new colonial foundation in Crete?

These questions become especially pressing when we consider this dialogue's many intertextual references to the *Republic*. However we understand Socrates' great utopian effort in that text, it is difficult to avoid the conclusion that Callipolis' philosophers have no political ambitions of their own. They would much prefer to spend their time philosophizing as far as possible from the Cave of real-world politics. They return to the Cave only because they are both persuaded and compelled to do so.[44] As Socrates emphasizes, moreover, genuine philosophers in non-ideal cities have utter disdain for politics, because of the injustice and madness of ordinary citizens. They keep away out of both fear and contempt (*Rep.* 496a–e). Socrates' emphasis, moreover, on self-cultivation—on the need to internalize the just regime in one's own soul—corresponds to precisely this apolitical, or even antipolitical stance. As for Socrates' city in speech, "it makes no difference whether it is or ever will be somewhere, for he [the philosopher] would take part in the practical affairs of that city and no other" (*Rep.* 592b, tr. Grube, rev. Reeve 1997).

Plato's *Laws* casts the Athenian Stranger in a different light. Within the dramatic framework of the *Laws*, the Athenian is not persuaded or compelled to speak with Kleinias and Megillus. He is under no constraint even to make himself known to the elderly Dorians; he begins as neither friend nor acquaintance of his interlocutors. Instead of speaking with Kleinias and Megillus, the Athenian could have chosen to develop his mathematical interests or to deepen his grasp of the stars and planets. He could have dedicated himself to writing or even to opening a philosophical school. He could simply have ignored Kleinias and Megillus at the outset and sought a more sophisticated set of philosophical interlocutors. True, his conversation is supposed to have taken place within one day,[45] but he represents himself as invested in the

---

44. For different interpretations of persuasion and compulsion in the *Republic*, see Strauss 1964a; Brown 2000.

45. Strauss 1975: 42: "Taking into account the *Laws* as a whole, we may observe that, since the day is very long, it is sufficient for elaborating a complete code of law; a complete code of law can be elaborated by a competent man in a single day of sufficient length."

political project of Magnesia—not as a participant, but as an adviser.[46] Who, then, is the Athenian Stranger? What motivates him to involve himself in this project?

In responding to such questions, scholars have tended to focus on the identity of the Athenian, proposing that he is Plato himself, or Socrates, or even Solon.[47] Better to hold that Plato has hidden the Athenian's identity intentionally.[48] Inquiring into the Athenian's identity may be the wrong question to ask. Instead, readers should focus on the Athenian's purposes, motivations, and attitudes toward the legislative project presented in the dialogue.[49]

A philosopher in his own right, the Athenian has not only acquired a deep knowledge of presocratic physical and cosmological theories, but also digested a great number of Platonic texts, including the *Republic, Apology, Symposium, Statesman, Philebus*, and others.[50] He is adept at using Socratic ideas in arguments of his own devising, as (for example) in his remarkable reformulation of the Socratic paradox in his account of criminal responsibility (860d–864c). He is an erudite student of the Greek poetic tradition—including Homer, Hesiod, Tyrtaeus, and Theognis (e.g., 629a–629e, 630a–c, 718e–719a, 904e). Like Socrates, he reworks poetic discourses for his own rhetorical and philosophical purposes. He has read Herodotus' *Histories* and Thucydides' *History* with care. He expresses intriguing, substantive views about both historians in his own thoughtfully crafted historiography in Book 3. He has also travelled widely in order to grasp "comparative politics." He has at least read about various foreign lands and spoken with their inhabitants.

---

46. Compare 753a (which also refers to persuasion and compulsion) with 968b, 969a, 969c–d, with Schöpsdau 2003: 371; 2011: 603.

47. Plato himself: Cicero (*de legibus* 1.15); Schofield 1999: 39; Morrow 1960: 75 ("We can properly substitute Plato for the Athenian Stranger on most occasions, if we remember that the real Plato, more than most authors, remains inscrutable"); Klosko 2006: 217. Socrates: Aristotle, *Politics* 1265a11; Strauss 1975: 1–2; Pangle 1980: 378–79; Solon: Schofield 2006: 3, cf. 75, says that the Athenian is "meant to remind us of the great legislator Solon"; cf. Samaras 2002. Zuckert 2009: 31–33, 58–62 provides a helpful account of the differences between the Athenian and the Platonic Socrates; for Zuckert 2009: 59–146, the Athenian is a philosopher whose Presocratic ideas are shown to be inadequate to his goals of political reform.

48. Zuckert 2009: 31–33 rightly argues that the Athenian is left "anonymous" for particular reasons—namely, that if he succeeds, he "will have replaced Zeus as the purported source of the laws" (32).

49. This is the approach taken, in different ways, by C. Zuckert 2009: 31–33; 2013: 183; and Morrow 1960: 74–76.

50. Strauss 1975 emphasizes this point, followed implicitly by Rowe 2010; cf. Lisi 2004; the interpretation offered by Zuckert 2009), by contrast, appears to rule out this salient point.

He has "encountered many drinking parties in many places" and has "studied all of them" (639d–e). He has investigated foreign politics and practices, on the basis of which he makes unerringly apt suggestions for Magnesia's legislative code. He is an accomplished philosopher (968b, 969a), as he reveals throughout the text, above all in the arguments of Books 9 and 10.

If the Athenian comments on the tragic qualities of this project, then he also communicates, at least to readers, his general attitudes toward political engagement as a whole. In another set of self-reflexive statements, which complement his ideas on the "truest tragedy," he says that he is investigating the character of different types of soul and different ways of life, so that "we will best convey our life through this voyage of existence" (803b1–2). He carries out this investigation despite his philosophical reserve or ambivalence: "The concerns of human beings are not worth taking very seriously, yet it is necessary to take them seriously. And this is unfortunate" (803b3–5). Despite his ambivalence, he says, he feels compelled, he finds it "necessary," to take human affairs [= politics] seriously. As he immediately indicates, though, he looks down on the human "puppet" from the vantage point of his wider theological contemplation (804b–c). On the other hand, he understands that "since we are here, if somehow we might do this [be serious about human affairs] in some fitting way, then perhaps it would be well-measured (*summetron*) for us" (803b5–7).

Where does this line of reasoning leave us? It shows, I would say, that the Athenian retains distance from politics even as he remains drawn to it for particular reasons of his own. Despite his aspiration to imitate the god, the Athenian recognizes that it is a proportionate and fitting task for him, as a human being, to care for other human beings. The Athenian is far from enthusiastically endorsing political engagement. Nevertheless, he persists in his legislative project—and, indeed, he shows great stamina, resilience, and courage in his effort to provide appropriate laws for Magnesia.

Can we describe the Athenian's motivations more fully and explicitly?[51] My suggestion is that, by engaging politically with the elderly Dorians, the Athenian is pursuing a certain eudaimonistic conception of his flourishing as

---

51. Roochnik (2013: 145) deserves credit for asking this question in the context of an interesting discussion of "serious play" in Book 7; he, too, considers the Athenian's statements to convey a sense of tragedy. Cf. also C. Zuckert 2013: 185, who says, correctly, that by dramatically illustrating his philosophers' concern with politics and legislation "Plato also shows that these rare individuals [philosophers] care about the lives of the less talented"; Clark 2003: 148 interestingly discusses philosophy and philanthropy, implicitly with a nod to the tragic qualities of this relationship.

a human being: that is, he hopes to embody the eudaimonistic principles that he strives to establish within Magnesia.[52] To be more specific, the Athenian believes that humanity's teleological fulfillment lies in the activities of the developed intellect and character. As a result, he can lead the best life of which he himself is capable by leading a rational, virtuous life. That life involves not only philosophical investigation of the world and humanity, but also care for other human beings in politics—whatever its inevitable disappointments. Philanthropic care serves as the natural expression of the virtues cultivated by the Athenian. His activity of philanthropic care contributes to his own flourishing as a human being. He is the rational eudaimonist that he calls upon Magnesia's citizens to be.

The Athenian's eudaimonism motivates him to develop his own virtues, beginning with courage. In the Athenian's own view, legislators who found new cities incur great risks in doing so. The enterprise itself requires courage. Early in Book 6, as he prepares to lay down the city's system of magistrates and office-holders, the Athenian worries about the ability of new citizens to select worthy candidates, since they are so unfamiliar with one another. Kleinias agrees that they are unlikely to do so. The Athenian responds that "they say that a contest doesn't allow for any excuses" (751d7). In other words: Kleinias and his colleagues have enthusiastically agreed to found a new colony; since the Athenian has undertaken to support them, he will not voluntarily leave his task unfinished (752a). When Kleinias compliments him for speaking well on this point, he responds: "Not only I have spoken well, at any rate, but I will also act in the best way I can" (752a6). Kleinias confidently agrees that they should carry out their deeds in accordance with their words (752a). The Platonic dialogues in general—and specifically, the *Laches*—emphasize that central to embodying courage adequately was living up in practice to one's own words or ideals. Socrates is typically portrayed as exceptional in this regard.[53]

During the dialogue, of course, the three old men often stress that they are simply exploring political and legislative ideas in conversation. They often find themselves, indeed, deferring their hypothetical legislation in order to

---

52. I offered a sketch of rational eudaimonism, with relevant literature, in Balot 2009b; its best known application to study of the *Laws* is Bobonich 2002. Kraut 2010 and Kahn 2004 provide helpful criticisms of Bobonich on ordinary *eudaimonia*; Irwin 2010: 101–7 offers a different perspective on eudaimonism, which he sets in the framework of natural law theory.

53. On Socrates' exceptionality in this respect, as portrayed in the *Laches*, see Balot 2014a: 129–48; on Socratic courage and "manliness" in general, see Hobbs 2000.

engage in wider reflections on humanity and the world.[54] At the same time, they present themselves, and experience themselves, as carrying out an important political task, one that requires an appropriate relation of *logos* to *ergon*. The Athenian emphasizes that in founding the city they are remarkably courageous and exceptionally willing to accept risk (*hôs andreiôs kai parakekinduneumenôs*, 752b). They are notably confident and fearless (*hôs eukolôs kai aphobôs*, 752b9) in at least one particular respect: they proceed without debilitating concerns about the new citizens' willingness to accept their ambitious legislative project. That concern—which arises repeatedly in Book 5—will not deter them.

The Athenian had already emphasized the need for courage at the very foundation of Magnesia. At the end of Book 3, Kleinias announced the project of establishing a colonial foundation (702c–d). When the Athenian and Megillus agree to join the project, the Athenian indicates that he considers law-giving and founding cities to be "truly (*ontôs*) the most perfect task of manly virtue (*teleôtaton pros aretên andrôn*)" (708d). You had thought that "manly virtue" prototypically comes to sight in war? No, the Athenian says: law-giving is its authentic field of application, for many reasons, including the potential disobedience or disunity of the new citizen body (708c–d).[55]

The city itself, of course, also cultivates traditional military courage (e.g., 763b-c, 814b: also among women, 824a, 830e–831a, 832c–d, etc.; cf. 791b–c, 815e–816a), as well as the "manly spirit" (731b–d) that will enable citizens to defend the law, help their fellow citizens, and prosecute criminals appropriately (e.g., 774b–c). The Athenian, however, lays stress on the novel, higher form of courage that characterizes the lawgiver—the political courage involved in legislating effectively, even when that project is likely to incur resistance, hostility, and laughter (781b–d, 790a). Kleinias comes to agree that laying down a coherent law-code is a "noble and serious pursuit

---

54. The Athenian's emphasis on the deferral or postponement of legislation: 737d, 768c, 768e with Laks 2000: 263–66; at 781d–e he has to "go way back" to propose appropriate legislation for women, which he can do because the three speakers are "enjoying leisure"; at 783b they still haven't completed the topic of education, cf. 788a; finally, at 796d the Athenian says that his account of the gymnastic art is complete; even at 796e he must still continue to discuss other parts of education.

55. Can we elaborate on the Athenian's opinion that legislation is the prototypical context in which courage is displayed? We will return to this question in later chapters, but let it suffice to say for now that the Athenian aspires to improve the human condition but wishes to avoid leading others astray, at the risk of committing injustice. He acts courageously upon his philanthropic ambition to help others, even though, like Socrates, he knows that he does not know the greatest things.

for real men" (769a, tr. Pangle 1980), a remark with which the Athenian agrees. It is difficult even to discuss such countercultural measures as the Athenian proposes, much less to effect them in practice (780c–d, 797a, 805b–c, 810d). The legislative enterprise often involves great perplexity, for example in considering how far to go in legislating for the details of everyday life within the home (788b–c, 810c). The Athenian's courage, as he strives to "run the risk" (*parakinduneuonta*) and "dare" (*tharrounta*) to legislate (810e), is perhaps summed up in his self-referential portrayal of the individual who speaks on the intractable, though all-important, subject of the city's erotic regulations:

> As things stand, it is likely that we need some daring human being, who honors frank speech in a special way and will say what he thinks best for the city and its citizens. He will order what is fitting and suitable for the whole regime, though being in the midst of corruption. He will speak in opposition to the greatest desires, with no human being to help him. All alone, he will follow reason alone (835c).

In his final words in the dialogue, the Athenian once again emphasizes the significance of the risk involved in the foundation (968e–969a).

The Athenian's persistent references to courage imply that he views his own legislative project as admirable. Despite his ambivalence toward political action, and despite his tragic sensibility, he believes that those who think independently and act decisively with a view to improving the human condition are meritorious. They exemplify their intelligence in action—specifically, in acting so as to care for others. To make this point differently: whatever his ambivalence toward politics, the Athenian endorses political activity as an expression of virtuous behavior. His behavior would not be virtuous, i.e., courageous in the first instance, if it were reckless or imprudent. In order to exemplify courage, his behavior must also be guided by *nous*. The Athenian's intelligence and courage in legislating are manifestations of his own rationally ordered soul.

The implication of this self-presentation is that politics itself has dignity and deserves respect. It is the field of action in which a virtuous leader, like the Athenian, uses his intelligence, courage, and other virtues, so as to care for others' souls or flourishing. It may be "unfortunate" that human beings are not gods. Even so, as a human being, no matter how god-like, the Athenian does justice to others by caring for them in politics. His political engagement, as a founder or legislator, is an expression of his care for others, but he is distant enough from politics to decline invitations to join the foundation himself (753a, cf. 968e–969a). Though he will take risks of his own, he ultimately wants Kleinias to assume control of the foundation. For that reason he attributes the title of "most courageous" to Kleinias (969a).[56]

With the Athenian, readers are invited to struggle over the relations between idealism and realism, between political opportunity and limitation, between the hopeful aspirations of founding and the tragic pessimism that often besets the founders' work. The Athenian's invitation to readers is expressed as the necessity of "judgment": while philosophers may hold up ideals for consideration, those who act must judge in each case what is appropriate to the situation:

> I think that in each case in which a plan is made, the most just thing to do is the following: the one who shows the model for what must be undertaken should in no way abandon what is most beautiful and true; but if any element of these things proves impossible, then he should avoid it and refuse to do it. But whatever of the remaining things is nearest to this and is by nature most akin from among the things that are suitable to do—this very thing he should contrive to accomplish. (746b–c)

Even after ideas are provided, practical agents and philosophers should cooperate in examining what is effective and what is too difficult (746c). The political craft is dangerous, endless, and forever uncertain. Fully adequate human lives require both investment in that craft and a tragic sensibility toward it. Ever ambivalent about his political role, the Athenian Stranger is "Looking with side-curved head curious what will come next/Both in and out of the game and watching and wondering at it" (Walt Whitman, *Song of Myself*, 4). However powerful his ambivalence and his tragic sensibility, though, the Athenian understands that it suits him as a human being to engage with others in order to improve their lives. His eudaimonistic project is both philanthropic and philosophical.

---

56. Of course, Kleinias' "courage" cannot be a fully adequate expression of the virtue, because he lacks *nous*. At the very end of the dialogue, the Athenian is not inclined to respond to Megillus and Kleinias' enthusiastic desire that he should share in founding the city (969c–d). In general, see once again 753a (which also refers to persuasion and compulsion) with 968b, 969a, 969c–d, with Schöpsdau 2003, 371; 2011: 603. One might compare the initial scene of the *Republic* on the use of force on Socrates.

The Argument

The Athenian's legislative efforts require considerable rhetorical and diplomatic skill—a level of sensitivity that enables him to meet his nonphilosophical interlocutors on their own ground. As a result, I have chosen to present my interpretation in order, as each episode and argument comes to sight for the reader. Especially in reading the *Laws*, of all Plato's dialogues, this approach is essential, because it alone enables us to appreciate the unfolding dynamics of the conversation in their particular dramatic and argumentative settings. My hope is that using the commentarial style will show what the genre of commentary can accomplish within this scholarly context. It is possible to invest this highly traditional scholarly genre with novel, philosophical purposes.

One potential drawback of this approach, to be sure, is that readers may lose sight of the general interpretation, as they work through the dialogue's numerous exchanges. Hence, this section provides an overview of my interpretation. Readers are encouraged to refer back to it throughout.

I begin by focusing on the Athenian's chief interlocutor, Kleinias, and his political and even cosmological views. From the outset, readers will understand that the dialogue is designed to address the education of Kleinias. Chapter 2 explores the Athenian's encounter with the elderly Cretan in the first two books. Its aim is to clarify not only Kleinias' self-conscious political views, but also his underlying character and ideals. Kleinias begins by expressing a cynical view of relations among states, in which peace is nothing more than a name. Acquisitive and aggressive, he is the product of his warlike Dorian culture. These characteristics mask Kleinias' deep fears and sense of vulnerability. His fears originate in his belief that wealth, power, and status are the ultimate objects of human striving. The uncertainty of these goods makes Kleinias particularly vulnerable to chance and to others' aggression. In response, Kleinias aspires to become an all-powerful, immortal tyrant, unaware that his own nature prevents him from achieving fulfillment by such means. Diplomatically uncovering these ideals, the Athenian exposes Kleinias' belief that nature is disordered and chaotic. The Athenian suggests a teleological response to Kleinias' "materialistic" views. He develops his own view by offering an account of the actualized potential of souls, goats, symposia, and cities. The two men's disagreements over the good life culminate in the Athenian's invocation of a "god" who will grant them consonance. This god refers to Magnesia's civil religion, by which the Athenian intends to convince Kleinias of his own eudaimonism—his view, in short, that virtue benefits its possessor.

In the course of this early discussion, the Athenian takes note of the need to educate three elements of Kleinias' soul: his desire (the seat of acquisitiveness), his spirit (the seat of aggression and fear), and his intellect (the seat of his belief in natural disorder). These are of course the three psychological elements outlined by Socrates in Plato's *Republic* (cf. Cooper 1999b), and they will return in the Athenian's educational program for Magnesia. The ensuing dialogue as a whole responds to Kleinias' acquisitiveness, aggression, fear, and belief in natural disorder. Remaining sensitive to character and drama, and their interconnections with the argument, is of central importance in understanding the *Laws*. Scholars who ignore Kleinias' character miss these crucial psychological elements that shape and inform the Athenian's educational project.

Chapter 3 builds on the Athenian's psychological analysis of Kleinias by setting it against the backdrop of human history altogether. In Book 3 of the *Laws*, the Athenian outlines a mythological history of humanity, from earliest times to the present. Whereas other scholars have wondered whether this book represents Plato's new-found attraction to history in developing his political philosophy, I read the Athenian's "historical" account as part of the work's literary design and psychological investigation: it is both rhetorically and substantively connected to the Athenian's analysis of Kleinias (Balot 2020b). The Athenian's goal is to provide a deep "archaeology" that explains the origins of Kleinias' character and outlook. Kleinias is nothing more than the latest in a series of ignorant, vicious primitives whose views of the human good have led to untold devastation and suffering. Ceaseless warfare and human misery are not, however, inevitable—contrary to Thucydides' *History*. Although human history appears to provide an empirical vindication of Kleinias' "Cretan thesis," the Athenian questions this "realist" outlook. The Athenian dares to imagine a more positive vision of human potential, embodied in a prudent obedience to law, which enables citizens to fortify themselves against tyrannical oppression. Souls and cities can be improved through cultivation of the virtues, above all moderation, in accordance with a correct account of natural human flourishing. Reinforced by the Athenian's analysis of Persia and Athens, these reflections point forward to his foundation of Magnesia in Book 4.

Metatextual cues indicate that Book 4 constitutes a new beginning, which is the subject of Chapter 4. Led by a "god," i.e., the Athenian himself, the new colonial foundation of Magnesia is designed to transcend traditional ignorance and militarism. Although the world itself remains inhospitable, the true legislator now holds out the hope of making decent human lives possible.

The true legislator is the culmination of a recognizable line of knowledgeable rulers, leaders, and craftsmen invoked by the Athenian throughout the first books. Knowing what to pray for, the true legislator wishes for a "young ty-rant" whom he himself can rule with *nous*. The Athenian hints that the true legislator, ruling via the young tyrant, is the city's best possible ruler. Though it always "stalks" and challenges the regime of law, however, the rule of *nous* proves upon reflection to be difficult (if not impossible) to realize in practice, because men like Kleinias will not accept it. Its mention here serves primarily to inspire Kleinias' unconditional support for the rule of law as the best po-litical antidote to oppressive tyranny. Instead of direct rule by *nous*, Magnesia will be governed by laws supported by a powerful religious ideology. The rule of law, reinforced by Magnesia's civil religion, is the disguised means by which the wise (e.g., the Athenian) can rule the ignorant (e.g., Kleinias).

At the city's point of origin, readers will see a particularly clear example of the need to distinguish between the Athenian as a philosopher and Kleinias (and the future Magnesians) as ordinary, non-philosophical citizens. To readers, the Athenian indicates that the best imaginable regime is governed by "intellect" (*nous*), which can be embodied by god-like philosophers; but in actual conditions, with actual human beings, as in Magnesia, it is neces-sary to establish the rule of law, supported by a powerful religious rhetoric and mythology. To Kleinias and ordinary citizens, the Athenian appears to follow the lead of the "god" in establishing a new colonial foundation, ruled by law and religion, that will make decent human lives possible. This "god" is in actuality his own intellect. As the "leader" of both his interlocutors and the foundation itself, the Athenian begins to establish a religious mythology that will encourage citizens to behave moderately and to obey the law.

Even beyond the political foundation, however, the Athenian also faces the difficult task of persuading Kleinias and the Magnesians that justice plays a central role in flourishing human lives. As he had previously called upon the god to produce consonance, so too does he now turn to persuasion by means of "persuasive preambles" (rather than philosophical argument). In Chapter 5, I show that the persuasive preambles help citizens to understand why obeying the law is good for them—not just for others or for the city. Through a hy-pothetical discussion with the poets, the Athenian reveals that his persuasive preambles aspire to educate the citizens' judgment in accordance with natural standards, especially if they initially adopt perspectives that differ from the legislator's own. For eudaimonistic reasons, the Athenian is motivated by care for the citizens' welfare as human beings. He likens himself to a free doctor. The free doctor's grasp of nature makes him a better diagnostician than the slave doctor, but also, more importantly, a more trustworthy supervisor of his patients. Like the free doctor, the legislator composes preambles based on and appealing to nature, which manifest his care for the citizens. These preambles range from persuasion to dissuasion and blur the categories of "persuasion" and "threat." Impossible to categorize simply, they also range from "emotional" persuasion to quasi-philosophical persuasion. The imagined legislator himself—a compelling figure by virtue of his superlative prudence, rhetorical skill, and dialectical abilities—must judge how best to employ this multidimensional tool in each context, so as to moderate ordinary citizens' passions and cultivate in them a genuine respect for the law.

After exploring persuasion and compulsion in these ways, the Athenian begins to legislate for Magnesia in Book 5 of the *Laws*. He turns first to the lowest part of the human soul, "appetite," or "desire" (*to epithumêtikon*). In Chapter 6, I show that the stage is set by the Athenian's comparison of Magnesia with the Callipolis of Plato's *Republic*. Because Magnesia's citizens will be acquisitive, desiring individuals, the Athenian explicitly distinguishes them from the god-like citizens of "Callipolis," the best regime outlined by Socrates in Plato's *Republic*. Hence, the Athenian explicitly legislates for a "second-best" regime—specifically with reference to its property arrangements, the object of the "second wave" in the *Republic*. In fact, the Athenian locates Magnesia's citizens on a spectrum between Callipolis' warriors and the citizens of Socrates' timocracy, the "second-best regime" of the *Republic*. By focusing on both institutional arrangements and the education of desire, the Athenian imitates Socrates' two-pronged strategy to limit materialistic acquisitiveness. Despite his emphasis on Magnesia's limitations, though, he also stresses his frequently countercultural ambitions for the city, which can be realized by human beings as they are empirically found. As successful as the Athenian may be in achieving his ambitions, I show that unsettling questions remain as to the motivations and quality of the Magnesians' achievement of virtue. Those questions are intensified by the Athenian's persistent emphasis on surveillance and punishment. We come to understand that Magnesia is neither a "community of the virtuous" (Bobonich 2002; Schofield 2006, 2010) nor an unregenerate human population (Schofield 2010); instead, the city is located, with the Athenian's own ambitions, in a tragic space between these two possibilities.

Having discussed the material foundations of the regime, I turn in Chapter 7 to examine *thumos*—the psychological seat of anger, shame, and self-assertion. In their early conversations, the Athenian recognized, with a certain dismay, Kleinias' attachment to a destructive, militaristic model of *thumos*, unmoored from intelligence, justice, and moderation. Hence, in addition to addressing the citizens' ingrained acquisitiveness, the Athenian also aspires to educate and elevate their *thumos*. In order to provide for the city's military security, he institutes rigorous training exercises, which he rendered less toxic by embedding them within religious rituals. Equally, he proposes to pacify common meals and to institute common meals for women, who would, as in Callipolis, receive military training, also a move to pacify rather than militarize the city. In offering his account of surveillance, punishment, and judgment, the Athenian strives to elevate *thumos*, in the hope that it may become a richer, more rationally reflective element of the citizens' souls. By means of their surveillance and watchfulness, citizens encourage others to live up to the city's standards of virtue. Citizens show care to one another in enforcing the city's norms and laws. Adequate care for others in these ways requires that citizens' thumoeidetic energies be appropriately informed by practical reason.

Chapter 8 completes our examination of the Athenian's education of *thumos*. The Athenian envisions civic participation and political leadership as the primary venues for the expression of *thumos*. The central books lay out a creative political system that both involves ordinary citizens and does justice to superior virtue and knowledge. Political institutions represent a compromise between strict, proportional justice and "equity," by which the claims (and power) of ordinary people are recognized. In describing the education suitable for the city's top political officials, the Athenian suggests obscurely that those officials will be superior in talent and education to ordinary citizens; but he leaves readers in suspense as to who they are, how they will be elected, and how a regime of law will accommodate these "god-like" individuals. Through their participation in elections and courts, on the other hand, all citizens play a role in determining, in highly practical contexts, just what is honorable, what deserves recognition, and what meets the lawgiver's standards. Ordinary citizens have gifts to offer, and, in participating politically, they develop their own faculties of imagination and judgment. Ordinary citizens do not, however, "deliberate" and "judge" for the city (i.e., through making binding decisions on its behalf, after discussion) or create laws for themselves. The city's elite courts play a paradigmatic role: leading magistrates, now functioning as judicial officials, deliver justice in high-stakes cases, while educating other citizens in the means of judicial process and forensic judgment. The Athenian's restatement of the "free doctor" analogy reveals that the free doctor is the model for the true judge of Book 9, who, like the city's paramount magistrates, appears to require a philosophical education in order to succeed in his role. That requirement becomes even more pressing when the Athenian unfolds the Socratic paradox at the heart of his penal code. From highest to lowest courts, even so, the Athenian stresses the need for judges to think honestly about their own possible limitations—even to audit themselves and their beliefs. He thereby introduces a generally Socratic ambition to the court system, which, in practice, different judges will be able to realize to different degrees.

In Book 10, the Athenian carries forward his discussion of the penal code by addressing the greatest crimes of all—crimes against the city's gods. Deferring consideration of the Athenian's three theological arguments, Chapter 9 focuses on his elaborate introduction of the "young atheist" and his surprising but precise "sociology of the impious." By impressing Kleinias with the grave threat posed to the city by atheism, the Athenian aims to persuade him of the city's need for philosophical defenders, i.e. the Nocturnal Council. He also positions Kleinias as his eager ally, a helper whose functions he describes in military language. These two motivations, however, important as they may be, do not exhaustively explain the Athenian's introduction of the young atheist. Late in Book 10, the Athenian distinguishes between honest, frank-speaking atheists and deceptive, materialistic ones. By doing so, he carves out space for a small group of naturally just, intellectually curious young people who become promising candidates for further philosophical study and even membership in the Nocturnal Council. His final characterization of "deists" and "bribers," meanwhile, enables him to re-engage with larger themes in the work, such as the opposition between justice and pleasure, and the need to find a place for Kleinias in the large, cosmic scheme he unfolds.

Chapter 10 turns to the Athenian's substantive arguments concerning Magnesia's civil religion. Although most scholars discern "Plato's final theology" in Book 10, the Athenian's three substantive arguments are psychological, ethical, and political in character. Appropriate to the context of the dialogue, they aim to educate Kleinias intellectually—the third movement in the Athenian's educational project. In offering him a satisfying religious myth, the Athenian responds both to the disorder of Kleinias' soul and to his implicit belief that chaotic, disorderly motion characterizes nature. On its face, the Athenian's first argument attempts to refute a materialist theory of nature by presenting the heavens as rationally ordered by the god's intelligence. This argument confronts important objections, which will provide material for future discussion with the young atheist. For Kleinias and ordinary citizens, however, a "mythopoetic" or allegorical interpretation is more appropriate: symbolically, the argument teaches him that to "imitate the god" means to abandon materialism and to embrace the Athenian's tele-ological, eudaimonistic presentation of virtue. By contrast with ordinary citizens, young atheists are invited to ponder the Athenian's account of the Sun's movements, which exposes unresolved but significant questions of theology and cosmic kinetics.

In the second argument, the Athenian strives to reform the deists' flawed conceptions of happiness. His presentation of the gods in this stretch shows that they care for justice by exemplifying it in their own souls, rather than by intervening to support misguided ideas of happiness. He offers the deists the gods that they need, not the ones that they want. Similarly, to liberate deists from their childish longings, he shows that human craftsmen such as himself, not the gods, work within the city to deliver the justice that deists desire. Within a broader framework, human nature functions naturalistically, without divine aid, to reward the just and punish the unjust.

The Athenian's third argument, nominally addressed to "bribers," will neither persuade nor dissuade them. Rather, it is best understood as an address to Kleinias. Having moved Kleinias from materialism to teleology, the Athenian now moves him from the pursuit of *pleonexia* to defense against it, on a cosmic stage.

I conclude by arguing that, altogether, Book 10 reveals that philosophers are essential to the city, in making citizens' larger belief-systems both sound and compatible with the city's orientation toward civic virtue. In order to live decent lives, ordinary citizens must subscribe to a religious mythology. This chapter offers a particularly clear demonstration of the strengths of a literary approach sensitive to multiple audiences, which understands the work as a unified whole, and which emphasizes the distinction between philosophers and ordinary citizens, including the Athenian's interlocutors.

Chapter 11 treats the Nocturnal Council and the "rule of *nous*." Scholars have either integrated the Nocturnal Council into the regime of law or dismissed it as an afterthought, incompatible with the dialogue as a whole. Engaging with the controversy between "integrationists" and "incompatibilists," this chapter charts a novel path. Readers should ask whether the Athenian's apparent change of tack in Book 12 might be deliberate. The appropriate question to pose is, Why would the Athenian install figures resembling philosopher rulers at the end of a dialogue focused on establishing an ambitious regime of law? Verbal echoes link the establishment of the Nocturnal Council with the foundation of Magnesia in Book 4; instead of "handing over the city" to magistrates who are the law's "slaves," as readers had been led to believe, the Athenian now proposes to hand it over to philosophers in the Nocturnal

Council, a major shift in orientation. Puzzlingly, however, he offers few legal or institutional details. The absence of those details is also deliberate: readers are invited to follow the Athenian in focusing on the Council's god-like knowledge. Close textual analysis of the dialogue's concluding section shows that the Athenian's presentation of the Nocturnal Council implies a downgrading of the quality and worth of the regime of law.

With these themes in mind, we turn to the book's conclusion (Chapter 12). Toward the end of Book 7 of the *Laws*, the Athenian offers a pregnant reflection on his own political project. He has established the Magnesian regime as a mimesis of the best life; and that, he says, is the "truest tragedy." According to the conventional interpretation, the Athenian's teachings concerning the gods, justice, and happiness prove superior to those of the traditional tragic poets, his rivals. While this interpretation fits the understanding of Magnesia's ordinary citizens, Magnesia's civil religion suggests the need to uncover, in addition, a deeper meaning. This chapter argues that the tragedy of the Athenian's political project lies in the necessary ignorance of the ordinary citizens for whom the regime, with its civil religion, is created. Their teleological purpose as human beings is frustrated because they fail to live lives of rational self-governance; their guiding principles derive from religious myths, rather than a rational grasp of nature. Ordinary citizens are encouraged to defer to the Athenian's authoritative myth-making. Their failure to live up to the promise of the human "puppet" is one element of the "truest tragedy."

The second element concerns the Athenian Stranger himself. In calling his political project the "truest tragedy," the Athenian also steps back in order to reflect on his own activity in the dialogue. As readers, we see the Athenian in the process of recognizing the constraints not only upon his citizens' progress, but also upon his own activities as an educator and reformer. His introspective habit yields a fertile vein of self-criticism. He thereby serves as a model for readers who, through exploring this intricate text, have come to appreciate both the opportunities and the limitations of political reform and educational ambition.

2

The Character of Kleinias

IN APPROACHING THE dialogue's first book, most scholars have focused narrowly on the Athenian's presentation of the human "puppet," an allegory of human psychology.[1] While this image is significant, it is essential to go beyond the traditional approach, not only by examining the role of the human "puppet" in the emerging argument, but also by grappling with the book's complex presentation of Kleinias. Kleinias introduces himself as a shrewd, cynical political observer with intriguing justifications for his own city's goals and way of life. Already in the opening scene, readers are invited to wonder about the relation of his express political beliefs to his deeper assumptions about nature. Prodded by the Athenian's questions, Kleinias reveals firm convictions about the anarchy and conflict that prevail in nature, including human nature. In watching the conversation unfold, moreover, readers come to understand that Kleinias' beliefs are shaped by his character—and, above all, by his passions. Implicitly developing Socrates' tripartition of the soul in Plato's *Republic*, the Athenian grasps the need to educate three elements of Kleinias' soul: his desire (the seat of acquisitiveness: *to epithumêtikon*), his spirit (the seat of aggression, shame, and fear: *thumos*, *to thumoeides*), and his intellect (the seat of his belief in natural disorder: *to logistikon*).[2]

The Athenian offers a teleological response to Kleinias' views of politics, human nature, and the natural world: that is, he proposes that human beings, cities, and the world itself are best understood when seen as rationally ordered

---

1. On this image, see, among others, Bobonich 2002; Scolnicov 2003: 123–24; Gerson 2003; Frede 2010: 116–20; Kamtekar 2010; Lutz 2012: 123–27; Bartels 2017: 86–92; Schofield 2016.

2. Scholars who ignore Kleinias' character (e.g., essays in Bobonich 2010; Laks 1990, 2000, 2001; Stalley 1983) miss these crucial psychological elements that shape and inform the Athenian's political project.

Tragedy, Philosophy, and Political Education in Plato's Laws. Ryan K. Balot, Oxford University Press.
© Ryan K. Balot 2024. DOI: 10.1093/oso/9780197647226.003.0002

wholes, whose nature is defined by particular ends or purposes. He justifies his teleological approach by offering a well-crafted account of souls, goats, symposia, and cities, which actualize their natural potential through the guidance of intelligent supervisors. The Athenian's attempt to educate Kleinias on these points foreshadows his educational purposes in the dialogue as a whole. Taken as a whole, the first book points beyond itself to themes and discussions in later books, which elaborate the education of Kleinias.

The Education of Kleinias as a Framework for the Dialogue

Understanding the character of Kleinias is crucial for understanding the dramatic trajectory, political arguments, and philosophical significance of the dialogue as a whole. Kleinias—far more than Megillus—is the Athenian's interlocutor throughout. He is the first to answer the Athenian's first question (624a). He speaks more frequently and at greater length than Megillus. Dramatically speaking, at least, the arguments from Book 4 onward are offered for the sake of Kleinias' prospective participation in the founding of a colony on Crete (702b–e). He belongs to a commission of ten Knossians tasked with establishing a law-code for the new city. Kleinias proposes to construct a "city in speech," with a view both to examining important questions and to providing useful ideas for the colony's foundation. It is his character that, in large part, determines the shape of the regime constructed by the Athenian.[3]

Kleinias' character, to be sure, is not singular; the author intends to pursue universal questions through a focus on this conversation with this particular character. Kleinias' outlook on ethics and politics is informed by his identity as a Dorian—the ethnicity in ancient Greece most closely associated with militarism, *thumos*, and, at its foundation, acquisitiveness. While scholars have developed certain nuances in Plato's portrayal of Kleinias the Dorian—such

---

3. Most commentators blur the distinction between Kleinias and Megillus. Morrow (1960: 17–73) outlines the differences between Crete and Sparta, from which they respectively hail. Pangle (1980: 394–95, 413–17, 430–34, and 438) emphasizes the differences in the Athenian's treatment of his interlocutors: he treats Kleinias as a shrewd founder, intellectually superior to the stolid Megillus. Lutz (2012: 54–89) offers an extended discussion of the Athenian's engagement with Megillus, who is a "representative Dorian citizen" (54)—more so than Kleinias; cf. Zuckert (2009: 66–67). For a more positive assessment of Megillus' role, see Friedland (2020), who also offers a detailed treatment of characterization in the dialogue. Clark 2003 argues that the Athenian is focused on healing or curing Kleinias in particular.

as his ignorance of Homer (680c2–5) and other facets of Greek culture—I focus on four salient characteristics. First, Kleinias holds a cynical, pessimistic view of politics, justice, and human nature. This view is rooted in his fear and suspicion of others, on the one hand, and his own acquisitive desires and tyrannical aspirations, on the other. Second, in addition to being driven by *pleonexia* (greed), he is also a passionate defender of his own status and privileges, a man of *thumos* (spirit). He imagines that the worst condition is that of being ruled by others, which is tantamount to a life of slavery. Third, Kleinias exhibits a soul whose impulses are in conflict with one another. In the language of the dialogue, he lacks "consonance" with himself. Finally, in ways that Kleinias himself cannot articulate or explain, he holds a materialistic view of the world. The anarchy of politics and interstate relations is rooted in the disorder, conflict, and necessities of nature.[4]

The dialogue's early characterization of Kleinias sets the stage for many subsequent discussions and legislative decisions. Most importantly, Kleinias' introductory comments in Book 1 foreshadow the young atheist's philosophical position in Book 10.[5] Unlike Kleinias, of course, that rebellious adolescent questions Magnesia's teachings about the gods—in particular, their existence and their incorruptibility. Even so, he shares with Kleinias two critical beliefs.

First, and more deeply, he, too, believes that nature is intrinsically disordered. He is more articulate than Kleinias; underlying his atheism is a developed philosophical theory that explains nature's anarchy—that is, a doctrine of philosophical materialism, which minimizes the role of *nous* (rational intellect) and stresses the random motion, mixing, and interplay of fire, water, earth, and air, all of which occur by chance.[6] Materialists emphasize purely physical "first causes" which render nature as such disorderly and chaotic. This theory is the startling philosophical expression of ideas that we first begin to glimpse, in embryonic form, in Kleinias. As we will discover, Kleinias' own view of natural disorder first comes to sight in his description of interstate relations, cities, and individuals in Book 1. His view is even more starkly revealed later, when he asserts that the heavenly bodies are mere "wanderers" who fail to keep to an orderly path, as everyone knows by observation—a remark that elicits the censure of the Athenian, who intends to show that

---

4. The following section is derived from Balot 2020b.

5. Cf. Zuckert 2009: 126–27; Benardete 2000: xii, 287–88; cf. also Clark 2003: 93.

6. On Archelaus as the source of these ideas, see, most recently, Betegh 2016.

the planets manifest god-like intelligence and that the cosmos is rationally ordered (822a).[7]

Second, according to the Athenian, the young atheist's materialist ontology underpins the belief that nature is opposed to convention—a belief that, in turn, appears to sanction tyrannical desires to rule others (889e–890a). In the young atheist's view, nature does not provide any normative basis for justice (889e). In that important respect, too, the young atheist draws out ideas and theses that underlie the characterization of Kleinias from the beginning. In Book 2, the Athenian elicits Kleinias' underlying acquisitiveness and tyrannical predilections. He asks Kleinias whether a man with worldly goods, tyrannical power, and even immortality would be unhappy because of his injustice; and Kleinias predictably demurs (661d–e). While Kleinias agrees that a rich and successful tyrant (who is *ex hypothesi* unjust) might live a "shameful" life, he refuses to accept that such a man lives an unpleasant life, or a life without benefit to him (661e–662a; see the section "Kleinias' Tyrannical Ambitions" below). In short, Kleinias harbors tyrannical desires. Kleinias foreshadows the young atheist in ways that make explicit the close connections between politics, ethics, and the character of the natural world.[8]

From the outset, then, Kleinias possesses tyrannical desires and sees chaos and disorder as fundamental attributes of the natural world. These two features of his character may not be causally linked. Like the materialists of Book 10, however, Kleinias is prone to slide illegitimately between empirical observations, on the one hand, and normative theses about how things *should* work, on the other. The Athenian's response to him was shaped by his conviction that, in order to suppress acquisitive materialism, it was necessary to develop, empower, and publicize a doctrine according to which the cosmos is structured in a rational, intelligible, and orderly way. The dialogue itself helps

---

7. On the contradiction between "wanderers" and cosmic order, see Bobonich 2002: 108–9. Later, at 886a, Kleinias considers it obvious that the motions of planets and stars are orderly—a sign that he has been persuaded by the Athenian.

8. On these connections, see further Mayhew 2008, Zuckert 2009, and Betegh 2016. None of these authors has developed this connection as a central theme of the dialogue as a whole or recognized the Athenian's attempt to oppose it by constructing his own teleological world view. While contemporary scholars have shown interest in the relation between politics, theology, and cosmology in Plato's presumptively "late" works, they have tended to prioritize theology and metaphysics, looking to Plato's *Timaeus* as the anchor of Plato's developed theological views: Stalley 1983: 172–75; Laks 1990, building on Morrow 1954; Bobonich 2002: 101–9, 208, cf. 454–59; Schofield 2006: 324–25; Laks 2000: 290–91; O'Meara 2017. By contrast, I prioritize the Athenian's ethical and political ideas rather than the rational cosmology he elaborates in Book 10, building on Strauss 1975; Pangle 1976; and Zuckert 2009: 51–146.

to explain why the Athenian chose this strategy. In the mind of Kleinias, one of Magnesia's prospective founders, politics operates according to the same disorderly and even antagonistic motions as nature.

Kleinias at First Sight: Cynical, Fearful, Acquisitive, Thumoeidetic

In the dialogue's opening exchanges, the Athenian inquires into the salient features of the Cretan regime, beginning with its common meals, physical training, and weapons. Kleinias' first response emphasizes the "nature" (*phusin*; 625c10) of Crete itself—its uneven countryside, for example, which led to the Cretans' adoption of light arms and their preference for fighting on foot rather than horseback. In his mind, the nature of the terrain carries with it certain self-evident consequences for the lawgiver's policies. The ultimate purpose, or *telos*, of his own Cretan *politeia* is warfare; in everything he legislated, Kleinias says, the Cretan lawgiver had war in view. In making this claim, Kleinias adopts an attitude of knowing superiority to "the many," who are too thoughtless to discern the continuous warfare that persists in all times and places (625e). Although he is not a philosopher, Kleinias presents himself as a "debunker," reminiscent of Plato's Thrasymachus, or Thucydides' Athenian envoys at Sparta or Melos, who deride the so-called "justice argument." In Kleinias' interpretation, peace is nothing more than a "name" (*onoma*, 626a3); "in actual fact," he says, "by nature all cities are permanently engaged in an undeclared war with one another" (626a4–5). The defining principle of the good society is an unqualified focus on war as the *telos* (626b–c).[9]

Kleinias moves quickly from observations about the nature of the terrain and about human nature (i.e., the omnipresence of war) to his conclusions about the regime's appropriate *telos*, war, and from there, to its most prized and all-important virtue, courage. What is Kleinias' own attitude toward the supposed inexorability or "naturalness" of interstate warfare? Is he offering a merely "value-neutral" analysis of interstate relations, as though he were an International Relations scholar of the "Realist" school? Does he embrace the rule of force? (It is hard to imagine a third possibility—namely, that he

---

9. For useful treatments of Kleinias' character and views, see Strauss 1975: 3–8; Pangle 1980: 379–87; Bobonich 2002: 121–36; Clark 2003: 4–11; Zuckert 2009: 64–73; Salem 2013: 50–53; and Sauvé Meyer 2015.

eschews "value neutrality" specifically in the sense that, like a pacifist, he repudiates the ambition to rule.)

The logic of Kleinias' presentation reveals his underlying fearfulness and acquisitiveness. When on campaign, he says, soldiers "are forced by the business itself to share common meals for the sake of establishing a guard for themselves" (*hup' autou tou pragmatos anankazontai phulakês hautôn heneka sussitein*, 625e). If wartime requires guards (again at 625e, 626a), then so, too, does peace: hence the lawgiver has given laws to guard (*phulattein*, 626a) us,[10] understanding that, unless a city wins its wars, it will not benefit from its possessions or practices. "All the goods of the conquered come into the possession of the victors" (626b3–4). Nature is a realm of force or necessity because of the threat of domination, which requires human beings to establish a "guard" (*phulakê*) for themselves.

What Kleinias is saying, almost despite himself, is that the Cretan lawgiver is interested in military success only instrumentally, as the means to protect material possessions; military prowess is not an end in itself.[11] If this statement captures Kleinias' understanding of his regime, then his description of warfare as the regime's *telos* is inaccurate. The *telos* with which he is most obviously concerned is, rather, the "guarding" and possession of material wealth that successful warfare makes possible. In light of his preoccupation with "guarding" his own "good things" or belongings, the Athenian discerns Kleinias' materialism, which will reveal itself most clearly in their discussion in Book 2. Kleinias' militarism serves his materialism.

Kleinias' initial presentation suggests that fear—a hyperawareness of the possibility of loss—lies at the heart of the Cretan regime's *telos*. Its warlike character results not from a Nietzschean effusion of strength, but rather from a feeling of vulnerability. Kleinias foreshadows a security dilemma, in which an international anarchy creates a competitive environment in which states vie to gain advantages over one another—initially and ostensibly, at least, for the purpose of self-protection. It is striking, and perhaps even tragic or lamentable, however, that the goal of adequately protecting the city became the overriding preoccupation of the lawgiver. As a result, a more aggressive or expansionistic understanding of courage came to predominate in the

---

10. The translation here is contested; I follow Sauvé Meyer 2015. Compare Brisson and Pradeau 2020: 683: "qu'il (the legislator) nous a confié la sauvegarde de ces lois"; similarly in Diès and des Places 1951.

11. Cf. Zuckert 2009: 65; Sauvé Meyer 2015: 83, 98.

Dorian cities. How, one might ask, was the lawgiver's fearful watchfulness transformed into a more aggressive form of militarism that pervades, and even defines, the Dorian ethos? How did this security dilemma give birth to belligerent acquisitiveness as a way of life?

Readers do not win clarity on such questions until Books 2 and 3. Instead, the Athenian now draws out the implications of Kleinias' views by proposing that his conception of the lawgiver's intentions is captured by Tyrtaeus' poetry (629a–c).[12] In a passage that echoes his exchanges with Kleinias, the Athenian argues that Tyrtaeus, like the Dorian legislators, also taught that only military prowess can make a human life good, even for the possessor of abundant wealth and other "good things" (629b). Upon further analysis, however, it becomes clear that Tyrtaeus' presentation of the "good man" is compatible with the activities of unjust "mercenaries" (630b), who are proverbial for their selfishness and acquisitiveness (cf. 667a). Tyrtaeus' good man is not nearly as good as the trustworthy and sound citizen described by Theognis, who exhibits the entirety of virtue in the greatest war—i.e., civil war (630a–c). The Athenian has confirmed at a deeper level that Kleinias' militaristic outlook is rooted in an underlying acquisitiveness. It will become essential, as he perceives, to develop a substantial educational program in order to address the acquisitiveness and appetitive drives associated with the lowest part of the soul—what Socrates in Plato's *Republic* calls "the desiring part" (*to epithumêtikon*).

At the same time, readers are now given to understand that Kleinias is also powerfully motivated by the passions associated with *thumos*—anger, self-assertion, aspiration, and shame—that is, the second psychological element in Socrates' tripartite schema.[13] He takes pride, for example, in the thought of winning a victory over himself (the "first and best of all victories," 626e), while he considers that "for someone to be defeated by himself is the most shameful

---

12. For an attempt to read this debate over the Cretan and Spartan lawgivers in the context of Plato's relationship to Xenophon's Lycurgus, see Schofield 2021.

13. Pangle 1976 emphasizes this element; cf. Pangle 1980: 454–56. Others have found it essential to focus on "Plato's conception of the structure of the soul in the *Laws*" (Sassi 2008: 128). Sassi 2008: 133–38 argues for *thumos* without a special part; see also Gerson 2003 (there is continuity between *Republic* and *Laws*, but no agent-like parts in either work), Kahn 2004: 357 (the *Laws* has no tripartition for contextual reasons), Wilburn 2013 (there is a distinctly thumoeidetic part), Fossheim 2013 (the *Laws* presents three distinct parts). See also the essays in Bobonich 2010, with the apt critique of Brisson 2011. My own view is that the Athenian himself does not pursue the issues of ethical psychology in this ambitious, fine-grained Socratic way; his purposes and audience are entirely different.

(*aichiston*), as well as the worst (*kakiston*), of all things" (626e). He harbors a powerful sense of vulnerability, which is encoded in his sense of shame at the possibility of being defeated. The worst form of political or military defeat is slavery: losing not only one's belongings but also one's own self. It is that ultimate form of loss that the young atheists later evoke—in the passage we considered previously, which is directly connected to the characterization of Kleinias—when they present domination and enslavement as the only available alternatives (890a).

Kleinias' sense of his own vulnerability carries with it significant political consequences. In the Athenian's parable of the three judges (627d11–628a3), in fact, Kleinias is willing to forgo the possibility of rule by the virtuous, because he is enticed by the prospect of a lawgiver able to reconcile competing factions. This lawgiver is willing to "set up a guard" (*paraphulattein*, 628a) so as to secure the continuing friendship of those factions. The Athenian is planting a seed in this parable: law (not military power) can itself become the "guard" that will provide security among fellow citizens who would otherwise necessarily come into violent conflict. As the Athenian illustrates more fully in Books 3 and 4, law is capable of guarding men like Kleinias from the oppression—even tyranny—of others. The Athenian himself would opt for the rule of the virtuous.[14]

In the course of examining Kleinias, then, the Athenian lays bare his aggressiveness, acquisitiveness, and fearful sense of vulnerability. These characteristics themselves rest on an even deeper foundation—namely, on Kleinias' implicit belief in natural conflict. The salience of that theme emerges when the Athenian drills down to the foundations of Kleinias' political ideas. He asks whether the war of all against all applies only to cities or also to neighborhoods, and then whether it applies to households, and then even to the internal psychological dynamics of individuals themselves (626c–d). Kleinias' view is that we are always and inexorably in conflict with ourselves, internally and psychologically; self-domination is the best of all victories (626e). Similarly, cities, too, are necessarily battlegrounds between those who are better and few and those who are many and worse (627a). For Kleinias, then, conflict is the essence of political life. The history of Greek cities, indeed of all cities, provides strong evidence for this view—as we will soon gather from the quasi-historical account offered in Book 3.

---

14. Strauss 1975: 5; Pangle 1980: 383–85: "the lawgiver's pursuit of concord attenuates his pursuit of virtue"; *contra* (for example) Schofield 2013.

Down to the Foundations: Kleinias' Materialism

Having drawn out the elements of Kleinias' views of politics and psychology, the Athenian now uncovers the depth of Kleinias' attachment to conflict as an explanatory principle. In his characteristically diplomatic way, the Athenian inquires into the building blocks of Kleinias' ideas, i.e., the elemental motions that make Kleinias' views plausible. After listening to the Athenian's description of conflict within the self, Kleinias responds in a telling fashion: "You have correctly carried the argument up to its source [*ton gar logon ep' archên orthôs anagagôn*] and have thus made it clearer, so that you will the more easily discover that we were correct just now in saying that all are enemies of all in public, and in private each is an enemy of himself" (626d, tr. Pangle 1980, modified). He infers that virtue, which is the best sort of victory, consists in self-domination rather than harmony or order. Power, rather than persuasion or agreement, is the governing principle of nature. Hence, for Kleinias, taking a "thumoeidetic" (spirited) perspective on life, being watchful, suspicious, and ever-prepared to fight—that is what it means to live according to nature.

Unbeknownst to him, Kleinias' particular vocabulary is charged: it reveals his character and beliefs in ways that go beyond his own understanding. Specifically, his response to the Athenian foreshadows later philosophical uses of the term *archê* ("source," "first principle") in the dialogue. For example, the Athenian employs a similar phrase in describing the "free doctor," a stand-in for the philosopher, who "uses arguments that come close to philosophizing, grasping the disease from its source (*ex archês*), and going back up to (*epanionta*) the whole nature of bodies" (857d, Pangle 1980). More importantly, the theological discussion of Book 10 is preoccupied with the "first principles" (*archai*) of motion. The Athenian himself argues, contrary to the materialist philosophers, that self-motion is the "source" or "first principle" (*archên*) of all motions (895b).

Implicitly, Kleinias' self-presentation shows that he is aligned with certain participants in a philosophical debate of which he is unaware. Specifically, his emphasis on conflict and disorder suggests that he subscribes to a materialist position. Whether he could express the point articulately or not, he believes that the world is naturally disordered—that it is fundamentally composed of matter in conflicting motion. His vocabulary and outlook call to mind the *archê* or "first principle" of things discussed by pre-Socratic philosophers, along with the *archê* or military "empire" pursued by Thucydides' Athenians. Kleinias thereby sheds light on the conception of nature that underlies his earlier thesis about the belligerency of interstate relations. In his view, nature is self-consistent, from the highest levels, political communities, on down to their smallest constituents in individuals' souls. Nature is pervaded by conflict, violence, and antagonism at the level of both its elements and its compounds: for example, in hostility and conflict within cities, or in the competing passions of the individual soul. No new properties emerge as we "scale up" from the (passionate) sources of motion in the soul to the human being as a whole, or from individual citizens to human associations such as cities. As we will discover, the Athenian will take this last thesis as his starting point. He observes the need to focus his educational program not only on the lower two elements of the Socratic soul, but also on Kleinias' "reason" (*to logistikon*), the highest element. Kleinias himself is a composite whole whose elements (desire, spirit, and reason) will be diversely addressed throughout the dialogue so as to enable them to become consonant and harmonious.

Although Kleinias is not a "young atheist," his views concerning political disorder and motion resemble those of the materialist philosophers who figure later in the work. Like them, he, too, believes that natural conflict and disorder sanction the desire for tyranny that he eventually reveals in Book 2. In emphasizing domination, Kleinias abandons the "defensive" perspective that lays stress on protection or "guarding." It was in response to Kleinias' own belief in natural conflict and disorder, and his desire for tyranny, that the Athenian began to develop a meaningful alternative—one that is ultimately disclosed in Book 10, when he elaborates on a cosmic vision of natural, rational order established providentially by the god.

The Athenian's Teleological Reply: Souls, Goats, Symposia, and Cities

In responding to Kleinias' character, ideas, and sensibility, the Athenian gives the first example of his own therapeutic persuasiveness. He aspires to create consonance in Kleinias' soul by persuading him to take a different perspective on conflict, whether between political factions or among the passions in a single individual. His vision of ethics and politics—outlined in the "table of contents" (631d–632c)[15]—is meant to supersede the "Cretan thesis" to which Kleinias has, at least provisionally, given expression.[16] Specifically, the

---

15. On the debate over the work's fulfillment (or lack thereof) of the plan announced here, see Nails and Thesleff 2003: 27.

16. "Cretan thesis": Lewis 2009b: 73, obviously by analogy with Thucydides' "Athenian thesis." As Lewis explains: "About the Kretan thesis we should notice three things: first, it reduces the

Athenian opens Kleinias to the possibility of distinguishing between the natural form of a city or individual (which involves a consideration of its *telos* and its intrinsically hierarchical order) and its individual parts or elements (which in practice, frequently come into conflict with one another). The Athenian opposes the harmonious possibilities inherent in form to the meaningless, antagonistic operations of individual elements.[17]

To make his references to "form" convincing, he points out that Kleinias himself has already suggested that any decent regime depends on a principle of "order" (626c). He also develops Kleinias' own implicit references to the *telos* of the Cretan regime (625e, 626c). In these ways, he builds on Kleinias' own views in order to persuade him that, at least ideally, cities can become rationally arranged, consonant "wholes" whose internal order renders them superior to the mere sum of their conflicting parts. Similarly, by working through the confusions of Kleinias' own commitment to virtue, the Athenian develops a teleological conception of the individual that culminates in his well-known image of the human "puppet" (644d–645b). His exploration of the "puppet" allegory must be understood within the context of the developing conversation—which is itself penetrated by significant dramatic cues. Already in Book 1, Plato stages a contest between Kleinias' convictions about disorderly motion, virtue, and desire, and the Athenian's arguments for a teleologically ordered conception of the soul and the city.

In order to make progress in their discussion, the Athenian "scales up" from the motions of the human soul, which typically present themselves as being disorderly and meaningless, to a hierarchically ordered model of the soul that arguably constitutes its flourishing. The key to his effort to overcome Kleinias' belief in meaningless, anarchic conflict was to establish his own view that the goods available to humanity are naturally and rationally ordered. Human beings cannot understand what is good for them merely by referring to their own random or unreconstructed desires; nor, similarly,

---

cause of important political phenomena down to psychic phenomena; second, it is presented as a claim about what is 'according to nature'; and third, it suggests as an ordering principle victory, but leaves off giving anything like a definition of victory." On "motion" in the context of Thucydides' presentation of warfare, see Rusten 2015.

17. For a contemporary teleological account of "form" and "life-form," which adds a new perspective to the scientific materialism of our age, see Thompson 2008. In considering the opposition between form and elements, one might also compare the distinction Benardete 2000: 18 draws between "eidetic" and "genetic." For an intriguing attempt to connect the life sciences to political philosophy, see Masters 1984.

would sound lawgivers legislate in an ad hoc fashion, according to social pressures (630e–631a). Rather, in order to make citizens "happy," to enable them to flourish, legislators must acknowledge a twofold, hierarchically arranged scale of goods.[18] The "human goods" (*agatha . . . anthrôpina*, 631b)—health, beauty, strength, and wealth—are goods of the body or instrumentally useful for it. These goods are hierarchically ordered in a comprehensible way: their descent from health to wealth (631c) is based, as readers will grasp, on their level of intrinsic as opposed to instrumental bodily goodness. On any respectable conception of bodily goods, wealth should serve health, rather than vice versa; health is the pinnacle of human bodily goodness.

Equally, the "divine goods" are hierarchically arranged, from prudence or intelligence (*nous*) to moderation and justice, and finally to courage (631c–d). *Nous* is the leader of the virtues because none of those other qualities—moderation, justice, courage—can exist without it. The virtues of character depend for their proper functioning on intelligence. No one can be just if he is ignorant of what justice (for example) demands in particular situations, if he lacks the appropriate sensitivity to circumstances or fairness. No one can be courageous if he lacks an understanding of the appropriate goals of courage, or if he lacks a sense of clarity and proportion in dangerous circumstances. For similar reasons, the human goods depend on the divine goods: health, beauty, and so on, will not even be good—they will be genuinely bad—if their possessor uses them without understanding or sensitivity. The Athenian will develop these points at greater length in Book 2.

What is good for human beings, viewed in this light, is defined, not by their chaotic and transitory desires, but rather naturally and objectively. The soul has a structure given to it by nature, in which it achieves its healthy condition when reason rules the other elements for the good of the whole. The Athenian furthers his implicit appeal to the rule of reason in his image of the human puppet.[19] He uses this image specifically in order to explain what he means by self-rule (644b–c) and by superiority to oneself (645b). Intriguingly, he provides a compelling framework within which to understand psychological

---

18. Useful treatments of this account of the human and divine goods include Frede 2010: 112–14; Bobonich 123–53 (which reads this passage closely in connection with 660e–661e); Strauss 1975: 7–9; Pangle 1980: 386–91; Sauvé Meyer 2015.

19. On this image, see, among others, Frede 2010: 116–20; Kamtekar 2010; Lutz 2012: 123–27; Bartels 2017: 86–92; Bobonich 2002; Scolnicov 2003: 123–24; Gerson 2003; Schofield 2016.

puzzles that Kleinias' own account left unresolved (626e–627b). Each human being, he says, has within him "two opposing and unintelligent counselors" (*sumboulô enantiô te kai aphrone*, 644c6–7), which are pleasure and pain, as well as "calculation" (*logismos*, 644d2), which is naturally set over them (644c–d). (Both Kleinias and Megillus remark on their difficulty in understanding the Athenian's point [644d]. They are only too happy to accept a more developed account of human psychology than they could ever have previously imagined.) The Athenian elaborates upon this description by comparing the human being to a "divine puppet" (*thauma . . . theion*, 644d7–8). According to this image, the human being's fully realized nature is defined hierarchically: by nature, the developed intellect governs the soul's moderated passions.

This teleological image offers a preview of the ambitious goals toward which the Athenian strives in legislating for Magnesia. At his most optimistic, he strives to enable his future citizens to rule themselves with reason. In describing the puppet, however, the Athenian also foreshadows the tragic limitations on his capacity to achieve these admirable goals. He emphasizes humanity's limited rationality and understanding, its susceptibility to pleasure and pain, and the need for its (obviously superior, but comparatively weak) "golden cord" of calculation to acquire "helpers" (*hupêretôn*, 645a6) in order to rule the whole. Our powerful passions, i.e., the desire for pleasure and the fear of pain, are represented by iron cords that pull against one another and often overpower the golden cord of reason (644e; cf. 718e–719a). These characteristics apply to Kleinias as much as to Magnesia's future citizens. Reason's struggle to rule the iron cords occurs in the neighborhood of virtue and vice (644e), a point that links this image to the Athenian's account of the hierarchically arranged goods available to humanity (631c–d). The human being realizes his true essence when reason's leadership in the soul is respected and firmly entrenched, but the accomplishment will be remote and difficult. Nevertheless, the Athenian says, both cities and individuals would flourish should they live according to correct reasoning about these typically conflicting psychological cords (645b).

Within the Athenian's teleological framework, as we now understand, disorderly motion represents the disintegration of rational order, a defective condition that reflects ignorance of humanity's genuine nature—or a failure, for other reasons, to live up to that nature. However things may stand in the dissonant souls of most individuals, including Kleinias, the Athenian argues that it is in the nature of these passions to obey reason voluntarily, and not to

seek a position of domination. It is only the Athenian's model of the consonant soul ruled by reason—and not Kleinias' model of the self-dominating
soul—that can explain how individuals have agency, and what it means,
after all, for an individual to be superior to himself (cf. 626d–627a).[20] The
Athenian's efforts to embed elemental motion and conflict within a stable,
rational, and teleological framework foreshadows his strategy in the cosmological debates of Book 10, which are central to his education of Kleinias' rational part (*to logistikon*).

Communities of Practice: Goats, Symposia, and Cities

As the conversation unfolds, the Athenian elaborates his teleological framework by moving from the individual to the social world. He invites his
interlocutors to reflect on the meaning, possibilities, and purposes of existing
human practices and ways of life. Mirroring his discussion of the individual
soul, he distinguishes between social practices as they happen to be found
empirically and social practices as they might ideally become in a more fully
developed state. His underlying idea is that the flourishing of communities
requires engaged human intelligence and leadership; communities must be
constituted by a human agent who actively interprets them, imagines different possibilities, and makes judgments about what is best only after thorough exploration of existing alternatives.

In order to illustrate his point, the Athenian draws attention to a mun-
dane, but presumably for that reason compelling, example—the rearing of
goats (639a). The example enables him to reflect on the difference between
disheveled, untended herds of goats and herds that flourish under a goatherd's
rational supervision. He imagines intervening in a dispute over the value of
possessing goats as herd animals. In adopting a position in this dispute, should
we rely only on the opinion of those who had observed goats devastating cultivated land through their grazing, because they lacked a ruler or shepherd?
The answer is obviously no, because "goats gone wild" cannot inform us about
the potential for growth, development, and flourishing of goats as herd animals. Instead, we should consider the possibilities that emerge when we examine herds of goats governed by a knowledgeable leader; and the same holds

---

20. Compare the treatments of Sauvé Meyer 2015 and Bobonich 2002, with which my interpretation shares elements.

true for all communities that have a natural ruler (639c). We should judge their character based on their potential to flourish when ruled adequately by a prudent and capable leader (639a–c). The history of herds of goats and other communities may obscure what is potentially admirable and orderly in them, simply because those groups may have fallen into chaos through indiscipline, the indulgence of excessive and unhealthy desires, and, above all, by the lack of prudent supervision. On the other hand, we might determine what constitutes success—that which is normatively desirable—by conversing with observers familiar with a variety of more apparently successful practices across cultures. In this intervention, the Athenian distinguishes between a normative vision of goats as they might be, if ruled correctly, and a mere description of goats who have been observed, in history, in a disordered and uncultivated condition.

The same argument holds, though in a more fully developed form, in the ensuing conversation about the educational significance of symposia.[21] The Dorians have grown to maturity in cities hostile to the perceived corruption generated by symposia (637b), whereas the Athenian recommends an investigation of the global practices of convivial drinking, quite literally, as they manifest themselves in Scythia, Persia, Carthage, Iberia, and throughout Greece (637d–e). As with goats and symposia, so, too, with human beings and cities: what we might call "comparative politics" (cf. 702c–d) makes an essential contribution to the process of educating ourselves about diverse possibilities and considering in that light the possible functional goals or purposes of these entities and the related question of what constitutes their flourishing condition. In all these cases, the Athenian rejects empirical observation as an incomplete source of understanding. While the history of souls, herds of goats, symposia, and cities may suggest that the world is fundamentally constituted by disorder and internal conflict, it is possible to look upon the world and to imagine more adequately realized forms of souls, herds of goats, and so on, that offer a different, more positive interpretation of their natures—one that shows nature to be, in its fully realized state, well ordered and rationally intelligible.

---

21. See the useful treatment of Belfiore 1986. Landauer 2022 integrates the Athenian's portrayal of the symposium into his analysis of leadership and political power in the dialogue, but he does not connect it to the Athenian's construction of a purposive, teleological framework within which to understand human social activities; cf. also the penetrating discussion of Strauss 1975: 13–21.

Kleinias' Tyrannical Ambitions

In the course of discussing education and music, the Athenian elicits Kleinias' agreement on the educational significance of the poets' representation of virtuous citizens. Poetic songs—or "incantations for souls," as the Athenian pointedly insists on calling them (*epôidai tais psuchais*, 659e2)—have as their purpose the production of "consonance" (*sumphônian*, 659e3) in the soul. Kleinias declares emphatically that the correct form of moralizing poetry is available only on Crete and at Sparta, but nowhere else in the Greek world. That remark leads to an important set of exchanges in which the Athenian explores Kleinias' underlying beliefs about the ethical virtues and the happiness or success of human lives altogether. More specifically, he brings out for readers the tyrannical desires that Kleinias harbors in his soul, along with his astonishing lack of psychological "consonance."

In order to elicit Kleinias' underlying beliefs, the Athenian tempts him to embrace the prospect of tyrannical power. He vividly calls to mind the possessions that any Dorian might fantasize about—not only conventional health and wealth, but also the tyrannical power and even immortality that ordinary people can only dream of. Then he challenges Kleinias by proposing a dramatically counterintuitive thesis: that these so-called goods are not only not good, but are rather actively *bad*, for unjust people.[22] He wants to see what Kleinias will make of the connection between justice and happiness, although the results are entirely predictable. Given Kleinias' beliefs about vulnerability, domination, and shame, what possible reason could he have for *not* desiring tyranny? If he is presented with only two alternatives—domination or slavery—then he will find his choice to be obvious. The desire for tyranny and immortal power is already logically "baked in" to his understanding of what is good for him, and to his account of the anarchy and conflict that characterize not only interstate relations, but also human psychology and even the natural world. Concern for justice (much less any belief in justice's benefits, instrumental, intrinsic, or otherwise) had not arisen in Kleinias' initial presentation of relations among cities, within cities, or within individuals.

The Athenian begins once again with the Spartans' "national poet" Tyrtaeus. This time, however, he reinterprets Tyrtaeus according to his own lights. Whereas he had earlier presented a Tyrtaeus who praised warriors above all for their courage (629a–b), the new Tyrtaeus ("if he speaks correctly, at

---

22. The best discussion of this "dependency thesis" is Bobonich 2002, on which more below; cf. also Sauvé Meyer 2015 for a helpful, and rather different, view of this thesis.

any rate," 660e7–8) understands that justice is the critical quality that makes individuals praiseworthy. This transition is a watershed. It makes sense for Tyrtaeus, in his first appearance, to say that courage is the linchpin of a good human life, because he was the quintessentially Dorian (though cf. 629a) poet who assumed that military prowess was instrumental to protecting one's own belongings and way of life. In his revised view, however, justice takes center stage; but the Athenian does not immediately explain why it would.

The explanation emerges shortly thereafter. Despite Dorian culture's emphasis on militaristic success, it was always necessary, in addition, for that culture to promote respect for the justice embodied in law. That is why, in the ensuing argument, the Athenian asks the Dorian law-giving gods, Zeus and Apollo, and then the Dorian lawgivers and fathers themselves, why they had always insisted that their children "live as justly as possible" (*zên . . . hôs dikaiotata*, 662e). The Dorian cultures had always prized justice alongside military virtue, and, in his re-presentation of Tyrtaeus, the Athenian means to explore the relation of these virtues. The Athenian's interrogation of justice and courage makes vivid, by contrast, the absence of any attention to justice in Kleinias' initial presentation of his lawgiver's purposes. His views of domination and submission left no room for justice.

What, precisely, has Tyrtaeus learned in the preceding thirty Stephanus pages? "The things called good by the many," the poet says, "are not correctly so called" (661a). He has become anti-conventional in his view of the good life. He has begun to question the "good things" whose nature Kleinias had taken for granted. To be more concrete: the warrior who wins battles and is otherwise conventionally "successful" is not necessarily successful, after all. The conventional goods (health, wealth, power) are the "best possessions" (*arista ktêmata*) for just and pious men, but the worst for unjust men (661a5–d4). Tyrtaeus implicitly understands that the warrior's courage might conflict with and wrongly override the demands of justice: he would not wish the warrior who fights courageously without justice to be "successful" in any way. Tyrtaeus has departed substantially from conventional belief, as embodied in his earlier views. In addition, the new Tyrtaeus now endorses, in embryonic form at least, the unity of virtue: courage would not be courage if it were not also just.[23] The Athenian concludes: "About this thing that I'm asking, then,

---

23. Of course, he may endorse other possibilities, e.g., the copresence of virtue; but the discussion obviously looks toward the Athenian's questions about the unity of virtue in Book 12. By 696b–d, at any rate, Kleinias appears to have understood that courage must be balanced by moderation if it is to be considered a desirable quality. Pangle 1980 has highlighted questions of the unity of virtue in Books 1 and 2.

do you and I have consonance (*sumphônoumen*), or how do things stand?" (661d).

It may be that consonance in Kleinias' soul can emerge only through consonance with the Athenian's arguments. To be sure, however, the Athenian already knows that Kleinias will refuse to accept his counterintuitive proposal. Kleinias' "Cretan thesis" had held that the city exists to protect the (conventionally understood) "good things" (*ta . . . agatha*, 626b3–4)—including its "possessions" and way of life (626b2)—from imperialistic victors in war. Hence Kleinias is predictably ambivalent. He rejects the idea that a person will be unhappy (*mê . . . eudaimona*, 661e4), even miserable (*athlion*, 661e4), if he lives with health, wealth, tyrannical power, exceptional strength, courage, and immortality, but also with injustice and *hubris* in his soul (661d–e). Kleinias refuses to believe that this person will be unhappy, or even lead an unpleasant life. He accepts at least that he will live shamefully (*aischrôs*, 662a2)—but, again, not badly (*kakôs*, 662a5). Although Tyrtaeus has changed his opinions, Kleinias has not. He knows what he wants out of life, the "good things" understood in his shallow and conventional (yet also ambitiously tyrannical) way. He does not, however, acknowledge any role for justice in the good life. Nor does he find "shame" incompatible with that life.

Kleinias proves to be conventional in two particularly revealing respects. On the one hand, he derives his conception of the "good things" from "the many" (661a4–5), despite the contempt he had earlier expressed for their "ignorance" (*anoian*, 625e5).[24] What the many call good (661a–b) includes "ruling as a tyrant and doing whatever one desires" (661b2–3), as well as "the possession of all these things while becoming immortal as fast as possible" (661b3–4). The Athenian hammers home the inclusion of tyranny (661d, cf. 661e–662a) and immortality (661c, 661e) throughout this passage. Everyone (perhaps especially the militaristic Dorians) wants to rule the world with tyrannical, or even divine, power. It is merely conventional to want tyranny. Kleinias is no exception.

Why does the Athenian add "immortality" to this list of desirable goods? Two ideas recommend themselves. First, death is the ultimate consequence of shameful defeat at the hands of one's enemies. Death is shameful. In military terms, those who are dead are as weak as they will ever be. Kleinias may be unfamiliar with Homer (680c), but he agrees with Homer's Achilles at least to that extent.[25] Only apotheosis will enable the Dorians to protect themselves and

---

24. On this point cf. Strauss 1975: 28–29; Bobonich 2002: 131–36.

25. Balot and Schillinger, forthcoming.

their "good things" adequately. Second, the Athenian is speaking to a trans-political desire of the Dorians. Whether he knows it or not, Kleinias is searching for a place, not only in the city, but also in the *kosmos*. Traditionally, the desire for immortality, via immortal fame (*kleos*), was a standard heroic quest, achievable principally through military exploits. But that egregious militarism was disruptive to a peaceful political life. By the end of the dialogue, the Athenian supplies Kleinias with a place in the *kosmos* that proves entirely appropriate for this man of *thumos*. In that way, the Athenian makes his transpolitical desires useful for politics, whereas earlier they were disruptive to politics.

On the other hand, however, Kleinias believes that living tyrannically (etc.) is "shameful." This belief, too, is a conventional one. He has inherited it from the "fathers and lawgivers" invoked by the Athenian. If tyranny is shameful, then the "happy tyrant" is (in some as yet unspecified way) a wrong-doer. Tyrannical injustice and *hubris* are (somehow) important defects, which cannot easily be ignored. It is unclear whether, or how deeply, Kleinias is conscious of the contradiction between this belief and his belief that the "happy tyrant" leads the best human life. Either way, he has inherited this contradiction from his own lawgiver. Neither the law-giving gods nor the lawgiver himself has achieved consonance on the all-important question of which life leads to happiness—that of justice or that of pleasure, assuming that these lives are contrary (662c–e).[26]

Knowledgeable readers will no doubt appreciate the Athenian's numerous pregnant allusions to Plato's *Gorgias*.[27] If the young atheist of Book 10 resembles Callicles, as we previously noted, then Kleinias in Book 2 resembles Polus—a confused thinker who desires tyrannical power as the human good, without any self-conscious concern for shame, justice, or the health of his soul. Like Kleinias, Polus also embraces a glaring contradiction: that injustice and *hubris* are shameful, albeit not lacking in benefit for the successful tyrant. As in the present passage, Socrates reveals that Polus lacks harmony with himself, beginning with the incoherence of his stated intellectual positions. He goes on to show, moreover, that incoherence, or dissonance, is the chief problem

---

26. Hedonism is perhaps a predictable outgrowth of human nature: from the outset, the Athenian emphasizes that the legislator's chief interest—consuming almost his entire inquiry, he says (636d–e)—is in pleasure and pain, which arise first in nature, and which are central to the development of both individuals and cities (636d–e, 653a–b, 653c). "By nature," the Athenian announces in the general prelude, "the human (*anthrôpeion*) is most of all pleasures and pains and desires" (732e4–5). On the choice of lives in this situation, and on the passage as a whole, see Strauss 1975: 28–31.

27. Sauvé Meyer 2015 at least notes the allusions.

with Callicles' position, too. The incoherence that besets all these characters can be traced to the same cause: Kleinias, Polus, and Callicles all inherit their conceptions of what is good (in brief: tyrannical power) from the many, despite their initial belief that they are free thinkers who operate independently of the many.[28] Polus' shame—and Callicles' susceptibility to shame—reveals that his soul is characterized by a fundamental dissonance, as well as by an unquestioned deep commitment to conventional norms.[29] Unlike Polus, though, Kleinias will not be shamed, at least not yet, into agreeing that the tyrant's life is bad and unpleasant (661e–662a).

These allusions to the Platonic *Gorgias* also suggest that Kleinias is similar to both Polus and Callicles in another critical respect: his tyrannical fantasies are motivated by fear. Callicles, in particular, continually reveals an awareness of, and a constitutive intolerance for, his own vulnerability.[30] He is frightened that others will defeat him in court, take advantage of him sexually or otherwise, and, at the limit, enslave or execute him. He is fearful and watchful; he desires the ultimate sort of power in order to quiet those fears. What we see in the case of Kleinias is similar. Cretans and Spartans are raised in such a way as to safeguard their possessions in the belief that the world is a highly dangerous, anarchic, and competitive place. The lawgiver decreed that keeping up a watchful guard was so central to the human experience that peacetime did not even exist; social life was necessarily maintained on a persistently wartime basis. Being dominated by others, in a natural and political world where victory and defeat were the only options, was both a constant threat and an intolerable evil. Hence, courage, power, and military aggressiveness were essential to avoiding that intolerable outcome. Peaceful co-existence with outsiders was no longer seen to be possible. The aspiration to possess tyrannical power then became an ideal of its own.

In sum, Dorian culture (like the Athenian culture underlying Plato's Callicles) is beset by a profound internal contradiction. It actively, though surreptitiously and perhaps unwittingly, promotes tyrannical drives in every citizen. At the same time, it promotes a conventional sense of justice and shame. Hence, it cultivates in its citizens a deep-seated internal dissonance. Kleinias experiences this dissonance as conflict, as a civil war of the soul, which can be settled only through domination, that is, a victory over oneself and others.

---

28. On these themes in the *Gorgias*, see Balot, 2024b; Ober 1998; Kamtekar 2005.

29. Balot, 2024b; Shaw 2015.

30. Austin 2013.

Consonance Achieved through the Advent of a "God"

How can the Athenian move beyond Kleinias' unhealthy paradigm of civic relations and individual psychology? Now we come to another point that is amplified by the Athenian's allusions to the *Gorgias*. The Athenian sharply differentiates his approach to Kleinias from Socrates' approach to Polus and Callicles. Instead of shaming him or drilling down to the foundations of his dissonance, the Athenian brings Kleinias' self-contradiction to the surface only for the sake of the dialogue's readers. Like Polus and Callicles, Kleinias, too, lacks consonance, but the Athenian refrains from conducting a full-scale audit of his soul. He recognizes the impossibility or futility of such a project. When Kleinias asks how they will ever reach an agreement, the Athenian responds: "How? O friends, if a god should grant us agreement, as it seems, since now, at any rate, we sing at variance with one another (*apaidomen ap' allêlôn*)" (662b, tr. Pangle 1980, modified; cf. 659e). Where Socrates turns to rational argument, the Athenian rings in the god in order to persuade Kleinias to cooperate. How will the god perform that role? The Athenian does not explain his point explicitly, nor does he address the question, even implicitly, right away.

The Athenian's own train of argument will enable the "god" to manifest himself. He states forthrightly what he himself believes about the just life and happiness. He wants to ensure that no reader is unclear on these points. In effect, he says: I believe that the just life is the most pleasant and beneficial life; I would compel the poets to avoid even implying that an unjust life can be pleasant or profitable; and in that respect, my citizens would have different opinions from all humankind, including the Cretans and Lacedaimonians (662b–c). Certainly, the Athenian does not argue his case against the supposedly "happy tyrant," as Socrates did in the *Gorgias* and the *Republic*.[31] Rather, he declares that his views appear more necessary to him than the natural, observable, and uncontestable fact that Crete is an island (662b). His ethical view resembles, to him, a fact of nature. It is naturalistically true, in his opinion, that the just life is the life of happiness.

To unpack that view in detail would require a long discussion, but the Athenian is not interested in having that discussion right now. Presumably, he has had it elsewhere, and to his own satisfaction. He is aware that the

---

31. Strauss 1975: 31.

discussion forms the subject of long dialogues such as the *Republic* and the *Gorgias*—and those dialogues have, I believe, helped to shape his own views—but he won't delve deeply into the discussion now, or anywhere else in this dialogue.[32] At all events, by calling this truth "necessary," the Athenian indicates his belief that this doctrine is clearly and obviously true, even more clearly and obviously true than the self-evidently true statement that Crete is an island (cf. 663d).

Such is the Athenian's view; what of the view of the Cretans, the Lacedaimonians, and the rest of humankind? The traditional law-giving gods, Zeus and Apollo, fail to make sense of the relation of justice to happiness (662c–d), but it is blasphemous to subject *them* to cross-examination. Unlike Socrates, who questions the god in the *Apology*, the Athenian is always concerned to strengthen religion, to promote the cause of piety. Only the gods' surrogates—fathers and lawgivers—can be examined directly. When they are subjected to questioning, they can be seen to contradict themselves: they admire the pleasant life as the happiest life, but they also require the young to live justly. They cannot explain whether or why the just life is happiest—that is, what "good and noble thing" it possesses, which is "better than pleasure" (662e–663a). The young (foreshadowing the young atheist) might well wonder: Why, father, did you command me to behave justly, when you wanted—didn't you—me to be happy? (662e). By this stage of his presentation, the Athenian is suggesting, at least, that the traditional gods, in having no good explanation for these things, cannot produce agreement among the three interlocutors. In referring to the god who will produce consonance, he is therefore emphatically, as he now indicates, not referring to the law-giving gods, Zeus and Apollo, not to mention their human surrogates.[33]

The traditional gods and lawgivers cannot save us; instead, they lead us to an impasse. How was the traditional lawgiver, then, to respond to circumstances in which he has no adequate account of the human good and yet must, for political purposes, produce *some* account of the relationship between justice, pleasure, and happiness? Every political regime embodies some such account. According to the Athenian, he was forced to turn to social shame and reputation. The lawgiver himself is imagined as imploring his citizens: "Come, are fame and praise from men and the gods, then, good and noble, and yet

---

32. Strauss 1975, followed by Schofield 2003, 2006 and Rowe 2010.

33. Strauss 1975.

unpleasant, and bad reputation the opposite? Least of all, O dear lawgiver, we will say. But it isn't unpleasant, is it, though good or noble, for someone neither to do injustice nor to suffer it at someone else's hands? Are the opposites pleasant but shameful and bad?" (663a). Kleinias answers: "How could they be?" In a nutshell, this exchange embodies the ethical teachings of the traditional gods and lawgivers. Having a good reputation makes it pleasant to live a life without either doing or suffering injustice; it is *ex hypothesi* good and noble to live such a life. Hence, the lawgiver has identified one way—that is, by means of good reputation—to make the life of pleasure and the life of justice coincide.[34] Taking that coincidence as his essential aim, the traditional lawgiver finds no other means to effect it.

Although Kleinias is attracted to this approach, however, it cannot provide a lasting solution to the deeper problem. These teachings are beleaguered by the preceding dilemma and bespeak a certain desperation, a genuine, political *aporia*. The lawgiver's approach leads right back to, and indeed, it is the foundation of, the ethical ambiguities Kleinias experiences. Kleinias secretly harbors a tyrant within. He restrains that tyrant only because his powerful sense of his own vulnerability leads him to obey the law willingly provided that others, too, will do so—almost in the manner of the "weak," law-abiding citizens imagined by Glaucon or Callicles.[35] Citizens beset by such internal dissonance, though, will hardly achieve the "friendship" and political "consonance" desired by the three old men (cf. 627e). Like Kleinias, the imagined citizens will have no solid grasp of the connections between justice, pleasure, and happiness. The Athenian has uncovered how even well-intentioned, though ignorant, fathers and lawgivers, basing themselves on traditional lawgiving gods, have managed to produce citizens like Kleinias—citizens who desire tyranny because they fail to grasp the connections between justice and their own flourishing. The traditional law is inadequate, because it is bound to lead to civic conflict, and to create psychologically "dissonant" citizens such as Kleinias.

---

34. Cf. the interpretation of Pangle 1980. The Athenian reinforces this argument by proposing that just and unjust men take pleasure in different things; as a result, he argues, it might be reasonable to consider which person's opinion carries more authority (663cd, cf. 654d).

35. It is ironic, then, that the lawgiver speaks of "fame" (*kleos*, 663a3; cf. *duskleia*, 663a4) in a heroic register. Perhaps the point is that the lawgiver has tried, mostly unsuccessfully, to convince his militaristic citizens that somehow obeying the law, neither doing nor suffering injustice, is itself heroic. If that is the traditional lawgiver's attempt to satisfy his citizens' desire for immortal fame, then we can see why they would continue to desire immortality in a more robust sense.

Consider carefully the structure of the Athenian's argument: You, Kleinias, harbor tyrannical desires. Only a god can deliver agreement to us. My view is that the just life is, in some sense, the flourishing life. Your traditional gods and lawgivers cannot make sense of their demands for justice, in light of the universal desire for pleasure and happiness. Perhaps they can point weakly to reputation as a mediating possibility that enables justice and happiness to coincide. That, however, is a flimsy solution. Here, to repeat, is the principle on which I believe we must agree: "It is necessary (*anankaion*), therefore, that the unjust life is not only more shameful and ignoble, but also in truth more unpleasant than the just and pious life (*tou dikaiou . . . hosiou biou*)" (663d2–4). Kleinias remains extremely skeptical: that is true, he says—"according to the present argument, at all events" (663d). The god has still not delivered consonance of any sort. Nor has the Athenian explained in any way how the god will intervene to help them agree.

It is precisely at this point that the Athenian introduces the possibility of lying to the citizens about justice and happiness. At the Athenian's suggestion, Kleinias agrees that this principle, about which he is so skeptical, should form the basis of a profitable lie (*pseudos*), to be announced in "songs (*ôidais*) and stories (*muthois*) and arguments (*logois*)" (664a). Its great benefit would be to encourage people to behave justly out of a decided willingness to do so, and not from compulsion (663d6–664b2). The Athenian had said that the god would deliver agreement; now a lie delivers agreement. (And it does: abandoning his former skepticism, Kleinias now responds: "At least with regard to these things [the benefits of the lie], it seems to me that neither one of us would ever be able to dispute it," 664b1–2). It is no coincidence that this agreement is based on a lie that has taken the place of a god: a civil religion is the means by which Kleinias, and presumably the future citizenry, comes to accept that the just life is the source of human flourishing. In a specific sense to be outlined immediately, the god supports the "lie," the noble "myth," whose message will be disseminated in "songs," in order that the Athenian and Kleinias will no longer "sing at variance with" (662b2) one another. Yet how is the god equivalent to a lie, as the logic of the Athenian's argument suggests?

We are now well positioned to understand the Athenian's appeal to the god who will deliver consonance (662b). The Athenian surely does not mean that one of the traditional gods, like Zeus, will come down from Olympus to broker an agreement among these disputatious human beings. Nor does he mean that the traditional, law-giving gods will produce consonance between them; that possibility has just been repudiated. The Athenian's meaning becomes clear if, and only if, we understand his words in a "metatextual" way.

He is referring to how things will work in this very dialogue. In the *Laws* itself, religion—a "god"—will provide the necessary means of persuasion by which less enlightened citizens can come to appreciate that the life of justice is essential to their happiness. The Athenian chooses a religious rather than an argumentative strategy, because he is convinced that Kleinias cannot be persuaded by a Socratic refutation of his view. Indeed, the unphilosophical Kleinias cannot even understand such conversations.

How will the god perform his assigned role? To look ahead, the Athenian is preparing to develop a civil religion according to which the god guarantees that just individuals will reap their appropriate rewards, while the unjust will be appropriately punished. According to this civil religion, the "god"—who appears in such memorable speeches as the address to colonists (Book 4: 715e–718a), and the second and third arguments of Book 10—providentially cares for justice and guarantees its efficacy in the human world, on the side of both reward and punishment. If, as the Dorians believe, the justice/happiness principle cannot be true by nature, then the god can intervene philanthropically, almost miraculously, in order to make it true, by caring for the just and by punishing the unjust. For the Dorians, the justice/happiness principle now seems to be a useful lie, but they will eventually recognize its truth. In the course of the *Laws* itself, they will come to see that the god's care for humanity makes the principle true. Thus, to be precise, the god serves as the foundation for what Kleinias supposes to be a lie: that the just life is the flourishing life.

Kleinias may well believe that a god will, literally, somehow produce consonance among the three interlocutors. The Athenian does nothing to discourage this belief. The logic of the discussion, though, and the Athenian's mention of the god right here, is arguably an attempt to communicate with the dialogue's readers. By the good offices of the god, the Athenian implies, in his role as a providential figure of Magnesia's civil religion, Kleinias will eventually come to agree that justice is the critical factor in human life that leads to happiness and fulfillment. The reason is that the unjust will be appropriately punished, while the just will receive recognition and reward from the god. To make the point differently, Kleinias will learn to prize justice from piety—like the citizenry of Magnesia itself. It is relevant that, in this passage, the Athenian refers three times to the connection between justice and piety (661b, 663b, 663d); "he does not speak of wisdom and good sense: holiness seems to take the place of these 'intellectual' virtues."[36] If Kleinias is ever

---

36. Strauss 1975: 28.

to credit justice with a role in producing human happiness, then it will be through a pious belief in the god's providential care for humanity. He will never, on the other hand, come to believe that justice naturally carries with it intrinsic rewards: that justice, all by itself, and prized just for itself, constitutes a leading source of human fulfillment.[37]

Scholars have frequently discussed the willingness of "Plato" to tell lies for the good of his imaginary citizens.[38] Whatever Plato may think, it is important that it is Kleinias, not the Athenian, who is prepared to lie to the future citizenry, because he refuses to believe, at least at the moment, that justice necessarily rewards the just with happiness.[39] For the Athenian, by contrast, the justice/happiness principle is true by nature. The rhetorical and logical movement of the passage should not obscure the Athenian's own unequivocal conviction about it. We have already examined his statement about Crete, the island. Now he says: "But even if things were not as the argument has just shown them to be . . . ," then we could, he says, lie to the citizens about it (663d, tr. Griffith). This statement is a contrary-to-fact conditional and indicates, without any grammatical ambiguity, that the justice/happiness principle is in fact true (in the Athenian's view).[40] Unlike the "just and pious" man without intellectual virtues, the Athenian's *nous* enables him to see that the just life is the most flourishing life by nature. From the Athenian's perspective, however, the civil religion that he develops for the Dorians' sake is still itself a myth, a "lie." The Athenian himself does not hold

---

37. Kleinias understands that a commitment to justice, at least as embodied in the law, is essential to preserving cities in the face of universal tyrannical desires. Even though he fails to grasp the intrinsic rewards of justice, he recognizes that justice is, at the very least, instrumentally important for the stability and security of cities. See Lutz 2012: 139–44 for an excellent discussion of the connections forged by the Athenian among justice, happiness, and divine providence, on which my account builds.

38. E.g., Pangle 1980: 415–16; Schofield 2006: 288–302. For Karl Popper, of course, this passage, along with others from the *Republic* and *Timaeus*, helps to build the case that Plato is a totalitarian and an enemy of the open society (Popper 2011). Stalley 1983: 63 is similarly harsh: "The disreputable argument is that, whether true or not, it will be useful to propagate the idea that the just life is pleasantest, since no one would allow himself to be talked into an act unless it produces more pleasure than pain (663b)." In a more sympathetic vein, Morrow 1960: 557 contends: "Sometimes the legislator indulges in something close to beneficent deception."

39. Alongside discussions of "noble lies," scholars have also explored the Athenian's precise thinking on the connection between justice and happiness, e.g., Annas 2017, Lutz 2012. The question of that relationship is an important one, of course, but it is not one that the Athenian himself pursues. He does not strive—in this dialogue, at least—to establish a precise philosophical position on these questions.

40. As England 1921 1:305 says, "He is careful, by the extremely hypothetical form of the question, to guard against the idea that he himself for a moment doubts the reality of his previous conclusion." Morrow 1960: 557n.30 is also emphatic about the Athenian's own endorsement of the view that "justice leads to happiness."

this (providential, caring, and philanthropic) view of the god. In Books 3 and 4, as we will discover, the human world is subject to chance and natural necessity. No one should expect the god to intervene philanthropically.[41]

The Athenian himself, however, *does* intervene philanthropically in the foundation of Magnesia. To a great extent, his intervention involves trying to embody in law ideas and principles that he views as naturalistically true, even if he cannot argue rationally for them before his Dorian interlocutors. Prior to the present section of the text, the Athenian had emphasized the need to explore whether their current argument about music and education was "true according to nature" (*alêthês . . . kata phusin*) or not (653d). His emphasis on the truth shines through in numerous places throughout the text.[42] In his ensuing discussion of Egyptian lawgiving, he had gone on to indicate that he considers it "true" (*alêthes*) and "worthy of consideration" (*axion ennoias*) that lawgivers can mandate "tunes which are most correct by nature" (657a). While he admits that many features of the Egyptian law code are "worthless" (*phaul'*), he admires the lawgiver's "firmness" in laying down unchanging laws (657a): if someone could understand these things clearly, then "it is necessary for him, in an act of daring (*tharrounta*), to order them in law" (657b). The lawgiver's role, he declares, belongs to "a god or some godlike man," just as in Egypt the songs of Isis have been preserved for so long (657a). The Athenian has shown us, in the sequel, how a godlike man—i.e., himself—can entrench certain (naturalistically) true principles in law, through "daring" (cf. 663d8: *etolmêsen*) to lie to the citizenry, i.e., to establish a civil religion that will enable them to glimpse what is true by nature in a different register.[43]

---

41. Allan Bloom's statement in another context is worth quoting in this connection: "The Stranger must have the consent of the other two to operate his reform of existing orders. Their particular prejudices must be overcome, but not by true persuasion of the truth; the new teaching must be made to appear to be in accord with their ancestrally hallowed opinions" (Bloom 1968, xxi). "True persuasion of the truth" is in this case impossible.

42. The Athenian is concerned with the truth throughout the work. Immediately beforehand, for example, he had emphasized exploring whether the current argument is "true according to nature" (*alêthês . . . kata phusin*) or not (653d). The Athenian later emphasizes the grave difficulties that attend upon convincing people of the truth, but he says that one must dare to try (835c). Apart from the present passage, he stresses truth and truthfulness, no matter what level of courage they demand: see, for example, 664c, 668a, 709c, 731e–732a, 738e, 746b–c, etc.

43. Note that the Athenian has also just shown, in re-presenting Tyrtaeus in Book 2, that he can change the poets' tunes as necessary, so as to "mandate tunes that are correct by nature." If poets can be easily compelled to change their songs, though, then the Athenian's interlocutors will require a more elaborate process of transformation, i.e., a god.

3

The Politics and Psychology of Human History

WHAT IS THE connection between Kleinias' tyrannical fantasies and his presentation of his own city's purposes—namely, his belief that the city exists in order to protect "good things" (*ta . . . agatha*, 626b3–4) from imperialistic victors in war? Kleinias' watchfulness—his *fear*—and his fantastical, self-aggrandizing desires are closely connected. As with Polus and Callicles in the Platonic *Gorgias*, Kleinias' fantasies grow out of his fears. Book 3 will uncover a fuller explanation of that connection.

In Book 3, the Athenian examines the possibility of moving from the desire to safeguard one's possessions to the projection of acquisitive, tyrannical desires. He explicitly links this theme to the initial discussion of the Dorians' law-codes (682e–683a; cf. 688a–c). He explores this theme, moreover, in the dialogue's most Herodotean and Thucydidean section.[1] Book 3 concerns the origins of society and the history of several celebrated regimes—Troy, Sparta, Persia, Athens. Human history shows that Kleinias' "realism" (that is, his

---

1. Schofield 2006: 197–199 frames his analysis of Platonic utopian writing as a "choice between Thucydides and Plato" (198). Farrar 2013 analyzes the dialogue's historical survey in related ways, helpfully distinguishing between humanity as it is and as it might be; although I am sympathetic to Farrar's view that "Plato" was "questioning where history itself fits, and putting it in its place" (34), I differ on various points, including Plato's relationship to Thucydides and his purposes in writing Book 3 and the *Laws* in general (Farrar 2013: 33: a "detailed blueprint for a good city."), not to mention the interpretation of Thucydides' *History* itself. For another kind of contextual analysis of Book 3, see Atack 2020. A more standard view of Book 3 is that of Klosko 2006: 226: "What is striking and original about the *Laws* is that he [Plato] makes use of conclusions that his historical investigation casts up." Cf. Schofield 2010: 18: "a historical survey, designed to discover basic principles of *politeia* construction which have to be observed if a political community is to achieve health and stability"; cf. Schofield 2012: 104–105. For the view that Plato based his political theory in the dialogue on history, see Samaras 2002.

Tragedy, Philosophy, and Political Education in Plato's Laws. Ryan K. Balot, Oxford University Press.
© Ryan K. Balot 2024. DOI: 10.1093/oso/9780197647226.003.0003

thesis about war and peace) is actually correct—but only at a descriptive level. World history reveals that the motions of war *have* persistently constituted the horizons of the human experience. Because of humanity's uncultivated spiritedness (*thumos*) and excessive desire (*epithumia*), combined with profound ignorance, states are constantly at war with one another; faction is the besetting difficulty of settled cities; and individuals lack psychological consonance. Kleinias can discover a great mass of empirical evidence that seems to confirm not only his psychological account of the individual, but also his cynical representation of interstate relations. In response, the Athenian reveals that humanity's suffering throughout history was hardly inevitable. Rather, it was the result of human ignorance and vice. The lives of individuals and cities can be transformed through taking a different perspective on the "human goods."

The Archaeology of Kleinias: Early Human History

The Athenian develops an intriguing vocabulary to describe humanity's lamentable history. Book 3 begins with the Athenian's inquiry into the *archê* of the *politeia* (676a).[2] He says that "many thousands of cities have arisen" during an "infinite period of time" (676b–c), and he wants to grasp the first *genesis* of regimes and the cause (*aitia*) of their transformations and destruction (676c). Political history is the history of a human world that is constantly in motion, rising and falling (676c), and getting bigger and smaller (676c). That world has always been governed by the motions of war and ruled by force. These motions can be aptly described in terms that resonate with philosophical theories of matter and motion, such as *archê, genesis*, and *aitia*. In light of the historical account in Book 3, Kleinias' view seems as plausible as ever, based on the evidence of human affairs: the underlying principles of nature, including human nature, are chaos, warfare, motion.[3]

Because human history attests to the plausibility of Kleinias' initial, militaristic outlook, the onus of persuading us otherwise will fall on the Athenian. He wants to argue that Kleinias' realism fails to answer adequately to human

---

2. For helpful remarks on the "beginning" in Book 3, see Sallis 2013.

3. For a treatment that compares Book 3 with Book 10 and emphasizes human agency and chance on the terrestrial level, see Nightingale 1999a, a piece that takes the historiography of this book seriously, as a "serious attempt to address the nature of history and the notion of historical causality" (301). Readers will see that my own view differs considerably.

beings' potential to live peaceful, flourishing lives governed by reason.[4] Here the Athenian builds on his discussion of "goats gone wild." Contrary to the accounts of Thucydides or Herodotus, the Athenian proposes that the persistent disasters of human history, however tangible and real, are the result of ignorance rather than human nature (687d–688b, 688c–d, 688e), construed according to his positive, normative vision (cf., e.g., 686d). Human history has produced a landscape that resembles devastated rather than cultivated land. How can we explain that devastated landscape? How can we dare to elicit from it a more optimistic vision of human life?

As a first step, the Athenian requires the Dorians to acknowledge that early history was a time of calamitous floods, diseases, and other natural disasters (677a). Readers, at least, will understand that humanity, thrown into an inhospitable and even cataclysmic world, was not provided for by the god.[5] It was left to its own arts, which were continually destroyed along with their makers (677c–d). In the beginning, herdsmen could barely live from their herds (677e). Fear is an understandable response to the isolation, difficulty, and devastation they came to know (677e, cf. 678c, 680d). As time went on, however, life improved: a sparse population, an abundance of land, and the lack of iron and copper ruled out warfare and conflict (678e–679a). "Neither arrogance nor injustice" (679c), nor any kind of competition or envy, could gain a foothold among the men of that time: they were neither poor nor wealthy, because their herding and hunting provided adequately, though not superabundantly, for them. Even though the Athenian is ostensibly pursuing the question of how laws and regimes came into existence, his more specific interest, at least initially, lies in explaining how an aggressive, militaristic ethos came to be instilled in the human communities that arose in this initially frightening and desolate, but then abundant and rather peaceful landscape.

One fact is clear: an important transformation from peaceful to warlike human beings has taken place over the course of human history. As human beings became more sophisticated and technically accomplished, they also built a world for which Kleinias—with his fearful suspicions, tyrannical desires, *thumos*, and sense of chaos—is a suitable representative and spokesman. The Athenian contrasts humanity's initial peacefulness with the

---

4. For an illuminating (albeit contrasting) interpretation of the Athenian's purposes in Book 3, see Zuckert 2009: 73–77.

5. Strauss 1975: 39; Pangle 1980: 424; Nightingale 1999a; Rowe 2010.

present-day arts of war, including factionalism within the city (679d–e), and with the "contrivances" (*mêchanôn*, 677b, cf. 679e) that men now use to pursue their greed (*pleonexias*), competitiveness (*philonikias*), and wrong-doing (*kakourgêmata*, 677b). The Athenian sums up the transition: "So from those people, in those circumstances, everything that we have now has come into being, both cities and regimes and arts and laws, and a great deal of wickedness, but also a great deal of virtue" (678a7–9). For the Athenian, humanity possesses an ineliminable potential for virtue, which he aspires to pursue, despite the aggression and excessive desires that have now become rampant.

The Athenian's explanation for this transformation is that the early human beings' peace and moderation were unstable. Their peacefulness was not based on any impressive ethical accomplishment. More than anything else, circumstances (moderate means of living, lack of metal weapons) accounted for their good will toward another (678c)—as well as, the Athenian says, their "so-called simplicity" (*dia tên legomenên euêtheian*, 679c).[6] In a striking reference to Thucydides' description of the Corcyraean civil war (3.83.1), the Athenian explains that these early human beings were ignorant and unsophisticated primitives. They had no critical faculties or even the capacity to question possible lies—for example, he says, lies about the gods (679c). They had natural virtues (courage, moderation, and justice) without *nous*, the leader of the virtues.[7] Their virtues, that is, had no anchor in their understanding of the world. Even if they were gifted with virtuous inclinations, they were ignorant.

Their ignorance explains why political regimes, and not simply ethical dispositions, were unreliable sources of peace, justice, and moderation. It should not surprise readers that politics quickly progressed, or disintegrated, to the level of tyrannical *pleonexia*. Remarkably, the Athenian explains that the first political regime, dynasty (*dunasteia*), was exemplified by Homer's Cyclopes. These Cyclopes lived in caves without any laws other than the tyranny of each man over his children and wives, plural (680b–c). Megillus appreciates that the Athenian is highlighting their "savagery" (*agriotêta*, 680d3)—though Kleinias does not grasp the point, since he is unfamiliar with Homer (680c). Megillus, though, and above all, Plato's readers, will immediately think of Polyphemus' deceptions and barbarism in Homer's *Odyssey*, as well as Odysseus' gloriously warlike but grotesque defense of

---

6. Rightly emphasized by Strauss 1975: 40.

7. For a justly critical account of "natural virtue" that lacks *nous*, see Bobonich 2002; cf. Pangle 1980: 425–426.

himself and his soldiers. Political regimes originate in barbarism. What is more, dynasty still exists "in many places both among Greeks and barbarians" (680b). The world is pervasively shot through, even now, with the savagery of barbaric Cyclopes. That is, unless our situation has deteriorated even further: according to the Athenian, the Cyclopean monarchy is the "most just" monarchy implicitly, because it is based on rule by the elder, handed down by parents or ancestors (680d–e); at least, the Cyclopes did not attack one another. Cyclopean monarchy is the best and most just form of monarchy? The Athenian shocks and amuses readers, unbeknownst to Kleinias, but he also indicates clearly the disposition of human beings whose potential for virtue remains undeveloped.

Farming communities would seem to herald a new, more peaceful, and more stable way of life. Odysseus and his bread-eating comrades survived their encounter with Polyphemus and formed cities. Whatever peace and stability they may have created, however, is almost immediately destroyed. These early communities took it as their first task to build defensive walls in order to protect themselves against "savage beasts" (*tôn thêriôn*, 681a): these "savage beasts" no doubt include the savage Cyclopes, along with other potential (human) aggressors; there are few armies of wild beasts.[8] These communities comprised the manly and the orderly (681b). If it is appropriate to detect a reference to Plato's *Statesman* in this description (306d–308b), then the *andrikoi* were driven by *thumos* and primed for war—as they had been, presumably, prior to arriving at the larger settlements, since their manliness was already ancestrally ingrained (681a–b), a point of pride (681c).

If the early human communities were primed to defend themselves, and even to engage in warfare, then humanity was already prepared for large-scale, far-flung militaristic ventures. Hence, still following Homer, the Athenian describes the foundation of Troy, now in the plain, leaving it up to his readers, and perhaps Megillus, to recall Troy's famous epithet "beautifully walled." Every reader of Homer understands that the Trojans relied on defensive walls to guard their city (cf. 685c–d for Troy's earlier military history). The Athenian does not particularly explain the Greeks' military expedition against Troy (682c–d), but Troy's well-known defensive walls were crucial to the effort to defend against Achaea's invaders. (Troy had already been sacked once, by Heracles, and relied on King Ninos' Assyrian Empire for protection, as the Athenian explains: 685c–d. Imperialism emerged at the beginning

---

8. See, especially, Pangle 1980: 427–428 on these inferences.

of human settlement.) The Achaeans were the "manly" and "savage" beasts against whom the Trojans defended themselves. We have now, perhaps, discovered the origins of the Dorian lawgivers' concern to establish a guard against predators. To repeat: no providential god intervened in these "epic" disasters of early human history. Fearfulness and imperialism dominated. The principal elements of Kleinias' psychology already shine forth from the earliest dawn of humanity.

It is at this stage that readers arrive at the heart of the story, insofar as it concerns Kleinias and his Dorian ancestry. The Athenian uses the recollection of the Trojan War to bring his interlocutors to a discussion of the foundation of Lacedaimon. The Achaeans' external wars led to internal *stasis*, as the "young men" refused to honor the returning heroes; they tried to slaughter them instead (682d–e). As the Athenian had suggested in Book 1, external war and internal war are intimately linked. The Athenian indicates that "the god" has led the discussion around again to the opening exchanges that concerned the Spartan and Cretan law codes (682e–683a; cf. 688a–c). Who is the god, if not the Athenian himself?[9]

The Athenian's selective history shows that human communities have always been trapped in a "security dilemma": under threat from others, and fearing attack, they have risen to defend themselves and thereby caused other cities to do the same. They have also developed enormous seagoing armies in order to, as Homer tells his readers, avenge insults. With the return of the Achaeans from Troy and, subsequently, the victorious return of the exiled "Dorians" (682e), we see that internal political violence has become as prominent as external warfare. The movement from external to internal conflict mirrors the same movement in Book 1, from interstate war to civil war to warfare within the individual soul. Within the framework of the "security dilemma," at all events, preemptive strikes will always blur the line between offensive and defensive war. By now we find nothing more than a world of war, fit for treatment by Thucydides. Early, primitive qualities of justice—which were never self-conscious or anchored by the intellect, and which resulted chiefly from chance or circumstance—have given way to the toxic aggressions characteristic of the life of "savages." That historical process, in short, provides a deep, "archaeological" explanation for Kleinias' own fearful suspicions, aggressive desires, and belief in the anarchical instability of the political world—and possibly the world at large.

---

9. Strauss 1975: 42: "the Athenian's providence for his interlocutors."

The Early History of Lacedaimon and the Dorians

This theme plays itself out with variations in the history of Lacedaimon. The three old men agree to explore, on the basis of their new understanding of history, lawgiving and regimes "from the beginning" again (683b). The Dorians founded three cities—Argos, Messene, and Lacedaimon—and decided that they should be ruled monarchically. These cities were held together by oaths and defensive pacts of a complex sort. Within cities, citizens agreed not to overturn the regime, so long as their monarchs refrained from oppressing them. Across the three cities, monarchs and citizens agreed severally to support one another if any king or any populace should be treated unjustly (684a–b). In other words, both rulers and ruled agreed to alliances in which they would neither do nor suffer injustice. This framework of defensive alliances anticipates that friendship is impossible. The underlying assumption is that individuals and states are untrustworthy, aggressive, and acquisitive. Even so, the founders' intention was the admirable one of leading the Greeks or, more specifically, of protecting the Greeks against the injustice of the barbarians (685b–c).

So, after all, what sort of "chance" (*tuchê*), the Athenian asks, destroyed this political alliance (686b)? The "brother kings" came to blows with one another before long (686a–b). Their lack of harmony made them all but incapable of leading the Greek effort against the Persians (692c–693a). The Athenian shows that their political failure to maintain "consonance" (*sumphônêsasa eis hen*, 686b3) originated in their ignorance, both of their own impulses and of what is most important in human life. Their ignorance would eventually destroy the alliance.[10]

The chief cause, as the Athenian explains in detail, was hardly chance. The only "chance" (so to speak) was that the Dorian leaders found themselves in possession of a beautiful, "amazing," powerful military force. The Athenian pretends that this "wondrous possession" (*thaumaston ktêma*) had simply "befallen" (*parapesein*) the Greeks (686d9–10). Possessing military power, though, was the foreseeable, indeed logical, result of cities' decisions to place themselves permanently on a wartime footing. The Dorians possessed military force because they wanted it, first, in order to protect themselves from

---

10. On the complexities of the Athenian's account of Peloponnesian history in this section, see the helpful accounts of Strauss 1975: 43–45 and Schofield 2013. Schofield 2013: 289 holds that "history is invoked as a way of investigating what makes a *politeia successful*"—though, in my view, the investigation does not in fact yield this result.

one another and from outsiders, and then, in order to seek to acquire more and more for themselves. The security dilemmas and aggressive drives that had characterized all human communities until that time encouraged the Dorians to put their energies into developing this fine, powerful army—and, as a result, to devote correspondingly less time to understanding how to use it well, in order to flourish (cf. *eudaimonoi*, 686e7).

The Athenian develops this thought by illustrating the Dorians' own understanding of the best use to which they might put their wondrous army. Consider his description of the mentality that prevailed at the time:

> If those who were organizing things at that time had known how to order the army properly, how would they have made the best of their opportunity? Wouldn't they have kept it firmly united and preserved it for the rest of time, so that they could be free and rule over whichever others they wanted, and so that they and their children could do whatever they desired among all human beings altogether, both Greek and barbarian? Wouldn't they be praised for these things? (687a4–b3)

Megillus enthusiastically agrees (687b–c). This fantasy of godlike power was originally rooted in a defensive alliance established for the sake of safety and freedom. That alliance and its associated motivations quickly, however, took on a more aggressive orientation. As in Thucydides, "freedom" (such as Athenian democratic freedom) was transferred from its domestic, political context to an imperialistic context in which it denoted the freedom to rule.[11] When human beings use power to fulfill whatever desires they may have, without intelligence, as the Athenian is suggesting (687b–e), it becomes difficult, if not impossible, to focus on maintaining a moderate guard on one's possessions without also conceiving of excessive and even tyrannical desires. As Megillus appreciates, at least in part, the leadership of *phronêsis* or *nous* is necessary to making one's possessions genuinely contribute to a flourishing and successful life (687e). Either way, the prehistory of Kleinias' own drives, passions, and cynical ideas about political life has now come into sharp focus.

---

11. See Balot 2009a, with Raaflaub 2004. Freedom has become a contentious topic among recent interpreters of the dialogue: Sauvé Meyer 2021; de Nicolay 2021; Schofield 2013.

The Regime's Goal: A Retrospective Account

Strikingly, the Athenian chooses precisely this moment to refer explicitly to the opening discussion of Book 1. He links the present discussion to the early contrast between the Dorian legislator's emphasis on courage alone and his own emphasis on the cultivation of all the virtues, led, he now says, by prudence (*phronêsis*), intelligence (*nous*), and opinion (*doxa*, 688a–b).[12] By referring readers back to that contrast, the Athenian indicates that the Dorians' focus on courage without intelligence constitutes a source of toxic manliness and aggression both within the city and in the wider world. It is impossible to contain an immoderate and unjust style of "courage" by limiting it to the defense of one's own possessions. Particularly when defensive military preparations are driven by constant fear, individuals and cities will, like Kleinias, begin to develop tyrannical fantasies of freedom, including the freedom to subjugate others. Courage will take on a destructive life of its own, when unmoored from the moderating impulses of justice and the clear vision of *nous*. Hence, the Athenian stresses that the kings destroyed themselves, not through cowardice—they had, indeed, a certain imprudent form of courage—but rather, through the rest of vice, especially ignorance "about the greatest things in human affairs" (688c–d). In their ignorance, they still resembled the early savages and primitives; what had changed was their development of unprecedented military power.[13]

History tells us, then, a sad story. In part because of the pressures of circumstance, and in part because of their ignorance, the first human lawgivers were toxically aggressive primitives with a thoroughly inadequate conception of human goodness. They admired large, powerful armies without recognizing that such impressive instruments of power are beneficial only if they are used with wisdom (686d–687b). They saw their good as lying in

---

12. Although Bobonich 2002 sees in this passage an upgrading of *doxa* that dignifies the understanding and virtue of ordinary people, he fails to acknowledge the dramatic context or other passages that deny the equivalence of knowledge and *doxa*; more correct is Thomas Pangle 1980: 433: "Intelligence must be much diluted in order to become an object of the laws' or the city's striving"; cf. Strauss 1975: 45–46. Strauss's discussion helps to reveal the way in which this passage's characterization of ignorance points ahead to the Athenian's examination of the Socratic paradox in the penal code (860c–864c).

13. Hence the evolution of the Athenian's argument is highly Thucydidean, in that progress in the development of technologies of power does not improve human life, but rather contributes to human suffering, i.e., pathos: see Immerwahr 1973. The difference is that the Athenian focuses on ignorance as the key cause, whereas Thucydides focuses on the expansion of desire: Balot 2001b.

the free satisfaction of desire through imperialistic expansion (687a–b).[14] Kleinias is nothing more than their most recent incarnation. Neither the primitives nor Kleinias recognizes that cities and individuals can flourish only if they are governed by, respectively, a prudent leader or the rational intellect (cf. 688a–b). History reveals the pattern when an authoritative guide draws out the salient themes, but it is by virtue of nature (not history) that the same thing has happened, can happen now, and will happen in the future (688d–e). In other words: Kleinias' character is shaped by his Dorian culture, to be sure, but his passions and attitudes reveal persistent, and highly unappealing, elements of human nature and political life, altogether.[15] The enduring power of these human characteristics leads the Athenian to offer a modified, and now less ambitious, exposition of wisdom and moderation.

Ignorance and Wisdom: A New Interpretation

The Athenian now offers a novel, and at first glance surprising, reinterpretation of ignorance, which turns out to be rife with implications for politics. Ignorance was the key failing of the early kings of Lacedaimon, and by implication it is the central defect of Kleinias and the present-day Dorians. Ignorance is (he now says) dissonance; wisdom is consonance. The "ultimate and greatest ignorance" (*amathian*), the Athenian declares, is the "dissonance (*diaphônian*) between pain and pleasure and reasoned opinion" (*pros tên kata logon doxan*, 689a). Dissonant individuals embrace what they believe to be bad and unjust, while repudiating what they believe to be fine and good (689a5–7). Ignorance is thus a lack of order in the soul, constituted by desires and aversions that disobey opinions based on reason. Consonant individuals, on the other hand, are those whose desires obey their opinions; they must be called "wise" (*sophous*), the Athenian now says, even if they cannot "read or swim" (689d; cf. 892d–893a)—that is, even if they are ordinary, conventional, and lacking in any significant intellectual ability.

This account of the "ignorant" or "wise" individual—we come to politics shortly—is bound to cause consternation. Knowledgeable readers of Plato, in particular, will bridle. How can mere consonance or dissonance prove to be equivalent to wisdom or ignorance? Readers may be disappointed to learn that wisdom no longer involves (for example) knowledge of the Form of

---

14. Strauss 1975: 44–45.

15. On the Thucydidean overtones of these ideas, see Balot 2001b.

the Good. Have law-abiding citizens, who are "virtuous" out of habit alone, now somehow earned the title of wisdom—even the greatest wisdom? Such readers may be puzzled, indeed, by the Athenian's blithe way of ignoring the difficulties besetting those who elevate "opinion" to the soul's throne, or his novel acceptance of unenlightened consonance (among the illiterate!) as "wisdom," or his nonchalance in blurring the standard Platonic distinctions between opinion and knowledge.[16]

What accounts for these surprises is the Athenian's rhetorical and political agenda. In offering this peculiar psychological analysis, he is looking ahead to the politics of Magnesia, to his theory of punishment, and to his theological speculations. Most immediately, he aspires to encourage obedience to the law among an unsophisticated citizenry. The best that he can hope for is to cultivate enough consonance to produce law-abiding behavior. We have just seen that the early kings' ignorance—the dissonance of their souls, their immoderate desires—led to disaster. The Athenian is now, by contrast, speaking of the citizens' "wisdom" or "ignorance." He focuses more attention on political followers than leaders. As a result, he immediately establishes an analogy between individual ignorance and the ignorance of citizens in a city ruled by law. He likens the parts of our soul that experience pleasure and pain to the demos (*dêmos*) and mass of ordinary citizens (*plêthos*) in a city, men like Kleinias (689b). Ignorance in the soul is opposition to its natural rulers, "knowledge or opinion or reason" (*epistêmais ê doxais ê logôi . . . tois phusei archikois*, 689b2–3; cf. 645b–c, in a resonant soul-city analogy). Similarly, a city's ignorance is the disobedience of the majority (*to plêthos*) with respect to its magistrates and laws (*archousin kai nomois*, 689b). So, far from upgrading ordinary opinion, as scholars have suggested, the Athenian is downgrading and "politicizing" wisdom.[17] His novel interpretation of ignorance and wisdom has directly political implications.[18]

Specifically, the Athenian is laying the foundation for his establishment of the regime of law in Book 4. He aspires to fashion the citizens of Magnesia as a collectivity of obedient followers, whom he will dignify with titles to wisdom, justice, and moderation. (Experienced readers of Plato will, no doubt, wonder whether the city allows for a more robust and ambitious

---

16. See again Strauss 1975: 45–46; Pangle 1980: 433–434.

17. Bobonich 2002, as opposed to Strauss 1975; Pangle 1980: 433–435.

18. Cf. Schofield 2013: 290: The Athenian is no doubt referring to the "folly in evidence when pleasures and pains or the mass of the people disobey reason (in the city in its guise as law)."

conception of wisdom; the Athenian does not disappoint in this respect, though he keeps readers in suspense until the end of the dialogue.) At least in his current presentation, wisdom has no relation to the philosophical quest for truth. Instead, it is a term of high praise for those citizens and officials who behave moderately enough to obey the law. No offices should be given to the "ignorant"; offices should be handed over to those obedient citizens who are now called "prudent" because of their moderation or consonance, even if they do not know how to read or swim (689c–d).[19] (This analysis leads the Athenian into a fertile discussion of the seven principles of rule, which will be explored in the next chapter.) The Athenian's novel account of "prudence"— that is, a form of prudence that amounts to nothing more than moderate, or consonant, obedience to the law—comes to be the future city's chief civic virtue.

This redefinition of ignorance and wisdom foreshadows two central passages late in the work. In mentioning those unable to read or swim, the Athenian looks ahead to the theological discussion of Book 10—or, more precisely, to his decision to leave the elderly Dorians on one side of a dangerous river, while he himself crosses and engages in a rich philosophical discussion (892d–893a). Like the elderly Dorians, Magnesia's citizens will be intellectually limited, unable to manage the swift currents of philosophical argument. Many lower officials, and virtually all citizens, will be equally limited—defined by their "prudent" consonance (and thus suited for obedience to the city's law code), rather than by a more ambitious prudence that consists in genuine philosophical understanding. Their nonswimming and illiterate "wisdom" cannot grasp the Athenian's theological arguments, which are suitable only for an entirely different kind of individual, who seeks wisdom in a different sense. As we will discover, in fact, the city's highest officials will receive a high-powered philosophical education, which fits them for the demanding tasks to which they are assigned. To carry out those tasks, they will need to be swimmers of a formidably high caliber.

Second, the Athenian looks ahead to his theory of punishment in Book 9, in which the "Socratic paradox" (i.e., "no one does wrong willingly") plays a major role. In that passage, after many twists and turns, the Athenian defines "injustice" as passion's tyranny in the soul, whereas justice, he says, is obedience to "the opinion about what is best (however a city or certain private individuals may believe this will be), even," he adds, "if it is in some way

---

19. On the image, see Schofield 2003: 4–6.

mistaken" (863e–864a, tr. Pangle 1980). As we will eventually discover, the Athenian means that justice consists in obedience to the law, full stop, even when obedient citizens are mistaken or fall short of full knowledge. If we put together his remarks about the orderly soul in Book 3 and in Book 9, then the Athenian's meaning is clear: henceforward, law-abiding Magnesians will be considered to possess the three most important virtues: wisdom, justice, and (*ex hypothesi*) moderation or consonance. By contrast, the "ignorant" citizens of Book 3, ruled by their passions, will be the "unjust" criminals of Book 9. The Athenian will refine these categories more fully in the discussion in Book 9, but for now it is worth bearing in mind the foreshadowing effect of this passage.

To repeat, however, Magnesia's citizens will not possess wisdom in any robust sense whatever their "consonant" obedience to law. As a result, they will possess a mere shadow of the fullest and finest versions of those virtues by which the city dignifies them. Simple obedience is an avowedly conservative, and a comparatively unambitious, goal. It should be, in fact, a great disappointment to those who hold that politics is the art whose task is to care for souls (650b6–9), if they understand that task to involve an ambitious conception of virtue according to which *nous* is the leader of the soul's virtues. The soul's obedience to opinion and law—perhaps to someone else's *nous*—is hardly equivalent to an individual's own rational self-rule, i.e., obedience to his own *nous*. The Athenian's lowering of his standards, so to speak, is based on his recognition that the early Lacedaimonians of Book 3, as well as Kleinias and his Dorian countrymen (688d1–5), whatever their natural dispositions, lack the intelligence that alone might enable human beings to flourish according to human nature. Having come to appreciate the deep flaws in Kleinias' character and his cynical, tyrannical views, readers will see that Kleinias and his fellow Dorians have failed to improve upon the lives of the earliest savages of the Athenian's story. The regime of law is intended to help them make progress. It does so by cultivating shadows of real virtue, especially political moderation, among the close kin of savages.

The Athenian's picture, however, is not entirely pessimistic, for two reasons. First, for the citizens of Magnesia, psychological consonance, embodied in obedience to the law, brings about important benefits. Their lives represent a significant improvement upon the lives of the early primitives and savages— as well as upon the lives of citizens in contemporary Dorian regimes. Second, although the Athenian offers this merely civic definition of prudence for now, he eventually finds a place for those citizens who have greater intellectual talents and who, in particular, seek philosophical wisdom. While ordinary, moderate citizens will, as the Athenian says, occupy certain offices in the city, Magnesia's foremost political officials, such as the Supervisor of Education, will be those with far greater, and indeed altogether impressive, educational attainments. The highest officials' wisdom will have to go beyond law.

Fortifying the Law against Tyrants

The Athenian expresses no doubt about the critical importance of ordinary citizens' obedience to the law. The traditional threat to the rule of law came, however, not from ordinary citizens, but rather from tyrants—from single individuals intent on ruling directly, independent of the law. That threat often inspired citizens to rise up valiantly in support of the rule of law.[20] When he inspects the soul of Kleinias, the Athenian recognizes an opportunity to turn his ordinary *thumos* in a positive direction, by reimagining it as a resource for strengthening the rule of law. Even if Kleinias harbors tyrannical desires, he also views it as most shameful to be defeated, or ruled, not to mention enslaved, by others. The Athenian uses Kleinias' fear of tyrants—those who might trample upon the law—in order to strengthen the prospects for the rule of law in Magnesia. As we have seen, Kleinias and his fellow citizens, even if moderated to some extent, are still motivated by thumoeidetic passions, by a sense of shame, and by anger at attacks on their own cities and way of life.

The Athenian seizes this opportunity to recruit Kleinias to the "rule of law" project, by calling to mind the frightening prospect of tyrants. Still within the framework of early Lacedaimonian history, he emphasizes the self-destructive role of single individuals—the early kings—in undermining their own power and destroying the power of the Greeks as a whole. The trouble, not surprisingly, was their ignorance; the Athenian now turns again from the citizens' ignorance to the rulers'. The early kings' ignorance was exemplified, the Athenian says, by their arrogant neglect of the Hesiodic proverb "the half is often worth more than the whole"—which is a disease, he argues, that is equivalent to *pleonexia* (690e; 691a: *to pleonektein*).[21] Ignorant and self-destructive *pleonexia* is particularly characteristic, the Athenian diplomatically suggests,

---

20. Teegarden 2013.

21. Balot 2001b. Compare the Athenian's description of the Spartan kings' dissonance as "the greatest ignorance even though it seems to be wisdom" (*amathia megistê, dokousa de sophia*, 691a) with his description of the doctrines of the "impious" as "a certain very harsh ignorance even though it seems to be the greatest wisdom" (*amathia tis mala chalepê, dokousa einai megistê phronêsis*, 886b).

of the kings of Argos and Messene (690d–e); note, though, that the Spartans have continued to fight the other two until this day (686b).[22] Human history has revealed humanity only in a diseased or feverish state, at first fearful, and then abandoned to its most acquisitive impulses, and thus most dissonant with itself (691a). As even Kleinias understands, however, the kings, not the populace, were responsible for the downfall of the alliance, because of the arrogance and *pleonexia* originating in their luxurious living (691a). Tyrannical ignorance and its associated aggression are the central political problem. The specter of the tyrant should frighten Kleinias and Megillus enough that they will want to establish laws whose power is beyond question, and to which all citizens, as we just saw, will be unquestioningly obedient because of their psychological consonance.

What crimes did the kings' ignorance lead them to commit? Readers should always keep in mind that the Athenian is telling this story in a particular, selective way—not one that corresponds to what he knew of history, or what we know of history, but rather one that suits his own political and rhetorical aim of reinforcing the rule of law.[23] Imagine the possibilities open to him. He could have added rhetorical flourishes highlighting the kings' mutual attempts to enslave one another (e.g., Sparta's enslavement of the Messenian helots), or he could have told lurid, tragic tales drawn from the House of Atreus. That was the path followed by most ancient Greek writers on tyranny. Instead, the Athenian focused on their trampling of the established laws. The kings were lawbreakers: that was their worst crime! They desired "to get more than the established laws ordained" (*to pleonektein tôn tethentôn nomôn*, 691a4). They therefore broke their oaths and "destroyed everything" through their dissonance, which was "the greatest ignorance even though it seems to be wisdom" (*amathia megistê, dokousa de sophia*, 691a). The greatest ignorance, fueled by acquisitiveness, is disobeying the law. The law needs enforcers and supporters to resist the rise of tyrants.

The Athenian's focus on these early law-breaking monarchs strengthens this point considerably. He now shows that the law, taken all by itself, or even reinforced by oaths, is weak. The early legislator, presumably as ignorant as the other savages of his day, was too imprudent to grasp the natural weakness of law in the face of tyranny. He made the mistake of granting unmixed power

---

22. Strauss 1975: 44.

23. For a different understanding of the Athenian's selective history of Sparta, see Schofield 2013: 290–292.

to a single individual, in the belief that a "young soul" could be constrained by oaths even after obtaining tyrannical power (692b, 693b; cf. 691b–c). He was not in possession of the political and legislative art—like the "political legislator" (*politikon ... andra nomothetên*, 688a1), who always looks to *nous* in establishing laws. The Athenian has, after all, subtly but devastatingly criticized the Dorian lawgiver as a friend and accomplice of tyrants.

The "young soul" who tyrannically destroys the laws is the work's first "young tyrant." (As we will discover, this passage looks ahead to the tyrants of Books 4 and 9.) The Athenian's description of him—a favorite image throughout the dialogue—is designed to evoke fear and loathing in Kleinias and Megillus:

> There does not exist, O dear friends, a mortal soul whose nature will ever be able to bear the greatest rule among human beings, if it is young and unaccountable (*nea kai anupeuthunos*), so that it is not filled in its mind with the greatest disease—ignorance—and thus earns the hatred of its nearest friends, which, when it happens, quickly corrupts it and destroys all its power. (691c–d)

This tyrant is "young," perhaps unexpectedly, to emphasize his ignorance: while he may have natural tendencies toward virtue, he does not have the mature knowledge or intellectual foundations that could anchor any "natural virtues" he may possess. Even in the best case, a tyrant with natural gifts will not be able to bear tyrannical rule if he lacks *nous*. This tyrant's youthfulness looks forward to the young tyrant of Book 4 and the young atheist of Book 10.

How, then, was the early law-breaking monarch or tyrant restrained? After all, only great lawgivers can prevent unaccountable tyrants from destroying regimes (691d). The Dorians had an ignorant lawgiver. In their case, the Athenian says, the god intervened to provide relief. Sparta's monarchical line was given twins who could share power; then divine lawgivers appeared who furthered the cause of the mixed regime, by adding the Gerousia and Ephors. Luck, in reality, is the "god" who saved Sparta, in the absence of a knowledgeable lawgiver. In the minds of Kleinias and Megillus, though, a new pattern has emerged, according to which the god (perhaps aided by an intelligent lawgiver) can save cities from aspiring tyrants. The Athenian will apply this pattern to the foundation of Magnesia in Book 4.

With regard to the foundation of Magnesia, this new lawgiver, who works, supposedly, under the direction of the god, will be, of course, the Athenian.

Readers should be especially conscious of his role in this crucial section of the dialogue. He is one of those "great lawgivers" who will prevent tyranny (691d), at first, by cultivating in Kleinias and Megillus a suspicion that all human beings want to be tyrants. He is the "political legislator" (*politikon . . . andra nomothetên*, 688a) who will look to *nous* in establishing the regime. He consistently works, however, to obscure his own role in the process. He wants to encourage the belief that the god has intervened in human affairs. The Athenian relates to his friends that "the god" revealed how to establish an enduring regime on principles that still apply right now (692b). It did not take any special wisdom on the Athenian's part, he says, to discern these principles when the model is so clear (692b–c). Why, then, one might ask, has the model been followed so rarely, if ever, in human history?

Readers will understand that the Athenian himself has constructed this story in a selective way. He is the author of the model; he has revealed the patterns. He will establish laws, with dispersed power, in order to ward off what has come to sight as the greatest of political disasters, tyranny. He will proceed, in Book 4, to add a critical ingredient. In addition to dispersing power, he will strengthen the law by giving it powerful religious foundations. He will call on the god to help once again. The regime of law in the *Laws* will become the antityrannical regime par excellence, supported by thumoeidetic citizens who are willing to surveil and punish their fellow citizens, and who understand that their obedience to the law is mandated by "the god." The regime's goal will be to avoid the worst disasters possible, through encouraging obedience to the law—a project which may, indeed, prove to be moderately painful (684c). Its key question will be how to reinforce the law, so as to make it resistant to tyranny.[24]

The Self-Destructiveness of Persian Tyranny

In his presentation of early Persia, the Athenian places renewed emphasis on the self-destructiveness of monarchies. Using the Persian case to illustrate the opposition between tyranny and the rule of law was familiar throughout Greece: Herodotus, for example, had made it clear to an ideologically conscious Greek audience that the Persians, led by a tyrant, had lost the Persian

---

24. The Athenian's question at this stage is how to legislate for unenlightened people who need law, when law is naturally weak. He devises various strategies for cultivating moderation and thereby avoiding the worst outcomes; cf. Lorraine Smith Pangle 2014.

Wars because of the Greeks' powerful resistance, which was based on the rule of law and the desire for freedom under law.

The early Persian Kings bear a striking resemblance to the early kings of Sparta, Messene, and Argos. Under Cyrus, however, the Persians fulfilled the dreams of the Lacedaimonian kings with their large armies: they "first became free and then became despots over many others" (694a). Inevitably, however, their successful imperialism was a "Trojan horse," because the "good things" acquired by empire led to instability. Even Cyrus the Great, like his monarchical predecessors, was beset by ignorance of the most important things. He had little idea how to use the material wealth he had acquired. He allowed his children to be corrupted by a luxurious upbringing. Because of his intense focus on warfare and military virtue, he failed to grasp the nature and significance of a correct education (694c–e). His sons fought with one another, until the Magian "Eunuch" took control; finally, Darius, who was not raised amid luxury, assumed power. Darius had the wisdom to govern by law and to regulate the empire's tribute by law (695c–d). Yet he made the same mistake as Cyrus and allowed Xerxes to be raised by luxurious women. The "Great King" is not truly "great" (695e); nor, by implication, were the early founders of the Persian regime.

The Athenian draws two lessons from this history. The first is that monarchs tend to destroy themselves because of their ignorance, construed in the broadest sense as dissonance. The Lacedaimonian kings did so, more specifically, because of their excessive arrogance and acquisitiveness. In Persia, the Athenian says, the royal children were scions of "outstandingly wealthy tyrants" (695e–696a) and therefore led terrible, self-destructive lives. They were no better than the early, savage primitives. The Persian tyrants, though, displayed their ignorance in a particular, telling way: "they destroyed friendship and community in the city" (697c–d) by imposing "more despotism (*to despotikon*) than was fitting" and restricting the people's freedom excessively (697c). In other words: they broke the sort of lawful compact that had once united the populace and monarchs of Sparta, Argos, and Messene. They, too, were destructive lawbreakers whose oppression of their peoples destroyed their cities:

> Once this [friendship and community] is lost, the rulers do not take counsel on behalf of the ruled and the demos, but for the sake of their own power. If they think that they can make even a small gain each time, they will overturn cities, destroy friendly nations and burn them down, and they will hate and be hated bitterly and ruthlessly. (697d)

The Athenian lays extraordinary emphasis on the cruelty and self-destruction of tyrants across history and throughout the world. The tyrannical character is universal, as are its self-destructive consequences. The evils of tyranny have become a standing principle of the Athenian's comparative political science. Once again, Kleinias and Megillus are being taught that tyranny is the greatest threat to the stability and well-being of cities. As the case of Darius shows, the best institutional means to limit the tyrant is the establishment of mean- ingful, powerful laws. This lesson encourages the elderly Dorians to recognize that passionate support for the law is the best means to moderate tyranny and to avoid "excessive slavery and despotism" (698a).

The second (and corresponding) lesson is the significance of moderation. The political prehistory of humankind has revealed the single most important virtue of any stable regime: moderation, or due measure. This virtue requires the elimination of unmixed offices. The new city will have to be fashioned as a mixed regime, constructed from the materials provided by the so-called mothers of regimes, monarchy and democracy (693d). This mixed regime, a regime of law, will enable citizens and leaders to avoid the excesses of each pure form; they will attain moderation, above all, through obedience to the law. At least partly, virtues flow from institutions, as they also reinforce them.

It is on this point, in fact, that the history of Sparta diverges from Persian his- tory. By contrast with the Persians, the Athenian says, the Lacedaimonians honor virtue over wealth and rank, provided that it is combined with moderation. After resisting their own tyrants and installing a mixed regime, the Lacedaimonians became a moderate meritocracy under law. By this stage of the conversation, the Athenian has persuaded Megillus to agree that all the virtues—including courage—can serve their true functions only if they are also moderate (696b–d).

Without arguing the case for the unity or copresence of the virtues, the Athenian is at least indicating to his Dorian interlocutors that the "new Tyrtaeus" was right to limit the activities of courage and technical skill by moderation and justice. The "pious statesman" (697c2) will, in Socratic fashion, honor the soul before the body, and the body before ma- terial possessions (697a–c), a lesson the Athenian will continually teach the Magnesians. As the antityrannical virtue par excellence, *sôphrosunê*, in the sense of self-control, consonance, and hence obedience to the law, will be the cardinal virtue promoted among ordinary citizens in the Athenian's regime of law.[25] However, as the Athenian emphasizes, moderation all by itself does

---

25. Annas 2017, esp. 149–161, also emphasizes moderation but reasons to its importance in a different way, and for that reason overstates its importance.

not deserve any great honor; it is merely a support to other virtues, which are worthy of honor (696d–e). The consonance of soul, a form of moderation, that the Athenian attributes to the best of ordinary citizens and dignifies with the name "wisdom" is not worthy of special recognition.[26]

Reinterpreting Democracy in Archaic Athens

By the end of the Athenian's treatment of Persia, readers might understandably conclude that monarchy has virtually nothing to be said for it. The Athenian has strongly encouraged this impression among his interlocutors. He will continue to do so throughout the dialogue, as I have argued, in order to strengthen support for the rule of law. What is striking, then, is that monarchy is one of the "mothers of regimes," out of which the new Magnesian regime will be formed. Readers will have to bear that principle in mind as the regime of law unfolds.

If monarchy has little to be said for it, then the democracy of early Athens, on the contrary, proves to be admirable. The early Athenian democracy, undergirded by a "sense of shame" (*aidôs*), restrained by laws, and hierarchically governed by those with knowledge, was a powerful, stable regime. The Athenians resisted the invading Persian tyrant because "*aidôs* was a despot" in the regime, "on account of which we [the Athenians] willingly lived as slaves to the laws in effect then" (698b; cf. 698c, 699c, 700a). Freedom—the democratic ideal of which democratic Athenians were the most proud—was, in the Athenian's telling, a source of corruption (698a–b), whereas slavery to the law (along with religious piety: 699c1) was the city's salvation, militarily and otherwise. In this respect, the Athenian rejects the Herodotean emphasis on freedom in favor of its polar opposite: slavery. It was slavery to the law that proved to be, as we have seen, a central resource in the Athenian's strategy of inspiring in the old Dorians a formidable desire to resist tyranny.[27] The ideal, as revealed by early Athens, was that those with knowledge should rule and make judgments, e.g., about musical performances (700c), while remaining ready to punish any disobedient member of the "ordinary mass" (*plêthous*, 700c3) or to beat "the great mob" (*tôi pleistôi ochlôi*, 700c7). Thoroughgoing

---

26. Cf. Strauss 1975: 50: "Surely, moderation in and by itself is no title to rule."

27. On the notion of *nomos despotês*, which was mostly associated with Sparta by fifth-century sources, see Millender 2002. This idea looks forward to Book 4, where the Athenian emphasizes slavery to the law. The Athenian is leading up to the idea that citizens will be slaves to the law, while those with knowledge should rule.

obedience to the law, along with deference to intellectual superiors, enables cities to resist tyranny and to flourish in peace and friendship at home. Does this model fail to mix the monarchy of wise superiors with a Spartan-like slavery to law among ordinary citizens? Could this model be the first projection of the regime envisioned by the Athenian?[28]

This particular Athenian model—not the monarchic model—will, indeed, become the paradigm of the regime of law founded in Book 4. This model, too, however, carries with it certain dangerous proclivities. Ultimately, a self-indulgent, hedonistic style of freedom—based on the idea that everyone is knowledgeable, and on lawlessness (701a)—unraveled Athens' early consensus founded on stable laws. Obedience is the key to a city that wants to be genuinely free, friendly with itself, and prudent (701b–d)—the very goals sought by Magnesia itself (cf. 693c–e, 694b). Citizens will have to be on guard, implicitly, to see to it that obedience to law does not slip away. That is why the Dorians have to be ready to surveil their fellow citizens and to apply the punishments that maintained order in archaic Athens (700c). Of all the regimes surveyed in Book 3, archaic Athens will be the most attractive, the one most likely to win the subscription and allegiance of the Athenian's Dorian interlocutors. Meanwhile, the Athenian indicates lightly that a knowing authority ruled in archaic Athens and punished disobedience (700c), while the majority were willing to be ruled (700d). Archaic Athens foreshadows Magnesia.

---

28. Cf. Strauss 1975: 53. It is unlikely that Cyrus's Persia foreshadowed the Athenian's model for Magnesia (as we will see, the wise [the Nocturnal Council] rule and the ordinary citizens obey the law), because of the Athenian's emphasis on common deliberation and "sharing in *nous*" among ordinary citizens and the monarch in Cyrus's regime (694a–b). These features are out of the question in Magnesia.

4

A New Beginning: Founding Magnesia

Non in depravatis sed in his quae bene secundum naturam se habent, considerandum est quid sit naturale. Aristotle, Politics, Bk i, ch. 2.

EPIGRAPH, Jean-Jacques Rousseau, *A Discourse on Inequality*

AT THE END of Book 3, Kleinias revealed that the other Cretans had put the Knossians in charge of founding a new colony. The Knossians commissioned ten men, including Kleinias, to establish a law code for the new city (702c). Accordingly, Kleinias recommends that the three men construct a "city in speech" (*tôi logôi . . . polin*, 702d). This announcement marks an important transition. Books 1 to 3 laid out the respective ethical and political ideas of the Athenian and Kleinias, as well as the prehistory of Kleinias' psychology. Kleinias proposes that they discuss the city in speech "as though they were founding it from the beginning" (*ex archês*, 702d). This phrase should be read metatextually: Book 4 constitutes a new beginning. That is, in fact, why the Athenian had offered a summary of the text's contents just before Kleinias' announcement, in another metatextual touch that closed the door on the first three books (702a–b).

The first three books have made readers aware of the Athenian's purposes. His goal is somehow to embody his own teleological, virtue-oriented ideas in a regime that acknowledges Kleinias' limitations and helps to calm his anxieties. The Athenian will have to be responsive to Kleinias' chief character traits while also transforming them, so as to turn them in new directions. Hence, when the Athenian and Megillus enthusiastically agree to join the project, the Athenian adds to Kleinias, "You are not declaring war, anyway" (702d). Having worked their way through Book 3's prehistory, readers will immediately grasp the deeper resonance of this statement. Because of his origins

Tragedy, Philosophy, and Political Education in Plato's Laws. Ryan K. Balot, Oxford University Press. © Ryan K. Balot 2024. DOI: 10.1093/oso/9780197647226.003.0004

in a militaristic culture, Kleinias might be expected to declare war instead of announcing a political founding. A new prospect, however, is on the horizon, in which the Athenian will attempt to transform these warriors into citizens. This project of law-giving and founding new cities, the Athenian indicates, is "really (*ontôs*)" most suitable for those with superior manly virtue (*aretên andrôn*, 708d). You had thought that "manly virtue" prototypically comes to sight in war? No—in reality, law-giving is its most perfect field of display.[1]

The "Existential" Framework

The Athenian elaborates on this point in an "existential" way: we are trapped in an inhospitable universe in which "chances and misfortunes of all sorts" legislate everything for us (709a). He is referring to war, poverty, disease, and destructive weather. Nature is a realm of necessity and chance, most of it hostile to human purposes. He immediately corrects himself, however, on the grounds that the "god," along with chance or opportunity and human art (*technê*), actually "pilots" all human affairs. Just as it is useful to have a skillful ship's pilot during a storm, so too, in founding a city, it is helpful to have "a legislator who knows the truth" (*ton nomothetên alêtheias echomenon*, 709c). Recalling the earlier discussion of the ignorant brutes and their misguided wishes, the Athenian stresses that the lawgiver will know what to pray for. He grasps clearly what he must acquire from "chance" in order to practice his art effectively (709d). Where the ignorant Lacedaimonian kings prayed for huge armies, the legislator, truly so called by virtue of his knowledge, will choose appropriate materials for his art. In the foundation's initial stages, at least, the god has been reduced to chance. He refuses to manifest himself personally.

What should readers infer from the Athenian's description? First, even after an invocation of the god, the world remains an inhospitable home for human beings, an uncertain landscape of chance and impending disaster. The god does not care for human beings providentially. Has anything changed,

---

1. Translators and commentators have been puzzled by the Athenian's specific reference to "manly" virtue in this sentence. England 1921a: 1: 425 asks, "Why should 'manly' excellence be specified?" The reason is that the Athenian intends to show that his form of "manly" excellence supersedes the traditional militaristic form cultivated by the Dorian cities. Whereas des Places (Diès and des Places 1951: 54) understands this point, translating "le courage viril," Griffith 2016: 145 misses it, translating "human goodness." The Athenian is making a special point of transforming, not universal human goodness, but the specific virtue—courage—that had traditionally been associated with militaristic men. See also the explanation offered by Schöpsdau 2003: 152–53, along with Pangle 1980: 439. The cultural background of this transformation is to be found in democratic Athens: Balot 2014a.

then, from the Athenian's earlier picture of a world hostile to human interests? Second, if we compare the two descriptions found in Books 3 and 4, then the answer is clear: while the world itself is the same, human art and knowledge are new. The "knower," the "legislator with truth," emerges as a person who, operating within the framework of chance, is able to make the world habitable for human beings. The knowledgeable practitioner of arts—above all, the statesman and legislator—will change the course of human history, by using intelligence to guide human purposes. Human beings will no longer be forced to rely on ignorant brutes and savages, such as the tyrannical monarchs of Book 3.

Despite his emphasis on ignorance and calamity in the first three books, the Athenian has, subtly but persistently, emphasized the power, even the necessity, of rule by knowledge. "Prudence" or *nous* is, of course, the leader of the divine goods (631c–d). No one could ever become a "worthy ruler" (*chrêstos . . . archôn*) of ships, the Athenian says, unless he possessed both the knowledge of navigation and a mind and body capable of seafaring (639a–b); the ruler of an army must have a general's knowledge along with courage (639b). Goats running wild, without a responsible ruler, should not inform anyone's opinion of goat-rearing altogether (639a). In general, the Athenian urges:

> Consider the case of any sort of association whatsoever, which has a natural ruler and which is beneficial under his rule, and imagine that someone praises or blames it without having seen it functioning correctly as a community with its ruler present, but had always seen it functioning without a ruler or with bad rulers? Do we suppose that such observers will ever say anything useful in either blame or praise of such communities? (639c)

When he turns to the symposium, the Athenian reiterates the point: "Do you understand that in every gathering and every community established for any sort of action whatsoever, there is a correct ruler for each one, in every single case?" (640a). It would be hard to overstate the Athenian's emphatic way of posing this question. Just as an army needs a general, the Athenian repeats, so, too, does a symposium need a ruler "first of all" (640c4). "Without a sober master or ruler" no symposium will function well or appear admirable (640e; cf. 671b–c, 671d–e). Equally, a city must acquire its knowledge of human psychology, of the human puppet with its golden and iron cords, and so on, "either from a god or from a man who knows these things," and on this basis set up the law for itself (645b). Finally, the true judge of music is the single individual who is superior in virtue and education (658e6–659a1). In these sections, there is no mention of any ruler or leader trampling the laws or pursuing untoward satisfactions, or of any knower's reliance on the gods, as opposed to the norms of nature.

The True Legislator and the Young Tyrant

Against the background of history's tyrannical monarchs, the legislator's "prayer," so to speak, opens a window onto one of the dialogue's most contested passages. What would the legislator pray for from chance, so that he could establish a healthy city by means of his art?

Athenian: Give me a tyrannized city (*turannoumenên . . . tên polin*), he will say; and let there be a young tyrant, with strong memory, quick to learn, manly, and magnificent by nature. The thing that we said earlier must follow upon all the parts of virtue, let that now also accompany the tyrannized soul (*têi turannoumenê psuchêi*),[2] if some benefit is to come from its other qualities.
Kleinias: The stranger seems to me, O Megillus, to be saying that the necessary accompaniment is moderation (*sôphrosunên*). Isn't that right?
Athenian: The popular kind, at any rate, O Kleinias . . . . (709e–710a).

Scholars have puzzled over the legislator's desire for a "young tyrant" and that tyrant's "tyrannized soul."[3] However we interpret these references, readers will bear in mind that this passage builds directly on the Athenian's description of expert craftsmen who intervene to benefit humanity through their knowledge. The lawgiver—a practitioner of the law-giving art—is imagined

---

2. At 710a1, I follow the manuscripts and Burnet, rather than the Budé, which prints *têi turannousêi psuchêi*.

3. My reading of the young tyrant section is indebted to, and builds on, Strauss 1975: 56–59; Pangle 1980: 438–45; Zuckert 2009: 80–89; Rowe 2010: 36–48; and M. Zuckert 2013: 94–97. Rowe (2010) shows no awareness of the degree to which the interpretation he recommends had already been developed by Strauss, Pangle, and Zuckert, among others. Schofield 1999 offers an ironic interpretation according to which the passage subverts itself, as follows: "The Stranger's fiction of an 'orderly tyrant' is a deliberate irony, warning us of the extreme unlikelihood of realising our political hopes by entrusting them to absolute rulers" (41). In a variety of ways this interpretation fails to do justice to the text, most importantly in its claim that the *Laws* rejects the possibility of uncorrupted philosophical rule. For a contrary account, see the helpful arguments of Kamtekar 1997, along with Zuckert 2009: 82–83; and chapter 11 herein, "The Rule of *Nous*."

as possessing "the truth," as founding the city on the basis of *nous* (709c). He is the "true lawgiver by nature" (*alêthês . . . nomothetês . . . phusei*, 710e). He is said to pray for certain preconditions that will enable him to practice his art effectively, so as to benefit his fellow human beings. If this lawgiver were going to pray, then the assumption is that he (by contrast with the tyrannical monarchs of Book 3) would know what to pray for—surely not a "gift" that would destabilize his own soul or destroy his city (cf. 687e–688c). If *nous* were going to found the city according to its own wishes, the Athenian is saying, then it would do so by means of an alliance with a young tyrant. Such is the Athenian's own interpretation of what a knowledgeable lawgiver *would* say in the situation. Allied with the young tyrant, the true lawgiver would create the best and most flourishing regime (710b), the regime that is according to nature (710c). Kleinias' persistent anxieties over tyranny (712c)—when the Athenian raises the question of the city's regime-type (712c)—betray his understandable concern that the Athenian wants to retain the tyrant as ruler once the true lawgiver's regime is founded.

The Athenian takes pains to distance himself from the fictional lawgiver.[4] As we have seen, however, he proceeds to give the combination of the true lawgiver, the young tyrant, and their regime high praise—as high as the praise given by Socrates to Callipolis at its founding (e.g., *Rep.* 541a–b). Despite distancing himself from the true lawgiver, the Athenian obviously identifies with him. His conflict with himself on this point is only apparent; it is resolved if we recognize that he is constrained by the need to address not only the dialogue's readers, but also Kleinias and Megillus. Understanding that Kleinias is adamantly hostile to tyranny, he wants to maintain his *bona fides* within the conversation. On the other hand, he implicitly suggests to readers that he envisions, at least hypothetically, another sort of regime—a regime of *nous*, in fact—that merits his highest regard. He favors the regime of *nous* over the regime of law that he will establish for Magnesia. This conflict will persist throughout the passage, and beyond. The Athenian is hardly at odds with himself, but in communicating his admiration for the rule of *nous*, he is subject to significant political and rhetorical constraints.

Why, then, would the true lawgiver pray for (of all things) a tyrannized young ruler of a tyrannized city? To answer this question, we have to observe that this passage is densely packed with allusions to Plato's *Republic*. The

---

4. Strauss 1975: 56–58.

young tyrant's qualities of character (i.e., having a good memory and being a good learner, courageous, and magnificent by nature: 709e) closely mirror those of the philosophers-in-training in Plato's *Republic*.[5] He is moderate in a "popular" sense—that is, self-restrained with regard to pleasure—not in a "dignified" sense (cf. *semnunôn*, 710a5–6), such as one might find in Plato's *Charmides*, or even in Book 3 of this dialogue. He is, from birth, not particularly ruled by his pleasures (710a–b). If he were to come to possess *nous*, and to establish it in his soul as the leader of its parts, then his moderation would, indeed, be the fully realized virtue, perhaps equivalent to *phronêsis* (cf. 710a6). The legislator is, moreover, obviously praying for that combination of philosophy and political power already familiar from the *Republic* (710c–e, 711d–712a; cf. *Rep.* 473c–e). In addition, the Athenian (with Kleinias' help) emphasizes, again and again, in language familiar from the *Republic*, that the combination of philosophical knowledge with political power will bring about the best regime in the quickest, easiest, and best way possible (710b, 710d, 711a–c, 712a; cf. *Rep.* 541a–b). Finally, the Athenian, like Socrates, speaks as though the true lawgiver will transform an existing city, instead of founding an altogether new one (710c–711a, 711c–d; cf. *Rep.* 473b–d).[6] Well-informed readers will not mistake these references—even if they pass by Kleinias and Megillus without recognition. The question remains, though, how we should interpret these allusions—as a dismissal of philosophical rule? Or even as an assertion of it? Or something else altogether?[7]

In light of Socrates' description of the tyrannical soul in the *Republic* and other texts, readers have understandably wondered why the true legislator would ally himself with a tyrant.[8] Normally, the tyrant's soul is enslaved by *erôs*; it is a prison-house of injustice, fear, and frustrated desire. His soul is "tyrannized" in that sense. The explanation is not that this passage is "ironic" or self-subversive. In the Athenian's presentation, the tyrant is young and

---

5. See, e.g., *Republic* 485a–487a, 494a–b, 503b–c, with Schöpsdau 2003: 161–63; cf. Strauss 1975: 56, who points out that the young tyrant is not required to be a lover of truth and justice. Strauss 1975: 56–57 argues correctly, I think, that "in speaking of the nature of the tyrant, the Athenian adumbrates the nature of the true legislator."

6. Schofield 1999: 38–39 has emphasized this point, but, as Kamtekar 1997: 247 points out, the idea is not surprising in the context of founding a new colony with colonists from all over the existing Greek world.

7. For these various options, see Schofield 1999; Strauss 1975: 56–59; Rowe 2010.

8. For example, Schofield 1999: 40–41.

"moderate" and has not yet developed this sort of "tyrannical" character.[9] As in the *Republic*, to the contrary, he has the natural character that would enable him, potentially, to become either a philosopher or a tyrant. If, like Alcibiades, he happens to be subject to unjust, imprudent, or even simply conventional, mentors and advisers, then his natural character may be subverted in the direction of tyranny (cf. *Rep.* 494a–495b). The key, however, is that this "young tyrant" will be guided and supervised by the philosophical legislator.

That point emerges clearly if we view the passage in relation to its counterpart in Book 3. While acknowledging the influence of the *Republic*, readers will remain focused, above all, on the Athenian's own presentation in the *Laws* itself. In addition to alluding to the *Republic*, the Athenian is also building on, and yet drawing a contrast with, his earlier discussion of the "young tyrant" in the Lacedaimon section of Book 3 (691c–d). The Spartans' ignorant lawgiver, who failed to understand or enforce "due measure" (691d, 692b), gave excessive power to a young soul who could not "handle the greatest rule among human beings" (691c). His unworthy, "inferior" soul (cf. 691c1) was characterized by *hubris*, that is, "arrogance" (691c3, 691c4)—the vicious counterpart of the new young tyrant's "moderation." He was "unaccountable": his own ignorance and desires drove his every action, without any restriction by laws or others (691c–d). Knowing how to preserve due measure belongs to great lawgivers, not to the Spartans' ignorant and imprudent lawgiver (691d). Out of "care for you" (*kêdomenos humôn*, 691d8), the Athenian says, the "god" had to save Sparta from its own lawgivers, by arranging for twins to be born within the royal line (691d–e), with a consequent dispersal of political power.

Many things have changed by the time we reach Book 4. First, the "lawgiver with the truth" knows how to preserve "due measure" in this situation. He is not ignorant but, rather, characterized by *nous*. The Athenian makes much of his intelligence amid chance circumstances; the saliency of his intelligence, even his capacity to rule, in Book 4 indicates that Book 4 represents a radical departure from the disastrously ignorant world of Book 3.

Second, the true legislator himself, with his *nous*, rules over the young tyrant, whose soul is tyrannized—by him. The young tyrant's soul is tyrannized, not by desire (as previously), but by the legislator's *nous* (which previously, in Book 3, was nonexistent). *Nous* will then take its proper place as the "leader," both of the tyrant, and of his "natural virtues."[10] The true lawgiver would

---

9. Cf. Rowe 2010: 37n31.

10. These "natural virtues" are in truth "pre-virtues," arising in the soul without benefit of *nous*: cf. Schöpsdau 2003: 164–67, with 631c7.

never ally himself with a self-indulgent tyrant who ruled unaccountably (like those of early Lacedaimon). Rather, he would choose, if only he could, a moderate young tyrant whose power is accountable to the legislator himself. Chance provides the materials, while he, with his intelligence, becomes the meaningful directing agent.

Third, no god is needed to save the "true legislator" from ignorance, or to save the regime from disaster. Whereas Sparta was rescued by a god (that is, by the chance appearance of twins in the royal line), the true lawgiver can pilot human affairs as successfully as possible, by design. If the god now does anything, then his sole task is to give the true legislator a "young tyrant" at the right moment. Note this all-important exchange between Kleinias and the Athenian: Kleinias asks how he could possibly think that a young tyrant was necessary to establishing the best regime for the city. The Athenian says that such a thing is "by nature" (*kata phusin*, 710c). What are you saying—that the young tyrant will be young, a good learner, courageous, and so on? Readers should take the Athenian's response literally: "Add 'fortunate,' not in another way, but in that, in his time, a lawgiver worthy of praise should arise, and that good fortune brings them together in the same place; for if this happens, then the god has done nearly everything that he does when he wants a city to do particularly well" (710c–d). The legislator proceeds naturalistically on the basis of *nous*. The god is reduced to chance ("good luck"), as in the case of the "caring" god who gave Sparta royal twins.[11] Apparently, however, Kleinias and Megillus still adhere to the traditional religious perspective.

Finally, and perhaps most importantly, the Athenian grasps these points himself and conveys them clearly to the dialogue's readers. By contrast with Sparta's ignorant legislator, he is the true legislator (cf. 692b–c). If we connect this point with the previous one, then the Athenian's presentation strengthens the true legislator's—and thus the Athenian's—resemblance to a providential and philanthropic "god," if one could ever exist. Or, to be more precise, the true legislator, or the Athenian himself, does the work that a providential god was traditionally assumed to do at the city's founding.[12] At least at the moment of the foundation, if not in the city itself, *nous should* rule "tyrannically"—that is, unaccountably to anything but itself, because what else should

---

11. This interpretation is anticipated by Strauss 1975: 57; Pangle 1980: 440; and Rowe 2010, although they do not draw the conclusion based on this line of reasoning. By means of the Athenian's presentation, a Machiavellian point is established: chance governs human affairs when human rationality or prudence fails to act.

12. Strauss 1975: 56–58; Zuckert 2009: 83; Rowe 2010: 39–40.

it be accountable to? Certainly, at all events, because of the benefits it will provide to the city, *nous* is *entitled* to rule the city. What we see in the text, in fact, is that the Athenian's *nous* does "rule" by means of his legislation and his authoritative management of the other "founders."

Why does the city itself have to be tyrannized to accomplish the true legislator's goals? The Athenian indicates that tyranny is, and is meant to be, as far removed as possible from a dispersal of power among various officeholders or power brokers (710d–e). The salvation of the Spartan regime—dispersal of power in a "mixed regime"—is anathema to the rule of the true legislator, who refuses to abuse his authority or oppress the people. He needs no "checks and balances" and would be merely hindered by them. The powerful should be the smallest in number but the most powerful, as in tyranny (711a), because the true legislator wants to enact the best reforms without constraint. He wishes to avoid compromising his vision. He wishes to legislate freely, without any need to negotiate politically with high-ranking colleagues who lack knowledge.

Out of the ashes of Book 3, then, there emerges a new, improved set of contrasts in Book 4. In Book 3, the vicious young tyrant, installed by an ignorant legislator, gave way to Sparta's mixed regime of law, by dint of the god's providential intervention (i.e., the twin royal heirs). In Book 4, the moderate young tyrant, ruled by a legislator who is "true" by virtue of his intelligence (*nous*), gives way to, indeed helps to found, a mixed regime of law that improves immeasurably upon Sparta's. This parallel has six terms (two young tyrants, two legislators, and two mixed regimes of law), all of which are active in the Athenian's presentation.

Evidently, the Athenian intends to establish a contrast between unaccountable, unmixed rule by a single individual and "mixed" rule by dispersed officeholders within a regime of law. The mixed regime of Sparta clearly transformed and improved upon the vicious rule of the young tyrant. The same contrast between unmixed and mixed rule still pertains to Book 4, but it now has dramatically different consequences. In virtually every respect, the true legislator allied with a young tyrant is diametrically opposed to the institutions of Magnesia, soon to be founded. He wants sole and exclusive power, based on his governing *nous*, unaccountable to anything but itself, and unrestricted by laws. If Sparta's mixed regime improved upon the vicious tyranny of Book 3, though, then it is questionable, even doubtful, whether Magnesia's mixed regime improves upon any regime that might be ruled by the true legislator. By contrast with Lacedaimon's vicious young tyrant, the true legislator and the young tyrant *are* able to "bear the greatest rule among human beings" without succumbing to *hubris* or immoderate desire. What, if anything, then, could tell against the true legislator's title to rule?

To avoid the conclusion that the Athenian advocates for the rule of the true legislator and young tyrant, scholars have argued that the "young tyrant" of Book 4 merely helps to found a new regime, whereas his counterpart in Book 3 actually ruled a regime.[13] Does the Athenian imagine that *nous* is required only at the time of the founding, in order to establish a healthy regime of law subsequently? On the contrary, the Athenian has a more robust vision of the true lawgiver; he wishes for a true lawgiver who will rule the city in concert with the young tyrant. He imagines, from the outset, a "tyrannized city" (711a6), not a tyrannical founding that yields a mixed regime of law. Kleinias finds the idea of a "tyrannized city" repugnant (711a7). The Athenian explains that the tyrant who wishes to change a city's way of life, e.g., in the direction of virtue, can do so by serving as a role model for his citizens, honoring certain activities and dishonoring others (711b–c). The young tyrant, under the true legislator's supervision, rules in order to benefit the citizens. He will be able to change the laws easily and swiftly (711c). When power is united with prudence, whether among the rulers or even in a single individual (711e–712a), then it brings a city "myriads of all good things" (711d3–4). In the Athenian's presentation, the true legislator not only wishes to establish laws, but also evidently intends to rule by means of law. That is why the Athenian emphasizes, as did Socrates in the *Republic*, the coincidence of political power with philosophical understanding in ruling (711d–712a).

If the Athenian has shown the dialogue's readers why the rule of *nous* is beneficial and why its absence is disastrous, though, then why does he fail to pursue that seemingly desirable option?[14] Arguably, the reason is that he finds this option to be politically inexpedient or, indeed, impossible, because of the

---

13. Many scholars (Schofield 1999: 39–40; Kamtekar 1997: 247–48; Annas 2017: 64) have emphasized that the true legislator is imagined as founding a regime of law rather than ruling a city. However, the Athenian also imagines, a là the *Republic*, a coincidence of political power with philosophical understanding in ruling per se (711d–712a). He blurs the distinction between founding and ruling: see Strauss 1975: 56–58; Rowe 2010: 43. The true legislator is a prototype for both the Athenian himself as legislator (Strauss 1975: 56–57) and the future rulers of the city, in particular, the Guardians of the Laws, who also form part of the membership of the philosophical Nocturnal Council. The "rulers" (magistrates: *archontes*) of Magnesia, in particular, the Guardians of the Laws, are also necessarily "legislators" (770a). As we will discover, the philosophers of the Nocturnal Council (also called guardians: 964b–d, 966b) rule the city on the basis of their philosophical understanding, by means of law (as well as rhetoric, education, poetry, and religion).

14. The situation could have been remarkably similar to Socrates' philosophical founding and legislation for Callipolis: on founding and legislating in the *Republic*, see Annas 2017: 13–14.

old Dorians' entrenched hostility to tyrannical rule. The Athenian is forced to distance himself from unequivocal advocacy for the rule of the true legislator and his young tyrant. Kleinias is, after all, very anxious about tyrannical rule (712c). Hence, in order to avoid angering or worrying his interlocutors excessively, the Athenian now does everything in his power to vindicate their preexisting belief that tyranny is dangerous and destructive. The most striking feature of this entire section, in fact, is one that scholars have noticed less frequently: it is not the true lawgiver's desire for a young tyrant per se, but rather, the way in which the lawgiver's "prayer" for a young tyrant is, seemingly incongruously, placed amid a dense cluster of references to the evils of tyranny. First, we have the calamitous tyrants of Book 3: the imperialistic Lacedaimonian kings, with their own "young tyrant," and then the Persian tyrants, not to mention early barbarians such as the Cyclopes. Then, in a short while, the Athenian will again drive home the disasters wrought by tyrants, from the arrogant and unaccountable autocrats repudiated by Kronos (713c) to the rulers who trample laws and destroy cities (714a).

How, then, readers may ask, with Kleinias, could the Athenian possibly be suggesting that tyranny (of all things), even when subjected to the rule of the true lawgiver, will enable the city to flourish? Throughout the discussion of the young tyrant, in fact, Kleinias is heartily disturbed by the Athenian's suggestion (710c, 711a, 712c), because what he hears in the name "tyrant" is not flourishing but, rather, oppression (711c). (The Athenian even exclaims aloud when Kleinias—like many modern scholars—simply refuses to believe that he means what he says (711a): the best regime is the one founded by a true legislator allied with a "naturally virtuous" young tyrant.)[15]

Doesn't Kleinias have a point? Isn't the Athenian contradicting himself or wishing a great evil upon the city, by his own account? I would say that the Athenian is not contradicting himself, but rather, speaking to two different audiences. On the one hand, he is sensitive to the impact of his remarks on

---

15. At 711e, the Athenian mentions Nestor as an example of the powerful rulers (*tôn dunasteuontôn*, 711c7–8, cf. 711d7–8) whose power must be combined with the moderation, justice, and prudence of the true lawgiver. Strauss 1975: 57 (cf. Pangle 1980: 441) rightly observes that the Athenian is arguing that power must be linked to prudence, and that this power "does not have to be the strength of arms; it may be the most outstanding strength of speaking, like that for which Nestor is famed." Nestor takes the place of the young tyrant; his power still needs to be associated with the virtues of a true legislator, above all, prudence and moderation. The paragraph starting at 711d6 is listing diverse sources of power, which must be linked to the knowledge of the true legislator; the conclusion to this line of thinking is finally stated at 711e7–712a3. Cf. Rowe 2010: 39n36, 46, along with the more puzzling interpretations of Schofield 1999: 43 (with 177nn59, 60, 65) and Kamtekar 1997: 248.

Kleinias and Megillus. He distances himself from the young tyrant in order to establish his *bona fides* as a lawgiver in their eyes. He wants them to understand that he stands with law rather than tyranny. His references to the evils of tyranny also have another benefit. They enable him to bring to the surface Kleinias' hostility, a thumoeidetic response. The Athenian elicits that response right now, precisely because he will shortly introduce the regime of law, to which he wants Kleinias' unconditional and enthusiastic commitment. Most tyrants really *are* harsh, evil, and oppressive to the city, because they lack popular moderation combined with the knowledgeable guidance of a true legislator. The Athenian can agree with Kleinias and Megillus at that level and, in the meantime, stir up enthusiasm for the new regime.

On the other hand, the Athenian is also making an announcement to more philosophically sophisticated readers. In his view, the best regime, if only it could exist, is not only *not* a regime of law, but rather its exact opposite—a "moderate tyranny" ruled by *nous*. Over the course of the work, it emerges that the regime of law is a far inferior substitute for the rule of *nous*. The Athenian emphasizes this point by alluding to the standard Greek opposition between tyranny and the rule of law throughout Books 3 and 4.[16] Tyranny and the rule of law define the limits of the political spectrum in the *Laws*. By associating *nous* with tyranny, the Athenian announces ostentatiously that the rule of *nous* is the polar opposite of the rule of law. From the perspective of law, any rule by *nous* would be ipso facto tyrannical in that free, moderate, and self-sufficient *nous* cannot justly be constrained by law or held accountable to anything or anyone except itself. That explains why, in this text, philosophical rule will have to be equated with (virtuous) tyranny. Tyranny is the regime-type that negates the rule of law and embodies its opposite (i.e., free and unaccountable rule) in the most unforgiving way. Even though he intends to found a regime of law, the Athenian still subscribes to the account of the best regime Socrates promoted in Plato's *Republic*. His attachment to philosophical rule will resurface throughout the dialogue, particularly in Book 12.

Has the Athenian adequately justified his own position to readers? Readers may object, in particular, that not even the true legislator can avoid being tempted by desire or undermined by passion, precisely on the psychological grounds stated by the Athenian. Can the true legislator's "mortal nature" firmly resist the pull of his desires and passions? Is the rule of *nous* that he foreshadows a "nonoption" for precisely this reason? The Athenian, after

---

16. On this opposition in Greek culture at large, see Canevaro 2017.

all, repeatedly emphasizes that no mortal nature can bear unaccountable rule without becoming corrupt and destructive. He pointedly restates this concern while introducing the new city's religious ideology. It is only after considering his restatement that readers will be able to sort out where the Athenian stands on these questions, and why.

Religion and the New Regime

The "oracular myth" of the young tyrant means, the Athenian says, that even if it is difficult to bring a city with good laws into existence, the method we described would be the quickest and easiest way to do so (712a4–7). Governance by *nous* would have been the quickest, easiest, and best option for securing a flourishing human existence. Kleinias fails to comprehend how or why (712a8). At least in part because of the Dorians' hostility to tyranny, the best path is not available. The more difficult and uncertain—and certainly diminished—option has to be pursued. The Athenian proposes to fit the preceding "oracular myth" to Kleinias' new city (712b1–2). He thereby sets himself this seemingly impossible question, to which the regime of Magnesia is the answer: How can *nous*, with all its associated benefits, somehow be embodied in a regime of law, since it is impossible for ordinary citizens to accept the direct, unencumbered rule of the true legislator allied with the young tyrant?

The Athenian invokes the "god"—now, apparently, not as a substitute for "chance," as before, but rather as a providential god who will hear their prayer and "graciously and with good will come and join us in ordering the city and its laws" (712b). By contrast with his attitude in the dialogue's opening exchanges, Kleinias is now less cynical about the god's existence and care for the city (712b). Readers will understand that this god, too, plays a vanishingly small role in the actual process of legislation. They will note both the similarity and the contrast with Book 3. The "god," i.e., chance, had intervened to save early Sparta from its ignorant lawgiver and to help establish a mixed regime of law. Now the god once again manifests himself in order to aid in the foundation of Magnesia's own regime of law. The difference is that Magnesia does not need saving from an ignorant lawgiver. A religious ideology turns out, in fact, to be a substitute for the direct rule of *nous*.

The religiosity of this section (712b–714b) contrasts sharply with the foundation by the true legislator and the young tyrant. The true lawgiver established the city on the basis of his own rationality and a naturalistic understanding of human nature, psychology, and political life. He does not rely on religious revelation or belief. When he wants to change the city's habits or character, for example, he does not turn to a religious myth or "lie." Instead, more naturalistically, he directs the young tyrant to model the appropriate behavior and to praise and blame citizens according to his standards (711b–c; cf. 631d–e). By contrast, religion serves a critically important purpose in adapting the legislator's rationality to the future regime of Magnesia. While the god is meant to fortify respect for the regime of law, he also disguises the Athenian's role—that is, the role of human *nous*—in founding the city and ordering its laws.[17] The rule of law, reinforced by Magnesia's civil religion, is the disguised means by which the wise (e.g., the Athenian) can rule the ignorant (e.g., Kleinias). In order to reach this startling conclusion, it is necessary to follow the twists of the Athenian's argument.

He begins by asking an apparently conventional question: What should the form of Magnesia's *politeia* be (712c)? Do they, as legislators, favor democracy, oligarchy, aristocracy, monarchy, or even tyranny? He leads the Dorians to believe that the knowing legislator will henceforward be absent. Whatever type of regime they may found, it will not involve direct rule based on the unassisted *nous* of the true legislator. As though to confirm this point, Kleinias shudders at the thought that the Athenian might favor tyranny for Magnesia (712c), since he equates tyranny with violence and oppression. Leaving the Athenian's suggested options aside, Megillus and Kleinias do not engage in wide-ranging speculation on the different types of regime. Rather, lacking imagination, they immediately reflect on their own regimes. Presumably, they suppose that their regimes will provide a model for the new city. They profess an inability, however, to name their regimes: Sparta, in particular, contains a confusing variety of magistrates and power holders (712d–e), as they had discussed in Book 3. They seem already to have arrived at an impasse; they do not know how to say "mixed regime." As in Book 2, though, the "god" will resolve their difficulties for them.

The Athenian responds diplomatically, by developing the history of Sparta from Book 3. Kleinias' and Megillus' regimes are genuine regimes, he says, in that they are not ruled despotically. By contrast, the traditional, unmixed regimes do not qualify as regimes at all. They are mere battlegrounds, captured by despots who enslave their fellow citizens (712d–713a). We learned in Book 3 that Sparta narrowly escaped the tyranny of "great and unmixed offices" (693b2–3). Basing their discussion on the lessons of Book 3, the three men

---

17. Strauss 1975: 58; Zuckert 2009: 83. Compare the discussion of 692b–c in chapter 3, where the god helped to obscure the Athenian's role in discerning the patterns of healthy political life.

agree, at any rate, that the best regime must be focused on resisting tyranny, the inevitable consequence of the pure regimes. Readers will understand, meanwhile, that Magnesia will have no true legislator with unencumbered rule, precisely because of the old Dorians' fear of and resistance to tyranny.

The early law-code of Sparta, however, was missing a preeminent god who would trouble himself to govern human beings with solicitude. Kleinias and Megillus refer to Zeus and Apollo as their lawgivers, to be sure. In his account of the Lacedaimonians in Book 3, however, the Athenian eschewed any reference to the gods, beyond the "god" (i.e., chance) who had caused twins to arise in the royal line. Even so—or perhaps precisely because the world without god is so uncertain and inhospitable—the Dorians are inclined to accept the Athenian's proposal that Magnesia should take its name from the "god who truly rules despotically over those with *nous*" (713a). The new regime of law will therefore be a "theocracy." Even though Kleinias welcomes this new advent of the god (712b), the idea mystifies him: Who is this god? (713a).

It is through his explanation of this "god" and of the Magnesian "theocracy" that the Athenian is able to create a regime of law in which *nous*—that is, his own *nous*—can still rule in disguise, behind the scenes, mediated by law and religion.[18] To Kleinias and Megillus, the Athenian is constructing the new city along familiar lines: a "philanthropic" god (cf. 713d6), albeit not one of their own gods, will provide the content necessary for a law-code,[19] while Magnesia's citizens and, above all, its magistrates, will thereafter obey that code. If they will not agree to human despotism, then divine despotism, imposed through law, is acceptable, because gods are already acknowledged to be superior to human beings. To readers, on the other hand, the Athenian is communicating that the new regime will be underwritten by a powerful civil religion. They are aware, of course, that the Athenian's *nous* is responsible for constructing the law-code, as the dialogue's action reveals.[20] Unbeknownst to the Dorians, the Athenian is the philanthropic god they are seeking.[21] The

---

18. Compare Strauss 1975: 57–58 and Zuckert 2009: 83–84, which anticipate Rowe 2010: 29, 39–40; cf. also Abolafia 2015: 372.

19. The old men's long walk to the cave of Zeus might remind readers of the Platonic *Minos* and its suggestion that Zeus is a sophist (319c).

20. Strauss 1975: 58 and Zuckert 2009: 83–84, which anticipate Rowe 2010: 31–32.

21. Zuckert 2009: 32 aptly comments: "The anonymous Athenian stranger represents the 'intelligence' or 'mind,' which he argues is the only true source of law and is itself divine"; cf. Zuckert 2009: 86; M. Zuckert 2013; Abolafia 2015: 372–73.

true lawgiver has not vanished; he has gone into hiding, though, because he cannot rule directly.

Instead of answering Kleinias' question about the god,[22] the Athenian tells the myth of Kronos in order, somehow, to explain his designation of Magnesia as a theocracy. One "oracular story" follows upon another in the Athenian's foundation of this new regime. Foreshadowing Magnesia's civil religion, he tells the Dorians a myth that is specifically designed to reinforce the city's objectives. They will be delighted to learn, in particular, that Kronos is sympathetic to their antityranny project, understanding, as he does, that human beings cannot govern themselves directly, because "human nature is not capable of wielding absolute power (*autokratôr*) over all human affairs without being filled with arrogance and injustice (*hubreôs te kai adikias mestousthai*)" (713c). Employing a remarkably similar vocabulary (cf. 691c–d), the Athenian alludes to the young tyrant of early Lacedaimon. Kronos wants to protect humanity from that sort of tyrant; Kronos has not met the true legislator and *his* young tyrant. The god's understanding of humanity's nature, and his concern to remedy the many difficulties to which it gives rise, grows out of his philanthropic care (713d). Kronos installed *daimones* as "kings and rulers" (713c–d) over human beings, like shepherds ruling despotically over cattle, to take care of us and to grant us peace, justice, and happiness (713d–e).[23] The Dorians accept the direct rule (the despotism) of divine beings because those *daimones* are unlikely ever to abuse their authority, and their superiority is taken for granted. The civil religion will, likewise, operate by reinforcing ideas—such as hostility to (human) tyranny—that promote and maintain the social order.

In the Athenian's interpretation, the myth implies that, since the god will not rule us directly, human beings must rule themselves through whatever inkling of immortality is in them, embodied in law, which is the name for the "distribution of *nous*" (713c–714a). An intelligent, philanthropic god in the heavens, analogous to Kronos, grants his imprimatur to laws constructed by his proxy on earth, i.e., human *nous*.[24] That is how law becomes the substitute

---

22. Strauss 1975: 57–58 and Zuckert 2009: 84, which anticipate Rowe 2010: 29–31, 39–40.

23. Peace, justice, and happiness are precisely the goods that the Athenian offers to the Dorians, above all, Kleinias, who began the dialogue as a warlike man, with tyrannical objectives and ready to live in a disordered (and thus miserable) society.

24. Strauss 1975: 58 correctly points out that by contrast with the Eleatic in Plato's *Statesman*, who draws the lesson that divine providence has ceased in the age of Zeus, the Athenian "is silent on this vanishing of divine providence"; followed, albeit less clearly, by Rowe 2010: 30, 40–41.

for, and the closest possible approximation of, the rule of the *daimones* whom Kronos had earlier "established as kings and rulers for our cities" (713c–d).

Rule of Law, Rule of Nous

By this stage, Kleinias and Megillus have accepted the Athenian's way of passing off the "true legislator" as an oracular myth. He is forgotten by all but the dialogue's readers. Noticeably, the Athenian has offered his interlocutors ample reason to resist concentrated "tyrannical" power of all sorts. Per the puppet image of Book 1, for example, "mortal nature"—desire, anger, and so on—is supposed to be incompatible with direct rule (even that of *nous*). It is impossible for *nous* (like the *daimones*) to rule directly, by means of unmixed offices, because the individuals in whom *nous* would presumptively be pre-eminent are too vulnerable to corruption. No individual is fully resistant to *akrasia*. (Of course, there is the related question of how individuals with *nous* would be recognized, and *a fortiori* how they would be *reliably* recognized, but the Athenian does not now raise those difficulties.) Hence, the Athenian has continually emphasized the dangers of tyrannical power. He eschews that possibility because he agrees, apparently, with Kronos that mortal nature cannot genuinely bear unaccountable power, without becoming arrogant and unjust.

He even restates the point once again. He emphasizes the dangers inherent in the rule of particularly aggressive and ambitious individuals over their fellow human beings:

> If a single human being or an oligarchy or even a democracy, with a soul that seeks out pleasures and desires and wants to be filled with these things, and is self-indulgent and afflicted by an unending and insatiably evil disease, if one such as this rules a city or some individual, trampling down the laws, then there is, as we just now said, no device of salvation (*ouk esti sôtêrias mêchanê*). (714a)

Why, then, is the question still a "live" issue? Why would any reader refuse to follow the lead of Kleinias and Megillus, and simply forget about the favoritism that is supposedly shown to the true legislator and his rule of *nous*?

The Athenian pointedly alludes to Plato's *Republic* in between his last two emphatic pronouncements on the dangers of unbridled power. Over the heads of his interlocutors, he mentions that "in as many cities as a mortal rather than a god rules, there is no relief from evil or toil" (713e). This statement obviously alludes to Socrates' introduction of the third wave, where "cities can have no rest from evils" apart from the coincidence of political power and philosophy (*Rep.* 473c–d, tr. Grube, rev. Reeve 1997). Many scholars have regarded the Athenian as making this allusion precisely in order to reject philosophical rule—that is, in order to reject the option represented by Plato's *Republic*.[25] Does the Athenian reject philosophical rule altogether, though, or does he force it to go underground in this particular dialogue?

Unlike Kleinias and Megillus, readers will recall that the Athenian emphasizes that the best regime is established via the tyrannical power of *nous*. Yes, the Athenian has often touted the dangers of tyranny. So, too, has he proclaimed, again and again, that the tyrannical rule of *nous* provides the most straightforward and best path for ensuring healthy regimes and flourishing individuals.[26] When he praised the rule of *nous* in that way, did the Athenian simply forget that mortal nature makes the best option impossible? Did he fail to grasp that the "best option" is not even an option, because of the weakness of human nature? Why even discuss it, in that case? Why not, instead, propose even more fantastical options as the "best option"? What if a divine race of *daimones* should descend from the heavens in order to rule humanity for its own good? The Athenian explicitly rules out fantastical options and "rules in" the possibility of the "true legislator" ruling tyrannically on the basis of *nous*. In other words: the Athenian discusses the true legislator because tyrannical *nous* is enough of a live option to provide a compelling basis on which to criticize the regime of law. It would fail to serve that purpose if it could simply be dismissed out of hand, as impossible for human nature. Philosophical rule is a "live enough" option to continue to worry, trouble,

---

25. Schofield 1999.

26. Rowe 2010: 41–42 notes this contradiction but resolves it by arguing that the Athenian makes an allusive appeal to the *Statesman* and the *Republic* in order to find a model for the ruler "who by application of impersonal, godlike reason will, or would, be able to save cities from shipwreck." These other dialogues, Rowe argues, carry forward the argument that the Athenian himself does not make; we are supposed to "import into our reading of the *Laws* whatever parts of the surrounding—and especially the following—argument of the *Republic* will appear to fit" (Rowe 2010: 42–43). This interpretive approach, however, is problematic, unless the *Laws* itself tells us what to import and how to interpret the importation in its new setting in a new dialogue. When we look at the logic of the text itself, we find that *nous* is being forced underground in the founding of the regime of law, only to resurface intermittently in the middle books, and then fully and dramatically at the end of the dialogue. This process, and the connection between *nous* and the rule of law, is the *explanandum* and has to proceed on the basis on a detailed examination of the text of the *Laws* itself.

harass, and provoke any readers who may too readily place their faith in the regime of law.[27]

Does the Athenian, however, provide any positive reasons to think that the true legislator or philosophical ruler would not, were he ever to exist, succumb to passion or desire? The answer is that he implicitly offers a number of responses to this challenge, but he does not develop them systematically. The first can be found in his discussion of tyranny in Book 2 (661a–d). Recall his counterintuitive thesis that the so-called "goods" are not only not good, but rather actively *bad*, for unjust people. It is equally true, however, that these conventional goods, while bad for bad people are good for good people. The list of goods included health, beauty, wealth, sharp senses, and, by becoming a tyrant, to satisfy all one's desires. It is counterintuitive enough to argue that these conditional goods are bad for bad people, such as Kleinias. That idea, though, is not as strikingly paradoxical as the thought that these goods, including tyrannical power, are good for good people. Tyranny is good for the true legislator, as it would be for the people he governs. The reason is that he knows how to use it well—unlike the Spartan tyrants with their big armies.

The second point corresponds to and cooperates with the first. The true legislator is defined by his knowledge of the truth and by his capacity to practice his art effectively. Knowing what to pray for, he prays for tyrannical power. He wants that power not in order to satisfy any wayward desires that may arise in him, but rather in order to have his wish follow his prudence (cf. 687e). Appropriate desires, including *erôs*, follow upon the clear vision of *nous* (688b). The Athenian does not explain the point in detail, nor does he address any possible, even reasonable, objections to that principle. If *ex hypothesi* the true legislator knows how to use tyranny well, then he should not be destabilized by it.

Third, later in the text, the Athenian confirms the possibility of rule by those whose souls are rationally ordered. In a well-known passage in Book 9, to which we will return (875a–d), he offers a nightmarish vision of the soul of a powerful individual who is overwhelmed by his own arrogance and acquisitiveness. He also, however, suggests the possibility of free, self-governing *nous*: "For no law or order (*oute nomos oute taxis oudemia*) is

---

27. The rule of *nous* is likely enough to exist to provide an adequate stalking horse for the regime of law, in the minds of readers. We cannot dismiss the rule of *nous* out of hand. Like the philosophers of Callipolis, or the *politikos* of *Statesman*, philosophers or lawgivers who rule with *nous* do provide a genuine, meaningful basis of criticism of the regime of law. Unlike a divine race of *daimones*, they are just possible enough to serve that function.

stronger than knowledge (*epistêmês*), nor is it right for *nous* to be a subordinate or a slave, but rather, to be ruler over all things (*pantôn archonta*), if it is true and really free according to nature; but now it doesn't exist anywhere or in any way, except to a slight extent (*nun de ou gar estin oudamou oudamôs, all' ê kata brachu*)" (875c–d, tr. Pangle 1980, modified).[28] He leaves things more ambiguous than we would like, but his statement also makes the rule of *nous* enough of a "live option" to serve the purposes it needs to serve in this dialogue.

Late in the dialogue, the Athenian confirms these points once again. In describing the Nocturnal Council, he says that those who will be the *real* guardians of the laws (*tous ontôs phulakas . . . tôn nomôn*) must *really* know (*dei . . . ontôs eidenai*) the truth about serious matters, and "be adequate (*hikanous*) to interpret them in speech and to follow them in deed, judging according to nature what comes to be both well and badly" (966b); note the verbal echo with "adequate" (*hikanos*) at 875c. In context, the Athenian is saying that the philosophers' comprehension of the forms of justice, moderation, beauty, goodness, and courage is not powerless in relation to their character and behavior. On the contrary, their knowledge is expressed in "following in deed" (*tois ergois sunakolouthein*) their grasp of these ideas (966b). The philosophers of the Nocturnal Council are not beleaguered by the defects of mortal nature, which are repeatedly said to undermine any exercise of political power that is not held strictly accountable by the law. Rather, their *nous* is self-sufficient, free, and fully in control of their souls.

Finally, the Athenian has repeatedly compared himself to a god. In this passage in Book 4, and elsewhere, as we will see, he does the work that the god is traditionally said to do. The drama—the action—of the dialogue makes that point clear, as he rules the elderly Dorians in founding the city, and as he

---

28. "To a slight extent": the Athenian leaves this phrase ambiguous in Book 9. Does it mean that free and liberated intellect exists only to a slight extent, i.e., that it is only (say) 60 percent free and liberated? That would seem to be the interpretation favored by Schöpsdau 2011: 348, citing *Tim.* 27c2. For the argument that the phrase has a temporal meaning, see Laks 2012, Laks 2022; the temporal reading, however, seems doubtful to me. Could the Athenian mean, on the other hand, that fully (100%) free and liberated intellect exists only in a vanishingly small portion of the human population? This is how Benardete 2000: 281 takes the phrase, helpfully referencing Socrates, no doubt because of the "divine dispensation" (though his conclusions differ from mine, because he ignores the phrase "to be ruler over all"); cf. also Lisi 2004: 17. This seems to me the only defensible interpretation: Schöpsdau 2011: 348 cites *Tim.* 51e6 as a *comparandum*. It is only in Book 12, though, in his description of the Nocturnal Council, that the Athenian indicates decisively that free and liberated intellect can exist in only a very small portion of the human population. Cf. Lewis 2009a: 654–55.

legislates for the city for its own benefit. One implication of that comparison is that he himself, as the true legislator, is beyond the defects of mortal nature. Given the action of the dialogue, it makes sense that the Athenian would hold out the possibility—as a live option—of beneficent philosophical rule, comparable to that of a philanthropic god.

In short, then, the Athenian persists in holding that the best regime is the regime ruled by a philosophical legislator with unaccountable power. The Athenian can still imagine, and put his trust in, the combination of political power and philosophical understanding that he evoked earlier, the one represented by the true legislator and the young tyrant (who are likened to the philosopher rulers of Plato's *Republic*). If this regime is impossible for human communities, then the explanation for that impossibility is not the philosopher's own frailty. The regime of law requires the suppression of the rule of *nous*, because Kleinias and men like him refuse to be ruled directly by other human beings—even fully knowledgeable craftsmen, should they ever exist.

The dialogue offers an image of two regimes: a shadow regime of *nous* and the regime of law, which suppresses it. Since the Athenian will be founding a regime of law momentarily, he offers (by way of reminder) a notable glimmer of its opposite, the rule of *nous*, which mostly goes undercover until its re-emergence in the second half of Book 12. Philosophical rule will surface occasionally throughout the dialogue as the "stalking horse" or "bad conscience" of Magnesia's regime of law. The Athenian cannot pursue the best option because of the Dorians' hostility to tyranny, not because of the weakness of mortal nature.

For Kleinias, as opposed to the dialogue's sophisticated readers, law is called forth as a defensive strategy, in regrettable conditions defined by mortal weakness. The use of law as a defensive strategy is the linchpin of the new regime. By making law paramount, the regime is able to restrain the excessive desires of powerful individuals, i.e., prospective tyrants. Law is our best method of ruling ourselves intelligently, within the constraints of a pessimistic view of human nature as subject to uncontrollable passions. A powerful regime of law enables us to avoid the worst possibilities inherent in human nature. If the elderly Dorians believe that tyranny represents the most cataclysmic of political disasters, then they will support the regime of law as the greatest bulwark against tyranny. They will also thumoeidetically surveil and punish any possible law breakers. By promoting the fear of tyrants, the Athenian can cultivate watchfulness and surveillance as standing practices of the regime.

Thrasymachus' Challenge and the Seven Titles to Rule

The Athenian showed in his discussion of the Spartan tyrant in Book 3 that the law is often too weak to restrain powerful individuals. Now he points out that law itself, like human individuals, is not invulnerable to corruption—specifically, to what might be called "elite capture." To make the point differently: if the rule of law is to characterize Magnesia, then the city will have to face, perhaps implicitly, a "Thrasymachean challenge" (cf. 714b–c). Don't rulers always make laws in their own interests? Why should we be confident, then, that the new regime of law will amount to anything more than arbitrary political power in disguise? Instead of providing an independent standard of justice, law might well serve as an instrument of power useful for promoting the interests of the existing regime and above all its rulers. Is the law capable of policing itself, so as to promote the common good (715b), and not the (narrowly construed) interests of the established regime, i.e. the powerful?

The Athenian does not explicitly address this challenge at an intellectual level. Instead, he addresses it at a practical level, by instituting a highly conservative legal regime and by emphasizing the need for magistrates to be unquestionably obedient to the law. Magnesia's magistrates will lack the power or agency to transform the law code into a vehicle that serves their own desires. On the other hand, the "true lawgiver," i.e., the Athenian, who embodies *nous*, will rule indirectly by means of the law code itself. He is entitled to that position of power by virtue of his *nous*. Moreover, for reasons already given, his desires will follow upon his prudence; in other words, he will have no motivation to use the legal system instrumentally for his own narrowly construed or conventional interests. Meanwhile, changes to the law code will be possible, in effect, only via the Nocturnal Council—a body of god-like men who, as we will come to understand in Book 12, rule the city with *nous* for the duration of its existence.[29] Once again, for the foregoing reasons, the Athenian is hardly concerned about the "capture" of the city's law code by the philosophers of the Nocturnal Council.

If we focus on this particular passage, however, then the appropriate question is: How does the Athenian orient Kleinias and Megillus to his own

---

29. On legal conservatism and innovation in Magnesia, see Balot 2020a. The argument there is that Magnesia's law code is made virtually unchangeable in order to provide for the city's stability and the citizens' sense of security and order; beneath the surface, however, the law-code is seen to be changeable. Its mutability is closely linked to the submerged power of the Nocturnal Council, which is made explicit only at the end of Book 12.

response to the Thrasymachean challenge? The answer is that he makes sense of this challenge by referring back to the seven "titles to rule" mentioned in Book 3. Presumably, the Thrasymachean challenge represents one way of thinking about "who should rule." (One telling detail is that Kleinias fails to recall the discussion of the titles to rule, 714e2; if they attend to the dialogue's dramatic action, then it will be evident to readers that the Athenian is, like *nous* itself in the ideal human psyche, the "leader," whereas the elderly Dorians are followers—and not very intelligent ones at that.) The Athenian dismisses three of these principles right away: the rule of parents, of the elder, and of the well born. He appears to want a single principle to determine their choice, because the principles themselves conflict with one another (714e; cf. 690d). Even in a mixed regime such as Sparta, different factions will make different claims to rule, based on factors such as noble birth, wealth, or strength.

Once we remove all the "noise" and complications of the different types of political regime, the Athenian argues, we discover that they have all been based on the rule of force. Cities are typically battlegrounds, with winners and losers (712e–713a, 714d). The Thrasymachean challenge is based on a well-founded and accurate understanding of history; that is why Kleinias appears to assume its point without argument (714d). Elite capture of the legal system is so common as to appear natural. The Athenian's strategy is to show that this "natural" fact is hardly natural and actually represents a questionable claim about justice (714d–e). He points out that "elite capture" embodies the rule of force, which equated violence with justice, and which Pindar asserted to be "natural" (714e–715a). If the rule of force pertains, he says, then "the winners" (*hoi nikêsantes*, 715a7) will refuse to share power. The Athenian argues that their cities will not even qualify as regimes. On the other hand, he agrees—as a descriptive point—that the rule of force, or "Thrasymachean politics," is the best description of all hitherto existing political regimes. The question remains whether any other "title to rule" might be superior to the rule of force.

Intriguingly, the Athenian chooses not to argue against Pindar or Thrasymachus directly—that was Socrates' strategy in the *Republic*. Instead, after pointing out that the rule of force leads to civic conflict (715a–b), he invites the god, once again, to grant the three old men consonance. The Athenian explains that he has initiated his discussion of the "titles to rule" in order to indicate that the lawgivers will not distribute offices based on wealth, size, or family—that is, some of the seven traditional titles, which have traditionally led to conflict. Instead, they will give office to whoever "wins the victory" (715c3) of being most obedient to the established laws.[30] That victory—he argues—makes the magistrate the servant of the gods, insofar as he is obedient to the law (715c, cf. 762e). With this religious gambit, the Athenian has, apparently, wrapped up his case: by obeying the law, we obey our *nous*, which is an inkling of immortality within us; and thus we obey the god. This response should presumably settle the controversy and, indeed, is reinforced in various guises throughout the text.[31]

Even so, one might wonder, how can this response solve the problem posed by Thrasymachus' challenge? How does it help the Athenian to make the case against the Pindaric law of force? And why would the Dorians find it persuasive? The key is that, by depriving the city's magistrates of power altogether, the Athenian's idea represents an extreme in the project of delivering an antityrannical politics. The magistrates cannot aspire to Thrasymachean tyranny if they have no power to shape the law code in accordance with their own interests. "Force," in that very traditional political sense, is hobbled. As always, the Dorians are inclined to support any institutional proposal that will prevent magistrates or other power-holders from misusing their power. In addition, if the Dorians are sympathetic to the idea that the Pindaric rule of force is "natural," as the presentation of Kleinias in Books 1 to 3 strongly suggests (cf. 690b6 with 714d), then the Athenian may have turned their minds by indicating that the god endorses Magnesia's rule of law. The god, surely, is more "natural" than the Pindaric law of force.[32]

How can any of these considerations be derived from the seven "titles to rule," which the Athenian invokes as the standards for determining who should rule (714e, 715b–c)? In light of the titles to rule, the Athenian's "solution" is surprising, and even arresting. He emphasizes how strange his idea must sound, referring to a "neologism" (715d). Rule must be exercised not by those who rule, paradoxically, but rather, by those who obey, precisely because they are the most obedient. The Athenian pinpoints this paradox when he says that these magistrates—"the ones usually called rulers" (*tous d'archontas*

---

30. This point is reinforced in the general prelude, where obedient service to the laws is superior to Olympic or military victories: see 729d–e (cf. 840b–c), with Schöpsdau 2003: 197. The idea of civic service as the greatest victory has a distinguished pedigree in Athenian political thought, traceable to Solon fr. 5.5–6, fr. 32: Balot 2001b: 97.

31. 762e, with Schöpsdau 2003: 415, who points out that the connections between divinity and law are stressed throughout the text, e.g., at 713a, 716a, 957c (cf. 965c).

32. That the Athenian is making precisely this suggestion is strongly reinforced by his first argument in Book 10, which again pits these two senses of nature against each other. Kleinias finds this argument absolutely compelling: 890d. Compare 690b8–c3, discussed below.

legomenous, 715c)—will actually be servants (*hupéretas*, 715c7). He calls them "servants," he says, not for the sake of a neologism (*outi kainotomias onomatôn heneka*, 715d1), but because he believes that the city's safety depends, above all, on the paramountcy of (presumably: common good–seeking) law over the rulers. Even with this clarification, however, the Athenian has still not sorted out the puzzle of how the "rule" of these magistrates, which is based on obedience, is justified in light of the seven titles to rule.

Worse still, the Athenian has left in abeyance the Thrasymachean questions of who has imposed those laws and in whose interests the law-code is constructed. Who will "rule," after all, if not the "rulers"? Who will provide the laws, since the god cannot do so, and since the city's rulers are nothing more than obedient servants?[33] By now, the answer to these questions should be obvious: the Athenian Stranger is the ruler who, in the text, provides the law-code, although he does not do so to serve his own interests. He does so for the sake of the city's welfare. He does not explicitly justify his own "rule," i.e., his law-giving. He does, however, implicitly offer a justification with reference to the seven titles to rule. It is crucial to follow his own arguments in order to bring this justification to the surface.

By contrast with ordinary political victories (not to mention those imagined by Kleinias in Book 1), the victory of *this* city's magistrates—*their* title to rule, so to speak—conspicuously does *not* appear among the seven titles to rule outlined by the Athenian in Book 3. Alert readers are meant to recognize that their title to rule is not parallel with the other titles to rule. In fact, to understand how their "rule" makes sense, readers must read the Athenian's arguments in light of his earlier and more elaborate discussion of the seven titles to rule in Book 3 (690a–d). Those titles to rule were as follows: parents over children, the well born over those not well born, the elderly over the younger, masters over slaves, stronger over weaker, prudent over ignorant, and the lucky (those who draw winning lots) over the unlucky (those who draw losing lots). The Athenian stresses, as in Book 4, that Pindar had asserted that the rule of the stronger was the most widespread and according to nature (690b). His chief disagreement, in fact, had been with

---

33. At this stage, it is essential to appreciate the contrast with the *Republic*. Scholars have often reminded us that Callipolis is also ruled by laws (Annas 2017: chap. 2), but in Callipolis, philosophical rule is explicit, and Socrates' and the philosopher rulers' roles in legislating are manifest to all citizens. As in the *Statesman*, they rule by means of law. The *Laws* depicts a law-governed regime in which the role of the original legislator (i.e., the Athenian) is obscured, and in which the role of the philosophers of the Nocturnal Council in changing the law is equally obscured, until the end of the dialogue. On these points, see Balot 2020a.

Pindar: "But the greatest title, as is likely, would be the sixth, the one commanding the ignorant man to follow and the prudent man to lead and to rule.
Indeed, O most wise Pindar, I would hardly say that this, in fact, is against
nature, but rather according to nature: the rule of law which comes to exist
naturally over willing subjects, without force" (690b–c). The Athenian shines
a bright light on his dispute with Pindar—that is, on the conflict between the
rule of force and the rule of prudence (or reason), a conflict that is based on
differing conceptions of nature and its norms (or commands). He does not
explain, however, how the rule of law over the willing is equivalent to the rule
of the prudent over the ignorant.

If we return to Book 4, then we can now discern a similar train of argument. The Athenian reiterates precisely this controversy with Pindar. In his
foundation of the new regime, the Athenian dismisses the first three titles
(parents, the well born, and the elderly; 714e). Passing over the rule of masters
over slaves (the fourth title), he says that the typical pattern of rulers making
laws in their own interests exemplifies Pindar's principle that the rule of force
is according to nature (715a). He does not explicitly say which title to rule is
to pertain in Magnesia, but it is clear that he intends to contradict Pindar, as
in Book 3, and to instantiate the sixth and greatest title in the new city: "the
rule of law over willing subjects, without force" (690c). In this iteration,
though, he passes over in silence the primary claim to rule, upon which the
rule of law is based—namely, the one "commanding the ignorant man (*men
ton anepistêmona*) to follow and the prudent man (*ton de phronounta*) to lead
and to rule (*hêgeisthai te kai archein*)" (690b–c).[34]

The Athenian's argument, along with his silences, leads to an interesting
consequence, visible not to Kleinias and Megillus, but to readers of the text.
Magnesia's victorious magistrates, to whom the city must be handed over, turn
out to be followers of the Athenian. Their claim to rule consists in willing
obedience to the law. The Athenian rules them by means of law, because of
his superior understanding. Hence, the rule of law over the willing turns out
to be equivalent to the rule of those who know (the Athenian) over the ignorant (most Magnesians, who are unphilosophical), who are willing to obey
(cf. 627e). The rule of law is the (disguised) means by which the wise rule the
ignorant.[35] The Athenian's indirect "rule"—that is, his lawgiving—is justified

---

34. In this iteration, moreover, he simply fails to mention the seventh title, that of "luck" based
on the drawing of lots.

35. Other scholars have arrived at a similar (though less radical) conclusion by other means,
by speaking of the "sovereignty" of *nous* as opposed to law in the *Laws*: see Adomenas

on the grounds that he is the prudent or wise man. The ignorant are those who lack consonance in their souls, in the sense that they are led by their excessive and unjust desires. The best and most just political solution is to place the "ignorant," who harbor tyrannical desires in their souls, in the position of obedient followers of the law.[36]

If the rule of law is the disguised means by which the wise rule the ignorant, then this consequence is not one that Kleinias and Megillus would find palatable if it were expressed candidly. The Dorians would hardly tolerate the implication that they are ignorant, that they are not fit to rule themselves. After all, Kleinias, in particular, claims to be wiser than the "many," and certainly not "ignorant" (625e–626a). Both old Dorians believe that they, unlike their younger fellow citizens, are justly entitled to question the law and to speak freely about such important matters (634d–635a). Moreover, they would repudiate the rule of any other human beings, as opposed to law (or gods or *daimones*), over them, because they are fearful and suspicious of any human beings (as opposed to the disembodied law) who would claim a title to rule over them. That would be a defeat, a cause of shame. All of these factors revolve around their powerful sense of themselves and their own importance—their *thumos*. They may not be well positioned to rule, but they certainly want to avoid being ruled directly by other human beings.

The striking fact, though, is that they do not mind being governed by a law code devised by the Athenian. The Athenian is "the wise" who will lead and rule over "the ignorant," as he does at every moment in the dialogue itself. Like a god, he appears out of nowhere in Book 1, as though a god has manifested himself to help Kleinias found a new city (cf. 712b). (What sort of city would they have founded without him? The militaristic, aggressive city, based on ignorance and devoted to manliness, which we observed in Book 3.) The Athenian's leadership, and even his quasi-divine status, will be increasingly emphasized as the text progresses. Dramatically, the foundation of Magnesia is a human action, based on human reasoning and decision-making. When the legislators are discussing how best to set up the city, the god is distant rather than philanthropic (cf. 709a–c); the human legislator (not the

---

2001: 46–47, building on Laks 2000: 281 (cited in Adomenas 2001: 47n19). "Sovereignty" is to my mind an anachronistic term, but both Adomenas and Laks are fundamentally correct to ask "who rules?" if the magistrates are *ex hypothesi* slaves to the law.

36. It is important that the city's highest magistrates, who make up the Nocturnal Council, do not fall into this category. As we will come to understand in Book 12, they rule as philosophers, like the Athenian. But these implications are held in abeyance at this stage of the dialogue.

gods: cf. 718b) is the key to the city's flourishing (709c–e).[37] It is the Athenian who asks relevant questions and makes sense of the answers. He is the "leader" and "ruler" of the present conversation: he embodies *nous*, and the Dorians are the followers. In outlining the sixth title to rule, the Athenian does not mention god; that title is based, wholly and emphatically, on the norms of nature.

What makes the Athenian's (unabashedly, to readers) hierarchical train of thought palatable—indeed, plausible to the old Dorians, as well as clear to readers—is the intervention of a "god." The Dorians are convinced that the god (not the Athenian) has given them their laws, because they gather from the myth of Kronos that the god is still present; he is philanthropically and providentially watching over the foundation of the city. That is why, in his ensuing address to the colonists, the Athenian emphasizes the significance of the "god" in preserving order throughout the cosmos and (by means of his personified helper and follower "Justice") in punishing hubristic men who ignorantly (*anoiai*) believe that they need neither "ruler nor leader" (*oute archontos oute tinos hêgemonos deomenos*, 716a). Magnesia's citizens will be "prudent," not ignorant, if they understand that they need rulers and leaders (who turn out to be the Athenian and other philosophers). Kleinias is convinced of the necessity of following the god (716b8–9), which means, the Athenian explains, becoming a "moderate" man (*ho sôphrôn*, 716d1) and participating in a variety of traditional religious rituals. Magnesians will have a strong sense that their founder, leader, ruler, and despot really is "the god."[38] The Athenian concludes: "Thus, if the gods agree, the laws will succeed in making our city blessed and happy" (718b, tr. Pangle 1980, modified).

Conclusion: Direct and Indirect Rule

The Dorians have repeatedly agreed to the Athenian's principle that communal activities require single, knowledgeable, and capable leaders if they are to have any chance at success (cf. Landauer 2022). There is no reason why the very same principle should not hold true when the group enterprise concerns law-giving for the proposed city of Magnesia. Why, then, is the Athenian's elaborate theological framework, his way of disguising his own role in the process of founding the city, necessary?

---

37. Strauss 1975: 58; and Rowe 2010.

38. Strauss 1975: 58; and Rowe 2010.

That question becomes even more pointed when we reflect on the numerous allusions to the *Republic* that are made in the very section in which the Athenian most stresses Magnesia's civil religion, along with the dangers inherent in unaccountable power—and in which he proposes as a remedy the unbreakable obedience of magistrates to a law-code that, embodying the god's own power and rationality, possesses ultimate authority. Why does the Athenian forgo Socrates' strategy in the *Republic*, according to which the productive class will exhibit "moderation" by willingly agreeing to the rule of philosophers, without any disguise or intermediary (431d–432a)? Readers will, no doubt, recognize the contrast between "moderation" in the *Laws*, which involves psychological "consonance" and adherence to the city's religion (cf. 716d), and "moderation" in the *Republic*, which involves harmony in the soul and willing acceptance of the philosophers' rule. What is the significance of this difference?

It is clear that Plato has not abandoned philosophical rule in this text. What has changed, primarily, is the presentation of the nonphilosophical citizens and their willingness to accept philosophical rule. Consider once again the Athenian's statement that there will be "no relief from evil or toil" for cities ruled by a mortal rather than a god (713e), alluding to the third wave in Plato's *Republic*, and specifically to Socrates' statement that "cities will have no rest from evils" (*Rep.* 473c–d, tr. Grube, rev. Reeve 1997), until philosophy and political power coincide. The Athenian's presentation in Book 4 suggests that the *Laws* will follow an entirely different pattern, in which human philosophical rule is obscured and replaced by a "theocracy" of law, at least, until philosophers resurface in the Nocturnal Council. The coincidence of power with philosophy had been exemplified by the young tyrant's alliance with the true legislator—an alliance decisively repudiated by Kleinias, who cannot tolerate the thought of being ruled by a tyrant. For reasons of their own, Kleinias and Megillus cannot adopt the solution chosen by the producing class of the *Republic*; that is, they cannot acquiesce willingly in the direct rule of philosophers in the city.

The political foundation of Magnesia follows upon the character of Kleinias (especially) and Megillus. These Dorians combine suspicion of others with an enlarged sense of self-respect. Their *thumos* makes it impossible for the Athenian to reveal himself as the embodiment of *nous* who guides this conversation and, as a knowledgeable lawgiver, constructs a law code for the new city. For the sake of the city's stability and moderation, in fact, the Athenian has *heightened* the Dorians' suspicion of any leaders, or any others at all, who might abuse their power to gratify their appetites. (Strikingly, only the young tyrant, not the old Dorians, is willing to be ruled directly by an-other human being, i.e., the "true legislator." Only the young tyrant exhibits the "moderation" characteristic of the citizens of Callipolis.) The character of Kleinias explains why the Athenian disguises his own role in the text and why he founds Magnesia as a theocracy.

These considerations bring the Athenian's quandary fully into view. How can he instantiate the sixth title to rule in Magnesia, for the good of the cit-izenry, when "the prudent," beginning with himself, cannot rule directly and must instead rule indirectly or in disguise? He accomplishes his goal by introducing a philanthropic god who cares both for justice and for Magnesia's citizens—one who can, moreover, provide a standard of justice that is inde-pendent of human individuals' quest for power and their Thrasymachean ploys. Although the Athenian is a well-informed Platonic philosopher, his strategy differs markedly from that of Socrates because of the context in which he finds himself. He does not argue against Thrasymachus; he does not explicate justice (cf. 714d). The rule of law—a peculiar sort of "theocracy"—has now been established. "Constitutional" questions have been settled, until the final pages of Book 12, when the Athenian's dedication to the rule of phil-osophical reason is once again dramatically uncovered.

5

Persuasive Preambles

TRADITIONAL FATHERS AND lawgivers were in conflict with themselves about the role of justice and happiness in the good life. While they encouraged a life of justice in accordance with the laws, they also promoted a life of hedonism as the happiest life, without ever explaining the relationship between the two (662c–e). Judging by Kleinias' self-presentation, one might fairly conclude that traditional fathers and lawgivers had left in place the citizens' belief that these two lives inevitably stand in conflict with one another. Having inherited their confusion, in fact, Kleinias disputed the Athenian's emphatic declaration that justice leads to happiness. The Athenian prudently circumvented their conflict on this point by ringing in a "god" to achieve consonance for them. To be more specific, Kleinias and the Athenian agreed to disagree on the substantive issues involved, while agreeing that no "lie" could be more profitable to the citizenry than the equation of justice with happiness. The Athenian's aim was to convince Kleinias, over the course of the work, to pursue justice (and virtue generally) for its own sake, as the most fulfilling life for a human being.

Without a doubt, the rational eudaimonism upheld by the Athenian is not a highly "intuitive" position for Kleinias or any other Greek. Ordinary citizens tend to be psychologically dissonant, precisely because they recognize the need for law-abiding behavior—justice according to the law—while also harboring tyrannical desires to acquire power for themselves, as the means to fulfill their wishes. How can it be, after all, that I am better off by moderating my appetites rather than pursuing their full satisfaction, by limiting my self-promotion rather than advancing my own interests (narrowly construed) to the greatest extent possible? How can it be that respecting the law, behaving justly, cultivating moderation, and so on, are in *my* interests, as opposed to others' interests or the city's interests? The Thrasymachean claim that justice

Tragedy, Philosophy, and Political Education in Plato's Laws. Ryan K. Balot, Oxford University Press.
© Ryan K. Balot 2024. DOI: 10.1093/oso/9780197647226.003.0005

is "another's good" seems so much more obvious—and, in fact, it can be, so to speak, empirically validated.

Facing this tidal wave of opposition, the Athenian occupied an unenviable position. His task was made even more difficult by the rhetorical and political constraints that prevented him, as a philosopher, from tackling these questions directly. By contrast with Socrates in the *Republic*, the Athenian was not in a position to argue the case with his nonphilosophical interlocutors. As he had turned to a religious ideology in founding Magnesia, so, too, does he now turn to more indirect means of persuasion.

Preambles and the Two Doctors at a Glance

It is within the orbit of these conflicts that we can best understand the Athenian's chief innovation in law-giving (722e): the use of persuasive preambles (*prooimia*) as prefaces to the laws themselves (722b–d). Roughly speaking, the preambles are meant to persuade citizens to obey the laws; the law proper is a command (*epitaxis*, 723a6).[1] According to the Athenian, the preambles enable the legislator to treat citizens like free men by persuading them to abide by the law willingly, instead of forcing them to do so. They constitute the means by which the legislator will avoid tyrannizing citizens by compelling them to obey under duress.[2] In highlighting his own innovation in this crucial respect (722e), the Athenian stresses not his retreat or compromise from an ideal, but rather his difference from and superiority to traditional, indeed, all hitherto existing, legislators. He wants the balance of his legislation to favor persuasion, rather than threat, sanction, and punishment, which he considers "worse and more savage" (*cheiron . . . kai agrióteron*,

---

1. Although the Athenian refers to preambles as being spoken at the beginning of the laws (719e9; cf. 722d–e), the *prooimia* encompass the entirety of the legislator's conversation and writings about law (cf. Laks 2000: 288: the "generic form of all the para-legislative statements," with 723c), including everything that the three elderly men have said thus far (722d).

2. Notably, however, even the wise legislator giving laws to free men will, in the end, use sanctions and force; the "unmixed" law itself (cf. 723a), whether prefaced by a persuasive prelude or not, always embodies the threat of violence; cf. 721e, 722c, 722e–723a. Laks 2000: 287–88 has helpfully emphasized this theme; cf. Laks 2022. The Athenian himself introduces a certain ambiguity in his terminology: the laws that have been called "double" (*diploi*, 722e6; cf. 720e) actually consist of "two things, a law and a preamble of the law" (722e). At times, then, the law proper plus the preamble will be called a "law" in this twofold sense. The violent part of the double law is "unmixed law" (cf. 723a, with Laks 2000: 288.) On these terminological and other related points, see also Morrow 1960: 553–60.

720e4), but his reference to a "third way" (722c2) suggests that both will be necessary in Magnesia.[3]

The Athenian introduces the preambles by way of an analogy between the lawgiver and two sorts of doctors, a free doctor and a doctor's servant (*hupêretês*, cf. 720a), also called a "doctor." The Athenian associates the slave doctor with a tyrannical legislator, who issues commands and threats without any explanation; he associates the free doctor with a gentler legislator, who prefaces his laws with persuasion and encouragement. The slave doctor practices medicine on the basis of his master's commands, along with his own observation and experience.[4] He treats only other slaves, not free men, and refuses either to give or to receive an account (*tina logon*, 720c3) of each sickness. Acting like a "headstrong tyrant," he boasts that he "knows with precision (*hôs akribôs eidôs*)" (720c, tr. Pangle 1980).[5] Within the analogy, the slave doctor's commands are equivalent to the unmixed, violent law laid down by tyrannical legislators (722e–723a). Free doctors, by contrast, learn their art, practice medicine, and teach it, all according to nature (*kata phusin*, 720b). The free doctor investigates disease "from the beginning and according to nature" (*ap' archês kai kata phusin*, 720d3). He discusses difficulties with his patients and their friends, both learning from them and teaching them "in so far as he is able" (720d). His efforts to learn show that he does not possess full and complete knowledge, nor does he boast of such knowledge. He understands his own limitations. He eventually gives orders or "prescriptions,"

---

3. Cf. Laks 2000. Intriguingly, at 722b the Athenian says that the double law will have "double the amount of practical virtue" (tr. Pangle 1980), which suggests that even unmixed law, all by itself, contains a single "dose" of practical virtue; its merit in cultivating virtue is greater than zero.

4. The "slave doctor" can theoretically be a free man or a slave (720b), but as Schöpsdau (2003: 240) points out, the free-born doctor's servant plays no further role in the image after this initial mention. It is clear from the Athenian's description that, despite his tyrannical commands, the slave doctor is far removed from the "true legislator" who rules with tyrannical power. While the slave doctor has no expertise, the true legislator is defined by his expertise. The free doctor is, in fact, an expansion of the image of the true legislator, who rules in concert with the young tyrant; arguably, in fact, the Athenian's particular image of the true legislator was designed specifically in order to distance the true legislator, who is defined by knowledge, from power itself, which does not uniquely characterize him. On this latter point, see Strauss 1975.

5. Notably, precise knowledge is a possession that not even the Athenian claims for himself, and one that he does not attribute to the free doctor, although he attributes precise knowledge to the philosophers of the Nocturnal Council (see chapter 11, "The Rule of *Nous*"). *Akribeia* ("precision," "accuracy") is a distinguishing feature of the city's higher philosophical education of a few talented citizens: cf., e.g., 818a, 965a–b.

but only after "taming" the patient through persuasion (720d–e), which makes him more favorably disposed and ready to learn (723a).

The Athenian's presentation of this analogy has occasioned a great deal of scholarly controversy.[6] Its interpretation remains a hotly contested issue, in part because of the apparent discrepancies between his general description of the preambles and the actual preambles offered throughout the work. If we examine the Athenian's argument in context, though, then we discover the analogy's fundamental point: persuasive preambles aspire to educate the citizens' judgment in accordance with natural standards, especially if they initially adopt perspectives that differ from the legislator's own.

Persuasion versus Force: Revisiting the Case of the Young Tyrant

The Athenian introduces this analogy as part of his attempt to clarify the status of his opening address to the citizens. Upon finishing his first address (715e–718a), the Athenian interrupts himself, so to speak, in order to identify the spectrum of means by which the law will enable the city to flourish. At times it will persuade, though at other times, when confronted by those who resist persuasion, it will punish "with force and justice" (718b). It is as if the Athenian, after delivering part of his general address, stops short upon realizing that he ought to clarify the relationship between the general address itself and the forthcoming body of laws. He points out, more specifically, that the lawgiver must communicate with the citizens on many important points that cannot be "presented harmoniously in the shape of law" (718b, tr. Pangle 1980)—topics such as those that characterize the general prelude itself.[7] As the ensuing discussion makes clear, he already has in mind the distinction between the lawgiver's persuasive speech and the law itself, understood as a forcible command that permits no negotiation or discussion.

Intriguingly, the Athenian proclaims his allegiance to the model of persuasion. Despite the range of means at his disposal, his aspiration is always to persuade citizens to embrace virtue, rather than to coerce them to behave lawfully (718c). He does not explain this allegiance, but, despite Kleinias' immediate agreement ("how could it be otherwise?" [tr. Pangle 1980]: 718d1),

---

6. See Bobonich 2002: 97–119; Laks 1991, 2000, 2001, 2005; Stalley 1983: 42–44; 1994; Bartels 2017: 134–40; Strauss 1975: 62–65; Morrow 1960: 552–60; Pangle 1980: 445–57.

7. He thus raises the question of what can and cannot be harmoniously presented within law: cf. Morrow 1960.

readers should not assume that the explanation is obvious. In fact, they may wonder how the Athenian's attraction to persuasion squares with his earlier embrace of tyranny as the best and most straightforward method of founding the regime (709e–710a). That earlier section, it turns out, illuminates the Athenian's account of the persuasive preambles.

A young tyrant (supervised by a wise lawgiver) is best, according to the Athenian, because he can establish laws without any negotiation or compromise, without any resistance from other members of the elite (cf. 710e–711a) or from the citizenry as a whole. As a result, the young tyrant, allied with the wise lawgiver, can change a city's habits (*poleôs êthê*, 711b5) without much effort, if he chooses:

> It is necessary for him first to travel along the path he desires, whether he wishes to turn the citizens toward the practices of virtue or the opposite. He must first sketch out everything by means of his own conduct, praising and honoring some things, while censuring others, and dishonoring anyone who disobeys in each of the activities. (711b–c)

Upon hearing this explanation, Kleinias asks why they should suppose that other citizens will follow someone who uses such a combination of persuasion and force (*tên toiautên peithô kai hama bian*, 711c)—two terms that are central to the Athenian's own law code.

Although the characters do not dwell on it, Kleinias' question serves two important functions. First, he points out that the true legislator with tyrannical power rules by means of both persuasion and compulsion. Strikingly, however, Kleinias assumes that other citizens might not follow: in other words, in his mind, they are not *forced* to do so. Kleinias' impression is confirmed by the Athenian's description of the young tyrant's method: he does not refer to force at all. The young tyrant models the correct behavior, no doubt under the supervision of the true legislator, and persuades the citizens by means of praise, honor, blame, and dishonor. Surprisingly, even though he is a young tyrant, he is not said to use force! The Athenian intends to preserve his method of cultivating virtue, as much as possible, in Magnesia. Paradoxically, however, while the true legislator with tyrannical power is said to rely on speech rather than force—despite Kleinias' redescription—the Athenian will have to rely, as in Kleinias' redescription, on a combination of persuasion and force in legislating for Magnesia. Because Magnesia is a step down from the best regime, the Athenian is not able to carry forward, wholesale, the true legislator's method of cultivating virtue. As we will discover, the

Athenian's "double method" of legislation both adds the punitive or violent element and expands upon the quality and means of persuasion involved.

Second, Kleinias' question draws attention to the problem of the tyrannized citizens' motivation. Have they been given strong reasons to accept the tyrant's model of behavior, or his standards of praise and blame? Do they have "internal reasons" of their own to imitate the tyrant?[8] Why *should* the citizens want to imitate the tyrant who acts at the behest of the true legislator? The Athenian does not stop to explain this point. His presentation, however, provides the basis for the answer he offers in describing the persuasive preambles. In describing the preambles, the Athenian will offer the citizens "internal reasons" to follow the law. He will explain in suitable language why following the law is best for them, beyond the avoidance of punishment. That suitable language will be a translation, for the citizens, of his own eudaimonistic belief that the just life is the most fulfilling human life. In that way, the Athenian's persuasive preambles offer a friendly amendment to his own vision of the true legislator acting with tyrannical power. The Athenian explains further how praise and blame, honor and dishonor, will function in the city. Strikingly, to repeat, the Athenian's "double law" turns out to be more "tyrannical"—in the sense that it relies on force as well as persuasion—than the persuasive methods of the true legislator with tyrannical power, as he himself describes them.

The Athenian's Purposes: "Tameness" and "Savagery"

We are now in a better position to interpret the Athenian's own explanation of the purpose of his preceding address to the colonists (718d).[9] He wants the audience to listen in a "more tame" (*hêmerôteron*) and "more favorably disposed" (*eumenesteron*) frame of mind to the advice being given (718d). He is unsure how great an impact his words will have, but they might make the audience "more favorably disposed" (*eumenesteron*) and "more ready to learn" (*eumathesteron*), provided that the listeners' souls are not "utterly savage" (718d). The Athenian is obviously concerned that his audience will disregard his advice or respond defiantly to it. Why would the audience be

---

8. Williams 1981.

9. With Schöpsdau 2003: 229, I take *ta toinun dê lechthenta*, "the things that were said just now," at 718d2 to refer to the address to the colonists: cf. 719a4, 719d4, with Schöpsdau's comments in 2003: 230–34.

"savage"—and what does "savagery," as opposed to "tameness," signify for the Athenian in this context?

In short, the Athenian maintains that the human being is the tamest creature on earth when it receives an appropriate education, but the most savage when it does not (765e–766a).[10] Savagery is, above all, associated with lawlessness or disrespect for the law (874e–875a), but also with violence (cf. 791d, 867d, 890, 919a, 950b), injustice (649e), and destructive acquisitiveness (909a–b). Book 3 reveals that "savagery" has been characteristic of warlike humanity since the time of the last flood.[11] Anticipating that the new colonists will be uneducated primitives, the Athenian wants to use his addresses to the citizens to make them less resistant to the law, less defiant in the face of the legislator's commands. If they are more accepting of law's provisions, then they will be "tamer." This term does not imply that they will be more "docile" or passive or acquiescent. Rather, tameness is a significant human achievement. The Athenian associates tameness with humanity's fulfillment of its nature (951b: "sufficiently tame and perfect") and its proximity to divinity (766a).[12] He is trying to communicate to an audience of potentially defiant colonists that it serves their interests, whether they know it or not, to accept the law willingly and to abide by it. What they are supposed to learn is how the law conduces to their own flourishing as human beings, to their becoming "sufficiently tame and perfect."

Hesiod and the Athenian on the Benefits of Virtue

These points are reinforced in the Athenian's ensuing discussion of virtue and vice, which proceeds with reference to Hesiod.[13] Lamentably, as the Athenian explains, his words may have little impact (718d), precisely because "the many"

---

10. On tameness, see Laks 2000, 2005, following Morrow 1960.

11. At their worst, the Athenian says, human beings become like beasts (*thêriôdeis*, 909a8) when, as necromancers, for example, they show enough contempt for others as to manipulate their fears concerning the dead and the gods to make money (909a–b). Human beings must establish laws for themselves, the Athenian says, or else they do not differ from the most savage beasts (874e–875a). For other general statements, see 880d, 937d.

12. Human beings share in the divine by means of their glimmers of rationality (cf. 644d2, 644d7–8, 728b, 804b; cf. 721c in the marriage prelude).

13. For a helpful treatment of Hesiod and other poets in this section, see Lorraine Smith Pangle 2014: 219–20. Too few scholars have recognized the significance of this Hesiodic section to the interpretation of the passage; it is essential to read the passages both in context and in sequence.

(*hoi polloi*, 718e1) do not pursue virtue energetically. Quoting Hesiod's *Works and Days*, the Athenian indicates that most citizens prefer vice to virtue: "The many show that Hesiod is wise when he says that the road to vice is smooth to travel and without sweat, since it is very short, but 'before virtue,' he asserts, 'the immortal gods have put sweat,/And a path to it that is long and steep'" (718e, tr. Pangle 1980).

The Hesiodic passage helps to explain the citizens' tendency to resist the lawgiver's edicts.[14] Because of their attachment to pleasure and immediate sense of their own good—their dedication to their own "savagery"—the citizens do not accept that the lawgiver's effort to cultivate virtue in them is in their own interests. They experience virtue as a burdensome, alien imposition on them. Savages do not want to become tame, because they find tameness to be an intolerable constraint on their freedom. Hence, they resent any law that aims at promoting justice or moderation. Recall that, for Kleinias and the traditional lawgiver in Book 2, the life of law-abidingness and justice was manifestly in conflict with the life of happiness.

The Hesiodic context is suggestive along these lines. Just prior to the quoted passage, Hesiod had recommended justice and law-abidingness to his acquisitive, unjust brother Perses:

> O Perses, store these things in your mind and listen to justice—and lay off violence altogether. For the son of Kronos ordained this law for human beings: for fish and wild beasts and winged birds, on the one hand, that they should eat one another, since there is no justice among them; but he gave justice to human beings, which is by far the best. For if anyone knows what is right and is willing to speak it, to him far-seeing Zeus gives prosperity. Whoever willingly lies under oath while giving witness and hurts justice and damages it beyond repair, that one's family is left unknown afterward. (Hesiod, *Works and Days*, 274–284)

Strikingly, Hesiod praises justice in parallel with the Athenian's praise of law (cf. 874e–875a), as distinctive of our "humanity," construed as a virtue or an ideal. Justice—or, for the Athenian, the law—distinguishes human beings from the other animals, whose willingness to devour one another is emblematic of their savagery. In showing respect for justice, Hesiod says, human

---

14. Note the explanatory *gar* at 718d7: "*for* there is not any great abundance" of people striving to become virtuous.

beings repudiate the violence of animal nature and achieve god-given prosperity: justice and respect for law (embodied, in the Hesiodic passage, in
truth-telling during a legal trial) are in the individual's interest, even if they
seem at first sight, to Perses, for example, to operate as constraints on his acquisitive desires. Perses is a typical savage who fails to understand his genuine
interests.

What the Athenian communicates to the elderly Dorians and, at a different level, to readers is that the preludes might help, even if to a small extent, in convincing the audience to pursue justice and to abide by the law.
His addresses will show the citizens that, however things may appear at first
glance, justice and law-abidingness are conducive to their own happiness,
whether it is god-given or not. For Hesiod, it is the god Zeus who confers
prosperity on the just. The Athenian believes that the just will prosper according to human nature, without Zeus. He is willing, however, to invoke
"Zeus" and other religious ideas in order to persuade his audience to accept
the point if they prove unable to do so without religious assistance; the god
will give them "consonance."

The Lawgiver and the Poets

The Athenian now turns, unexpectedly, to entertain a certain critique of his
address, which he imagines being offered by the poets (719c–e).[15] Although
the lawgiver should censor the poets, as they have agreed (719b), perhaps
the poets, conversely, still have useful advice to offer. The poets first draw a
contrast between themselves and lawgivers: lawgivers have to speak singly
about each topic, whereas poets often contradict themselves by imagining
characters who oppose one another. In the preceding address to the colonists,
for example, the Athenian had mentioned burials of three sorts—luxurious,
measured, and skimpy—and had simply chosen the middle term, without any
qualification or explanation. By contrast, poets represent diverse characters—
a wealthy woman, a middling property owner, and a poor man—and therefore
give voice to praise of different and conflicting types of funerals (luxurious,
measured, and skimpy), depending on the case. The poets ask: Shouldn't the

---

15. This section, too, is too often ignored by scholars interested in the political significance of
the preludes; see Strauss 1975: 61–62; Pangle 1980: 446–47, who reach different but complementary conclusions from my own. M. Zuckert 2013: 101–2 provides an illuminating analysis
of the Athenian's discussion of the poets in this section.

lawgiver explain what he means by a "well-measured" funeral—that is, what constitutes proper measure in a funeral?

Readers may wonder why the poets, or the Athenian, had to go through this elaborate presentation in order to ask an apparently simply question. The Athenian could have said: we have left unclear our notion of a "well-measured" funeral, and the concept itself is not self-evident. Obviously, then, we have to be more specific; here, after all, is what we mean. Why didn't he simply say that? Why introduce three imaginary characters in poetry?

In presenting the issue as he does, the Athenian is making manifest the need to explain the law to diverse citizens, who approach the law from different, potentially conflicting perspectives. Each of those citizens believes, at the start, that he or she is creating an appropriate—a well-measured—funeral ceremony. The rich woman praises the funeral that is "overly elaborate," as the poets say (719d–e),[16] but it would hardly make sense for her to praise her own design as "overly elaborate"! That description constitutes criticism rather than praise. Instead, the wealthy woman would praise her funeral as a beautiful remembrance for a loved one, as a fitting and richly deserved tribute to an extraordinary life—or something along those lines; and similarly, with the poor man's praise of his own "skimpy" funeral: no one praises his own "skimpiness." The key is that such differently situated citizens all believe that their respective approaches to funeral expenditure are well-measured and appropriate. They are in conflict, *ex hypothesi*, because they have diverse judgments. It is up to the lawgiver to settle their conflicts in judgment when the correct approach is not obvious.

In this situation, the lawgiver could, as the poets propose, simply describe what "well-measured" expenditure really is, according to his own (i.e., the natural) standards. He could then impose his own understanding on the city. This approach, however, recommended by the poets, would constitute a merely superficial solution. Barring any further explanation or discussion, those with different judgments (the wealthy woman, the poor man) would experience the law as simply an alien imposition, one they neither understood nor agreed with—even if they were forced to obey, and even if the law were perfectly in accord with nature. (They believe, after all, that *their* views are perfectly in accord with nature.) The lawgiver could state clearly "how much" constitutes good measure and still find that most of his citizens object to the law, because their sense of good measure differs from his. If we appreciate these points, then we can see that the poets' advice is helpful but limited. The

---

16. Note that in her case alone, the poet says: "I would praise etc."

poets themselves have not grasped, in a full and clear way, the implications of their objection for the lawgiver.

By contrast, however, the Athenian has grasped the genuine import of their objection. The real implication is that the lawgiver should not only specify the terms of his judgment, but also, and even more importantly, work to convince citizens with different judgments to change their minds—to see things his way, because they will be better off if they do. In this case, he might, for example, point out to them that extravagance leads to arrogance, while penury leads to servility (e.g., 728e–729a); and both those conditions embody an unhealthy dissonance. The Athenian is understandably concerned that his citizens might react "savagely," i.e., defiantly, to this sort of advice. He aspires to provide an explanation that will reduce their defiance, by explaining to them *why* his judgment is correct according to nature and therefore advantageous to them as individuals, however matters may appear at first glance.

"Caring" Legislation: Persuasion toward Eudaimonism

Now that the poets have raised the question of conflicting judgments as a political problem, we should ask once again: Why is the Athenian particularly concerned about the citizens' defiance of or resistance to law? First, he recognizes that the citizens of Magnesia, as mere human beings, will not tolerate the highest and most ambitious legislative enactments. At times, they will resist, and the lawgiver is forced to pay careful attention to their limits, so much so that persuasion itself is often not even an option for the "uneducated mob" (722b7). Second, and more generally, as a forcible command, law often manifests itself to citizens as an imposition—as a constraint or limit that they would not otherwise have chosen for themselves. This sense of law as a constraint that limits one's happiness or pleasure shines through clearly in the Athenian's conversation with the traditional father and lawgiver in Book 2.

If we think of laws on taxation or military conscription, then it is not difficult to imagine that to the Greeks—or, indeed, people of all epochs—it felt as though the law treated citizens instrumentally, that it sacrificed the happiness of citizens at the altar of the city's good, or that it sacrificed individuals for the sake of the community.[17] It is in this sense that the imposition embodied

---

17. See Balot 2014a on the traditional city's conception of "courage," which had, arguably until the democratic reconceptualization of courage in the fifth century BC, always seemed a self-sacrificial duty, good for the city but destructive of the individual.

in law is often experienced as an "alien" imposition. In most Greek cities, as the Athenian emphasized, law serves the interests of the rulers, to the detriment of the ruled (714b–d). As Thrasymachus had argued in Plato's *Republic*, justice is the interest of the stronger (cf. 714c) or of the established regime. There is no hope that Magnesia (unlike, for example, democratic Athens or a Rousseauian republic) can solve this problem by imagining citizens as self-legislating, because Magnesians receive their laws from the lawgiver.

The salient point, then, is that the Athenian needs to make a convincing case before an audience of citizens who are, understandably, liable to think that law-abidingness is a pseudo-virtue of the weak or foolish. They have been trained by a history of savagery to adopt the cynicism of a Callicles or Thrasymachus, even if they lack the ability to articulate their cynicism fully. The citizens' sentiment would be intensified in cases like the one raised by the poets, where the judgment of diverse individuals differs substantially from the lawgiver's on points that they consider significant. (They might even wonder whether any judgment at all can be justified—or is the imposition of law simply a matter of power, all the way down? This worry explains the Athenian's repeated emphasis on nature in his presentation of the preambles.[18])

It is for these reasons that the legislator strives to convince citizens that he genuinely cares about their happiness and flourishing as individuals. The Athenian emphasizes, for example, that the lawgiver's writings should appear "in the shape of a father or mother who loves them and has good sense" (859a3–4). The lawgiver should not act like a "tyrant or despot, giving orders and issuing threats, and walking away having written commands on the walls" (859a4–6). Since the lawgiver cares deeply about his citizens, he will counsel them in his writings regarding what is noble, good, and just, "teaching what sorts of things they are and that it is necessary to practice them if one intends to flourish" (858d). The lawgiver, understood as the Athenian desires, will not use the citizens instrumentally for the sake of the city's benefit. Rather, he will make laws devoted entirely to their own flourishing as individuals, and he will strive to communicate publicly just how the laws achieve this purpose. This conception of the lawgiver as a caring parent corresponds to the Athenian's presentation of the citizens as children who seek gentle treatment from their doctor (720a). By enabling the citizens to grasp more clearly virtue's advantages for them, the Athenian hopes to make them more eager to become virtuous, notwithstanding Hesiod's warnings about "the many."

---

18. On this emphasis on nature, see Pangle 1980: 446.

It is crucial that convincing the citizens of his care for them is not simply a persuasive technique. The Athenian actually *does* care about the citizens, for eudaimonistic reasons of his own. He manifests this care by persuading them, to whatever extent possible, of the rational eudaimonism that motivates his own activity.

Free Doctor and Slave Doctor: Persuasion, Trust, and Nature

The question is how the Athenian can best make his case to the citizens. He explains his thinking on that question by referring to the analogy with the two doctors. Two essential features distinguish the free doctor from the slave doctor: while the free doctor practices his art according to nature and frequently appeals to nature, the slave doctor does neither; and while the free doctor teaches, learns, and gives an account, the slave doctor refuses to give an account and treats his patients high-handedly. These differences have two consequences: that the free doctor is superior to the slave doctor as a diagnostician, and, more importantly, that the free doctor is better at winning his patients' trust both in his scientific abilities and in his care for them. The first consequence follows from the free doctor's willingness to investigate illness thoroughly and according to nature (720d). By contrast, the slave doctor refuses not only to give an account of his remedy, but also to receive an account of his patient's malady (720c). This difference is clear from the Athenian's presentation, but it is less central to the analogy than the question of trust.

At the heart of the analogy, rather, is the question of whether or not the respective patients will trust in the medical abilities and the care or beneficence of the doctors. The slave doctor, like the young tyrant, is high-handed in his approach. He refuses either to listen to patients or to explain their illnesses to them. He also refuses to explain why his prescriptions are in each patient's best interests, in situations where the connection may not be obvious. Why, for example, must an ailing patient eliminate certain foods that he enjoys, or subject himself to amputation of a limb that seems, at present, perfectly healthy? Since the slave doctor hurries off without giving an explanation, the patient is left to wonder whether and why the proposed cure is appropriate to his condition. He has been given no reason to follow the slave doctor's prescriptions, because he has not been given the means to see why those prescriptions (of all things) are likely to restore his health. In short, after a house call or a visit to the infirmary (720c), the slave doctor's patient will be neither "favorably disposed" to his command nor apt to understand it (723a–b; cf. 718d). Communicating arrogantly and immodestly with his patients (cf. 720c6), the slave doctor does not inspire trust in either his remedies or his care for the patient.

By contrast, both the free doctor's appeals to nature and his conversational, persuasive style are intended to convince his patients that he cares deeply about their welfare, and that his prescriptions accurately indicate ways to help them live healthy, flourishing lives. In diagnosing disease, the free doctor has many advantages: he investigates thoroughly and according to nature, he listens to the patient and his friends, and his own grasp of medicine is based on nature. More importantly, though, his conversations with the patient and his family enable him to grasp the patient's starting points, from which his own efforts at persuasion must begin. He wins the patient's trust in his medical abilities by thoroughly examining the disease. On the other hand, he conveys his own trustworthiness by taking the time to give an account of the patient's condition and to explain why his proposed cure is conducive to health. He takes his time; he is not hurried. Even if the cure seems extreme or inappropriate, at first glance, the patient will have reason to believe both that the doctor has offered it in good faith, and that, for reasons he now understands, it is likely to conduce to his recovery.

In addition to communicating care for his patient, the free doctor strives to maintain a connection with nature that the slave doctor entirely lacks. "Nature" is a persistent theme in the Athenian's presentation of the analogy. The free doctor learns his art by following nature (720b) and investigates disease according to nature (720d). The benefits are that he becomes a better practitioner and that he conveys competence and trustworthiness to his patients in the course of his explanations. The slave doctor enjoys neither benefit. By analogy, the lawgiver should also and equally maintain a connection with nature, both in order to enact law correctly and in order to persuade the citizens that the laws are made with their interests in mind. The Athenian concludes his presentation of the preambles by emphasizing that preambles exist for each law according to nature (722e, 723c–d).

To take an important example of the appeal to nature, the lawgiver should, according to the Athenian, order the laws of marriage according to nature (*kata phusin*, 720e10). The preamble lays great emphasis on the natural desirability of marriage, as a means to procreate and thereby to participate in the natural immortality of the species. According to the Athenian, the human species shares in immortality by nature (721b), and everyone desires immortality by nature (721b), e.g., in desiring to be famous after death. The human species is naturally linked (*sumphues*, 721c3) with all of time and partakes of immortality by continual regeneration. It is impious for anyone willingly to deprive himself of this natural destiny by refusing to care for a wife and children.

What is the point, more specifically, of the Athenian's emphasis on nature in this preamble? To understand his point, it helps to take note of his audience: he is speaking to a young man who might form the erroneous opinion that "the bachelor's life brings him profit and ease" (721d4–5). This young man has a different starting point, a different perspective on the question, like the wealthy or the skimpy givers of funerals. He is likely to react defiantly to the Athenian's marriage legislation. How to convince the young man that he has formed his judgment in error? That, despite the *prima facie* desirability of the playboy's life, he would be better off marrying and having children? The Athenian would be unwise simply to impose his marriage law on a recalcitrant and unyielding population of young men; that would inspire hatred of the law and disobedience in the breach. At best, the young men would obey out of fear or compulsion, in a way that would diminish the ethical quality of their behavior. For, after all, the young man strongly believes that his own judgment is correct, and that the lawgiver is merely imposing on him for the city's good, not his own. The Athenian's attention to nature, though, provides a convincing independent standard of judgment. By appealing to nature, he shows the young man that the lawgiver is not simply sacrificing the would-be bachelor at the altar of the city's goals (e.g., its military manpower), or imposing an arbitrary standard to please (for example) unsympathetic old men. Instead, he communicates that he intends to enact laws that take as their chief purpose the fulfillment of each individual's own nature, on the assumption that a life according to that nature is the best and most flourishing human life.[19] He thereby manifests his care for the bachelor.

---

19. In the later and fuller marriage preamble (772e–773e), the Athenian emphasizes the need for mixing of wealthy and poor, energetic and orderly, and in particular the need to avoid seeking wealth through marriage. These measures are designed to benefit both the city (773a, 773b) and the individual household (773a), as well as the individual himself, who participates in immortality (773e). The image of wine mixed properly under the supervision of a "sober god" to make possible a "noble partnership that creates a good and measured drink" (773d, tr. Pangle 1980) suggests that the preamble is appealing both to the citizen's own advantage, narrowly construed, since his character would be improved by an appropriate partnership, and to his sense of the common good of the city, which benefits from measured households. There is no need to hide or obscure the benefits to the city; the key is only that the individual must benefit, too, and recognize his benefit, so that his good will coincide (and can be seen to coincide) with that of the city.

Reason and Emotion in the Preambles

This preamble has the character of persuasion as opposed to threat. It might, indeed, make the citizen more favorably disposed to the law itself, because he comes to understand more clearly its contribution to his own happiness (as well as the city's good). Can we say, on that basis or any other, that the preamble is particularly "rational" or "cognitive," as opposed to emotional or rhetorical?[20] This distinction is less useful than first appearances may suggest, in part because of the difficulty of distinguishing between cognition and emotion altogether. However that question may stand in general, this particular preamble appeals both to the individual's natural desires and religious anxieties (his "emotions"), as well as his larger conception of himself as a member of the species (his "rationality"). It involves both rational and emotional persuasion—and the Athenian himself does not draw attention to any distinction along these lines.[21]

The Athenian does, however, draw attention to another type of contrast: that between a positive model of persuasion and a threatening model of dissuasion. Does the Athenian offer his citizens a positive goal to achieve, with enthusiasm and encouragement, or does he hold out threats—based, for example, on shame or fear—that dissuade citizens from particular actions or self-conceptions? This distinction grows naturally out of the Athenian's own way of contrasting the legislator as caring parent from the legislator as tyrannical martinet. However, even this more adequately grounded distinction seems to run afoul of the Athenian's attempt to contrast persuasive preambles with the violence of law proper. The trouble is that the Athenian's own account is ambiguous. There is often a blurring of violence and persuasion: unmixed law (723a), while "violent," is not itself violence, but rather the threat of violence in speech, a form of speech that dissuades before compulsion is applied. On the other hand, certain types of "persuasion" found in the preambles, especially but not only in the penal code, are explicitly threatening; as Laks correctly argues, it is often difficult to discern where "persuasion" ends and "force" begins.[22] Nevertheless, this distinction can shed light on whether and

---

20. Zuckert 2009 recognizes the fusion of rationality with "appeals to pleasure" and "threats of painful punishment" (113); cf. also the discussion of the interrelations of reason with emotion in Bobonich 2002: 114–16. For a different perspective that illustrates the weakness of practical reason among ordinary citizens, see Lutz 2012: 127–32.

21. As Morrow 1960: 558 puts it, correctly though too optimistically, the preludes are "persuasion at the high level of rational insight suffused with emotion."

22. Laks 2000: 285–90, on which my discussion builds; Pangle 2014: 221.

how a particular prelude might encourage citizens to embrace virtue for its own sake, or for purely instrumental reasons, or out of fear, or for motivations (even mixed ones) that fall somewhere along the spectrum.

Often the preambles will follow this first model—of marriage—in educating practical judgment toward a life of virtue, in response to untutored judgments that would otherwise lead citizens along worse paths. The preambles provide a larger context for judgment. Beginning with starting points that the individual will understand (such as the desire for fame after death), the preamble leads him to see his activity, and indeed his own happiness, in a different, more capacious light. This practical, action-guiding type of preamble is not richly "rational" in the sense of embodying philosophical training,[23] but it is obviously connected to the philosophical discussions of Plato's *Symposium*, some of which concern ordinary people's achievement of immortality through childbirth.[24] Implicitly, the Athenian Stranger has read that Platonic dialogue (along with many others). He entertains its potentially interesting ideas about popular desires for immortality. He then reformulates those ideas for the present, nonphilosophical audience, with a view to their didactic potential within his own law code.

Demonstrative Preambles: The Use of Philosophical Dialectic

At its height, however, the Athenian's persuasion of the citizens ascends to a more fully adequate philosophical level. This more demonstrative method of persuasion, in which the Athenian teaches the citizens directly, in a philosophical or dialectical spirit, is illustrated in a later discussion of the two doctors (857c–e)—a section that we will treat more fully in its own context. In that passage, all existing legislators are represented by slave doctors, who treat patients on the basis of experience rather than reason. If a slave doctor were to encounter a free doctor discussing things with his free patient, he would ridicule him. In the eyes of the slave doctor, his free counterpart is not treating the sick man so much as educating him, as though he wished

---

23. Pangle 2014: 221 is right to say, "Preludes cannot serve as 'free doctors' but can at best dispose some citizens to obedience and some to thoughtfulness."

24. On the connection with the *Symposium*, see Rowe 2010, although I have a different understanding of the significance of the connection. The Athenian uses the philosophical resources of other Platonic texts he has read, but not in order to point readers to firm conclusions that are established in other dialogues (since those dialogues only rarely establish firm conclusions).

to make him a doctor instead of a healthy man. The Athenian describes the free doctor's conversation with his patient—the thing ridiculed by the slave doctor—as follows: he "uses arguments that are close to philosophizing (*tou philosophein engus*),[25] taking hold of the disease from its source (*ex archês*), going back up to the whole nature of bodies (*peri phuseôs pasês epanionta tês tôn sômatôn*, 857d, tr. Pangle 1980, modified)." (It is important that at least this initial part of the description is intended as a sympathetic one, offered by the Athenian himself; the slave doctor has not yet started speaking; since the slave doctor finds the situation ridiculous, he would presumably describe what he witnesses very differently.)

Three features of this image shed light on the Athenian's efforts to communicate effectively with the citizens. First, the Athenian emphasizes the rational and argumentative quality of the free doctor's conversation with his patient. When he mentions the "source" of the disease and the "whole nature of bodies," he alludes to the language of the early discussion with Kleinias in Books 1 and 2. He also, and especially, looks forward to his conversation with the young atheist, where the discussion of the "whole nature of bodies" (as well as "origins") becomes explicitly philosophical. In connection with his conversation with the young atheist, it is striking that the slave doctor ridicules the free doctor for educating the sick man with a view, not only or even primarily to healing him, but rather with a view to making him a doctor. As we will discover, the Athenian's conversation with the young atheist is, indeed, designed to transform him from an adolescent questioner with philosophical interests into a full-fledged philosopher. That transformation, in itself, is a mode of healing the adolescent.

Second, and consequently, this rational, dialectical quality of the doctor's conversation with his patient applies only to a narrow range of the preludes across the entire dialogue. This doctor is treating a very special sort of patient, not an average one. Few patients will become doctors; few citizens will become philosophers. The Athenian's image conveys to readers the character of the highest form of persuasion found in the work, in the prelude of Book 10. Many other preludes, by contrast, proceed on the basis of much less abstract, systematic, and philosophical appeals. While it would be unfair to call those other appeals "nonrational," we will see that they are distinguished from this one by their practicality; by their appeals to desire, shame, and fear; by their attempts to guide action; and by their lack of philosophical or dialectical ambition. The didactic approach of the first argument of Book 10 is both too

---

25. One of only two mentions of "philosophy" by name in the dialogue; the other is at 967c.

complex and too austere for most Magnesians, who must understand it in an allegorical way.

Intriguingly, the Athenian's ambitiously philosophical method also applies to his response to Kleinias in this section of the work, in Book 9. Kleinias fails to understand why the city should punish thieves equally, whether their thefts are great or small (857b). His objection leads the Athenian into a difficult, speculative, and even possibly incoherent philosophical discussion of criminal responsibility and appropriate punishment. This discussion is significant for our understanding of Magnesia's justice system, but the Athenian's exploration of the Socratic paradox ("no one does wrong willingly") is well beyond Kleinias' comprehension.

Third, the slave doctor's ridicule reminds the reader of the ridicule faced by the Athenian in laying out his legislation. His legislation meets with laughter from both the citizens and the existing Greek culture, including its poets and lawgivers (e.g., 781a–c; cf. 810c–d, 839c–d, 842b). Although he legislates on the basis of reason and nature, his proposals are strikingly countercultural. Others who rely on more tyrannical conventions will find his approach absurd or impossible. It is clear how the reader is meant to evaluate both the Athenian and his counterpart in the image, the free doctor. It is also notable that, over the course of the dialogue, the elderly Dorians gain in respect and trust for the free doctor who guides or even heals them.

Just as the free doctor provides a model for the Athenian's activity as a lawgiver, so, too, does the Athenian's relationship with the elderly Dorians provide guidelines for the interpretation of the free doctor himself. Over the course of the entire dialogue, the Athenian persuades Kleinias and Megillus that he is beneficent or philanthropic. In that respect, his relationship with the elderly Dorians becomes itself a model for the lawgiver's caring, beneficent attitudes toward the citizens. It is possible to interpret his discussion of the preludes in that light. The lawgiver begins with his citizens' starting points and works his way upward, just as the Athenian begins from Kleinias' and Megillus' patriotic devotion to their own regimes and ways of life, and reshapes their concepts from within, so as to gain their trust and allegiance.[26] He listens carefully to their views about the nature of things and often himself appeals to nature in order to persuade them of his own views. The Athenian is entitled to be conceived of as a "free doctor"; on the other hand, Kleinias' continual insistence on providing laws themselves, not just preludes (e.g., 723d–e), shows that his status as a "free patient" is still ambiguous and that

---

26. Cf. Strauss 1975, followed by Annas 2017.

his achievement of freedom is still in progress. He still identifies himself, to a worrisome degree, with the high-handed tyrannical legislator.

Conclusion: The Legislator's Judgment

The dialogue's diverse preludes occupy varying positions on the spectrum from rational persuasion to force. Much of the Athenian's effort in constructing the regime of *nomos* is focused on the large region lying between full rational comprehension and the more violent or tyrannical forms of "persuasion" that rely on shame, threats, deception, and punishment. The Athenian enables readers to appreciate both the higher reaches of self-development among ordinary human beings and the depths to which a society must resort to maintain obedience to the law. In exploring these questions, the Athenian also invites readers to grasp the significance of his elevation of Kleinias and Megillus from their traditional militaristic societies to a new and more idealistic community. The possibility of transforming warriors into citizens makes the discussion of that in-between sphere important and relevant.

In their highest expression, the preambles provide the Athenian with his best opportunity to educate the Magnesians to approximate, to some extent, his own rational eudaimonism. At the same time, most of the preambles fall away from those heights of rational persuasion. They illuminate the Athenian's references to the need to provide the golden cord of rationality with "helpers," with assistants capable of managing the soul's iron cords. In doing so they raise questions about the very possibility of establishing a community of virtuous citizens, thereby inspiring a tragic sensibility. Can humanity fulfill its promise to govern itself rationally or to live virtuously? To what extent is it realistic to expect citizens of "mortal nature" to live within a "community of the virtuous"?

The Athenian leaves these questions indeterminate, sometimes expressing hope and at other times expressing pessimism. His accent, however, is on the shortcomings and limitations of human nature. As we will see, the Athenian frequently stresses the need for surveillance and giving information, for instilling in citizens a fear of shame and humiliation, and for frightening citizens with the prospect of painful punishments both in this life and in the next. It will always be the lawgiver's responsibility, in his particular circumstances, and given his own human population, to evaluate how ambitious his legislation can responsibly become.[27]

---

27. This theme is present from the very outset of the conversation, as the Athenian indicates at 636a–b: judgment is required in prescribing exercises to bodies and gymnastics and common meals to cities.

6

The "Second-Best" Regime: Human Nature, Property, and Acquisitiveness

HAVING BEGUN TO found Magnesia in Book 4, the Athenian now sets its property relations in order. The Athenian himself draws attention to the city's distribution of property as a central political concern specifically in Book 5, just after finishing his general address to the colonists. Following the Athenian's lead, we are well positioned to examine the questions of property distribution and materialistic acquisitiveness—two issues that illuminate Magnesia's strategies for cultivating virtue. By exploring the Athenian's efforts to cultivate virtue, specifically in relation to materialistic desire, we will come to understand the significance of the contrast he draws between the best regime and the second-best regime at the beginning of Book 5. In the *Republic*, of course, Socrates presents acquisitiveness and bodily desire as the hallmark of the "epithumetic," or desiring, part of the soul. Examining the Athenian's own way of addressing the epithumetic part of the soul gives us a clear perspective on the limitations of and prospects for his ambitious ethical and political project.

Before turning to these central issues, however, it is essential to make sense of the Athenian's initial comments on the character of the citizen body itself. He again raises the specter of tyranny only to dismiss it from the current proceedings. He reminds readers that the regime being founded will have to use "gentle" as opposed to "tyrannical" methods, even though he himself believes that harsh, tyrannical approaches are characteristic of the best regime.

Tragedy, Philosophy, and Political Education in Plato's Laws. Ryan K. Balot, Oxford University Press.
© Ryan K. Balot 2024. DOI: 10.1093/oso/9780197647226.003.0006

Purifying the Citizen Body

Understandably, the Athenian's first legislative move is to ensure the soundness and health of the citizen body. In particular, the legislators are forced to select an appropriate citizenry, by eliminating lawbreakers, either at the foundation or in the course of the city's life. With a view to securing a "pure" citizenry, the Athenian distinguishes between harsh, tyrannical measures (involving retribution, exile, and death) and gentle methods (euphemistically called "colonization"); he regards the former as superior. Despite his own preferences, though, he states that Magnesia will rely on the gentle measure of colonization—evidently because the three old legislators are not tyrannical (735d–736a). Fortunately, though, because they are merely speaking rather than acting, the Athenian says, they can simply assume that the citizenry has already been purified (736b).

What is the point of these initial reflections? In this short but complex passage, the Athenian is already endeavouring to distinguish between "first-best" tyrannical regimes and the "second-best" regime contemplated in the *Laws*. He does so through allusion to other Platonic texts. In likening the tyrannical method to the practices of animal breeders (735b–c), the Athenian is evidently (to readers, not his interlocutors) alluding, all at once, to Socrates' discussion of eugenics in the *Republic* (e.g., 459a–461), to the discussion of rearing and purging in the *Statesman* (e.g., 271d–275e, 293d) and to the image of the herdsman in the myth of Kronos (713c–d; *Statesman* 271d–275e). These texts contemplate the rule of knowledge or wisdom (however understood). Readers will appreciate that the political authorities depicted in these texts are ready and able to employ what the Athenian now calls "tyrannical" measures. In founding Callipolis, for example, Socrates proposes to exile (if not execute) everyone over the age of ten; since the exiled are not punished as criminals, this measure could be interpreted as being even "harsher" than the tyrannical measures envisioned by the Athenian (541a–b; cf. *Statesman* 293d).

By contrast with these other Platonic regimes, as the Athenian emphasizes, Magnesia will be a "gentler," nontyrannical city. The Athenian confirms this point immediately. "Someone" (*tis*), he says, might refuse to accept Magnesia, the "second-best" regime, because he is unfamiliar with a lawgiver who lacks tyrannical power (739a). Who could that "someone" be? Surely not Kleinias or Megillus. These elderly Dorians fiercely oppose tyrannical power because they are familiar with it. Rather, the Athenian answers the reader, who wonders why he would refrain from instituting a "first-best" regime—why he chooses gentle measures even though they are inferior. The reason is not that he lacks wisdom. Instead, he lacks tyrannical power. He is legislating for ordinary people who repudiate tyranny. As we saw when examining the true legislator and the young tyrant, the Dorians have come to identify free citizenship in Magnesia with resistance to tyranny.

If the Athenian is forced to create a "second-best" and "gentle" regime, then he is equally compelled to construct a less ambitious and less virtuous regime. Why? The teachings of *Laws* Book 4 and the "third wave" of Plato's *Republic* coincide: the coincidence of philosophical lawgiving with political power is essential to the creation of the best regime. In the absence of that ideal combination of wisdom with unconditional political power, it is necessary—perhaps regrettably—for the lawgiver to negotiate with citizens about the laws, norms, and regulations of a city. The lawgiver must be gentle rather than high-handed toward his citizens. Nonetheless, after suppressing wisdom combined with tyrannical power in Book 4, the Athenian persistently keeps that stalking horse before readers' eyes, in order to expose the disappointments and constraints of Magnesia's regime of law.[1]

Ultimately, three forms of compromise are necessary. First, throughout the dialogue, the Athenian must negotiate, persuade, and compromise with Kleinias and Megillus themselves. He must pay attention to the elderly Dorians' sensitivities. His efforts at persuasion are not always successful. In Book 2 he resorted to invoking the "god" in order to produce consonance. Later, he fails to persuade Kleinias of his proposed erotic arrangements for the city (837e).

Second, the Athenian must bear in mind the future citizens' capacities. He mentions, for example, that the common possession of land, households, and farms would be "greater than the birth, rearing and education we are assuming" (740a). The Magnesians could not tolerate it. The Athenian highlights the same problem later in Book 5: the lawgivers may not find citizens who will tolerate limits on the acquisition of money or the prescribed childbirth practices (746a). The lawgivers will need to retreat from their models and to make concessions to expediency and practicability (746a–d).[2]

---

1. The Athenian presents the best regime as one governed by a true legislator, who legislates without negotiation or compromise with ordinary citizens; but, as in the *Statesman* (cf. Cooper 1999b), the true legislator is also not oblivious to the need to educate ordinary citizens and to provide them with "internal reasons" to obey the law.

2. Scholars have often understood these provisions as a "retreat" from the ideal (Laks 2000: 269–71; Cohen 1993: 312–13), though we will see that the Athenian's provisions are too complicated to fit into this undifferentiated rubric. On the general question of the relation between *Laws* and *Republic*, see also Laks 1991.

Third, the necessity for negotiation and compromise also helps to explain the Athenian's reference to a third regime (739e). As the Athenian emphasizes, the lawgivers are not at present devising a law-code for an actual foundation. The present conversation outlines a city in speech, "for the sake of a sketch or outline" (*schêmatos heneka kai hupographês*, 737d7), which provides ideas for that future process of negotiation and compromise; the Athenian does not provide a blueprint (702d, 736b, 778b, 857e–858c).[3] Future legislators will have to consider carefully what is practicable and appropriate in their own circumstances (746b–d).[4] These future legislators are the ones who might establish a "third" regime or beyond, one that represents a step (or more) down from the present, "second-best" regime.[5] In the future, it will be necessary to take into account features of geography and climate, which make them more or less favorable for producing good human beings (747d–e). The vagueness of the Athenian's references to the future indicates that if any of his proposals are to be realized in practice, then they will have to be reconsidered and redeployed in other contexts, by future legislators capable of exercising their own judgment.[6]

By contrast, the philosopher kings of the hypothetical Callipolis (like the *politikos* of Plato's *Statesman*) rule Callipolis openly via law, education, and norms, without "recruiting" their inferiors or inviting their assent, much less obscuring their own presence behind the rule of law.[7] The guardians and "producers" of Callipolis are presumed to assent to the rule of philosopher kings by virtue of the city's moderation (431d–432a). Plato's *Laws* outlines an entirely different project, in which the Athenian must negotiate with ordinary people who will disagree with the lawgiver on important topics, and whose views make a difference. Their views "count" in important ways, precisely because they hold certain privileges of citizenship that the guardians and producers of Callipolis do not enjoy. The Athenian's pointed recollections of the tyrannical legislator—one of the stalking horses of the regime of law—are

---

3. Cf. Annas 2017: 65.

4. Cf. Annas 2017: 65; Morrow 1960: 11–12.

5. Cf. Laks 2000: 274; Laks 2001: 108.

6. Note the reference to future *nomophulakes* as students of the Athenian, Kleinias, and Megillus (770b-c, imitating the language of 737d7; cf. 771a). Future lawgivers are invited to learn from the dialogue, but they will need to exercise their own judgment in attempting to realize any of its political ideas in practice. I address the question of practicability more fully in chapter 11, "The Rule of *Nous*."

7. Cf. Strauss 1975: 64.

meant to show that the need to negotiate with the elderly Dorians and with Magnesia's citizens specifically rules out the possibility that "friends will hold all things in common."

Magnesia and Callipolis

After these important preliminaries, the Athenian says explicitly that the current foundation will be a second-best city (739a). He makes this point vivid by contrasting this city with one inhabited by gods or their children (739d). In the "first-best" city, the city of gods, he says, the old proverb holds true as much as possible: the "things of friends are really (*ontôs*) common" (739c). Women, children, and property are common. To the greatest extent possible, everything that is by nature private is also common, such as the eyes, ears, and hands. The city will praise and blame together, as it will feel delight and pain in the same things. These conditions create the greatest unity and hence the maximal achievement of virtue (739c–d). According to the Athenian, this regime provides a model (*paradeigma*) that the current regime should emulate.

Most readers—though not Kleinias or Megillus—recognize that the Athenian is alluding to the Callipolis of Plato's *Republic*.[8] At least in this passage, however, he is not alluding to all features of that hypothetical city, such as philosophical rule or the equality of male and female guardians. Rather, he is alluding to Socrates' so-called "second wave": "that all these women are to belong in common to all the men, that none are to live privately with any man, and that the children, too, are to be possessed in common, so that no parent will know his own offspring or any child his parent" (457c–d, tr. Grube, rev. Reeve 1997). This provision applies, of course, only to the guardians of the city (e.g., 461e). As Socrates describes it, this "wave" confers the greatest possible benefit on the city: unity (462a–b). The citizens experience pleasure and pain in the same way, even becoming like a single person or organism in that respect (462b–e). As Socrates explicitly states (464b–c), this "wave"

---

8. See Lisi 1998: 89–90 for discussion of recent scholarship; Lisi 1998: 98–105 on the relationship between *Republic* and *Laws*, arguing that both texts not only offer theoretical models of the best regime, but also considerable nuance in explaining their respective positions on theory and practice; Lisi himself holds the interesting view that Magnesia is a preliminary step on the way to possible philosophical rule in the future; cf. Lisi 2004. Papadis 1998: 112 holds a more traditional developmentalist view. In a variety of writings Laks (1991, 2000, 2001) argues that Magnesia retreats from Callipolis because of its focus on actual humanity rather than abstract form. For a helpful critique of Laks, see Lisi 2004. Lewis 2009a: 640–41 notes certain differences from Socrates' Callipolis. Ausland 2002 argues that this section does not clearly allude to the *Republic*, as does Bobonich 2002: 10–12, 425–27.

cooperates with the earlier provisions according to which the guardians will have their living quarters and possessions in common (464b–e; cf. 416b–d, 458c–d). So alien to them are private property and materialistic acquisitiveness that they would not even touch silver or gold (417a) or hold any currency privately (417a–b).

Why does the Athenian choose to make his points by alluding, over the Dorians' heads, to Plato's *Republic*—with which only he and the reading audience will be familiar? Why not simply emphasize the importance of political unity and then proceed with the foundation? Although Kleinias and Megillus are unaware of his purposes, the Athenian intends to signal to readers that Magnesia is a city filled with constraints, limitations, and disappointments. Because of the compromises he will necessarily make, the Athenian is forced to limit his ambitions. He cannot propose a foundation in which philosophers rule directly and in which private property and the nuclear family are abolished among the guardians. He wants readers to bear these points in mind; that is, he wants them to compare and contrast Callipolis and Magnesia.

Several other questions also present themselves. First, why does the Athenian focus on Socrates' "second wave," rather than Callipolis' other salient features? Second, why does the Athenian omit any reference to Callipolis' third class, i.e., the "producers," who are governed by the "epithumetic" part of the soul? Third, why does this passage occur right here, rather than elsewhere in the old men's conversation? (The answer is probably not that Book 5 of Plato's *Laws* is meant as a direct counterpart to Book 5 of Plato's *Republic*, although that similarity may be suggestive.) Finally, what is the Athenian's attitude toward the practicability of Callipolis (and, in turn, Magnesia)?

The Second Wave, Producers, and Private Property

Why does the Athenian focus sharply on the "communalism" of the second wave, as opposed to other salient characteristics of Callipolis? All the guardians of Callipolis, including both philosophers and warriors, live under the communistic regime to which the Athenian alludes. Both philosophers and warriors are, therefore, held by the Athenian Stranger to be gods or the children of gods. In the *Republic*, of course, the philosophers form a special subset of the guardians and are ultimately distinguished from those guardians who are merely "warriors," and who lack the deep philosophical understanding possessed by the rulers. Even those warriors, however, are given high praise by Socrates, although their lives hardly approximate to the "divine" lives of

Callipolis' philosophers (though, cf. 469a). According to Socrates, though, all the guardians, including the warriors, are "Olympic victors," whose lives are markedly better than those of "cobblers, farmers, or other craftsmen" (466a–b). Their victory is "the preservation of the whole city" (465d, tr. Grube, rev. Reeve 1997), and they will, in turn, receive their upkeep from the city. They will have a full and rich life, one blessed with great happiness, and defined by moderation (466b–c).

From the perspective of Magnesia's citizens, then, the second, "warrior" class of Socrates' Callipolis—not to mention the first and most god-like (497b–c, 500c–d)—will be "gods." Even the warriors of Callipolis represent too ambitious a goal to aim at; the citizens of Magnesia are significantly downgraded with respect to their capacity for virtue. (Imagine, then, what the Magnesians should think of Callipolis' philosopher-kings, if only men like Kleinias and Megillus could imagine them. Figures resembling Callipolis' rulers will emerge only in the final exchanges of the *Laws*). Like the "producers" of Socrates' Callipolis, the Magnesians will have individual households, with private property, and so on, as well as nuclear families. The second wave is too far above them—as it is above the Callipolis' producers—even to propose it for Magnesia.

Are the citizens of Magnesia, then, likened to the producers of Callipolis? It is important that the answer to this question is no. Even though Magnesians will enjoy private households and nuclear families, they will not engage in the productive crafts, not to mention commerce, precisely because those crafts are "illiberal," "banausic," money-making (846a–847a; cf. 919d–e).[9] Citizens will have "leisure" to spend on the city's activities and their own self-development, rather than on the accumulation of wealth (806d–807e). It is plausible, in fact, to infer a particular reason that Callipolis' producers are not mentioned. Readers are being actively discouraged from comparing Magnesia's citizens with them; they would represent too diminished or unambitious a target for the Magnesians to aim at.[10] Rather, the Magnesians are to be imagined as citizens who aspire to become like Callipolis' warriors but inevitably fall short.

Within the *Republic*, however, Socrates offers another, potentially more direct comparison that sheds light on the ethical status of Magnesia's citizens. Magnesia's citizens are close cousins, not of Callipolis' warriors but, rather, of

---

9. Sauvé Meyer 2003.

10. Kraut 2010: 68–69, by contrast, holds that even the producers of Callipolis live better lives than the Magnesians, because they are continuously supervised by philosopher rulers, instead of simply obeying the law.

the citizens of the first defective regime discussed by Socrates, timocracy or timarchy (545b).[11] Timocracy is the "second-best" regime of Plato's *Republic*. At the beginning of *Republic* Book 8, Socrates and Glaucon remind us that the rulers and the warriors of Callipolis will forgo private property and receive their upkeep from the producers (543b–c). That communistic regime, however, is now displaced by the civil discord that follows Callipolis' demise (547a–b). The first defective regime is "the one praised by most people, namely the Cretan or Laconian" (544c, tr. Grube, rev. Reeve 1997), which is ruled by, and is analogous to, honor-loving citizens (545a). Readers of the *Laws* will immediately appreciate the connection: Magnesia is, after all, the second-best city, i.e., the first defective regime after Callipolis. The Athenian is legislating for Cretans and other Dorians, who are honor-loving citizens of their regimes.

What is the significance of this connection? When the aristocracy of Callipolis dissolves, a civil war ensues, and the leaders compromise on a "middle way": "They distribute the land and houses as private property, enslave and hold as serfs and servants those whom they previously guarded as free friends and providers of upkeep, and occupy themselves with war and with guarding against those whom they've enslaved" (547b–c, tr. Grube rev. Reeve 1997). This description does not fit Magnesia precisely: its citizens have not, for example, enslaved their craftsmen and agricultural workers in a civil war. On the other hand, its citizens are highly militarized and preoccupied with defense of the city, and their craftsmen and agricultural laborers are, indeed, partly or even mostly slaves.[12] Socrates' description of timocracy resembles Magnesia in further particulars: the "fighting class" will be prohibited from engaging in money-making crafts and labor; it will share communal meals; and it will be preoccupied with physical training (547d, cf. 548e, 549a)—all characteristics of Magnesia's citizens. Like the Magnesians, members of this class will also favor physical training over literary education (548b). These similarities are striking; their cumulative effect is strengthened by Socrates' explicit reference to Crete and Laconia.

Since we are considering the Athenian's focus on Socrates' second wave, the key point is the timocrats' attitude toward wealth. Socrates' picture is unequivocal in this respect. The timocrats secretly desire an abundance of wealth

---

11. Strauss 1987: 79 notes this comparison; Kraut 2010: 64 argues, by contrast, that the (ordinary) virtues of Magnesia's citizens should not be associated with the "diminished psychic conditions" described in Books 8–9 of the *Republic*.

12. Sauvé Meyer 2003; Morrow 1960: 138–52; Stalley 1983: 106–8.

(548a–b), since they share in "the money-loving nature" (549a, tr. Grube, rev. Reeve 1997). It is that ingrained acquisitiveness, along with the wealth eventually won by certain timocrats, that eventually destroys the regime, compelling it to become an oligarchy (550d). The possession of a private household, a nuclear family, and a competitive wife are all said to play an important role in amplifying the acquisitive impulse (549c–e). This description gives rise to useful questions for readers of the *Laws*: How great is the similarity between Magnesia's citizens and Socrates' timocrats? Where, in ethical and political terms, do the Magnesians fall along the spectrum that runs downward from the warriors of Callipolis' aristocracy to the timocrats of Socrates' timocracy? Finally, even if the Magnesians fall short of Callipolis' warriors, can the Athenian improve upon timocracy through (for example) education?

However these questions may stand, readers will recognize that, despite the dangers of private property and the nuclear family, Magnesia does not, as currently described, descend so far as to share the pathologies of oligarchy, as Socrates envisions them. Magnesia is not a regime wholly governed by materialistic desires. By contrast with Socrates' oligarchy, Magnesia does not become two cities, with rich and poor ranged in hostile opposition to each other (552d), nor will it consent to using mercenaries (551d–e), nor will a segment of its population serve as farmers, craftsmen, and warriors all at once (551e). Magnesia will not allow for abjectly poor citizens, in part because property is inalienable, by contrast with Socrates' oligarchy (552a). Magnesia does not resemble Socrates' oligarchy in an ethical sense, even though its political institutions contain certain oligarchic features, such as wealth qualifications for particular offices (consider, for example, *Laws* 759e: sacred treasurers, cf. *Republic* 551a–b), or fines for nonattendance applied only to the upper classes (e.g., 756c–e, 764a, 765c).[13]

---

13. On Aristotle's own interpretation of Magnesia as oligarchic, see *Politics* 2.1266a5–30 with Morrow 1960: 158–59, 230–31. Brunt 1993: 260, 274–75 offers reasons to discount the Aristotelian assessment that Magnesia most resembled an oligarchy. Magnesia has recently experienced its own "democratic moment," as scholars have argued that the *Laws* in one way or another shows Plato's greater appreciation of democracy or of ordinary people or both (Samaras 2002; Bobonich 2002; Schofield 2006). Contextual and historical scholars have demonstrated that Magnesia's legal system and culture owe a great debt to Athens, often to an archaic, idealized, or "ancestral" Athens, but also to contemporary democratic Athens: Morrow 1960, Piérart 1974, with a clear statement at 465–66; Samaras 2002: 249–66 (emphasizing the Solonian "ancestral" model). Brunt 1993: 256–59 has shown, however, that Magnesia is anything but democratic according to ancient Greek standards (not to mention those of our own day); Kahn 2004: 344–45 helpfully remarks on Magnesia's rigidly antidemocratic exclusion of artisans and farmers from citizenship.

The Athenian makes significant gains in choosing to convey his meaning through the comparison with Plato's *Republic*. Instead of simply emphasizing unity as central to Magnesia's welfare, he enables knowledgeable readers to "locate" the virtues and qualities of Magnesia's citizens at a glance by setting them in relation to Callipolis' "warrior" class and to Socrates' description of timocracy. Callipolis' warriors (not to mention its philosophers) represent an unattainable ideal for Magnesia's citizens. The Athenian does, on the other hand, have ambitions to cultivate virtue in his citizens—ambitions that will help them, he hopes, to go well beyond the savagery and brutality that have, on his showing, characterized most of human history. If the Magnesians represent warriors who live under a private property regime, then their habituation to virtue will enable them to transcend the greed and injustice that characterized (for example) the imperialistic Lacedaimonians in Book 3. The major question, perhaps, is whether and how the Athenian can improve on the timocratic regime, or where Magnesia's citizens will fall, somewhere between Callipolis' warriors and Socrates' timocrats.

Socrates on Curbing Acquisitiveness

Socrates' timocrats inhabit a regime that is much less regulated, and much less ethically ambitious, than either Callipolis or Magnesia. The timocrats give vent to their acquisitiveness, with destructive consequences, and are limited (if at all) only by the force of law (548b) and by whichever elements in their souls still seek honor and victory (548c, cf. 550a–b). They lack the rule of reason (*logos*), however, combined with music and poetry (*mousikê*), which Socrates calls the "lifelong preserver" of virtue in the soul (549b, tr. Grube, rev. Reeve 1997).[14]

By contrast, both Socrates and the Athenian Stranger adopt two-pronged strategies for curbing acquisitiveness. While they both rely on laws and property arrangements, on the one hand, they also stress the capacity of education to moderate and inform desire. The Athenian invites readers to compare and contrast his proposals with those of Socrates in the *Republic*.

As Socrates presents them, Callipolis' warriors (not to mention its philosophers) were remarkably successful at setting appropriate limits to their desires. Socrates only rarely mentions the possibility that they might indulge, contrary to the laws and to their education, in greed (cf. 466b–c).

---

14. On timocracy and the other regimes of *Republic* 8–9, see the helpful treatment of Hitz 2010.

He had, of course, given all the guardians an extended literary education. He revised the Greek poetic tradition according to which gods and heroes sought their own good unjustly and through acquiring more and more wealth (390d–391a, 391c, 408c; cf. 392a–b).[15] In part by means of this education, Callipolis' warriors came to acquire right reason in their souls, in the form of correct opinion, even if their souls were ruled, for their own benefit, by the philosophers' rationality rather than their own.

Socrates had, moreover, curbed their avarice, in part, through the communal property regime (417a–b, 464b–e). According to Socrates, Callipolis' warriors are spared a great deal of trouble by their lack of private possessions and households. They would not destroy the city by fighting with each other over property and possessions (464c–d). They would be free of lawsuits and judicial contests (464d), all sorts of discord (465b), and "all the dissension that arises between people because of the possession of money, children, and families" (464d, tr. Grube, rev. Reeve 1997). They would also avoid numerous domestic troubles originating in the need to raise children, pay off debts, and provide money to their wives (465b–c). To repeat, however: those warriors were eventually, and remarkably quickly, corrupted once Callipolis fell—which reveals that their innate desires for more were by no means eradicated from their mortal natures.

Socrates' use of external supports to assist in the cultivation of virtue was not restricted to curbing acquisition. To take just one example, the warriors' courage was supported by the presence of their children at battles (466e–467a), combined with the threat of severe sanctions—demotion to the status of craftsman or farmer (468a)—to eliminate cowardly behavior (468a). The incentives for courageous behavior, on the other hand, were not simply the nobility of courageous action for its own sake, but rather, the honors bestowed by the city and special sexual opportunities (468b–d), as well as the prospect of having a glorious funeral (468e–469a). In all the domains of virtue, Callipolis' warriors were motivated both by their own sense of the intrinsic rewards of virtue (cultivated by the city's education) and by the extrinsic "supports" created by the city to help them behave correctly. The myth of Er illustrates, though, that even if they were partly attached to justice and other virtues for their own sakes, their lack of philosophical understanding implies that they will go awry often and, especially, with respect to important questions such as their choice of life itself.

---

15. Balot 2001b: 237.

Magnesia's Private Property Regime: The Ethics and Politics of Limiting Acquisitiveness

The Athenian's approach resembles Socrates' in its concern with both property arrangements and education. His development of Magnesia's ethical education and of the city's appropriate property arrangements, however, will always take place within a "second-best" framework. His explicit contrast between Callipolis and Magnesia is closely connected with its local context in the dialogue. The Athenian had concluded Book 4 by proposing to consider, in the next stretch of conversation, how the citizens should be disposed toward their souls, their bodies, and their property (724a–b). He had already offered a prelude that addressed the gods, those who come after the gods (i.e., demons, heroes, and so on), and the ancestors (724a, referring to 715e–718c). The Athenian's contrast between Callipolis and Magnesia arises roughly in the middle of Book 5, shortly after he finishes his general address (or "prelude," 734e4; cf. 724a) to the colonists (715e–718c, 726a–734e), and as he lays down a number of provisions regarding the city's land, its division of households, and its property regime (736c–738e, 740b–end of Book 5). In short: after the general prelude, the Athenian draws his all-important contrast between Callipolis and Magnesia, just before establishing the disposition of landed property as a central, even foundational, political question.[16]

Readers coming to Book 5 from the psychological and historical study of Books 1 to 3 will no doubt already have in mind the salient role materialistic acquisitiveness played earlier in the dialogue. Kleinias himself, his city, his ancestors—and indeed virtually *all* human beings, thus far in history—have shown themselves to be susceptible to the ethically corrupting and politically destructive influence of greed. Throughout Book 5, this motif emerges from time to time, until it becomes a dominant theme when the Athenian establishes Magnesia's private property regime. In the general prelude itself (726a–734e), the Athenian briefly addresses "honoring the soul" (726a–728d), touching on questions of responsibility for wrongdoing to which he will return—and admonishing future citizens, above all, not to honor the soul less than the body, by (for example) indulging in *erôs* for shameful material gain (727e–728a). Then, in the section on the body, citizens are first warned against either excess or deficiency in money and property—as in the *Republic* (728e–729a). Greed and the acquisition of material abundance

---

16. Strauss 1975: 71–72.

harm the city and one's own children (729a), who should be given awe rather than gold (729b). The Athenian has drawn the attention of both readers and future citizens to the dangers of avarice, both ethically and psychologically, by the time the general prelude is complete. He pinpoints the general idea by stressing that the greatest evil for most human beings is excessive self-love, excessive friendship for oneself (731d–e), a direct rejoinder to the communistic notion that "all the possessions of friends should be in common."[17]

What is less clear by that stage, however, is the political (as opposed to ethical) significance of greed and, in particular, its attendant social ills. The Athenian argues that the bedrock of a stable regime—the *sine qua non* of the legislator's further efforts—is a measured equality of property combined with the absence of excessive materialistic desires. In Book 3, the Athenian had remarked that the Dorian founders of Lacedaimon enjoyed the advantage of being able to create a rough equality in property holding, without encountering serious contention, because the region had no great debts from the past (684e). Recalling that moment in the conversation (736c–d), the Athenian now remarks on the good fortune of the present foundation: as a new colony, Magnesia will experience no calls for the redistribution or cancellation of debt.

Even so, in order to clarify his two-pronged—i.e., ethical and political—approach to the problem of acquisitiveness, the Athenian finds it essential to explain how the lawgivers would escape this difficulty if confronted with it: "Let it be said now that it is through a combination of justice and the absence of love of money (*dia tou mê philochrêmatein meta dikês*); and there is no escape, either broad or narrow, other than such a device" (737a).[18] The Athenian discerns an intimate link between the social benefits of just distribution and the ethical education required to limit excessive acquisitiveness. Those cities in need of a cancellation of debts and redistribution of property can be brought to good measure only slowly and with great difficulty, and only through instilling the belief that poverty results, not from having few possessions, but from insatiable greed (736e). This recognition of greed's destructiveness, the Athenian says, is "the chief basis of the city's preservation" (736e). Although the Athenian leaves unclear the precise relationship of inequality in wealth to greed, he considers it essential for political stability that

17. On self-love and moderation, see also Annas 2017: 154–55.

18. With the Athenian's response one may compare Aristotle's critique of Phaleas of Chalcedon: equality of possessions will not solve the problem of material acquisitiveness. On Phaleas of Chalcedon, see Balot 2001a.

Magnesia maintain a rough equality in property (737c), combined with strict limitations on the citizens' desire to acquire wealth (737d). The Athenian understandably envisions greed as both an ethical and a political problem—a disruptive passion that invites the lawgiver's best efforts at both ethical education and a just distribution of property.

Classical scholars have written extensively about the Athenian's ethical education of the Magnesians—that is, his use of drinking-parties, dance, song, and ritual as educational devices designed to educate the Magnesians' desires, to instill moderation and harmony in their souls, and to encourage them to practice the virtues of citizenship.[19] As readers of the dialogue know, the Athenian develops these themes at length in Books 1, 2, and 7.[20] The Athenian's proposals are reminiscent of those of Socrates in their emphasis on cultivating harmony or consonance in the citizens' souls (653e–654a, 659d–e). In particular, the Athenian is concerned to ensure that all citizens take pleasure in genuinely beautiful and noble things; that they recoil from genuinely ugly, shameful, and vicious ones; and that they rationally affirm their correctly habituated desires, in accordance with the law's pronouncements about what is noble and what is shameful (653b–c, 654c–d, 655e–656b, 657a–b, 658e–659a). Building on these ethical ideas, the Athenian exposed the traditional lawgiver's dissonant opinions about the lives of pleasure and justice (662d–663a); the implication is that a dissonant ethical education has manifestly destructive social consequences. That implication becomes irrefutably clear in the "history" provided in Book 3 (686b, 689a–e, 691a, 696c). Dissonance is the greatest ignorance (689a–e). The just society, then, results from the citizens' habituated capacity to take pleasure in moderation, justice, and a fair distribution of material goods (cf. 663b, 664a–b)—as the Athenian re-emphasizes at the beginning of Book 5 (736e–737d).

Having laid out his ethical strategy in the earlier books, the Athenian now, in the present context, addresses the disruptive materialistic passions through legal, institutional, and political means. Magnesia's property regime is intentionally designed to limit acquisitiveness and to promote civic friendship.[21] To accomplish these goals in second-best circumstances, the Athenian proposes a property regime that is not entirely private: citizens are to consider their

---

19. For example: Peponi 2013; Prauscello 2014; Folch 2015; Cusher 2014. The foundational treatment remains Morrow 1960.

20. On Book 7 in particular, see Cusher 2014 and Lutz 2012, along with the conclusion to this volume, chapter 12, "The 'Truest Tragedy' in Plato's *Laws*."

21. On civic friendship, see Schofield 2013.

shares as belonging to the entire city, and to cherish them as children cherish their mothers (740a). Land is private in one sense but public in another and stronger sense (877d–e); more importantly, it is divine (740a; cf. 741c). The god "Lot" has determined the distribution of households and has decreed that land is inalienable, under threat of harsh punishment (741b–c).[22] Hence, the number of households—5,040, a mathematically useful number—is unchangeable, also by decree of the city (737e, 740b). These provisions specifically limit acquisitiveness, by rendering vast money-making impossible and by making banausic occupations unattractive (741e).

Other measures serve the same purpose. For example, retail trade and innkeeping, both of which inspire shameful forms of greed and money-making, will be kept to a minimum, reserved for noncitizens, and carefully regulated, at that (918d–919d).[23] Additionally, private possession of gold and silver is outlawed, as is the private possession of foreign currency (742a–b). Taken as a whole, the Athenian's provisions convey the point that the citizens are to honor "similarity, equality, sameness, and what is agreed" (741a6–7), a way to produce unity, friendship, and trust (743c–d). Readers will see that these provisions combine features of Callipolis' regime with others that become intelligible against the background of the failings of Socrates' timocrats. To all these features, the Athenian adds a significant religious component— the god Lot, the land as a goddess, the Earth's sacredness to all the gods (740a, 741b–c)—in order to engender respect for the city's laws on property.

In devising these measures, the Athenian also makes concessions to circumstance, as befits his realism and his second-best regime.[24] Perfect equality of possessions is impossible (744b). It may also be undesirable, because the city will prize equality of opportunity and the virtuous use of wealth and poverty (744b–c). Moderation and civic friendship require, however, that there be limits to economic inequality among the four wealth classes that are now established (744d–745a). Hence, the extraordinary acquisition of wealth will be eliminated; surpluses, in fact, must be dedicated to the city and to the gods (744e–745a). The absence of any prospect of unlimited acquisition will both

---

22. On the many ways in which land or property in Magnesia is not "private" in any robust sense, see Laks 2013: 170–73.

23. Cf. Sauvé Meyer 2003.

24. What, again, is the third-best regime? Perhaps the future Magnesia to be founded by Kleinias and his colleagues? Cf. Laks 2000: 274 and Strauss 1975: 75. For a detailed explanation of the actual impracticability of this fictional city, see Brunt 1993, who speaks of the "delusion that the *Laws* is a realistic, practical treatise" (281).

induce moderation and maintain civic friendship.[25] The Athenian strives to compel any necessities encountered by Magnesia to yield virtue—of a sort—among the citizens.

Intriguingly, along similar lines, the Athenian also proposes that each allotment be divided into two parts—one near the center, and one near the city's borders (745c–d). Citizens will thereby come to know the city in all its diversity; citizens will be less likely to be strangers to one another (738e, cf. 738d). They will also, one and all, have an interest in the common defense of the city's borders, should the need for defense arise. In this way, the Athenian shapes the (unavoidable) private property regime to serve at least two ends of the city: freedom from external control via self-defense, and friendship or solidarity among citizens who know one another's characters.[26] By contrast with ordinary legislators, the Athenian pursues virtue rather than wealth-maximization, on the grounds that happiness is brought about by goodness; the excessive pursuit of wealth makes virtue, and so happiness, impossible (742d–743c; cf. 743e, 870b–c). One of his chief strategies is to use the city's imperfect circumstances to promote the goals of stability, self-defense, solidarity, and virtue (specifically, in using wealth). In these ways, he brings the citizens closer to Callipolis' warriors and erects barriers to any slippage in the direction of Socrates' contentious and unhappy timocrats. However, as citizens who draw income for themselves and their families from their private households and agricultural land (743d), they remain at a considerable distance from Callipolis' warriors (cf. *Rep.* 417a–b).

Retreat and Compromise—or Surprising Innovation and Aspiration?

While others have emphasized the conventionality of the Athenian's arrangements or his retreat and compromise from a hypothetical, "first-best" ideal, the Athenian's measures are actually a sign of considerable ambition.[27] The Athenian intends to fit his own regime of *nomos* between the ordinary Greek cities—which are chaotic and brutish—and the regime of Callipolis, or philosophers, or Kronos, or gods, which are too "high" for human beings

---

25. On the basis of consideration of the practicalities of income and ownership, Brunt 1993: 265 makes a strong case that in Magnesia, "the division into property classes is . . . meaningless."

26. On this theme in Aristotle's political thought, see Balot 2006: 250–53.

27. Conventionality: Morrow 1960; retreat and compromise: Laks 1990, 2000; cf. Cohen 1993.

as they are. Although the Athenian "retreats" from the ideal, "first" regime (739c–e), he also speaks with hope and even pride of these second-best arrangements (807b).

Given the pessimistic outlook on human nature expressed by the Athenian, the implications of his proposals are startling. It is *not* impossible for human beings, as they are, to tolerate, and even to benefit from, restrictions on private property that go well beyond the conventional property regimes of ordinary Greek *poleis*. The Athenian's willingness to inscribe these provisions in a second-best regime shows that he has in mind significant ambitions for the future Magnesians. At the same time, of course, he hedges these ambitions around with qualifications. He cautions that they have been speaking as if they were "nearly telling dreams" or "as if they were molding a city and its citizens from wax" (746a, tr. Pangle 1980, modified): "the one who points to the model (*paradeigma*) for what must be undertaken should in no way abandon what is most beautiful and most true" (746b), but it is necessary to recognize that some of its features may be impossible. Even so, in the most favorable conditions (e.g., 736b, 737b), the balance of provisions may be found to be "expedient" rather than "too difficult" (cf. 746c). In addition to emphasizing humanity's limitations, then, the Athenian also highlights the capacity of human beings, as they are found in their "non-divine" condition, to accept and benefit from significant restrictions on the liberties that characterized the lives of ordinary Greek citizens.

The point extends beyond property arrangements. Consider, for example, the Athenian's account of the leisure enjoyed by Magnesians. After describing the lifestyle of a Magnesian citizen, and laying stress on his freedom from merely necessary activities (806e–807a), the Athenian points out that spending his leisure being fattened like a cow would be wholly inappropriate, even self-destructive (807a). Instead, the Magnesian citizen should devote all his time to self-development:

> For as compared to a life spent striving to win at the Pythian or Olympian games, which has no time for any other activities, the life that we are describing, which is most correctly called a "life," is doubly lacking in leisure, or even much more so, since it is dedicated to caring for the excellence of the body and the soul in every respect. For no other side-task should prevent him from giving his body suitable labors and nourishment, nor again the soul its learning and habits, but the entire night and day is barely sufficient for someone doing this to take full and adequate advantage from these things. (807c–d)

While the Magnesians may rank below Callipolis' god-like guardians (who are also compared to Olympic victors: *Rep.* 466a), they, too, can justly be compared to Olympic athletes, as citizens who care intensely for their bodies and souls (cf. 839e–840b on the Magnesians' superiority to actual Olympic victors). Their "leisure" will consist in permanent occupation on behalf of the city, self-development, and management of their household affairs (807d–808a).

Readers should be struck by the unconventionality of such minute-to-minute management of the citizen's activities, as well as by the ambitions of those activities. The Athenian explicitly inveighs against self-indulgence and excessive freedom (807a), precisely because most Greek citizens would expect a life of "leisure" to consist of freedom from necessary labor.[28] He wants to be clear that leisure is an activity—and an intensely active one, at that. He envisions the Magnesians as having prodigious energy for civic activities, which enables them both to benefit the city and to cultivate themselves (808a–c). Even if they are not gods or the children of gods, Magnesia's citizens are, by comparison with ordinary Greek citizens, outstanding examples of what the human *thauma* can achieve. Despite their embodied, desiring human nature, the Magnesians are expected to accept these unorthodox measures from their lawgiver, within the second-best city. Human nature is capable of accommodating them.

The Athenian makes a wide range of other surprising and even counter-intuitive proposals throughout the dialogue, often flagging them as such for Kleinias and Megillus and for readers. The Athenian recognizes, for example, that his proposal that there be common meals for women will be met with ridicule, especially among those who are unfamiliar even with common meals for men (781a–c; cf. 839c–d, 842b); additionally, women would scream in protest in other cities but, perhaps, not here (781d). Similarly, Kleinias recognizes how countercultural it would be if, as the Athenian proposes, women were given an equal military training with men (804d–805b). In this respect, in fact, the Athenian is proposing that the Magnesians follow the noble practice of—not the Spartans or even the Egyptians—but rather, the Sarmatians (804e), a striking inversion of the ordinary Greek/barbarian hierarchy! The common belief that studying the stars and the cosmos is impious is simply mistaken (821a); instead, it is blasphemous to be so ignorant as to think that the moon, the sun, and other stars "wander" (821b–d, 822a).

---

28. For other reflections on the wide gap between Magnesian life and that of ordinary Greek cities, see Brunt 1993: 253–55.

Kleinias is surprised when the Athenian suggests that all thefts, great or small, from sacred or profane places, should receive the same punishment (857a–b). The Athenian is very obviously, throughout the text, establishing "laws that are different from those used by the many" (836b).

The Socratic metaphor of waves of laughter and ridicule, familiar from the *Republic*, is not as remote from this text as readers may initially suppose. The Athenian expects to be met with ridicule and opprobrium, both by Kleinias and Megillus and by the wider Greek culture. In the midst of describing his educational proposals, the Athenian remarks on the difficulty of speaking against convention and of the need for daring and an acceptance of risks (810c–d). Recognizing how countercultural their proposals have been thus far, Kleinias urges the Athenian to continue (810d). The Athenian wants to comment on those "myriads" of people who have often recommended that young people be educated by learning poetry by heart (810e–811a). Since poets say things that are both worthwhile and disgraceful, the Athenian argues, it is necessary to find a "model" (*paradeigma*, 811b8, cf. 811c6) that provides a standard of judgment for poetry. The Athenian proposes that the present "speeches" (*logoi*) will suffice (811c–e; cf. 957c–e). In other words: the Athenian himself, like Socrates in the *Republic*, also legislates in the face of waves of ridicule and opprobrium, taking a road that is "hateful to many" (*echthodopou . . . pollois*, 810d). Yet these teachings of the lawgiver will be internalized by the city's educators (811e), to be taught to students in an appropriate form, and by its judges, to countervail other speeches that tend to make citizens worse (957c–e).

The citizens of the second-best regime will go well beyond the brutishness characteristic of ordinary cities and displayed so powerfully in Book 3. The limit of the Athenian's ambitions emerges from his provisions on sexual and erotic measures.[29] He introduces the topic by describing a human being—a remarkably close replica of himself—who speaks in a daring and outspoken way, without allies, against the corrupt existing culture, and himself "alone following reason alone" (*logôi hepomenos monôi monos*, 835c), i.e., without the god's assistance. The erotic passions are the most difficult desires to educate and even to restrain, far more so than acquisitiveness (835e–836b). At this stage of the conversation, highly unusually, Megillus takes over as respondent from Kleinias, because Kleinias is unconvinced by the arguments of the Athenian that are designed to restrict erotic desires and activities;

---

29. On this complex topic, see especially Lutz 2012; Strauss 1975: 119–22; Zuckert 2009: 110–11.

the Athenian will have to use "incantations" to persuade him later (837e; cf. 842a). Conceding that his measures are second best (841b–c), the Athenian agrees to establish a law that allows for extramarital sexual relations, as long as they escape notice (841d–e). This measure represents a marked concession amid a series of measures that remain unrelentingly aspirational. Recall that, for the Athenian, everything must be suffered before the regime is allowed to be transformed into one that makes people worse; even the city itself should be abandoned or destroyed before that possibility should be allowed (770d–e).

At times, at least, the Athenian creates the impression that Magnesia is highly successful in achieving his ambitions. In particular, he expresses pride in the Magnesians' achievement in curbing their excessive acquisitiveness. In discussing training for war, for example, he distinguishes Magnesia sharply from other cities. He explores why most cities nowadays do not concern themselves adequately with military exercises and contests. The answer is not, as expected (cf. 831b–c), their ignorance, but rather an "erotic desire for wealth":

> The first is a passionate desire for wealth which leaves a person no time to care for anything other than his own private property. When each citizen's soul is wholly caught up in this pursuit, he would never be able to care for other things, apart from profiting day by day. Whatever learning or practice leads to this, each man privately is most ready to learn and to pursue, while deriding other things. We should say that this is one cause of a city's unwillingness to take seriously either this or any other noble and good activity; but, because of an insatiable desire for gold and silver, every man is willing to put up with every art and contrivance, both more noble and more disgraceful, if he will become wealthy, and to do anything, whether it is holy or unholy or wholly shameful, without any qualms, if only it gives him, like a wild animal (*kathaper thêriôi*), the power to eat things of all sorts and likewise to drink them, and gives him complete and utter satisfaction of his sexual desires (831c–e).

By contrast, the Athenian remarks, Magnesia will escape this cause (of inadequate preparation for war): "On account of these laws (*ek toutôn tôn nomôn*) they [i.e., Magnesia's citizens] would be least likely, I think, to be greedy (*philochrêmatoi*)" (832d). Hence, uniquely among existing regimes (832d; cf. 950c–d), Magnesia will be able to prepare for war through its highly developed "gymnastic" regime, without any significant distractions.

The Athenian obviously believes that, whatever the shortcomings of its private property regime, Magnesia will be praiseworthy in this critical respect.[30]

This passage clarifies several distinguishing features of Magnesia. Most importantly, Magnesia's citizens will not be ruled by the epithumetic or appetitive desires that govern the souls of Callipolis' producers or of most Greek citizens. The Athenian alludes to those desires directly when he mentions avarice for not only wealth but also eating, drinking, and sexual desire—all desires characteristic of the lowest part of the soul in Socrates' account, and deriving from the body. Most cities are thoroughly epithumetic, but not Magnesia. The "beast" mentioned here recalls the savage (human) beasts of Book 3, who were equally driven to seek more and more through conquest. Magnesia's citizens are not beasts; they have transcended that degraded and uncultivated condition. Instead, as the Athenian often emphasizes, Magnesia's citizens will enjoy the "leisure" to engage in civic activities and self-development, albeit primarily of a gymnastic and warlike sort (cf. 806d–807e, 828d, 846a–847a). They thereby become "tamer."

What justifies the Athenian's pride in Magnesia's achievement is that greed is a stubborn, natural, and persistently disruptive characteristic of all human beings. Excessive materialistic desires, however, have not evaporated in Magnesia, in the way they may seem to have done in Callipolis. For example, the Athenian proposes that voluntary homicide motivated by great desire should receive the most severe penalties (870a–c). The desire that is the strongest and most common among the many is greed: "Money has the capacity to give birth to countless desires for insatiable and limitless acquisition, because of their defective nature and lack of education" (870a). Magnesia still produces criminals who try to bribe the gods for the sake of unjust gain; such citizens are guilty of great ignorance, impiety, and greed (906b–d, cf. 909b). Other citizens, likewise criminals, may pursue a shameful desire for gain by practicing forensic rhetoric (938b–c). Apart from these criminals, however, most ordinary citizens of Magnesia do not indulge their materialistic desires to nearly the same extent as Socrates' timocrats, who "passionately adore gold and silver in secret" (548a, tr. Grube, rev. Reeve 1997).

---

30. Notably, by contrast with Sparta, another regime that clamped down on excessive acquisitiveness—but ineffectively, as illustrated by the example of Regent Pausanias; cf. Balot 2017.

Evaluating the Athenian's Success

The issues raised by property, material goods altogether, and acquisitiveness provide an illuminating test case for the Athenian's ambitious program of civic virtue. The central question is whether the Athenian's accomplishments in curbing acquisitiveness are genuinely founded on the rational eudaimonism he embraces. What is the quality of the Magnesians' moderation? What motivates them to restrain their acquisitive desires? How well have those desires been educated? For the city's achievement of virtue, properly under- stood, is dependent not on the citizens' obedience *per se* to law in action, but rather on the quality of their obedience—that is, whether their motivations for behaving virtuously are more or less admirable, more or less rational and self-conscious, more or less driven by a love of what is good for its own sake or by other, more diminished motives, such as social shame and humiliation or the fear of punishment.[31]

In describing the task of future legislators, the Athenian indicates that the lawgivers seek to produce virtue through a wide range of possible means:

> The substance of our agreement was this: however a man might be- come good, with the excellence of soul appropriate to a human being— whether it is the result of some pursuit or habit, or some possession or desire or opinion or particular studies, whether he is born a male or female member of our community, young or old—every effort will be focused on this thing that we are describing, throughout the whole of his life. (770c–d)

Given these diverse strategies, it is obvious that not all citizens will be motivated to embrace the life of virtue for its own sake. Few will rationally grasp, with *nous*, that justice, moderation, and courage (not to mention *nous* itself) constitute the fulfillment of their natures. No. Human nature, in the Athenian's presentation, is characterized by weakness and psychological dis- sonance, by conflicting opinions and appetites, and hence by a sense of shame over the soul's disorder. Our golden cord needs "helpers," assistants, which educate, persuade, supervise, and, at the limit, forcibly constrain the iron

---

31. General treatments of this topic include Bobonich 2002; Stalley 1983: 45–56; Laks 2005; Kraut 2010; Irwin 2010; and in general, the essays in Bobonich 2010; Strauss 1975; Pangle 1980; Lutz 2012; L.S. Pangle 2014.

cords of passion. It is important to explore whether the need for such helpers diminishes the quality of the Athenian's achievement.

The Education Provided by the General Prelude

Midway between habituation through song and dance and outright coercion lie the Athenian's lengthy public discourses, epitomized by the general prelude. Utilizing an appeal to both cognition and the emotions, the Athenian strives to educate the citizenry from their first arrival. Among much else, he attempts to persuade the new colonists to see their souls and bodies in the correct light, giving them a framework for appropriate acquisition and appropriate self-respect in relation to material possessions.[32] To take one example, he explains the significance of paying back one's debts to parents, with property, bodily things, and things of the soul, as a matter of giving back what is owed, or justice (717b–c). Upon their deaths, parents should receive moderate funerary services because they are the most beautiful and well measured (717d–e); the provision of adequate material resources for rituals in their honor is a sign of appropriate respect (717d–718a). The well-measured are similar to and dear to the gods (716c). The Athenian reveals that living a good life in these ways is likely to help the new colonists think, feel, and behave in ways they admire. They will find themselves on the path to consonance, matching their opinions about what is good to their emotions and practical behavior.

In eschewing force and offering clear explanations, the Athenian resembles the free doctor. In two respects, however, the general prelude differs from the model of the free doctor. First, the Athenian justifies his advice, at least initially, by suggesting, in a Hesiodic vein, that the gods reward those who live justly (718a). In cultivating a particular self-image in his citizens—one based on moderation and justice—the Athenian relies on an explicitly religious framework of desert and punishment. In doing so, he also diminishes the citizens' sense that justice is its own reward—their sense, that is, that justice is intrinsically good. Unlike the free doctor, he does not rely solely on the nature of bodies (or souls) themselves. Second, even in the early discussion of the gods (715e–717b), the Athenian integrates both positive aspirations and threats of punishment. Those who feel superior because of their riches or other human goods are abandoned by the gods and ultimately punished for the destruction

---

32. Nussbaum 1980.

they cause (716a–b). The goddess Nemesis watches over young people's treatment of their parents and enforces respect, under threat of punishment (717d). At the outset, the Athenian's persuasion of the Magnesians draws on characteristic elements of both free and slave doctors.

The Athenian returns to his general address at the beginning of Book 5, taking as his subject the human soul, the possession that is "most one's own" (*oikeiotaton*, 726a3) and most "divine" (*theiotaton*, 726a3). In his examination of the Persian regime, he had already pointed out the necessity of first honoring the "good things" related to soul, then the "good things" related to body and, finally, those that come from money or property (697b–c). The Persians made serious mistakes in this regard, which led to their downfall (697e–698). We expect, therefore, a discourse on how to establish the correct distribution of honor in all these areas.

Strikingly, however, the Athenian draws attention almost exclusively to mistakes that we all make in respect of our souls: no one honors the soul appropriately, since we fail to appreciate our defects (727a).[33] If the Athenian is attempting to cultivate self-respect, then he is doing so by adopting a negative, censorious posture. Young people praise themselves excessively; human beings typically refuse to accept responsibility; they delight excessively in pleasure; they fail to show courage in times of difficulty; they prize the body over the soul by admiring beauty rather than goodness; and they pursue their erotic desires for material gain, instead of feeling shame (727a–728a). The Athenian concludes his treatment of the soul with certain threats directed at these characteristic human failings: the unjust become similar to the wicked and suffer from that association. Punishment would at least provide a cure; most criminals, however, will be left only with retribution, either to suffer without cure or to be destroyed (728b–c). In the absence of any explanation of these ominous and quasi-religious threats, the Athenian has clearly tipped the balance in favor of the slave doctor's approach.

When the Athenian offers a more positive framework, his address becomes utterly commonplace. He stresses, for example, that moderate beauty and strength are prized, because they make the soul moderate rather than either arrogant or servile (728d–e). The same goes for possession of property— whereas excess leads to civil strife, deficiency leads to slavery (728e–729a)— and for inheritance, where the key consideration is the children's consonance (729a–b). Morrow's assessment of these teachings is apt:

---

33. Consider the Athenian's address in light of the general Socratic preoccupation with "care of the soul": Larivée 2003b.

These beliefs are not merely what seemed true to Plato, but what moral teachers have generally taught and men have usually acknowledged. Not many of us would really doubt the validity of the principles that Plato wishes his citizens to accept and live by; most of this doctrine is completely obvious.[34]

While the Athenian's aspirations are unconventional, his general practical advice, in this section at least, is platitudinous. Would the Magnesians need a "free doctor" to convey to them banalities about moderation and child-rearing? No. These ideas are obvious. On the other hand, the Athenian's effort to persuade citizens that justice and moderation are intrinsically beneficial is neither obvious nor substantially furthered by this type of address. Instead— for all that we see in the general prelude—his primary strategy for curbing acquisitiveness is to employ religious threats and certain traditional platitudes. Barring certain qualifications to be entered in the next chapter, the Athenian does not offer an ambitious rational account of the individual's own good. New colonists, of course, are not prepared for any such account: their education comes from threatening and punitive measures, along with superficial rationalizations of virtuous behavior. The question is whether the Athenian eventually transcends those measures or not.

Pleasure in the General Prelude

Toward the end of the general preamble, the Athenian explores "the human things" (*ta ... anthrôpina*), on the grounds that "we are talking with human beings and not gods" (732e). Hence, he focuses on the role of pleasure and pain in human life: "By nature the human is most of all pleasures and pains and desires" (732e). Previously, the interlocutors had agreed that pleasure is the chief source of human motivation (663b). Now the Athenian reconsiders the role of pleasure in the virtuous life by discussing the comparative pleasures and pains associated with lives of moderation and the other virtues, as opposed to lives of indulgence, sickliness, and cowardice (732e–734e).

Readers of Plato's *Philebus* will be disappointed by the superficiality of this discussion.[35] The Athenian ignores the nature of pleasure itself; he also refuses

---

34. Morrow 1960: 559.

35. Cf. Stalley 1983: 66–70 for an assessment of this discussion of pleasure; Stalley finds the Athenian's view compatible with that of the *Republic* and *Philebus*. My discussion is focused, by contrast, on anchoring this discussion within the context of the dialogue.

to argue for virtue's priority to pleasure. Instead, he leaves intact the end-like status that pleasure holds in the minds of most human beings. The noblest life deserves praise, accordingly, because it "is better in providing that which we are all after—that is, greater enjoyment, and less pain, throughout the entirety of life" (733a). There is no question of the Athenian himself embracing hedonism.[36] Yet commentators have tended to worry this point, because the Athenian makes no reference (as is typical of Socratic argument or even of his own treatment of pleasure in Book 2: e.g., 661b–c, 662b–c, 663b) to good or bad pleasures or to standards of evaluation that differ from pleasure.[37] Such is the grip of pleasure on the standard human being that the Athenian does not dare to question its fundamental role in ordinary practical thinking. The Athenian concludes his introduction with a flourish, by explicitly appealing to nature (733a), but not in order to isolate an independent standard by which to criticize pleasure. Rather, he is, to all appearances, preoccupied only with maximizing pleasure.

What follows is a set of highly practical and commonsensical, not to say tedious or even shallow, remarks on the number, size, and intensity of pleasures, as the Athenian examines the desirability of one life as opposed to another. Given these various factors, which way of life—that of virtue or vice—should we choose by nature (*phusei*, 733d4)? Through several homespun reflections, the Athenian illustrates that the calm, self-controlled pleasures of a virtuous life are greater than those of any other life, "necessarily and according to nature" (734b). The virtuous and healthy life, though less intense than its opposite, produces, on balance, a life of greater pleasure than any other. Licentious and immoderate appetites lead to more pain than pleasure. The Athenian's unsurprising conclusion is that the moderate, courageous, prudent, and healthy life is superior to its counterpart in pleasure. The individual who lives such a life will enjoy a "happier" or "more flourishing" life than will his opposite (734d–e).

How should readers evaluate the general prelude's finale, especially when its length and rhetorical position (as the first and most general address to

---

36. For a consideration of this question, see Bravo 2003, who tries to reconcile what he sees as the hedonistic and antihedonistic strands of thought in the dialogue.

37. Consider, though, the Athenian's earlier arguments that music should not be judged simply on the basis of pleasure, since the goal is to create young people who delight in what is noble and recoil from what is ugly or immoral (654cd, 655cd, 655e–656a). Those who take pleasure in noble songs are benefited, and vice versa (656a). Thus some pleasures are harmful and some are beneficial. Pleasure itself must be judged by correct judges—i.e., old men of sound character and practical intelligence (658b–659b).

colonists) speak to its great significance? First, this section outlines a positive ideal of behavior and does not rely on shame, fear, or other coercive measures; it constitutes persuasion, rather than dissuasion. Second, as in the case of the first marriage prelude (720e–722a), the Athenian attempts to instill in the citizens an appreciation of virtue based on an appeal to their own interests, as they understand them. He wants to convince citizens that their own lives will be better and more fulfilling if they pursue virtue; virtue is not a mechanism of social control or an alien imposition. Rather, virtue is the path that most clearly leads to a satisfying human life. Third, by making a hedonistic argument for virtue, the Athenian gives readers a sense of his own understanding of the psychology and intellectual capacities of Magnesia's ordinary citizens. As in the rhetorical persuasion to virtue in Plato's *Menexenus*, his level of reasoning lacks depth.[38] (One might call the resulting hedonistic calculus "rational" in some sense or other, despite the concomitant appeal to emotion and desire, but what is at issue is the *quality* of the rationality at play in this section. It is not highly impressive.)

Despite the intelligibility of the Athenian's purposes, however, his argument raises serious difficulties for his political project. His reasoning may, indeed should, prove confusing to citizens who, understandably, come to believe that pleasure is the ultimate standard by which virtue itself must be judged. That erroneous view, to be sure, is not one that the Athenian would ideally aspire to cultivate. Why, then, does he take the risk of making such an argument in the first place? The straightforward answer is that persuading the citizens to pursue virtue, if at all possible, even on this highly circumscribed basis, is worth the risk of possibly leading them astray by promoting a hedonistic calculus of virtue. Even so, their pursuit of virtue would then be motivated less by an appreciation of virtue's intrinsic goodness than by the misguided belief that virtue is worthy of choice chiefly, or exclusively, for its instrumental production of pleasure. Their cultivation of virtue would be accordingly diminished.

On the other hand, it is possible that the Athenian's hedonic appeals, and even his instrumentalization of virtue, are part of an imagined "ascent" by which citizens will eventually arrive at a more complete, more satisfactory, grasp of the goods internal to virtue. For readers accustomed to typical Socratic arguments, it will be a challenge to bear in mind how slowly the Athenian is forced to proceed as he leads the elderly Dorians, and the new

---

38. See Balot, 2024a.

colonists themselves, to see pleasure and virtue in a different light. He had given readers a clue to his idea, however, when he referred to the different perspectives on pleasure taken by the just and the unjust individual. The law-giver, he says,

> will persuade, somehow or other, by habituation or praise or arguments, that just and unjust things are shadow-figures. To the unjust and evil man himself, what is unjust appears pleasant, the opposite of the way it appears to the just man, and what is just appears most unpleasant. To the just man, on the other hand, everything appears the opposite on both counts. (663c)

In persuading the Magnesians to cultivate virtue on hedonistic grounds, the Athenian is attempting to lead them to more virtuous habits and practices in everyday life. Ideally, a learner will come to appreciate the worth and significance of virtue for its own sake, after inhabiting for some time, even if in a shadowy way, the perspective of justice, moderation, and so on, in daily practice.

How might this more optimistic possibility unfold? Behaving justly and moderately will at first produce a greater balance of pleasures, one may hope. Then, just and moderate behavior will begin to become intuitively comfortable, as the individual becomes accustomed to it. From there, pleasure itself (one hopes) will begin to take on a different appearance, one that depends more reliably on the justice or injustice of the individual. Learning how to take pleasure in the right things is the key to musical education (802c–d; 654c–d) and dance (815d–816d; 655d–656b), as it is central to psychological consonance altogether. The possibility of progression in an education to virtue explains why the Athenian is not incoherent to argue, in a later discussion of music, that the virtuous and the vicious might experience pleasures that are roughly equal in magnitude; but some pleasures are beneficial, while others are positively harmful (802d). It is possible, then, that the Athenian's opening gambit initially relies on a hedonistic account of virtue, in imitation of the educational system that encourages individuals to grow into the pursuit of virtue for its own sake.[39] (Even Kleinias, who is attracted to hedonistic

---

39. Note that already, at 667b–668a, the Athenian had argued for the primacy of "correctness" and "benefit" as opposed to pleasure in the judgment of food and drink, as well as in the experience of learning and the production of images and music. The critical point is that learners should take pleasure in the right things for the right reasons—in other words, that

self-indulgence [e.g., 661e–662a, 792b–c, 837e; cf. 694d–695b], eventually becomes suspicious of pleasure's power to rule the soul because of its harmful consequences [863bc, 863e–864a].)

The Golden Cord's "Helpers": Surveillance, Informing, and Punishment

It gradually emerges that, in most of the preambles, the Athenians favors strategies of social control that resemble the issuing of orders and threats rather than the gentle persuasion of a free doctor.[40] As the dialogue moves beyond the general prelude, readers come to see that the Athenian maintains an unblinking realism about the Magnesians' nature. Despite his successes in cultivating decent behavior among the Magnesians, the Athenian has not rendered them psychologically consonant. Their ethical training is not adequate for this purpose. Neither are the positive promises made in, or on behalf of, the preambles. Even education in seemingly innocuous subjects such as mathematics can go awry, unless "someone takes away by other laws and pursuits (*allois nomois te kai epitêdeumasin*) the illiberality and greed (*tên aneleutherian kai philochrêmatian*)" that might otherwise erupt in students of this subject (747b; cf. 644a).

Instead, and to be specific, the Athenian's strategy is to emphasize surveillance, punishment, and religion as the keys to limiting the citizens' pursuit of their desire to get more. On this basis, Magnesia will become an outwardly decent regime, but the Magnesians will not embrace virtue for its own sake. Law, if well designed, is beneficial and educational, but it is unable to instill more than a shadowy appearance of virtue in ordinary people.[41] The regime's ethical achievement is not highly impressive.

Again, materialistic acquisitiveness provides a helpful point of departure. The Athenian returns to the subject of acquisitiveness, and explicitly outlines a system of deterrence, in the course of describing the law's (mostly ineffective) measures to control erotic desire: "It is no wonder if the customs (*nomima*) we laid down earlier overpower (*kratoi*) most desires (*epithumiôn*);

---

pleasure should supervene upon genuine benefits and the appreciation of the truth. Cf. Pangle 1980: 420–21.

40. The material in this and the subsequent section comes from "preludes" in either a narrow or a broad sense. Whatever does not come from preludes specifically does, nevertheless, reinforce the Athenian's attempts at persuasion and compulsion in the preludes themselves.

41. Compare the more positive assessment offered by Annas 2017.

for the ban on the acquisition of excessive wealth is a considerable aid in producing moderation (*to sôphronein*), and the entire education has measured laws that promote the same end; and, in addition to these things, the eye of the rulers is trained to focus on them, and to watch over them constantly, as well as the young" (835e–836a, cf. 849a on market regulators).[42] (An example of a "custom," as opposed to a legal sanction, is the use of enchantments and blame to discourage the pursuit of material gain through marriage: 773d–e). Two points emerge from the Athenian's statement on deterrence. If customs *overpower* desires, then the Athenian has produced "self-mastery" (*enkrateia*; cf. *kratoi*, above) in Magnesia, not harmonious consonance or moderation. More important, his expectation is that the city's customs, including its prohibition of excessive acquisition, will work together with the magistrates' surveillance to promote moderation—"as far as these things are humanly possible" (*hosa ge anthrôpina*, 836a). Something beyond the laws and customs is necessary—surveillance—but even surveillance will not eliminate outbreaks of disruptive acquisitiveness from time to time.

The city's constraints on materialistic acquisitiveness achieve a certain success, by contrast with the measures regulating erotic desire. Whatever their success, though, they also reflect on the quality and character of Magnesia's ordinary citizens. Those citizens are not motivated by a steadfast, rational, and internalized belief that the virtues of justice and moderation are good for their own sakes, or that their own flourishing depends on practicing those virtues for the right reasons. Rather, the citizens are motivated to behave correctly, at least in part, because of the city's laws and punishments, which function in connection with the extensive network of surveillance prescribed by the Athenian. If they had the power to do wrong unaccountably—for example, if they were given Gyges' Ring, or were able to commit crimes secretly, and without fear of shame or harsh punishments—then, according to the Athenian's general statement on "mortal nature" in conditions where accountability is lacking (874e–875c), they almost certainly would.

Accordingly, Magnesia has an astonishingly well-developed system of surveillance and punishment, both in general and with respect to property in particular. The magistrates, and especially the *nomophulakes*, play an important role in this system (754d–755b). Anyone, for example, who buys or sells one of the 5040 (inalienable) allotments will suffer harsh penalties, including having an account of his crime inscribed on cypress tables, to be kept

---

42. For this interpretation of the sentence, see England 1921: 2: 341–42.

in the temples forever. The magistrate with the sharpest eyes is to watch out for transgressions and punish the disobedient (741c–d).

The city's system of surveillance, however, extends far beyond the magistrates' supervision of citizens. Indeed, one notable contrast between Callipolis' warriors and Magnesia's citizens is the emphasis placed on the Magnesians' need to conduct surveillance themselves and to inform on one another. Surveillance is horizontal as well as vertical. With respect to property, in particular, citizens are allowed to acquire money and even to move from one property class to another (744c–d, 744e–745a). If anyone acquires more than four times the value of an individual allotment, though, then he is legally required to dedicate the surplus to the city and to the gods. If he defaults in that duty, then any other citizen can denounce him, which leads to monetary penalties; remarkably, the informer himself has an economic incentive beyond that of civic duty, namely, a monetary reward of half the surplus (745a). Strikingly, and perhaps confusingly to citizens, the law encourages them to conduct surveillance on other citizens' materialistic desires, not only or even primarily out of a sense of justice or reverence for the law, but rather, to satisfy their own acquisitive desires (cf. 868b).

Similar penalties—monetary fines and public humiliation—are prescribed for all whose possessions exceed those listed in the public records of the *nomophulakes*, while "anyone who wishes" (754e) may accuse such transgressors in court on the charge of shameful gain (*aischrokerdeia*) (754d–755a; cf. 850a). No penalties for false or malicious accusations are mentioned here (though cf. 943e)—which tends to encourage a greater number of accusations than would otherwise be likely. Occasionally, the city uses punishment rather than material incentives to encourage one citizen to inform on another. If Magnesians who travel abroad keep foreign currency after they return, which is against the law, then the money will be confiscated; anyone who had been aware of the crime but failed to inform the magistrates would be subject to both a fine and a "curse and reproach" (*arai kai oneidei*, 742b).

Examples of such measures could be multiplied. They provide us with a striking window into Magnesia, in part because of their ubiquity. There are incentives, for example, to inform (and corresponding punishments for failing to inform) on those who find treasure and keep it (913c–914a). Early in the dialogue, the Athenian had emphasized surveillance, speaking of "testing" souls in the symposium (that is, making trial [*peira*] or using a touchstone [*basanos*], 649d), in order to watch just how individuals—possibly even a "difficult and savage soul" (*duskolou psuchês kai agrias*, 649e)—would react under the influence of wine (649d–650b; cf. the "testing" of new citizens at 736b–c: *diabasanisantes*, 736c2). And so on. The point of the Athenian's unrelenting emphasis on surveillance, informing, and punishment is that individuals cannot be trusted to behave correctly for the right reasons—that is, on the basis of a belief in the importance of justice and moderation for their own sakes. Rather, they obey the law because they fear harsh punishments, monetary fines, and the sanction of public humiliation. Even surveillance itself is motivated by the fear of punishment and the expectation of monetary rewards, instead of respect for the law as such. It is striking how little we see of such measures in Socrates' Callipolis. Are they not, however, the chief reason that Magnesia's civic life is more moderate and decent than that of Socrates' timocracy?

To a certain extent, the Athenian's measures originate in native Athenian norms that were designed to foster civic engagement.[43] Solon had invented an independent, third-party prosecutor (*ho boulomenos*, "the one who wishes") for just this purpose. We can see this idea reflected in certain of the Athenian's prescriptions on surveillance and informing.[44] The Athenian's prescriptions on surveillance, informing, and punishment, however, go well beyond the Solonian measures. In a passage that has dismayed modern scholars, the Athenian says that, while citizens who refuse to commit injustice are honorable, those citizens who report others' injustice to the magistrates are twice as honorable (730d). What is more, "the man who joins the magistrates in inflicting punishment to the best of his ability, let him be publicly proclaimed the great and perfect man in the city, the winner of the prize for virtue" (730d).[45] This presentation of virtue, needless to say, goes well beyond anything found in Solon's poetry or laws. Contrary to the modern scholarly tendency to be "dismayed" by this proclamation (an important element in the "general prelude"), this emphasis on surveillance, informing, and punishment is not an outlier: these features are present everywhere in the Athenian's system of laws, customs, practices, and norms.[46]

---

43. Morrow 1960 is the standard text on this subject.

44. E.g., 856b–c: informing on political revolutionaries; 932d: informing on those who neglect or mistreat parents; 868a–b, on third-party prosecutions of murderers who pollute public spaces, as well as of those kinsmen of the victim who fail to pursue the murderer.

45. On "perfect" citizens, cf. 643e5; on a perfect human being, cf. 653a–b; Annas 2017.

46. Annas 2017: 103–4: "Here we come up against the fact that Plato, and ancient society generally, has a blind spot here about what is lost when an individual is made the object of social pressure, including—and perhaps especially—ethical pressure." See chapter 1 herein, for commentary on this remark and the approach it represents.

Perhaps these features (which are *features*, not "bugs," of the system) should not be cause for so much dismay: they represent the Athenian's "realist" strategy for addressing the inevitable shortcomings of real, passionate, desiring people who are, despite the power of their passions, ordered to curb their acquisitiveness and to become moderate. Such measures are, in the Athenian's presentation, simply what it takes to produce virtue—or, rather, virtue-like behavior—in ordinary people, absent the rationality combined with serious musical education and law that produced the "civic" virtues in Callipolis' warriors.

The measures of surveillance, informing, and punishment surveyed thus far are all related to questions of private property and materialistic acquisitiveness. Since the Magnesians are not trustworthy on their own account, since they do not appreciate the intrinsic benefits of virtue and act accordingly, the Athenian has developed a set of "workaround" solutions to fill out the impact of the law. As a result, the citizens of Magnesia will likely behave correctly and enjoy the benefits of a comparatively stable, secure, and peaceful political life, without ever cultivating virtue in a rich or significant sense. The Athenian's measures, though, apply much more broadly to all civic activities—not just to property and acquisitiveness. The Athenian's approach to materialistic greed and its disadvantages is emblematic of his strategy for controlling, educating, and legislating for Magnesia's citizens throughout the work. The present discussion enables us to see precisely what is involved in crafting a decent, moderate regime for ordinary citizens of a militaristic disposition, who would otherwise strive to carry on the imperialistic traditions uncovered in Book 3.

Exemplary Punishment and Deterrence within a Religious Framework

A similar analysis applies to the Athenian's treatment of punishment. Punishments for all sorts of crimes—not only property-related crimes—are discussed, of course, and at great length, in Book 9. The Athenian connects his contrast between Callipolis and Magnesia to the remarks that introduce Book 9: he emphasizes how shameful it is that the lawgivers must assume that wrongdoers will arise, and that it is necessary to establish both deterrence and punishment for the presumably well-educated citizens of Magnesia (853b–c). He reminds readers, however, that the lawgivers are human beings legislating for other human beings; they are not children of gods, like the ancient legislators, nor are they legislating for the children of gods (853c).[47] This statement clearly alludes to his contrast between Callipolis and Magnesia and helps to define his project further. The implication is that, in order to be kept in check, "mortal nature" (cf. 853e–854a for its weakness), requires measures that are, apparently, shameful, such as harsh punishments used as deterrents (853c, 854e–855a). Punishment is meant to be educative not only for the criminal but also for the city: for example, all citizens who are not otherwise occupied with civic tasks are expected to attend murder trials (855d).

These effects of punishment are amplified by the Athenian's use of a variety of frightening stories about the fates of souls after death and about divine punishment, in addition to the many types of social pressure that we have thus far examined.[48] After offering incisive and even subversive reflections on criminal responsibility, the Athenian descends to the worst types of crime, such as the "voluntary and completely unjust murder of kinsmen," for which the punishment is carried out not only on earth but also by "Justice, avenger of kindred blood," who ordains a strict *quid pro quo*: someone who intentionally kills his mother, for example, will be reborn as a woman and killed by his own child (872d–873a). This type of "myth" (872d–e), along with other stories of punishment in Hades, retribution, and demonic luck, is likely to be more useful than true (cf. 865d–e, 870d–e, 877a–b, 880e–881b). As Stalley points out, "The Athenian repeats stories about the vengeance of the gods and of the souls of the dead even though he officially regards vengeance as irrational (729e, 865d–e, 870d–e, 872e–873a)."[49] So, too, with the prelude addressing temple robbers, which explains their evils as motivated by "a certain gadfly that grows naturally in human beings as a result of ancient and unexpiated injustices" (854b3–4). Many of these mythic stories are explicitly designed to motivate citizens to abide by the law out of fear of divine retribution (e.g., 870e, 873a, 880e–881b).

---

47. Does the Athenian, in calling himself a "human being" legislating for other human beings, mean to distance himself from the true legislator or Kronos' *daimones*? I think that in Book 9, he does: this book that is specifically on punishment would have no place in Kronos' regime. Humanity is forced to reckon with its own "hard cases" that arise because of human nature. As we will see, however, the Athenian reasserts the sharp distinction between himself and the elderly Dorians in his later account of responsibility, injustice, and punishment, which flies well over their heads.

48. This paragraph is adapted from Balot 2014b. On punishment, see also Stalley 1983: 137–50; Saunders 1991.

49. Stalley 1983: 148.

These religious themes were already prominently on display in the Athenian's general address to the colonists. The Athenian emphasizes the significance of the "god" in preserving order throughout the cosmos and (by means of his personified helper and follower, "Justice") in punishing hubristic men who ignorantly (*anoiai*) believe that they need neither "ruler nor leader" (*oute archontos oute tinos hēgemonos deomenos*, 716a).[50] Such men are left behind by the god and, meeting with the vengeance of Justice, destroy themselves and their cities (716b). Nemesis keeps watch over relations with parents (717c–d). Avenging gods—above all, Zeus—carefully surveil relations, and especially contracts, between citizens and strangers, as well as the wrongdoing suffered by suppliants (729e–730a). The themes of divine surveillance and punishment become even more pronounced in Book 10 (901d, 902b–c, 903b–d, 905a–b).

Conclusion: Political Achievements and Their Limits

By focusing on Magnesia's property arrangements, and by studying the Athenian's contrast between Callipolis and Magnesia, we have uncovered a new way to characterize the Athenian's project. The Athenian is a Socratically educated realist, who attempts to cultivate virtue in human beings as they are—that is, insofar as they are peculiarly limited by their mortal natures. He refuses to entertain the possibility of legislating for a city of gods, their children, or even god-like human beings. The future citizens of Magnesia will always remain at a great distance from the philosophical comprehension of virtue as intrinsically satisfying. and as central to the highest and most fully realized human life. The Athenian urges his interlocutors and the dialogue's readers to bear in mind the fundamentally recalcitrant human beings who are his charges.

Even if the preambles are designed to cultivate something approximating rational eudaimonism, the Athenian assumes that the Magnesians' dedication to virtue will be largely extrinsic—that is, motivated by social rewards and sanctions, by public praise and blame.[51] We may infer these extrinsic motivations from the Athenian's emphasis on shame and public humiliation and, at the limit, fear of punishment. The Athenian is hardly averse to

---

50. See my discussion of this idea in the previous chapter.

51. Kraut 2010: 68–69 offers a complementary view.

deterring wrongdoing through the use of severe, and even seemingly disproportionate, penalties, which are not only curative for the criminals themselves, but also exemplary for the city as a whole. These extrinsic motivations
are fostered, furthermore, by a surprisingly wide-ranging system of surveillance and information-giving. Citizens are expected to police one another,
under the supervision of magistrates. The Athenian stresses the usefulness,
and even virtuousness, of citizens who devote themselves to preventing others
from violating the law or otherwise going astray. Central to the Athenian's
project of surveilling the citizens, moreover, is his strong encouragement of a
religious ideology in which the gods promote justice and maintain a watchful
eye over the city and all its citizens, even when they operate without others'
knowledge.

At the same time, the Athenian also has ambitions to further the teleological growth of his citizens, as they progress through the city's diverse means
of education. As a close reader and admirer of Plato's *Republic*, the Athenian
holds out the Socratic Callipolis as a paradigm for the present foundation—
or, more precisely, for the third, or even more remote, regime that could hypothetically arise out of the legislative materials he provides. As the Athenian
emphasizes, Magnesia will stand at a great distance from ordinary cities,
which will hardly ever, if at all, ascend from the savage world of war, aggression, and domination in which they have hitherto been immersed. Within
the framework of the Athenian's realism, his achievements should not be
underestimated. As the Athenian stresses, however, his success in Magnesia
also required a great deal of burdensome legislative effort on his part, including heavy-handed constraints on citizens themselves. He also points out,
moreover, that even Magnesia itself is too ambitious to be realized in practice;
he envisions a third regime and beyond, on a descending scale. It is frustrating
and even tragic, in his view, that ordinary citizens will not achieve any impressive degree of civic virtue. Hoping beyond hope, we might somehow construct
a sub-Magnesian society that fails even to measure up to Magnesia itself, with
its diminished cultivation of virtue. As we will discover, the Athenian finds
this truth about politics to be a painful one.

The resulting picture of the limits and possibilities of political life is inevitably a frustrating one. The frustrations that readers may experience are
the deliberate result of the author's design. Plato invites readers both to admire the Athenian's ambitions and accomplishments, his novel ideas and his
strategies for inspiring ethical progress, and constantly to bear in mind the
deficiencies of Magnesia as a political society. On balance, the weight of the
text is on the side of pessimism: on the need for continual surveillance and

sanction even to make a decent life possible. The Athenian is not excessively optimistic about the results that can be achieved, even by a "true legislator" in favorable circumstances with the right citizenry. Perhaps, however, certain of the Athenian's ideas will be useful enough to live on beyond the dialogue. We take up that suggestion in our subsequent discussion of his transformation of a militaristic society into a peaceful community of citizens.

7

Warriors into Citizens:
The Re-education of Thumos

WHEN WE FIRST meet Kleinias, the elderly Cretan lays stress on his shrewd understanding of the Cretan lawgiver's purposes. By contrast with others, Kleinias understands that the world is ineluctably a world of war; peace is nothing but a name. To Kleinias, the world of war is the primary arena of manly ambition: it implies the opportunity to pursue unlimited acquisition, of both material wealth and power. Hence, his lawgiver had emphasized courage as his society's cardinal virtue. At the end of Book 3, though, readers learn that Kleinias is also preparing to play an important political role in the life of Knossos—namely, by helping to found the new colony of Magnesia. Even beyond his tyrannical fantasies, Kleinias has his own political ambitions, building on what he takes to be his astuteness in worldly affairs. By contrast with his materialistic desires, which we have explored in detail, these ambitions speak to Kleinias' desire for honor. In characterizing Kleinias as both acquisitive and ambitious, Plato directs well-informed readers to the two lower parts of the soul, as Socrates describes them in Plato's *Republic*: the "epithumetic" part, the seat of bodily appetites and materialistic desires, and the "thumoeidetic" part, the home of ambition and aspiration, the desire for honor, feelings of anger, and the sense of shame and self-respect. Having explored material wealth and bodily desires in relation to Magnesia's property regime, we are now well positioned to grapple with the Athenian's reconsideration of the desire for honor, with specific reference to his education of *thumos*.[1]

---

1. A classic account of *thumos* as an element of the tripartite soul is Cooper 1999a. Pangle 1976 is one of the few pieces that pay adequate attention to *thumos*, followed in this respect by

Tragedy, Philosophy, and Political Education in Plato's Laws. Ryan K. Balot, Oxford University Press.
© Ryan K. Balot 2024. DOI: 10.1093/oso/9780197647226.003.0007

The Athenian's education of *thumos* shows him at his most optimistic. Unwilling to tolerate the status quo of angry conflict, he strives to induce a calmer, "tamer," and more moderate attitude toward the ends of the political community. In this phase of his legislative activity, the Athenian refuses to accept that Magnesia will inevitably become embroiled in a world of war, force, and domination. Even if conflict is an unavoidable dimension of the human condition, he wants to demonstrate the falsity of the belief that warfare is humanity's proper aim or goal. Instead, he strives to convince his interlocutors that human beings can develop and sustain a peaceful, fulfilling political life. He accepts the Thucydidean view that, human nature being what it is, his city will never escape the need to defend itself militarily. On the other hand, he repudiates traditional aggressiveness and rejects the conventional elevation of courage to the highest rank of the virtues. Hence, without aspiring, quixotically, to eradicate the aggression originating in *thumos*, the Athenian turns to education and persuasion. Humanity's thumoeidetic tendencies can serve useful purposes within a regime of law. The Athenian's persuasion of Kleinias and Megillus depends on a thorough reconsideration of the role of *thumos*, which begins with the effort to extirpate entrenched but self-destructive assumptions about human happiness.

A Brief Archaeology of Thumos: Books 1–3

As always, the Athenian begins with his interlocutors as he discovers them— self-assertive and proud members of a militaristic culture, who are ready to defend their way of life against criticism (628e–629b, 630d, 667a). The very content of their patriotism concerns their cities' thumoeidetic attitudes, practices, and behavior: they are proud of their cities' punitive attitudes toward the pleasures of drunkenness (637a–b) and of their capacity to rout barbarians (638a). Before he redirects their punitive energies, the Athenian will invite these firmly thumoeidetic Dorian citizens to open themselves to self-criticism. As the psychological element that both asserts and protects the "self," however, *thumos* is specifically oriented toward preventing this possibility. The Athenian had to convince his interlocutors that criticizing existing legislation might promote their self-interests; it would not necessarily

Zuckert 2009; see also Fossheim 2013. On the musical education aimed at cultivating the spirited part, as discussed in earlier books of the dialogue, see Wilburn 2013, which also discusses gymnastic training and the law as other sources of education for the thumoeidetic part of the soul.

reduce their self-respect. As a result, they should react to an open-minded investigation "not harshly," but with good will (634c). Even if he successfully engineers a self-critical conversation (634e–635b), however, it remains to be seen whether he can reshape the ingrained anger and self-assertion characteristic not only of Dorian culture, but also of human nature altogether. At any rate, the question is crucial, because many injustices originate in a "difficult and savage soul" (*duskolou psuchês kai agrias*, 649e).

Central to that project is his effort to convince the elderly Dorians that the appropriate end of political life is not war, but rather peace and friendship. In light of Dorian culture's entrenched militarism, this plank of his new outlook is nothing short of revolutionary. Once again, so far from retreating or compromising, the Athenian holds out the prospect of overcoming the epic, not to mention tragic, militarism of human history. Early in the dialogue, the Athenian contested Kleinias' interpretation of his own lawgiver's ultimate purposes. Whereas Kleinias emphasized the city's fundamental orientation toward war, the Athenian argued that peace was superior to both external war and civil war, which are regrettable lapses, mere signs of disease (628c). The true statesman and "legislator precisely so called" (*nomothetês akribês*, 628d) understands that the "flourishing" (*eudaimonia*, 628d) of both cities and individuals depends on legislating the things of war for the sake of peace, rather than vice versa.

How to make that claim convincing? In the initial conversations of Books 1 to 3, the Athenian deploys several strategies to bring home to his interlocutors the benefits of peace and friendship and the destructiveness of conflict, whether it arises inside the city or with external enemies.

With regard to civil conflict, on the one hand, the Athenian first reduces the scale of the conversation to an intellectually manageable level. He invites Kleinias to imagine how best to address the brothers of a single family who come into conflict: is it through establishing the rule of the best, even if that involves the destruction of the rest, or through reconciling those brothers in friendship (627e–628a)? Whatever the Athenian's own response, Kleinias expresses little doubt that reconciliation and friendship are the worthiest goals within a family.[2] When prompted by the Athenian, Kleinias recognizes

---

2. Strauss 1975: 5 is one of the few commentators who raises the question of which of the three options the Athenian endorses. To most others (e.g., Schofield 2013), the answer to this question seems obvious: it hardly merits commentary. In fact, however, it takes a long time for readers to reach the Athenian's own conclusions on this point. On this passage, see Lutz 2012: 39–40; Pangle 1980: 384.

that his line of reasoning applies also to the city. Any citizen, and any law-giver, would choose "both friendship and peace that came about through reconciliation" rather than peace achieved through the victory of certain citizens and the destruction of others (628b6–8). The Athenian plans to build on these judgments in his elaborate re-education of traditional *thumos* in Magnesia.

In order to strengthen his case, the Athenian also projects his arguments onto the wide, panoramic backdrop of human history. He argues at length in Book 3 that humanity's warlike impulses and military technologies have led, not to an improvement of the human condition, but rather to the large-scale destruction and diminishment of all human prospects. The Athenian does not deny that the Greeks had to repel the Persian attack, and did so successfully—however poorly, in his view, many Greek cities (e.g., Argos) behaved during the Persian War period (692d–693a). He accepts that both self-defense and appropriate self-respect can be found in maintaining a reputation for military force (cf. 692c, 951a). The Athenians, in particular, were notable for their heroic stand at Marathon (698b–e) and their leadership of the Greek cause afterward (698e–699d). On the other hand, the experience of both the Lacedaimonians (687a–b, 690d–691a, 691c–d) and the Persians (697c–698a) as imperialists demonstrated clearly that even the successful oppression of others leads to one's own self-destruction, chiefly because of ignorance (688c–d). The Athenian's underlying criticism is directed not specifically at Dorian culture, but rather at the militarism that has long plagued humanity as a whole.

When we arrive at the foundation of Magnesia, then, the Athenian is anxious to avoid the errors of history's militarists, while still providing adequate means to defend the city militarily. His chief difficulty, in this context, is to uncover a way to re-educate *thumos*. How can the Athenian best integrate *thumos* into the city? How can he redirect its typically ungovernable impulses in civically constructive and appropriate directions? To do so will involve not only building on the insight that courage is fourth among the virtues (666e–667a; 688a–b, 705d), but also convincing Kleinias, Megillus, and the new colonists that honor is best won through civic attainments rather than military ones. Peace, not war, provides the appropriate context for achieving the highest human goods, even the greatest perfection of human nature. In short: the Athenian takes as his task the transformation of inveterate warriors into peaceful citizens, of "savage" and "harsh" brutes into "tame" and "perfect" human beings (cf. 643e, 653a9, 951b) oriented toward the peaceful activities of civic life.

To be clear, in "taming" the citizens of Magnesia the Athenian hardly intends to eradicate *thumos*. Rather, he pays close attention to the need to rechannel it in healthy directions, because he anticipates that anger and spirit-edness will frequently, and necessarily, surface in the life of the city. Hence, the Athenian calls to mind these very associations—of making citizens "tame" and "ready to learn"—when he outlines the purpose of the persuasive preambles, just after founding the new city. In connection with the preambles, in fact, Fossheim has persuasively argued that "the *Laws* is tailored to a psychology with broadly three kinds of motivational structure in play: reason, taking in and responding to arguments and truth; appetite, reacting to mere pleasures and pains; and thumoeidetic motivation, concerned with self-esteem and as such responsive to pride, shame, and the noble and beautiful."[3] As Fossheim has shown, we can discern the Athenian's concern with *thumos* in preludes such as the one on premeditated murder, for which the Athenian identifies three causes: greed, the love of honor (cf. *philotimou psuchês hexis*, 870c5), and the fear of being exposed in disgrace or wrongdoing (869e–870d). Or, again, in the marriage prelude, the Athenian intends to solve a problem created by the potential conflict between "manly" and "orderly" types in early human communities (681b) by encouraging spirited types to marry the more orderly and phlegmatic (773b–773d).

Thumos has, it is now clear, hardly disappeared in the transition from savage early life to the Magnesian political community. The question is how it can be appropriately integrated. The Athenian devised several strategies for this purpose. First, he offers a telling account of the education of cit-izens in respect of war and its ends: war is for the sake of peace, and not vice versa. The challenge was to make the citizens generally peaceable, while also offering them a superlative military training oriented toward the city's self-defense. Such training remains essential, because even though Magnesia itself repudiates the traditional "world of war," it will always be necessary, given human nature, to defend the city from inevitable security threats. Second, the Athenian stressed that his citizens' spirited natures could be educated so as to serve the laws by enforcing communal norms, standards, and practices against any defaulters. The citizens had to maintain alert-ness against possible infractions and be ready to punish criminals with the anger they deserved. On the other hand, the Athenian strove to introduce a gentleness and humanity toward criminals by inviting citizens to question

---

3. Fossheim 2013: 90.

traditional notions of responsibility. Finally, the Athenian intended to elevate *thumos* once he had tamed it, by transforming it into an appropriate, self-respecting desire for honor in the city. Citizens could earn the respect of others by engaging in the prescribed activities of civic life, including service in the courts. They could thereby not only enforce communal norms, but also learn to exercise their higher, more distinctly rational capacities for judgment. The education of *thumos* eventually manifests itself as the education of rational judgment deployed specifically in maintaining the community's standards, enforcing respect for its laws, and, in certain cases, providing political leadership.

Upending the World of War: The "Playful" and the "Serious"

In announcing peace's superiority to war, the Athenian had to confront the cumulative weight of traditional norms of manliness and aggression. "Real men"—like the imperialistic early Lacedaimonians and the Persian kings—viewed the oppression of others as the highest political goal; courage or "manliness" (*andreia*) was the highest human virtue; and tyranny over one's own people was the summit of each man's fantasies. Could the Athenian liberate the Magnesians from human history and tradition, so as to enable his citizens to pursue their natural vocations as "tame," moderate, and rational human beings?

The Athenian's strategy was to use the city's religious ideology to convince both Kleinias and Megillus, and the new colonists, to reconsider their understanding of what is "serious" and "playful" in human life, and the importance of each. In responding to the Athenian's early arguments for peace instead of war, Kleinias had already referred to the Dorian lawgivers' *spoudē* (serious effort) for the sake of war (628e). The Athenian's sensitivity to this concept—what should we, as human beings, be serious about, and indeed, how seriously should we take what is often thought to be "serious"?—is noteworthy. He returns to questions of war and peace and seriousness and play at a critical juncture in Book 7, when he reflects that "the concerns of human beings are not worth taking very seriously, yet it is necessary to take them seriously, and this is unfortunate" (803b3–5). (Kleinias reacts "thumoeidetically" to the idea that human affairs are trivial and insignificant (803b–c); in his view, traditional manly business is the most important of all pursuits.) Although we will return to the meaning of this sentence later (see chapter 12, "The 'Truest Tragedy'"), it is worth exploring now how the Athenian reconfigures the ideas of seriousness and play against the background of his reflections on war and peace.[4]

The Athenian begins to reverse traditional relations between war and peace by setting them within the framework of relations between divinity and humanity. He announces, in a seemingly obvious way, the importance of treating seriously whatever is serious, and of not taking seriously whatever is not serious. Although this statement is apparently banal, it is designed to initiate a thorough revision of the category of seriousness. Human beings tend to take mortal affairs—warfare, political success, moneymaking—excessively seriously, but those human concerns are actually not worthy of our attention. By contrast with such "human affairs," the Athenian asserts, only the god is "worthy of a certain blessed seriousness" (803c3–4). Humanity is a plaything (*ti paignion*, 803c5) of the god. As a result, he infers, every man and woman should live his or her entire life with this self-image in mind, "playing at the noblest games" (*paizonta hoti kallistas paidias*), contrary to what is now thought (803c). Human beings can live well, in other words, by living up to their natural character as "playthings," by "playing" at what is truly serious—namely, in acts of religious devotion, not warfare.

The Athenian recognizes that his initial statement sounds like gibberish, particularly because his efforts to promote peace instead of war run counter to contemporary practice. Others (including, above all, the Dorians) believe that "serious things are for the sake of playful things," by which they mean, he says, that war, the most serious human activity, should be managed correctly for the sake of peace, i.e., self-indulgence in conventional, materialistic happiness (803d). This understanding of the serious and the playful is misguided, but not because it moves in the wrong direction; the Athenian does not now, after all, want to revert to the view that peace is for the sake of war. On the contrary, he agrees that war, a regrettable necessity, should be undertaken for the sake of peace (cf. 628d). Rather, his point is that the Dorians—and presumably all others (cf. 803c8, 803d2)—fail to grasp the genuine character of the "serious" and the "playful" altogether. People are wrong, in the first place, to equate peace with the "play" of self-indulgent pursuits or to equate warfare with the most serious and honorable of all activities (Kleinias, for example, had advanced this conception of the serious and the playful at the beginning of Book 1); they cannot then use those misguided concepts of peace and war to reach any reasonable conclusions about the relation between the two. On

---

4. On this passage, one may compare the results of the postmodern treatment of Kurke 2013.

the contrary, he says, one finds in war no play or education that is "worthy of account" (*axiologos*)—which we say is the "most serious thing—for our part, at least" (*hemin ge . . . spoudaiotaton*, 803d). War is neither serious nor playful! Each person should spend most of his life, and the best part, in peace (803d), "playing at" religiously significant "games," such as sacrifices, singing, and dancing—which are, after all, viewed in the appropriate light, the most serious things.

In other words: if we understand humanity correctly (as a "plaything") in its relation to divinity, then human beings will dedicate their play—i.e., their ritual activity in peace—to the most serious things, i.e., education and, above all, the worship of the gods. Our nature demands, not that we fight one another, but rather that we view warfare as a lamentable distraction from the educational and religious pursuits that embody our true purpose. Our ritualistic "play" will become, in that light, our most serious activity of all, insofar as it constitutes our recognition of the greatness and seriousness of divinity. To that extent, the Athenian breaks down the distinction between "the playful" and "the serious."[5]

In a further and striking twist, however, the Athenian concludes by suggesting that in performing appropriate ritual "play" human beings will not only cultivate the gods' beneficence but also prevail over their enemies (803e). It is possible, no doubt, to read his conclusion as implying that the city will prevail militarily because of the gods' favor, which is won through ritual activity; and Kleinias may well understand the statement in that light alone. Another interpretation, though, helps us to grasp the Athenian's vision of Magnesia's own form of "serious play"—that is, his sanctification of military exercises and his persistent emphasis on the warlike overtones of the city's ritual singing and dancing. On the one hand, he understands the necessity of actual military training, which does, indeed, help cities prevail over their enemies.[6] On the other hand, he appreciates the need to "defang" this training, by making soldiers less eager to fight without adequate forethought. He does so by transforming military activity into a form of religious ritual, which preserves its character as physical training for war, while assigning the activity a new meaning. That meaning is "play," interpreted as a ritual activity dedicated to the highest and most serious beings, the gods. In this sense,

---

5. Cf., again, Kurke 2013. For more traditional interpretations, see Morrow 1960: 399–401; Schöpsdau 2003: 547–52.

6. Cf. 763c, on the military training cultivated both by hunting and by the *krypteia*-like service of the "guards" or Field Regulators.

cultivating the gods' beneficence through ritual activity does help the city prevail over its enemies, though by means of natural consequences, not through any intervention by the gods.

In laying out his vision of military organization altogether, the Athenian confirms these points. He stresses, for example, that choral dancing should be conducted for the sake of war (942d). This purpose was his focus in earlier discussions: choral imitations, such as the armed games of the Kuretes or the Dioscuri, will always involve dancing in complete armor (796b–c), while dancing the "Pyrrhic" involves imitating the postures and movements of armed combat (814e–815b).[7] Children will always bear arms as they march in honor of the gods (796c). The Athenian stresses that military training should take place in the guise of making an "artistic" or "athletic" contribution to festivals and sacrifices. He inaugurates Book 8 by announcing a need to legislate for the city's festivals. Notably, almost the entire first half of this book lays heavy emphasis on military preparation and the training for war within the framework of these festivals. The city will enjoy "certain noble games" (*tinas . . . paidias . . . kalas*) that accompany sacrifices and closely resemble actual battles (829b).[8] Magnesia's citizens will be "athletes in the greatest contests" (830a1), who conduct military exercises every day, even if of a minor character and however laughable to others (830d), and who engage in a frightening but true-to-life form of "play" (*paidia*, 830e6), which the Athenian likens to choral activity (*choreia*, 831b5). The poets (proven warriors, aged fifty years or older: 829c–d) should sing songs of praise and blame, evaluating the contestants' "athletic" abilities and their lives as a whole (829c). The Athenian sets genuinely efficacious military training within a religious framework that renders the city less militaristic.

Examples of the associations between the festivals, singing and dancing with arms, and ritualized forms of military training could be multiplied, but the point is clear: the city will conduct high-powered military training because other human beings will always represent a grave threat to its security. That military training, however, is thoroughly sanctified. It is mixed together with religious ritual and thereby dedicated to what is "most serious," namely, the god. To repeat, the Athenian wants not only to protect Magnesia from

---

7. On the Pyrrhic dance, see Morrow 1960: 358–62. As Morrow 1960: 360 and 360n.209 point out, it was traditional for Greek cities to use the Pyrrhic dance as a means of physical education and training for war.

8. On this section, see Morrow 1960: 377 for links to the ancient Greek ritual and competitive context.

foreign threats, but also to re-interpret, to whatever extent possible, the significance of military activity in the citizens' lives. Their military activity is, after all, dedicated to maintaining the city's peaceful religious and political life. It is not an instrument of oppression—either of other factions within the city or of other cities altogether. Warfare does not take on a life of its own, superior to civic affairs, nor does its cardinal virtue—courage—come to be enshrined as the city's noblest and highest ideal. Warfare is not even "serious," much less "playful," except insofar as "militarized" dances, songs, and exercises become contributions to the measured, playful activity of building solidarity and worshipping the gods.

At the same time, however, to accept this idealistic "rebranding" of warfare at face value would be excessively optimistic. Another dimension of the Athenian's management of warfare and its associated impulses should also capture the reader's attention. Specifically, the Athenian recognizes the primacy of *thumos* in the character and traditions of his new colonists. His emphasis on gymnastic training therefore becomes focused above all on warlike "play." All the city's gymnasia and exercises are construed as contributions to making the city fit for war (813d–e, 814d on wrestling, in particular). Military games either entirely take the place of traditional sports such as wrestling or the pankration (cf. 832e, 833d–e, 834a, with 796a–b) or add warlike overtones to them by, for example, requiring runners to compete in armor rather than unarmed (833a–b; cf. 834c–d, 796a).[9] Intriguingly, the Athenian attempts to satisfy the warlike impulse, and therefore to pacify it, precisely by militarizing traditional athletic events. His integration of militaristic exercises into festival competitions and rituals is not only functional—that is, designed to protect the city militarily—but also psychological in its intent.

All the same, the Athenian's emphasis on such paramilitary "play"—on marching in unison, on contests in armor, and on prizes of victory at the city's games—speaks to his inability to eradicate the pugnacious impulses characteristic of *thumos*. By means of religion, and by means of prescribed "leisure" activities, the Athenian could, at most, defuse those impulses. By allowing them a measured expression within the carefully controlled rituals of the city, though, he is able to moderate them. He can correctly think of them as elements of "warlike education and play" (*paideian te hama kai paidian polemikên*, 832d). They can be redirected to the winning of prizes in warlike

---

9. In general, on education, training, and festivals, see the most helpful account of Morrow 1960: 297–89, along with the contextual reading of Schöpsdau 2003.

contests (832e), where the citizens' competitive, aggressive desires may be at least partly satisfied and thereby moderated.

Militarizing Women, Pacifying Institutions

One of the Athenian's most interesting innovations is the provision that women and men should receive an equal—or roughly equal—military training (794c–d, 804d–e, 805c–d, 813e–814a, 814c). After introducing the idea that both boys and girls should learn the various arts of war, even if not to the same degree of precision, the Athenian comments on the ignorance and prejudice that now prevail about such matters (794d2–3; cf. 805a). The common practice of denying women a military role is against nature. The Athenian makes this point indirectly by railing against our conventional tendency to favor the right hand over the left: ambidexterity is our natural condition (794d–795d). To make a mistake about ambidexterity is trivial in relation to playing the lyre, but with respect to warfare the point is significant (795b). The Athenian offers the Scythians, of all people, as a model; shortly thereafter, his cites the Sarmatians as his model ("countless myriads of women around the Black Sea," 804e; cf. the Amazons, 806a–b). (Readers should note how frequently the Athenian uses the example of "barbarians" to propose new ideas of which he himself approves. Unlike his contemporaries, the Athenian learns important lessons from the barbarian "other"; unlike Herodotus, in particular, he is no mere "tourist."[10]) They operate the bow on either side of their bodies (795a), while athletes such as wrestlers also use both sides (795b). We can be trained to use our left hands as well as we do our right; by implication, women can be trained in war as well as men can. The convention that keeps women from fighting in wars is a harmful mistake, since by nature they are capable of making a genuine contribution to the city's military force.[11]

What is the rationale for the Athenian's revolutionary decision to militarize the "other" half of the population, contrary to ordinary Greek practice (cf. 805a–b)? And what is its impact? In part, the Athenian justifies these provisions on the grounds that a true legislator should not fail to provide laws for the entire citizenry, rather than only half of it (806c; cf. 780d, 781a–b). In part, he offers the instrumental rationale that the city's fighting force

---

10. Redfield 1985.

11. On military training for girls and women, see Morrow 1960: 329–31; Stalley 1983: 104–6; on the theoretical basis of the Athenian's treatment of women as citizens, see Santas 2003: 239–42.

could use more, rather than fewer, soldiers, and that women are up to the task (805a–b, 806a–b, 814a–b). Is there more to it than that? Three mutually reinforcing possibilities recommend themselves.

First, the Athenian's decision to train girls and women in the affairs of war makes Magnesia ever more closely approximate to Callipolis.[12] Socrates' "first wave" involved the proposal that male and female guardians should be, at least theoretically, equal: equally philosophers and equally military guardians (451d–457c, 458c–d, 540c).[13] The Athenian's move therefore complements his earlier efforts to make Socrates' "second wave" manifest in the life of the Magnesians. The "third wave," suppressed for a time in the regime of law, will also eventually return (see chapter 11, "The Rule of *Nous*").

The other two points follow from this equality, because they both depend on women's access to military training and their resulting familiarity with the affairs of war. We can understand the Athenian's purposes more clearly if we consider, by comparison and contrast, the Aristophanic presentation of men and women in (for example) *Lysistrata* and *Ecclesiazusae*. Both comedies were, of course, familiar reference-points for readers of Plato's *Republic*. Because of its focus on war and peace, *Lysistrata*, in particular, illustrates the enormous gap that traditionally divided ancient Greek men and women on the subject of warfare, at least in representation, if not also in reality. As Aristophanes' presentation reveals, the men jealously guarded their "privileges" as the city's sole defenders. Accordingly, they took it as their prerogative to make all decisions concerning war and peace. They believed—understandably, from a traditional, badly informed perspective—that their status in the city depended on their military role. In the Aristophanic play, the men's identification with militaristic bravado encouraged them to develop a "toxic masculinity," which sought out occasions on which they could display their manly virtues—their distorted conceptions of "courage"—whenever possible.[14]

---

12. Also noted by Morrow 1960: 329.

13. Both Socrates and the Athenian add certain qualifications to their emphasis on equal military training for men and women. Men and women are to be equal in theory, but both Socrates and the Athenian Stranger still adhere to certain elements of the traditional androcentric culture and traditional beliefs in male superiority: cf. e.g., *Rep.* 455c–d, 456a, 456e, 457a, with *Laws* 781b, on the inferiority of female nature; the Athenian envisages the female fighting force as staying behind to guard the city while the "whole mass of the army with all its power" (814a, tr. Pangle 1980) leaves the city to fight outside, thereby placing the female forces in the second class. He also distinguishes between the level of expertise that men and women are supposed to acquire (813e) and suggests that while it will be taken for granted that boys will receive military training, girls will somehow "have to agree" to it (794c–d); cf. also Santas 2003 on both texts.

14. Balot 2014a: 256–77.

By contrast, the Athenian's cultivation of gender equality tends to make all citizens more "equal" and more "similar" than they would otherwise have been. This is the second point: gender should not be a source of (quasi-) factionalism in the city. Women's knowledge of military affairs holds out the possibility of creating greater friendship throughout the city, across the traditional gender barriers that led to the unfortunate (and avoidable) consequences represented by Aristophanes. Men and women would become more familiar with one another's lives, and thus citizens would be, as the Athenian often stressed, better known to one another, and as similar to one another as possible (816d1). Moreover, the undoing of traditional gender roles would help the city avoid the difficulties, well known to (for example) the Persian court (694d–e, 695c–696a), consequent on female luxuriousness in the household and its corruption of boys' upbringing (806c; cf. 806a). If women are envisioned as participating in the military, then men will take on a greater role within the household: men and women will work together on household affairs (808a–b).[15]

The third point is that the Athenian's proposal is likely to create a less militaristic and less imperialistic city—a city at peace. An initial reaction might be that militarizing more of the population is likely to lead to a more thoroughly militarized city. In fact, the opposite is the case, because militarization results, not from the city's cultivation of an entire population of thoughtful and civic-minded soldiers, but, rather, from the ethos that governs its attitudes toward peace and war. If the men of Magnesia do not win special respect within the city for fighting in foreign wars—in other words, were their sense of "manliness" or courage not dependent on their military prowess in foreign wars—then their incentives for fighting would be fewer. Although the city still honors soldiers for defending the city (e.g., 921e–922a), warfare is not a special source of prestige for any particular group (defined, for example, by gender).[16] Even if Magnesia's women form part of the city's fighting force, moreover, their role is envisioned as defensive (814a–b). It is striking that Aristophanes' women are peaceful, cosmopolitan, and egalitarian, rather than militaristic, "nationalistic," and hierarchical. It seems likely that the Athenian's introduction of a defensive, female force will lend weight to his

---

15. Note *Republic* 460b, where men and women work in the city's daycare facilities.

16. Except citizens, of course; metics and slaves will not be part of the city's fighting forces (though cf. 804d, with Levin 2010: 210–11). The role of noncitizens in Magnesia is an important area of inquiry that deserves further investigation; cf., for now, the recent study of Levin 2010, along with the treatment found scattered throughout Morrow 1960.

basic idea that if wars are at all necessary, then they should be fought strictly in order to preserve the peaceful political, educational, and religious activities of the city.

Closely related to both the private property regime (807b) and the Athenian's revision of traditional gender roles in military affairs is his proposal that both men and women share in common meals.[17] At the beginning of the dialogue, Kleinias had explained that his lawgiver had established common meals in peacetime after witnessing their necessity on military campaigns. While campaigning, soldiers keep up their guard by eating together; and since "peace" is only a name, and warfare always exists whether we know it or not, common meals should be held in peacetime, too (625e–626a). The Athenian says—at least—that he accepts the historicity of this explanation (780b, 780e), though, of course, he does not accept this explanation as a justification. It was incorrect, at all events, for the Dorian legislators to leave women's affairs unattended, with the result that cities experienced myriad evils (781a–b). He emphasizes over and over that he now has a proposal that will strike many—even the Dorians, who accept common meals among men (cf. 842b), and even women, who would thereby achieve greater equality (781c–d)—as entirely absurd, although it is correct according to nature (780c–d; cf. 779e, 781b–c, 839c–d) and "good and appropriate" (781d). More specifically: although common meals for women never came into existence (781a), the city's happiness depends on regulating "all practices for men and women in common" (781b), contrary to current Greek practice (805a). Both male Magnesians and female Magnesians, therefore, should have common meals. (Note the qualification, however, that the common meals for men will be separate from those of women; children, moreover, are present at the women's common meals, but not at those of the men [806e]).

Notoriously, the Athenian does not describe the common meals in great detail and leaves this part of the legislation unfinished (cf. 842b).[18] As the Athenian points out (780a–b, 807b), there are indeed difficulties involved in reconciling a gendered system of common meals with the nuclear family; scholars have wondered how the author might have reconciled the two, had he elaborated the description of common meals in greater depth. My suggestion, though, is that the tension itself may be deliberate. Common meals help to counteract the private property regime based on the nuclear family.

---

17. On this interesting proposal, see Morrow 1960: 389–98.

18. Morrow 1960: 389–98; Rabieh 2020.

Like the provisions discussed in the previous chapter, common meals help Magnesia approximate to the communism of Socrates' Callipolis.

However those precise details may stand, the Athenian's underlying point is that the common meal, ordinarily and originally a military institution, should be maintained in civilian life, but not for the militaristic purposes described by Kleinias. Rather, the Athenian wishes to "pacify" this military institution by making it serve civilian purposes. The Athenian indicates that these meals will become possible only because the city's necessities, such as farming, will be managed by slaves (806d–e). The citizens themselves will thereby be freed to pursue, not bodily self-indulgence (cf. 807a), but rather, the cultivation of excellence in both body and soul, beyond even an Olympic level (807c–d). Seen against this background, the purposes of the common meals become clearer: the creation of equality between men and women, promotion of solidarity among citizens, and education of all citizens and the young (who will be present: cf. 806e) in the city's norms and laws. Naturally, the meals will be supervised by male and female rulers (806e), who will conduct surveillance over the citizens—particularly important for the women, who are, according to the Athenian, naturally more secretive and cunning, and are habituated to life indoors (781a–c). To reinforce the city's religious ideology, the meals are concluded by ritualized libations in honor of the gods (806e–807a).

Warfare: A Permanent Condition, Humanized by the Athenian

The Athenian emphasizes the military implications of the city's ritual activity because he is under no illusion about the prospects of establishing a permanent peace. He mentions the need to plan for catastrophes, such as epidemics or the "destruction brought on by war" that might decimate the city's population (740e–741a; cf. 814a). These are ever-present threats. Magnesia will need to protect itself; it will need a highly trained and courageous defense force, one that practices often and involves both male and female citizens (e.g., 829a–b).[19] Hence, the Athenian devotes a long section in Book 12 to military

19. At 829a, the Athenian introduces an intriguing argument: to live happily, whether in the case of a city or an individual, it is necessary to avoid doing or suffering injustice. Avoiding the commission of injustice is straightforward; by contrast, avoiding suffering injustice is difficult, because it requires being completely good. If a city is good, the Athenian argues, then it will be at peace; if not, then it will experience internal and external war. This judgment gives the reader an indication of the Athenian's evaluation of Magnesia. The argument as a whole is intriguingly

organization. By contrast with his education and currying of the individual "colt," who will lead the city (666e–667a), he emphasizes in this context the necessity of strictly following the orders given by the "ruler" (*ton archonta*, 942b); he even goes so far as to proscribe any sort of independent activity by individuals, specifically because strict obedience and soldierly coordination contribute mightily to victory in war (942c–d).[20] Like ordinary Greek cities, Magnesia practices conscription, gives prizes for military excellence, and holds courts-martial to hear charges of cowardice and desertion (943a–d). As often, though, the Athenian establishes a traditional framework only in order to introduce radical innovations in it—on the basis, in this case, of novel thinking about rendering justice in military courts. It is important that these military courts were staffed by juries composed of a soldier's peers: the cases of hoplites will be heard by hoplites, of cavalry by cavalry, and so on (943a–b). At least in courts-martial, all the citizens, high or low on the social scale, participated in delivering justice to one another. For that reason, the Athenian's discussion sheds light on the city's broad dissemination of norms of *thumos*, justice, and judgment.

The Athenian envisions what would have been considered an unusual set of practices in those courts, specifically with regard to charges of "shield-hurling" and other forms of cowardice (943d–945b).[21] He emphasizes the need for careful investigation of all such cases, under the watchful eyes of Justice, who is the daughter of Awe. He shows marked sensitivity to the role of luck in battle and to the ambiguities of interpreting combatants' behavior in the "greatest of contests." What if a soldier's retreat from battle, for example, showed good judgment rather than cowardice in particular circumstances? Is it possible

---

Socratic, but the Athenian interprets the train of thought in a flat-footed way and explains its logic moralistically rather than Socratically.

20. The Athenian's language in this section is in tension with his criticism of the Dorian regimes for their collectivism and lack of attention to the individual, in his analogy with the "colt" who needs to be groomed (666e–667a). His emphasis here is specifically on military organization. This section therefore corresponds to his idea that the Dorian societies were constructed, as a whole and pervasively, with military success in mind. We will return to the image of the "colt" in Chapter 9, "The Athenian's Theology, Part I," where it is shown to imply that Magnesia will educate citizens not only to participate in military life, but also to transcend that life in other peaceful and political activities of the city.

21. For the argument that the Athenian's presentation of court procedure has identifiable equivalents in Athenian law, see Morrow 1960: 276–77. My point is that the Athenian builds on these known procedures with specific (and carefully rationalized) points in mind—in this case, the necessity of thinking through more precisely the norms of responsibility and accountability that are at play in the courts. For brief philosophical discussion see Stalley 1983: 160–64.

for both courage and cowardice to appear even in retreat, depending on different individuals' ways of retreating, their motivations for doing so, and their judgments of their own particular situations—for example, in the contrast between Laches and Socrates during the Athenians' retreat from the Battle of Delium (*Symp*. 220d–221b)?[22] Should a soldier who misses a battle for legitimate medical reasons be considered a coward ever afterward when others reproach him as though he had simply lost heart?[23] Such cases require both careful consideration of the facts and a willingness to reject simplistic judgments based on traditional ideals of courage or "manliness." Even if courage has been demoted to fourth among the virtues, it retains its significance; it is still worth thinking hard about it. All citizens are encouraged, indeed required, to do so, in courts designed with their specific competencies in mind.

Based on such a reflective account of military infractions, the Athenian displays compassion toward those who, for reasons beyond their control, would have been disgraced as cowards in other, more traditional regimes. He stands for a true and fair assessment of merit—of courage and cowardice, properly understood—not an excess of shaming punishments that may be undeserved. To illustrate his point, the Athenian offers a hypothetical story about the Iliadic hero Patroclus (who stands in, he says, for myriad others): What if Patroclus, having lost Achilles' arms, had been brought back to his tent, not dead, but alive, and had then recovered? Would we then assume that the hero Patroclus was a coward? The answer, of course, is no—and the same answer should apply to those who are victims of nothing more than bad luck, such as a flash flood (944a–b). Our vocabulary should distinguish between cowards who throw away arms and deserve punishment (a "shield-hurler," or *ripsaspis*) and other soldiers who throw away arms because they are merely the victims of circumstance (an "arms-thrower," or *apoboleus . . . hoplôn*, 944b–c). Cowards—those who deliberately behave as "shield-hurlers" out of fear, in order to save themselves—should be punished for the sake of their

---

22. Cf. Balot 2014a.

23. My allusion here is to the case of the Spartan Aristodemus, who missed the Battle of Thermopylae, supposedly because of an inflammation of the eyes; his complex case, and the harsh treatment he received at Sparta afterward, provides a clear example of the ambiguities that often attend investigations of military cowardice (cf. Hdt. 7.229–31; 9.71, with Balot 2014a). The Athenian was much less responsive to considerations of luck and particular circumstances earlier in the dialogue, when he unequivocally condemns "marines" for their disgraceful willingness to flee hoplite encounters and take to the waiting ships (706c–d); no doubt, he expressed a more traditional attitude earlier in the conversation, in order to gain the trust of traditionally militaristic men such as Kleinias and Megillus.

improvement (944d). By contrast, the merely unlucky have nothing in particular to learn (944d).

Alongside his humanity toward unfortunate soldiers, however, the Athenian also displays harshness toward genuine cowards, "who win a shameful life" instead of courageously meeting a noble death (944c–d). Perhaps unfairly in light of his official theory of punishment (which we will discuss in the next chapter), the Athenian preserves the category of "cowardice" as such. His prescribed punishment also serves to undermine the military equality he elsewhere seeks to establish between men and women: he says that cowards should, as much as possible, be transformed from men into women, a precise reversal of the mythical story of Caeneus the Thessalian (944d–945b). Because of his love of his life, the coward will not only be liable to a fine (945a–b) but also will remain alive for the maximum length of time—just what he thought he wanted—in disgrace: he will be prevented by law from ever fighting for the city again (944e–945a). Such is the Athenian's (perhaps constrained and therefore defective) effort to strike a balance between harshness and gentleness in punishing soldiers. This effort, less defective in other cases, surfaces throughout his general re-education of *thumos* for civic purposes.

In working through these unconventional ideas, readers should bear in mind two different perspectives on the military courts. On the one hand, the Athenian emphasizes the need to do justice to a soldier's merits and deficiencies, in the most accurate way possible. He urges juries to evaluate questions of responsibility and just desert more deeply than usual, because otherwise, individual soldiers will suffer miscarriages of justice, a serious defect in the eyes of Justice, the daughter of Awe (943e). On the other hand, the Athenian emphasizes the active agency of prosecutors and juries in such proceedings. He exhorts prosecutors to shrink from falsely accusing others— whether voluntarily or involuntarily, he adds (943d–e). They should avoid making "errors in judgment about cases of necessary shield-throwing" (*mê diamartôn tis ara tôn anankaiôn apobolôn*, 943e). They should carefully separate, to the extent they are able, "the greater and the more repugnant evil from its opposite" (944b). In other words, the Athenian specifies virtues of judgment that will, ideally, characterize Magnesia's citizens in their capacity as jurors. He provides examples of the kinds of practical—yet also occasionally philosophical—reflections and considerations that they should bear in mind in judging such cases. He thereby enriches the city's judicial discourse and develops the citizens' rational capacities. This process exemplifies the elevation of *thumos*—which is still concerned with punishment, still concerned with upholding the community's standards—toward the rationally reflective capacity that the Athenian wants it to become. We will discover further evidence of this process in the Athenian's education of Kleinias in Book 10.

Fierce, though Gentle, Dedication to the City's Laws: Surveillance and Punishment Reconsidered

Magnesia's citizens are expected to be fiercely devoted to defending the city's laws from lawbreakers, especially those with tyrannical aspirations. The Athenian strove to inspire particular fear of and indignation toward those who would trample upon the laws for their own benefit (cf., e.g., 714a). In the context of the ancient Greek rule of law, however, it was possible to argue that any violation of the law, not only a tyrannical coup, was potentially capable of destroying the rule of law as such. The Athenian himself refers to this idea early in his account of the penal code, when he discusses laws regulating the cases of "the traitor, the temple robber, and the one who destroys the city's laws through violence" (857a, tr. Pangle 1980, slightly revised; cf. 864d). Compare the Athenian's inflationary rhetoric when he says that if one of the Field Regulators skips a common meal or spends a night apart from his company, he can be held up as a betrayer of his share in the regime (762c). Citizens were called upon to restrain and punish wrongdoers because, in the absence of such efforts, if violators were allowed to commit crimes with impunity, then the significance and power of the law itself would be diminished. Punishing every infraction thereby became a central duty of citizenship, insofar as it constituted an essential contribution to maintaining the rule of law.

For the sake of appreciating the context in which the Athenian's proposal made sense, consider, for example, Demosthenes' expression of similar ideas in the culmination of his speech *Against Meidias* (Dem. 21):

> Do not, men of the jury, betray me or yourselves or the laws. For if you would only examine and consider the question, what it is that gives you who serve on juries such power and authority in all state-affairs, whether the State empanels two hundred of you or a thousand or any other number, you would find that it is not that you alone of the citizens are drawn up under arms, not that your physical powers are at their best and strongest, not that you are in the earliest prime of manhood; it is due to no cause of that sort but simply to the strength of the laws. And what is the strength of the laws? If one of you is wronged

and cries aloud, will the laws run up and be at his side to assist him? No; they are only written texts and incapable of such action. Wherein then resides their power? In yourselves, if only you support them and make them all-powerful to help him who needs them. So the laws are strong through you and you through the laws. Therefore you must help them as readily as any man would help himself if wronged; you must consider that you share in the wrongs done to the laws, by whomsoever they are found to be committed; and no excuse—neither public services, nor pity, nor personal influence, nor forensic skill, nor anything else—must be devised whereby anyone who has transgressed the laws shall escape punishment. (Dem. 21.222–225, tr. Vince 1986)

Obviously, Demosthenes' hyperbole should not mislead us into thinking that any legal infraction would immediately lead to anarchy. At the center of this rhetorically inflated passage, however, lies a critical and unshakeable point: that citizens are called upon to defend the law in person, in order to secure peace and justice for themselves and for the city as a whole. Any infraction of the law is, from this perspective, a serious matter. This idea was not distinctively democratic, but, rather, characteristic of the Greek polis as such. It was this sense of honor, of anger, and of public-spiritedness that the Athenian called upon in his provisions on surveillance and punishment. We will have to consider whether and to what extent the Magnesian version of these qualities differed from those found in the Greek polis altogether or in (for example) the Demosthenic speech.

The Athenian aspired to cultivate decent, moderate behavior in all citizens by means of an extensive network of surveillance, information-giving, and punishment. This network operated not only vertically, from magistrates to citizens, but also horizontally, from one citizen to another. Although we explored the impact of this network on citizen behavior in the last chapter, we considered these questions from the perspective of "recipients" rather than "agents"—that is, we wondered about the impact of passively receiving such measures rather than actively pursuing or enforcing them. The idea of transforming warriors into active, thumoeidetic agents of surveillance and punishment, however, was central to the Athenian's re-education of *thumos* in Magnesia. It is essential to consider these proposals also from this more active perspective—from the perspective of the punishing agent.

In the Athenian's presentation, the activities of watching others, admonishing them, informing on them, and (if necessary) punishing them were critical parts of the citizen's self-image and were motivated by a sense of honor, spirit, and civic pride.[24] Consider, for example, the Athenian's most important adaptation of Solonian legal practice: his invitation to "anyone who wishes" (*ho bouloumenos*) to prosecute offenders in court. As in Solonian Athens, this invitation to third-party prosecutors encouraged civic engagement and participation. "Anyone who wishes" may accuse transgressors in court on the charge of shameful gain (*aischrokerdeia*) (754d–755a; cf. 850a). This same invitation to civic engagement applies to any number of prescriptions, such as informing on political revolutionaries (856b–c), informing on those who neglect or mistreat their parents (932d), and prosecuting murderers who pollute the public spaces, as well as those kinsmen of the murdered who fail to pursue the murderer (868a–b). Occasionally, there were economic incentives for informing on others (745a) and punishments for failing to inform when it was necessary (e.g., 742b, 913c–914a). In general, though, the Athenian expected citizens to be motivated by honor alone in carrying out these purposes.

One window into the Athenian's expectations is his establishment of a hierarchy of civic honors. He was ready to award the highest prize of civic honor to the citizen who eagerly assists the magistrates in inflicting punishment (730d): "The man who joins the magistrates in inflicting punishment to the best of his ability, let him be publicly proclaimed the great and perfect man in the city, the winner of the prize for virtue" (730d).[25] The citizen who prevents others from acting unjustly is "more than twice as honorable" (730d, tr. Pangle 1980) as the citizen who merely forbears from acting unjustly. Greater than any Olympic victor is the citizen who gains the greatest reputation as having served the laws better than any other (729d–e). In all these respects, we can discern the Athenian attempting to redirect his citizens' thumoeidetic energy from fighting on the battlefield to enforcing laws and social norms within the city. He is transforming warriors into citizens.

Holding Citizens and Magistrates Accountable

One way in which we can understand this activity is by analogy with political accountability. The Athenian proposes that the highest fulfillment of civic duty lies in holding one's fellow citizens accountable for their behavior,

---

24. Levin 2014: 191–93 is one of the few scholarly treatments of "horizontal" surveillance in the dialogue, though I believe that Levin both overstates the confidence of Plato (*sic* Levin, who does not refer to the Athenian Stranger) in ordinary citizens and understates his confidence in members of the Nocturnal Council. For a helpful contrast, see Lutz 2012: 127–32.

25. Contrast the interpretation of Annas 2017.

with a view to encouraging them to exhibit justice, moderation, courage, and care for the city in all their activities. This activity calls upon the exercise of *thumos*, in that it embodies a sensitivity to upholding particular standards or ideals of behavior. Citizens hold one another to account, on the shared understanding that they all belong to the city as much as to themselves or their private families. In holding one another to account in everyday life, Magnesia's citizens build on and develop the Athenian practice of holding citizens and magistrates to account in the courts. In democratic Athens, the practice of forcing litigants to "give an account" of themselves often extended to their characters and lives as a whole. The practice reflects the close connections between political norms, legal requirements, and ethical life in the Athenian democracy. Arguably, the Athenian "giving of accounts" also provided the generative context in which Socrates' own life of self-examination and self-auditing originated, and in which his demand that his interlocutors audit themselves, and give an account of themselves, became intelligible.[26] It is this set of connections that the Athenian mobilizes in his praise for the citizen who scrutinizes and watches over others with a view to their obedience to the law, if not their overall ethical development. While the Magnesians cannot give a Socratic account of themselves, they nonetheless, as a community, and with reference to the law, hold one another accountable.

Analogously, the Athenian provides that the city's magistrates will also be held accountable for their behavior in office; political accountability is a critical component of the Athenian's regime of law. This provision ranges widely, from the lowest levels of magisterial activity to the highest civic functions. In his discussion of minor officials known as the "Field Regulators" (*agronomoi*), the Athenian makes a general point about the pervasive auditing that characterizes Magnesia's political system: "It is necessary that no juror or magistrate render justice or perform his official duties without being subject to an audit (*anupeuthunon*)" (761e). If Field Regulators are accused of transgressions, for example, then they will be tried by a jury of villagers and neighbors for lesser offenses, and in the common courts for greater offenses (762a–b). The Treasurer of Hera—along with, possibly, all the unmarried[27]— is audited in the matter of fines to be paid by the unmarried (774b), while magistrates who fail to act on their knowledge of various crimes (e.g.,

---

26. Balot 2013.

27. England 1921 1: 611 supposes that all citizens concerned would have to testify at the audits of Hera's Treasurers; on this audit in particular, see Schöpsdau 2003: 456–57.

associating with anyone convicted of striking his parents, 881b–e) will be accused at the time of their audits. As in democratic Athens, magistrates will be held to account either by their fellow citizens or by other magistrates who have been specifically chosen for the purpose.

Toward the middle of Book 12, the Athenian elaborates on the role of those specifically designated "Auditors." The office itself is one of the city's highest and most important: auditing constitutes ruling over rulers by those who are superior in virtue (945b–c), i.e., "divine" (*theious*) men (945c). Because of their responsibilities in rendering justice among magistrates, the Auditors must be "amazing in the whole of virtue" (*thaumastous pasan aretên*, 945e). They are selected according to an elaborate procedure; they are given prizes for excellence and proclaimed to be the city's best men; they are priests of Apollo and the Sun; and they are given nearly heroic honors at their funerals and in their gravesites (946b–947e). This amplification of honor indicates that these highest and best magistrates of the city perform two, at least, of the city's most important tasks: surveillance and judgment of others. Being twelve in number, the Auditors divide the city's magistracies into twelve parts and record their judgments publicly in writing in the marketplace. In passing judgment on other magistrates, they ensure that aspiring tyrants will not even take their first steps toward overturning laws. Performing their duties well is essential to the city's unity and thus to its flourishing (945d–e). Numbering among the city's highest officials, they are the exemplars of virtue to which all citizens should look up admiringly. This hierarchy implies that one of the best activities of citizenship is exercising judgment of the best and highest sort.

Intriguingly, but consistently, the Auditors, too, are held to account both for their judgments and for their character.[28] Their particular judgments are held to account by virtue of the possibility of appeal before the select judges (946d). Their conduct in office will itself be audited (946e). After they have passed their audits—presumably at age seventy-five, at retirement (946c)—they will still be held accountable for good behavior, in default of which they will face prosecution (947e–948a). Even the Auditors can falter after passing their own audits (947e), but that possibility is not likely (see, further, chapter 11, "The Rule of *Nous*"). In the case of ordinary Magnesians, however,

---

28. For an examination of the role of the Auditors, and the historical context of audits in democratic Athens, see Morrow 1960: 219–29. The key difference is that at Athens a popular court had the final say over a magistrate's *euthuna*, whereas in Magnesia, as we have seen, the principal verdict was given by a small board of highly qualified magistrates (though appeal to the court of select judges was possible: Morrow 1960: 225–27).

the watchfulness of their fellow citizens creates an environment in which they will be held to the standard of ceaselessly practicing virtuous behavior. The Athenian's hope, if not his expectation, is that such practices will lead them further and further along the path of loving what they ought to love and hating what they ought to hate (cf. 862d). If the Athenian's view of human nature is correct, then such endless practicing, within the framework of the city's laws and educational regime, provides the best means for the cultivation of virtue in ordinary citizens.

The Complex Judgments Required of Citizens

The Athenian's effort to transform aggressively thumoeidetic warriors into moderate, appropriately thumoeidetic citizens involves a substantial component of emotional education. By examining this component, we come to grasp that the admirable citizen's psychology of honor is informed by complex, and occasionally contradictory, ideas. Having begun as the anger or spirit of a traditional warrior, his *thumos* is transformed into a rich seat of emotions and judgments that is characteristic of a high-functioning citizen. In effecting this transformation, the Athenian imitates Socrates' education of the guardians in Callipolis (consider, for example, *Rep.* 410b–412a), in attempting to balance *thumos* with gentleness: "It is necessary," he says, "for every man (*panta andra*) to be spirited (*thumoeidê*), but also as gentle (*praion*) as possible" (731b). His attempt to balance these antithetical attributes is central to his effort to educate *thumos*, but it emerges that cultivating *thumos* properly requires a wide-ranging reconsideration of what is just (*dikaios*) and noble (*kalos*) altogether.

The Athenian's "unification of opposites" leads him to offer a detailed, and not entirely coherent, explanation of how and why good citizens are expected to integrate these antithetical attributes.[29] He first draws an overarching contrast between curable and incurable injustice. It is permissible, he says, to show pity to the unjust when their illnesses are curable, but best to show anger to the purely unjust, who cannot be corrected. For the moment, at least, he says nothing about how to distinguish the curable from the incurable. He adds, however, an unusual psychological reason for pitying the curably unjust: namely, that "every unjust man is involuntarily unjust"—or, in other words, that no one does wrong willingly (731c). Since the soul is our most honored possession, he says, no one would willingly acquire an evil that afflicts his soul. Hence, the

---

29. On the notion of unifying opposites, both in Periclean rhetoric and in Platonic texts (above all, *Statesman*), see Balot 2014a.

unjust man is pitiable, and gentleness is the appropriate response to cases of curable injustice—though not to cases of incurable injustice (731d).

Two features of the Athenian's argument are striking. First, it is surprising that he calls to mind this "Socratic paradox" in Magnesia, and especially in the general prelude, where he is, in general, concerned to suit his legislation to an audience of new colonists, who are far from original thinkers or critics of tradition. Presumably, they subscribe to the commonsensical legal fiction that agents are responsible for their actions, except in obviously extenuating circumstances. They will be more concerned, as judges, with the facts of particular cases—whether crimes have been committed or not—and less with questions of individual psychology, such as whether individuals are genuinely responsible agents or whether they can be therapeutically "cured." They will also be more concerned with promoting the welfare of the community than doing justice to the individual in cases of potential conflict. Second, if the Socratic paradox is true, then the Athenian's conclusion fails to follow from his argument. In other words: if no one is voluntarily unjust, and if involuntary injustice should motivate pity, then all wrongdoers should be pitied— not only those whose injustice is curable. The Athenian fails to explain why the incurably unjust should, as a matter of justice, be subject to anger rather than pity. The obvious answer is that expressing anger at incurable injustice might benefit the community, but the unfortunate "remainder"—the injustice done to individuals whose injustice is, by this argument, involuntary— will be painfully obvious (pending a possible revision of the Athenian's stance in Book 9, which we will consider in the next chapter).

However those matters may stand, though, the Athenian clearly introduces the Socratic paradox in order to reduce anger and to begin to establish a "curative" theory of punishment. Criminals should be educated, if at all possible, rather than subjected to mere retribution. By informing citizens of the murky psychology of injustice, he aims to moderate their ingrained thumoeidetic tendencies. He cultivates their sense of humanity or pity.[30] In doing so he poses a challenge to the ordinary Athenian practices of calling upon his audience's anger and pity.

Typically, as Demosthenes' speech makes clear, orators urged jurors to feel anger when outlaws threatened to tear the fabric of the city's rule of law. The Athenian practice of punishment was typically punitive and retributive.[31]

---

30. Pangle 2014.

31. Allen 2000.

It was designed to reinforce or re-establish the honor of the male citizen as judge and punisher, presumably because the crimes under consideration, by their mere existence, constituted a threat to that honor. While democratic Athenian jurors remained conscious of voluntary action in the normal sense, they hardly adopted a curative perspective on the judicial process, as the Athenian recommends. (Defendants, of course typically sought to elicit pity from jurors by offering a sympathetic narrative of their own lives, even, as Socrates stressed in the Platonic *Apology*, parading their downtrodden families in court.[32])

From the Athenian Stranger's perspective, the democratic emotions of anger and pity, as expressed in Athenian jury-courts, were misguided. These democratic emotions targeted the wrong goals (i.e., re-establishing honor and hierarchy) and were moved by a misguided understanding of justice and associated goods. For example, the Athenian's special, "Socratic" reason for showing pity to wrongdoers differs mightily from standard juridical appeals, which were based simply on the untoward consequences of suffering punishment at the hands of juries. This Socratic reasoning serves, in the first instance, to reduce anger at wrongdoers (admittedly, only in cases of the "curably" unjust). Moreover, and more importantly, this line of reasoning highlights the Athenian's expectation that citizens will reason carefully, thoughtfully, and sympathetically about the psychological backgrounds of individuals who have been accused of crimes. They will have to develop and employ significant powers of judgment when they conduct surveillance or render judicial sentences. They will also have to bring their spirited emotions into line with those rational judgments about the appropriate responses to supposed criminals, in light of their capacity to be cured, and in light of the involuntariness of their injustice.

Needless to say, by raising these issues in the general prelude, the Athenian is both posing dilemmas for the city's legal code and placing heavy demands on the citizens' judgments and emotions. Already in the general prelude, in fact, he points to the existence of a dilemma by criticizing a certain type of human being who intends to honor his soul by refusing to accept responsibility for his actions: "When a human being does not consider himself responsible (*aition*) for his own faults (*hamartêmatôn*) on each occasion, even evils that are very grave and numerous (*tôn pleistôn kakôn kai megistôn*), but rather blames others, and always excuses himself, he thinks that he is honoring his own soul, but he is far from doing so; in reality, he is harming

---

32. On these themes, see Johnstone 1999; Allen 2000.

it" (727b–c). Understandably, the Athenian wants to encourage citizens to take responsibility for themselves; shirking responsibility for error or evil is, indeed, worthy of harsh criticism. That message is one that he undoubtedly intends to convey to all citizens, either explicitly, in the present address, or implicitly, in the city's entire educational and political system. On the other hand, his endorsement of the Socratic paradox seems to conflict with the admonition that criminals should accept responsibility for themselves. This dilemma is virtually unavoidable for anyone who accepts the Socratic paradox.

At first glance, this dilemma might lead readers to dismiss the Athenian's ideas on the grounds of philosophical incoherence: why should a person hold himself responsible for his behavior when he is apparently not, in cases of injustice at least, responsible for the motivations, desires, and judgments that lie behind that behavior? Yet the Athenian's idea makes greater sense at a practical level, if we consider his suggestions from two equally important, but conflicting perspectives.[33] On the one hand, from a "first-person" perspective, people must learn that they should take responsibility for themselves, because their own attitudes and actions play a major role in the development of their characters. It would hardly make sense for a legislator to encourage citizens to do nothing—to fail to accept agency or responsibility—on the grounds that, at some deep level, they are not responsible for any injustice in their souls. On the other hand, from a "third-person" perspective, we should also accept that others' faults may be, at a deep level, involuntary, in the sense that they did not, with full knowledge and awareness, accept "evils" into their souls. It would, though, be wrong for us to apply this perspective to ourselves, before trying, at least, to develop ourselves ethically. This line of reasoning does not settle the incoherence, but it does provide practical guidance and help to make sense of the Athenian's initial address.

Even so, the existence of this dilemma creates difficulties for those, such as Magnesia's citizens, who are tasked with important roles as judges in court, and as citizens who regularly conduct surveillance on their fellow citizens. How to be harsh or gentle in the right way, in appropriate circumstances, and at the right time? Should we be forcing teenagers to accept responsibility for themselves, while also showing pity to adult criminals on the grounds that they are involuntarily unjust and merely need a talking-to? The need for judgments of this sort—a need that is heightened in the novel, Socratic world imagined by the Athenian—places significant demands on citizens. At the

---

33. Cf. Pangle 1980: 455–457.

very least, citizens will be encouraged to become ever more thoughtful and reflective concerning the development of virtue among their fellow citizens. When is it right to be harsh—and how and how much—and when is it right to be gentle?

The citizens of Magnesia will have to reflect on those questions in particular cases by referring them to the city's ultimate goal of instilling intelligence, moderation, justice, and courage in the citizenry. In that sense, surveillance, giving information, and even punishment are civic tasks that require citizens to show care for one another in the cultivation of virtue. These civic tasks give new meaning to the idea that Magnesia should be characterized by "friendship." Friendship, newly understood in this way, involves not simply solidarity and tolerance, but also a sense of deeper caring about one's fellow citizens' development of themselves as individuals, for their own sakes. That activity of care requires both imagination and sensitivity to others' psychology. These demands of citizenship play a special role in the Athenian's effort to transform warriors into citizens. The *thumos* involved in surveillance and punishment has already become a much deeper, more reflective, and more intelligent faculty than readers may initially have supposed.

Intriguingly, the Athenian immediately links these points to a discussion of the significant evils of self-love. If Magnesia's citizens need a particular reason to show sympathy toward others, then the Athenian gives them one: "The greatest of all evils for most human beings is inborn in their souls; by forgiving himself for it, everyone fails to contrive any escape from it" (731d–e). Human nature itself is stacked against the achievement of virtue. The evil of self-love grows naturally in our souls. While informed readers may wonder about the implications of this statement for the existence and benevolence of a providential god, the more immediate point is that anyone with a tendency to judge harshly should step back in order to reflect on the difficulties with which human beings are beset by their very nature. Hence, in their capacity as judges and enforcers of communal norms, citizens also need to take into account their fellow citizens' psychological profiles, and the barriers erected by human nature itself, before giving vent to their spiritedness against wrongdoers.

If we take the Athenian's remarks on self-love seriously, however, then another important difficulty comes into sight. His remark reflects not only on potential criminals and their motivations, but also on citizen-judges themselves. We are not only naturally partial to ourselves, he says, but also, as a result, limited in our capacity to judge others fairly. Each of us naturally "judges badly" (*kakôs krinei*) when it comes to "the just, the good, and the noble" (*ta dikaia kai ta agatha kai ta kala*), because "he supposes that it is necessary to honor his own thing before the truth" (*to hautou pro tou alêthous aei timan dein hêgoumenos*, 731e–732a). The implication is that citizens are assigned a formidably difficult task as judges themselves, since they, too, are partial and naturally self-loving human beings. Magnesia's citizen-judges, too, like those they judge, can be counted on to embrace "their own things" over what is genuinely just, good, and noble. Worse yet, our natural self-love, or partiality toward "our own things," clouds our judgment and compels us to suppose that our ignorance is actually wisdom (731e–732a).

Readers might be inclined to interpret this point narrowly, as though it concerns only ordinary conflicts of interest between a judge and a fellow citizen or defendant. Does this point, however, also extend more broadly, carrying with it the implication that citizens, as judges, will prize the city's good—their own thing, in that sense—over doing what is just or right to individual citizens? And, if so, does the Athenian have a particular way of addressing the potential conflict between doing justice to an individual and benefiting the city? After all, that conflict arose in an acute form in the Athenian's directing citizens to punish harshly all those whose injustice, though involuntary, is also "incurable." Even if the Athenian's directions imply a greater attention to mercy and humanity in judgment, he also leaves in place the possibility that injustice will be done to those who, for reasons beyond their control, are incurably noxious to the community. He reconsiders the quandaries of the individual and community only in Book 9 (862e–863a).

8

Developing the Citizens' Thumos in Elections and Courts

THE ATHENIAN STRIVES to transform warriors into citizens. He turns the energies of a traditionally militaristic people to civic business. To that end, he elevates *thumos* by showing that it can be informed by an increasingly sophisticated capacity for judgment. Henceforth, citizens will dedicate their thumoeidetic energies not to militaristic expansion, but, rather, to envisioning appropriate standards of honor and dishonor and to enforcing them in the city's institutions. The Athenian furthers this project when he establishes the city's magistracies, a significant arena for both seeking and awarding honor. While certain citizens satisfy their ambitions through holding office, all citizens exercise their civic judgment in the election of magistrates. They award honors to particular individuals and reject or dismiss others, on the basis of a developed understanding of the city's norms, standards, and ideals. The Athenian strives to foster political justice by mixing oligarchic and democratic elements. He also, however, attempts to do justice to the natural superiority of virtue and knowledge. While making concessions to ordinary citizens, he gradually unveils a political hierarchy that culminates in the Nocturnal Council.

Citizens as Political Leaders, Citizens as Voters

The Athenian immediately turns to the establishment of offices in Book 6. Before describing the duties of each magistracy, however, he stresses that potential magistrates must be adequately tested from childhood onward (751c). He emphasizes the danger of granting power to unsuitable individuals—it brings the "greatest injuries and harm to cities" (751c)—in a way that brings

Tragedy, Philosophy, and Political Education in Plato's Laws. Ryan K. Balot, Oxford University Press.
© Ryan K. Balot 2024. DOI: 10.1093/oso/9780197647226.003.0008

to mind the tyrannical violation of the laws. Even the greatest regime of law requires virtuous magistrates and officials (751b–c), in the absence of whom a tyrannical "capture" of the legal system is ever more likely. The city's electors must be capable of distinguishing between worthy and unworthy candidates (751c–d).[1] Eliminating the threat of tyranny—maintaining a republican freedom from oppression—requires virtue among both leaders and ordinary citizens. It is illusory to believe, with Kant, for example (*Perpetual Peace*, "First Supplement"), that laws can, all by themselves, moderate a "race of devils."

In both magistracies and courts the city distributes responsibility, and thus honor, differentially. Key magistrates, not the citizens as a whole, make the most important political decisions and staff the most important juries. Officeholders assume positions of honor and are constantly called upon to exercise their judgment in the conduct of their duties. Even so, the citizen assembly as a whole, including the poorer citizens, plays an important role in electing officials, just as it plays a central role in the lower levels of the judicial system. In both contexts, ordinary citizens are expected to show reflective judgment. The city's electoral procedures are designed not only to yield the best leaders, but also to develop the citizens' own capacities to judge and enforce the city's standards of honor.

Honor, Class, and Justice

The Athenian envisions a sliding scale of honor, which originates in his provision of four wealth-based classes (744c–d). He aspires to mix the city's different elements; mixing monarchy and democracy is essential to creating freedom, friendship, and prudence in the city (cf. 693d–e). In practice, however, the Athenian mixed together oligarchic and democratic elements. The political prominence of magistrates, as opposed to the demos, is reminiscent of classical Greek oligarchies. This feature is balanced by the regime's meritocratic, i.e., democratic, openness to the candidacy of any citizen, including the poorest, for even the city's top magistracies. Nonetheless, as Aristotle recognized, Magnesia's election procedures usually give precedence to the wealthy, by making detailed provisions that obligate the upper classes to vote, while merely permitting the lower classes to do so (e.g., 756c–e, 764a, 765c). The Athenian calls these oligarchic–style selection procedures, in turn,

---

1. Even if we are, per Kant, making laws for a race of devils, the republican tradition has always recognized that officials' civic virtue is essential to working the machine of governance effectively; for an interesting recent reflection on this theme in contemporary politics, see Wu 2020.

a "middle ground (*meson*) between a monarchic and a democratic regime" (756e).[2]

Intriguingly, the Athenian identifies the privileges of the wealthier classes (not the most virtuous or "best") as "monarchic." The wealthy classes are prominent in election procedure, if not necessarily among the magistrates themselves. (How many magistrates would actually be wealthy in a given year is an empirical question on which have no evidence). Their prominence is surprising, especially in light of the Athenian's criticism of the traditional equation of the "rich" with the "good" (742e–743a). The Athenian's approach is a compromise: the very existence of four property classes (744c–d) grows out of his concessions to "mortal nature," because "proportional equality" (i.e., giving unequal things to unequal people), as opposed to simple equality, would reduce factionalism and quarrels. The city will therefore distribute "honors" (*timas*) and "offices" (*archas*) differentially and in accordance with this principle (744c). In elaborating upon these points (757a–758a), the Athenian emphasizes that, strictly speaking, this best and highest form of equality gives greater honor to "those who are greater with respect to virtue" and lesser honor to those who are "the opposite with respect to virtue and education" (757c). Such a distribution can be called "political justice" (757c). Yet, because of the potential discontents of "the many," necessity compels cities, for the sake of stability or friendship, to make use of the lot, which weakens the strictness of genuine political justice (757e–758a).

The Athenian leaves his conclusions on the best "mixture" vague and open (cf. especially, 757e–758a), as a signal to future lawgivers that they will have to apply their own contextual judgments (cf. 757d). Even so, he expresses regret

---

2. Morrow 1960: 528–30 offers a helpful summary of the regime's oligarchic and democratic elements. Brunt 1993: 260, 274–75 offers reasons to discount the Aristotelian assessment that Magnesia most resembled an oligarchy, even as he shows (Brunt 1993: 256–59) that Magnesia is anything but democratic according to ancient Greek standards (not to mention those of our own day); Kahn 2004: 344–45 notes Magnesia's rigidly antidemocratic exclusion of artisans and farmers from citizenship. One central democratic element is, as Morrow says (1960: 528–29), that "there is no property qualification for attending the assembly, for sitting on courts of law, or for holding any of the offices, except a few minor ones, and in these exceptional cases the motive seems to be more a desire to lighten the burdens of citizenship for the poor than to exclude them from honor and office." Some examples of a property qualification for a "minor" office: the office of the Treasurers of sacred funds, who should be chosen from the highest property class (759e–760a); the City Regulators, who should be drawn from the highest class (763d); the Market Regulators, who should be chosen from the first and second classes (763e); those who award prizes at gymnastic contests (both human and equine!) come from the second and third classes (765c). Morrow's own view (1960: 530) is that Plato's "free creations"—e.g., the *nomophulakes*, the *euthunoi*, and the Nocturnal Council—make Aristotle's judgments about oligarchic and democratic elements "irrelevant."

over giving the discontented "many" an unjustly large share. He forgoes commentary, however, on the political necessities that require the city to give prominence to the wealthy (e.g., in election procedures, and cf. 757a), despite the implausibility of equating the wealthy with the virtuous. However those matters may stand, the Athenian expects all citizens to participate in elections and thereby to develop their reflective capacities for judgment.

Toward the end of the dialogue, the Athenian mentions the creation of a hierarchy of civilian honor, which helps to explain the different political roles played by magistrates as opposed to ordinary citizens. The city grants the greatest civilian prizes of recognition to those who do exceptional honor to the lawgiver's writings (922a). Insofar as they judge and surveil others, all citizens will have to grasp the point of these writings, presumably at varying levels of depth; but the city's preeminent official, the Supervisor of Education (*paideias epimelêtês*, 765d), will be specially charged with doing so, so that he can act as an "interpreter" (*mênutês*) and "nurturer" (*tropheus*) for the others (809b). He will be selected from among the Guardians of Laws by other magistrates, in the temple of Apollo, by secret ballot; after scrutiny, he will hold office for five years (766b–c). The Athenian establishes an electoral procedure designed to remove this vote as far from the general assembly as possible—a clear indication of the sliding scale of honor that underlies "political justice."

After describing the various subjects overseen by the Supervisor of Education (song and dance, military training, reading and writing, arithmetic, and astronomy, all to a certain practical level: cf. 809e–810b), the Athenian pinpoints the novelty and difficulty of this important position. He remarks, in a self-consciously anticonventional spirit (810d–e), that a traditional Greek poetic education is potentially dangerous, because the poets have mixed in harmful ideas with certain admittedly noble ideas (811b). In this bewildering context, the best guidance for education of the young comes from the Athenian's own sayings, in this very conversation (811c–e). The Supervisor of Education is thereupon charged with an intellectually daunting job whose difficulty matches its significance: he is to familiarize himself with the vast body of existing literature, in whatever form it appears, and to note which passages agree with the Athenian's own ideas. He will then use the most appropriate passages, from the Athenian himself, and from elsewhere, to educate the citizens (811e; cf. 822e–823a). Seemingly at least, the intellectual accomplishment that underlies this task is formidable.

The Athenian's presentation of other officials—*nomophulakes*, priests, and auditors, not to mention military commanders, city and country regulators, members of the council, and so on—gives evidence of the same "sliding scale" of honor. Among the magistrates, the Athenian himself gives pride of place to the Guardians of the Laws, whom he describes first and at length (752d–755b). The legislator should took care to appoint "the first magistrates in the safest and best way possible" (752d). The Guardians of the Laws must be chosen with "complete seriousness" (752e), because of their great prominence in managing the city's affairs. "The mention of the guardians appears like a recurrent refrain . . . in the laws of the later books."[3] The Athenian emphasizes the visibility of the city's highest officials. He envisions the three highest magistrates investigating crimes against the public, in trials that are commenced and concluded by the people's assembly (768a). Such positions of great honor are recognized as such by the other citizens, as illustrated in the breach by those "honor-loving" criminals whose envy leads them to attack, even to murder, "the best of those in the city" (870c).

Education for Top Offices?

Are the city's highest officials distinguished by ambition alone, or have they received special training or privileges? What qualifies them for the city's leading positions? The responsibility for making difficult educational judgments, with far-reaching consequences, and then putting them into practice, illustrates the gravity of the office of Supervisor of Education. His is "by far the greatest of the highest offices in the city" (765e, tr. Pangle 1980). Ideally, at least, he will embody, to the greatest degree, the citizen who most does honor to the lawgiver's writings. He will disperse the responsibility— and the honor—to a variety of assistants, both male and female (813c). His "bureau" will require exceptional insight, powers of judgment, and (given the written record of existing literature) wide-ranging erudition. Moreover, because of the importance of early education for the eventual "perfection in virtue that befits the thing's own nature" (765e), readers will expect that the Supervisor should be highly educated with regard to virtue itself. Will the Supervisor of Education need a special education in order to carry out his assigned tasks? The Athenian does not raise, much less begin to answer, that question until Book 12. Well-informed readers of Plato, though, would be remiss if they failed to ask it.

---

3. Morrow 1960: 198.

The same question also arises in connection with other magistracies, in particular, the Guardians of the Laws. They are meant to fill in the details left out of the lawgiver's outline (770b–c). They are also assigned the forbidding task of reviewing the present legislation and judging whether it meets the goals of cultivating virtue in all citizens (771a). The Athenian says that the three elderly men should try, to the best of their ability, to make the Guardians of the Laws "both lawgivers (*nomothetas*) and guardians of the laws (*nomophulakas*)" (770a). The Guardians of the Laws also constitute the pool of candidates for each successive Supervisor of Education and play the most important judicial roles in the city. Already at their introduction in Book 6, then, readers may wonder whether they too—especially given their awe-inspiring task of judging the Athenian's own legislation—either have received or will receive a special education that fits them out for these duties.

These questions grow organically out of the text and derive from the very experience of governing imagined by the Athenian. How can these top officials do their work successfully without a philosophical education? That is the question that will press itself on any conscientious reader. Yet the Athenian presents these individuals as practical, political officials. They are chosen by a process of election—admittedly, as we will see, an unusual and rigorous one—that involves the entire citizenry. For all that he has said thus far, any citizen can legitimately be considered for the city's top offices, independent of his socioeconomic class. Why is the Athenian unwilling to discuss these issues directly and explicitly? Does he mean to imply, after all, that practical citizens, nonphilosophers, are able to carry on the work of a philosophical legislator in his absence?

As readers discover only in Book 12, these questions are linked to the complexities of the composition and education of members of the Nocturnal Council. Until we reach the Athenian's description of the Nocturnal Council in Book 12, however, he refuses to offer any comments on the education of magistrates. He gives readers the impression that even the most important magistrates will lack special training or education.[4] The Athenian gives no explicit indication of a system of educational tracking. In the elections themselves, everything is left up to the citizens' own judgment; candidacy for office is open to all citizens.[5]

---

4. Cf. Bobonich 2002: 392–95.

5. This impression is qualified, to some extent, at 952b, at the very end of the dialogue. See, once again, Morrow 1960: 528–29.

Even so, the Athenian offers occasional indications that suggest otherwise. As Brisson has proposed, the text gives evidence of a "hidden co-optation" of the city's elite, from youth onward; and I would like to add considerations along the same lines.[6] From the beginning of his discussion of the city's institutions and magistrates, the Athenian distinguishes between two groups of citizens by analogy with the "woof and the warp." One leaderly group of citizens must have "a certain firmness (*tina bebaiotêta*) in its character (*en tois tropois*)." The other group will be "softer" (*malakôteron*) and possess "a certain just equitable quality" (*epieikeiai tini dikaiai*) (734e–735a).[7] The leaders, he says, must be superior to the others in virtue (734e). Hence, the city must discriminate between them and those who have "been tested by only a slight education" (*tous smikrai paideiai basanisthentas*, 735a). One group of citizens is "tested" by a significant education and therefore proves superior in understanding and virtue, while another is "tested" by only a slight education.[8]

A similar idea surfaces in Book 6, when the Athenian convinces Kleinias that their first task is to establish offices for the city, along with laws to govern elections and official duties (751a–b). Then he stops short: legislating is a "great accomplishment" (*megalou . . . ergou*, 751b5–6), but even a "well equipped" city (*polin eu pareskeuasmenên*, 751b6) with "sound laws" would become ridiculous and harmful without suitable magistrates (751b–c). The Athenian is, accordingly, concerned to see to it that "the powers of the magistracies" (751c6) will be given to the correct individuals. Does he merely hope or fantasize that Magnesia's citizenry will vote well? Or does he have another strategy in mind?

The ensuing discussion clarifies his point. He now revisits the distinction between potential magistrates and the ordinary citizens who will judge and elect them. Those who assume the magistracies—along with their

---

6. Brisson 2005: 111. In general, Brisson 2003 (cf. Brisson 2005: 110–16) makes the interesting and plausible argument that the Athenian intends the young *agronomoi* to be co-opted as members of an elite who may eventually, at age thirty, become junior members of the Nocturnal Council. My argument concerning the recruitment of the city's rulers is compatible with, indeed supported by, Brisson's.

7. This particular terminology alludes to the "firmness" that the Athenian (and Kleinias) mention in describing the Nocturnal Council (960e, 967d4), while the reference to a "yielding quality" or "reasonableness" that is "just" refers to the Athenian's subsequent discussion of "equity" (*to . . . epieikes*, 757d8–e1)—which is, as we have seen, the principle by which ordinary citizens are included in the regime, contrary to strict justice.

8. In his note on 734e6–735a2, Schöpsdau 2003: 289 comments on the weaving image but pays little attention to the Athenian's contrast between these two groups of citizens; cf. Morrow 1960: 208. Strauss 1975: 71 grasps the significance of the distinction.

families—must have received "adequate testing" (*basanon hikanên*) from their childhoods onward, until the time they are elected (751c).[9] Other citizens will be educated in accordance with lawful habits (*en êthesi nomôn*) and will learn how to distinguish correctly between strong and weak candidates for office (751c–d). The Athenian carves out space for two distinct groups: one, a well-educated elite, trained more precisely from childhood onward to assume leadership positions in Magnesia, and the other, a lawfully educated body of ordinary citizens who will, he hopes, show good judgment in electing members of the political elite to office. These distinctions correspond to the distinctions at play in the Athenian's discussion of political justice. Is it possible that underlying his concessions to the many the Athenian envisions a corps of philosophically trained magistrates, so that, after all, the city need not weaken the perfection and precision (cf. *akribous*) of genuine political justice in favor of "equity" (*to epieikes*, 757d–e)?[10]

Later, in discussing education in arithmetic, geometry, and astronomy, the Athenian distinguishes between ordinary education and the pursuit of these subjects "in a strictly accurate way," a term he reiterates for emphasis (*hôs akribeias echomena*, 818a1–2; *di' akribeias*, 818a6, tr. Pangle 1980; cf. 757e1). Scholars have interpreted this passage as foreshadowing the education of the Nocturnal Council (cf. 965a–b).[11] It also refers back, though, to the more precise education of certain "firm" citizens whose superior virtue somehow—in a way that remains unexplained until Book 12—fits them out for the city's higher offices. At the end of this section, the Athenian links this superior group of citizens to the as-yet-undefined political body known as the Nocturnal Council: "That is the truth, Kleinias—but it is difficult, after giving a preliminary set of guidelines in this fashion, to proceed to actual laws; rather, if you agree, let us legislate in a more precise way (*akribesteron*) some other time" (818e, tr. Griffith 2016, modified). In this response, he is

---

9. Obviously, this testing cannot refer to any simple sort of *dokimasia*, per England 1921a I: 545, because it lasts from childhood to election; cf. the clearer account of Morrow 1960: 217–19. "Adequate" (*hikanos*) is another "keyword" that arises frequently in the Athenian's presentation of the Nocturnal Council: e.g., 964c–d, 965e, 966b, 968a, and Chapter 12.

10. Like "firmness" and "adequacy," these terms—"precision" and "accuracy," as opposed to "equity"—combined with his references to superior character and education, carry a transformative significance toward the end of the work (compare, for example, the Athenian's emphasis on "precise accuracy" at 964d5, 965a6, 965b1). Readers are gradually led to discover that these verbal indicators stand on the side of superior human beings, who deserve and are expected to receive a philosophical education, as opposed to ordinary people, who benefit from "the equitable" and receive a lesser education.

11. Morrow 1960: 507.

foreshadowing the education of the Nocturnal Council (which is also "impre-scriptible" just in this way).[12] If we read these passages together, however, then he is equally referring back to the select group of citizens who are apparently being groomed for political leadership, by virtue of their superior virtue and "precise" education.

In the ensuing discussion of "divine necessity," the Athenian provides an obscure description of the course of study that he has in mind (818b–e). In response to Kleinias' question about the necessities that are "divine," he says that if one could not understand these subjects, then one "would never become a god for men, or a *daimon*, or a hero who is able to exercise supervisory care over human beings in a serious way" (*ouk an pote genoito anthrôpois theos oude daimôn oude hêrôs hoios dunatos anthrôpôn epimeleian sun spoudêi poieisthai*, 818c). No human being could become "divine" (*theios*, 818c3), for example, if he were unable to count or to familiarize himself with the orbits of the stars. These elementary subjects, however, are merely the preliminaries to something that the Athenian now calls "the most noble subjects of learning" (*tôn kallistôn mathêmatôn*, 818d). How to study the preliminaries, before going on to study the more advanced subjects, is something that the three old men will have to pursue later in a "more precise way" (818d–e; *akribesteron*, 818e5).[13]

Like the Athenian's discussion of the "warp and woof," this passage connects education with political power. In making this connection, the Athenian also refers back to Kronos and his *daimones*, who exercised divine, supervisory care over human beings (713b–e). In the myth, he had explained that human beings could not rule other human beings without yielding to "insolence and injustice" (713c). On the contrary, as Kronos recognized, human beings needed a ruler drawn from a higher species. Now the Athenian is making the opposite point. Certain human beings might be entitled to rule other human beings, after all, despite their shared humanity, by virtue of their advanced education. That advanced education raises them beyond the human species, to the level of a *daimon* or divinity. Since Kronos had set up *daimones* as "kings and rulers" (713c) readers should ask themselves whether the Athenian is somehow preparing to establish certain citizens as kings and rulers of Magnesia, precisely because of their superior education and virtue. If so, then those kings and rulers would have to be "divine" men (cf. 969b2–3, 945c2).

---

12. Cf. 968d–e, with Cherniss 1953: 373 and chapter 11, "The Rule of *Nous*," for discussion.

13. On this passage and these themes, see chapter 12, "The 'Truest Tragedy.'"

In this intentionally obscure passage, then, the Athenian indicates that the city will institute a well-designed preliminary curriculum that will, somehow, lead up to higher studies. Those unspecified higher studies will, in turn, justify the "serious supervision" by certain human beings over others, in the manner of a god or *daimon* or hero. Why doesn't the Athenian state these points more clearly and directly? Full discussion of that question will have to wait until Book 12. Until then, Plato, the author, keeps us in suspense. Readers will understandably be tantalized by the thought that the tasks assigned to the Supervisor of Education and the Guardians of the Laws demand a higher education. Readers will wonder what is happening as the Athenian unfolds his description of the regime of law, while also vaguely referring to superior magistrates and superior human beings. His procedure creates not only suspense, but also dissonance. How can a regime of law accommodate superior, even godlike human beings? How will the city find the magistrates it needs, given its mixture of democracy and monarchy? To what is the Athenian constantly alluding in such obscure ways? Will he actually return to these subjects in the end? And why does he adopt such a puzzling method of proceeding in the first place? Like Kleinias and Megillus, readers are put in the position of simply having to trust the Athenian to do justice to these complexities in his eventual description of the Nocturnal Council.

Electoral Procedure: Practical Intelligence and Civic Courage

If Magnesia's leading individuals pursue their ambitions in seeking political office, then ordinary citizens will further their education in judgment and their enforcement of communal standards, by nominating, judging, and electing candidates for office. Beyond serving, when chosen, as guardians of the land (*phrouroi*, 760b–c), and beyond taking part in religious festivals and military training, citizens spend a great deal of time participating in elaborate electoral rituals. Or, at least, so it appears from the intricate, not to say byzantine, descriptions of elections offered by the Athenian. Certain magistrates are, to be sure, chosen by other magistrates (e.g., Supervisor of Education: 766b–c; judges in the common courts: 767c–e), but it is important that others are to be chosen by the entire citizenry. The Athenian stresses, albeit in the context of judging foreigners, that ordinary people, whether from Magnesia or not, possess a "divine quality that aims well" (*theion de ti kai eustochon*) when it comes to distinguishing better and worse human beings (950b–c). Despite the lesser education of ordinary citizens, and the city's sliding scale of honor, they, too, have important gifts to confer on the city's political life.

Widespread political participation does more than create "friendship" through the inclusion of all citizens. Through such participation citizens develop their practical reasoning specifically about what and whom the city should honor, and on what grounds.[14] All citizens play a role in determining, in highly practical contexts, just what is honorable, what deserves recognition, and what meets the lawgiver's standards.[15] Serving according to their different military classes, for example, they will award military prizes for excellence (943b–c). On a more regular basis, though, they will grant honors to their fellow citizens by voting for them in elections in elaborate procedures that, although they are weighted toward the wealthy, are also designed to call upon and develop ordinary citizens' judgment, insight, practical reasoning, and discernment.

Consider, for example, the proposed procedure for selecting the Guardians of the Law (753b–d), which is to be undertaken with "complete seriousness" (*hapasêi spoudêi*, 752e2).[16] The procedure's "seriousness" derives from its religious character, its lengthy duration, and its involved, iterated patterns of nomination and objection. Each citizen nominates a particular candidate by placing a wooden tablet with the candidate's name and patronymic, tribe, and residential district on the altar of the city's most honorable temple. Every voter must include the same information about himself or herself. During the next thirty days, any other citizen who so wishes is allowed to remove any tablets to which he or she objects. By reiterating this procedure, the magistrates narrow down the number of potential candidates until, finally, anyone who wishes can bring forward his preferred candidate by walking between the parts of a sacrificial animal. The top thirty-seven candidates will, after scrutiny, be named Guardians of the Law.

---

14. Cf. Bobonich 2002: 380–81, though Bobonich does not specifically link these civic capacities to honor and *thumos* or show how they unfold in different contexts and with varying significance.

15. Cf. 921e–922a, along with 767e–768c, 772c–d, 850b, with Morrow 1960: 165, 271. As Morrow shows, the people as a whole judge what is to be honored in both military and civilian contexts; the demos understands that courage, while still honorable, is to be demoted from its traditional place atop the table of virtues.

16. The Athenian mentions other, presumably transitional methods of selection at 752e–753a and at 754c–d; the precise relationship of these methods to one another and to the ordinary procedure outlined at 753b–d, which is a subject of scholarly debate (cf. Morrow 1960: 204–5; Schöpsdau 2003: 363–79), will not affect the present argument.

This elaborate procedure has substantial consequences; it calls upon the citizens' judgment and courage to state their choices formally and publicly and then to defend their decisions informally, in conversation with others.[17] The procedure encourages discussion among citizens over the course of several weeks. The city does not, like democratic Athens (for example), present a single issue for a vote on a single day and then quickly move on. The reiterated pattern of voting means that citizens will reconsider their own choices in light of those of others, presumably with time to discuss and revise if necessary. Citizens must learn and keep in mind all the city's cumbersome electoral procedures. They must know—or learn about—the character of the leading candidates, wherever in the city they originate. Since there are no secret ballots, it takes courage both to nominate candidates and to object to others. The most eager candidates will be watching such moves carefully. Citizens will observe the patterns of support among their families, friends, and neighbors, as well as across districts and tribes. Relatives and friends will question one another, exploring the choices in detail: the importance of the office will no doubt make these elections a central subject of conversation at the common meals and elsewhere. Politics (rather than war or moneymaking) will become the focus of citizens' interests and lively exchanges. Will patronage networks develop? Will political alliances become a threat to the city's unity? These dangers are presumably endemic to political life and will, in the course of the city's existence, be supervised by the existing Guardians of the Laws and the other magistrates. The city's focus on political activity is a worthy means to cultivate virtue and a worthy method of diverting citizens' attention from the typical militarism of traditional Greek cities.

Similar virtues are called upon in other popular elections. In the election of Generals, for example, one can imagine that it would take courage to reject a nominee put forward by the Guardians of the Laws and then to put forward one's own nominee (755d): one's objection would no doubt be noted by a candidate who could easily become one's military commander. (The same point holds for Rank Commanders [755e] and the Cavalry Commanders [756a]). In another context, the Athenian spells out the significance of such courage (835c). In the election of the Council (756b–e), a protracted procedure of nomination, voting, and re-voting provides time to reflect and discuss, as well as to consider one day's election in light of the previous one. Citizens will have time to explore the possible composition of the entire Council,

---

17. For a different and more hierarchical understanding of the consequences of the Athenian's election procedures, see Landauer 2022.

although the Athenian envisions using the lot to determine the final selection of candidates. Finally, in his discussion of the selection of magistrates for music and gymnastics (764c–765d), the Athenian mentions that at the scrutiny of these magistrates—possibly a general point—statements are solicited regarding the experience of each of the chosen candidates (765b). We might imagine that in the scrutiny of other candidates other citizens will speak out about the character and judgment of the persons being considered for the city's top magistracies.[18]

By comparison with the ordinary democratic procedure at Athens, Magnesia's system requires far more engagement and reflection.[19] By contrast with Athenian citizens, though, Magnesia's citizens would not have gained as much practical, civic understanding from "working the machine" of governance, especially in the case of the top magistracies.[20] Even in their capacity as voters in the Assembly, more importantly, Magnesia's citizens do not develop their deliberative capacities by making significant judgments, as a group, for the city as a whole. They do not hold public debates that culminate (for example) in voting on questions such as war and peace. Magnesia's Assembly, and even its Council, has a very limited deliberative function.[21] In part the reason may be, as Morrow has argued, that the Athenian meant thereby to rebuff the increasing elevation, in Athens for example, of decrees and popular judgments, as opposed to the law.[22] Who deliberates in Magnesia? Readers

---

18. On the scrutiny in general, see Morrow 1960: 215–19.

19. In general, Magnesia's electoral procedures go well beyond what ordinary Greek citizens would require, or even tolerate. On the other hand, as a method of choosing magistrates, classical Greeks generally considered elections (as opposed to selection by lot) to be an oligarchic practice.

20. On the idea of "working the machine" of democratic governance, see Ober 2005a. On the decisive importance of the Guardians of the Laws in Magnesia, see Morrow 1960: 195–215; Morrow in general appreciates how far the Athenian has moved from the institutions and offices of democratic Athens—in particular, in that the Athenian vests great political power in the magistracies and allows for little to no decision-making among ordinary citizens (e.g., Morrow 1960: 209), though he tends to assume too readily that in the absence of evidence "Plato" simply means to have recourse to Athenian democratic practice, an assumption I question; Reid 2020 offers an account of Magnesia's offices.

21. It is surprising how little scholars (for example: Bobonich 2002: 381) have paid attention to this cardinal point, but Morrow 1960: 174–78, 199–200 understands it, noting in the meantime that the Boule (Council) of Magnesia has no probouleutic function: Morrow 1960: 174–75. Cf. also Brisson 2003, 2005 on the larger point.

22. Morrow 1960: 177. As Brisson 2003: 225 notes, "The Assembly and the Council have nothing to say about the definition of the city's ends" (my translation).

will have to wait to discover that the Athenian entrusts the city's deliberative functions almost entirely to the Nocturnal Council.[23]

The Education of Citizen Judges

The Athenian also strives to create institutions that deliver justice to all citizens and to educate the Magnesians' judgment in the process. This education is the final step in his cultivation of traditional *thumos*. By demanding high standards of judgment from his citizens, the Athenian shows readers that participation in the city's political life helps to develop both their rational and emotional faculties.

When the Athenian first introduces courts in Book 6, he stresses their importance by remarking that cities would not be cities without courts (766d). All cities are called upon, as a constitutive feature, to manage the disputes over justice that inevitably arise among citizens. It follows that the activity of judgment, though difficult, is central to the citizen's self-image as a citizen: in both public and private lawsuits, it is essential that all citizens, including those lowest on the social and economic ladder, play a role in judging cases (767e–768a, 768b; cf. 766e–767a; 768c). "For anyone," he explains, "who does not share in judging will not consider himself to be part of the city" (768b). While the most competent courts will be made up of magistrates (767c–e), the neighborhood and tribal courts will be made up of ordinary citizens selected by lot (766e–767a, 768b, 768c). The full Assembly will have authority to judge cases of alleged crime against the public, with ordinary people and magistrates playing different roles.[24] The result is a dense pattern of judicial participation by all citizens, even despite the magistrates' preeminence as judges.

Whether in the lowest or the highest courts, the Athenian stresses the difficulty of judging well. Such difficulties manifest themselves especially in large courtrooms or in those populated by defective judges (766d): thus the great importance not only of constructing the judicial system well, if only in outline, but also of educating jurors in practices of rational discernment. Judges must be able to question those on trial, and to speak to defendants and one

---

23. This restriction is particularly unusual because the ordinary citizens made up the bulk of the city's fighting force (apart from the cavalry and the commanders), a fact reflected in the Assembly's seating arrangements (755e; cf. 753b; cf. Morrow 1960).

24. See 767e–768a, with Morrow 1960: 164 and Brunt 1993: 257 on the complexities of the Athenian's statements about the Assembly's jurisdiction.

another, in order to grasp the particulars of each case (766e). The meaning of this provision, which differs considerably from ordinary Greek practice, will become clear in the Athenian's subsequent images of the courtroom in Book 9 (855e–856a). It is important, however, that both ordinary citizens qua jurors and the court of highest competency will both use highly involved procedures of question and answer.

Ordinary citizens will be convened regularly by the litigants themselves, in order to judge disputes among their friends and neighbors. Such courts are the most "authoritative" (*kuriôtaton*, 767b2) for that kind of case. Their members, who both know the litigants and are well known to them, possess the local knowledge that will enable them to render more adequate judgments in matters that are close to home (766e–767a). Implicitly, they will need to know the law and to possess the clarity of judgment required to apply it to particular cases.

These lines of reasoning are further clarified by the Athenian's provisions for the *Agronomoi* and their assistants, and for the ordinary villagers who hold them accountable (760b–763c). Serving for two years at a time, these tribal units rotate throughout the twelve districts of the countryside and familiarize themselves deeply, in all seasons of the year, with the habits of each locality.[25] They create fortifications, make water flows more efficient and attractive, and maintain gymnasia for themselves and the local inhabitants. Serving in this local capacity constitutes a civic education in itself; this group of officials and their younger assistants embodies a dense pattern of political participation. Their "serious (*spoudê*) work" (761d5), however, is to provide protection against enemies from without or within—in particular, the Athenian says, to judge the alleged injustices among neighbors (761d–e), either as a group of five or a group of seventeen.

Already readers grasp that the civic education provided by serving as an Agronomos or assistant will include the development of reflective judgment needed for making decisions in local courts. To that extent, admittedly a modest one at this level, their work will be continuous with that of the lawgiver himself. The Athenian's description takes a particularly illuminating turn, however, when he considers the potential defects of these arrangements (761e–762b). No judge or magistrate, he says, is free from audit (*anupeuthunon*), except those "quasi-regal" judges of the select court (761e).

---

25. On the numbers involved, and potential confusion of the texts, see Morrow 1960: 186n81; Brisson 2003: 221–22; 2005: 113n23. On the *agronomoi* and their possible link to the Nocturnal Council, see Brisson 2005: 112–16, a development of Brisson 2003.

If they should behave arrogantly (*ean hubrizôsi*) or "impose assessments on an unequal basis" or steal or accept bribes, or render unjust verdicts, then they will suffer reproaches throughout the city (761e–762a). They will agree to submit, in lesser cases, to juries of the neighboring villagers. In greater cases— or in particular when officials refuse to submit to the local courts, or try to escape punishment by means of the monthly rotation of offices—the locals are to bring their disputes to the common courts. What is the significance of these details?

Four points are salient. First, at a local level, ordinary citizens are given the wherewithal to resist their magistrates' attempts to dominate or oppress them by means of their official powers. The Athenian is prescribing remedies against even the pettiest forms of tyranny. He thereby cultivates a sensibility among both magistrates—who must always be aware of the constraints of the law and their accountability to their fellow citizens—and among citizens— who integrate in a granular way the need for vigilance and the self-respect that comes through maintaining their freedom from oppression.

Second, by laying down such careful provisions at the local level, the Athenian shows that justice will be done in every corner of the territory. He thereby makes practical the idea that he had announced in the first part of the general address to the new colonists: that Justice, "who takes vengeance on those who abandon the divine law" (716a), follows the god always, as he rotates according to nature. Justice pursues those who are "puffed up with boastfulness" or feel "exalted because of riches or honors," those whose souls burn "with *hubris*" (716a–b, tr. Pangle 1980, modified). Others may think of an arrogant lawbreaker as a "somebody," he says, but the lawbreaker will swiftly undergo punishment at the hands of the goddess Justice. The general prelude uses religious language to express truths that the Athenian renders naturalistic and concrete in his institutional and educational system.

Third, the Athenian mentions in passing, the judges of the select court are "quasi-regal" (*hoion basileôn*, 761e6). The select court is chosen by all the city's magistrates in a given year. Gathered together in a single temple, they pick out the best judge from each board of magistrates, the one who seems likely to give "the best and most pious" decisions during his year-long tenure on the court (767d).[26] The language likening these judges to kings will have

26. As Morrow 1960: 263 points out, the Athenian's description of the court, as well as its competence and its freedom from accountability, suggest links to the Nocturnal Council; but the Athenian does not spell out how these links could be created. Presumably, at least, the scrutiny procedure (767d) will play a significant role in restricting membership to those with philosophical training, such as the retired younger associates of the Nocturnal Council.

important consequences in the Athenian's description of the higher and more competent courts. To anticipate: certain magistrates, in their capacity as judges, are *not* subject to audit (761e), because they are capable of ruling as kings over other human beings.[27] In itself that is a striking foreshadowing of the capacities and competencies of certain magistrates. This court is distinguished, among other things, by its being "as incorruptible (*adiaphthorôtata*) as human power, at least, can make it" (768b7–8, tr. Pangle 1980). Presumably, the reasons are both the judges' level of understanding and self-rule, and the measure of accountability provided by the attendance of the magistrates who had elected them (767d–e).

As Morrow points out, in fact:

> Again, one would expect that for service on this court Plato would require something like that philosophical competence, that insight into principles of reason from which right law derives its authority, which is a cardinal doctrine of the Laws. Perhaps it is intended that this court, either directly or indirectly, is to be linked to the Nocturnal Council, the body set up to explore just these fundamental principles of law and social policy. But if this is Plato's intention it is nowhere made explicit, and no formal mechanism is provided whereby it could be assured.[28]

That is exactly right: the Athenian's presentation of the highest magistrates suggests their need for philosophical understanding, which is not made explicit at this stage in the text. The Athenian reveals his meaning in the fullest light only at the end of the dialogue (see chapter 11, "The Rule of *Nous*"). Morrow's interpretation, however, corresponds closely to the idea that the Athenian envisions a vast process of subterranean recruitment of the most talented citizens, who will rule the city.[29]

Finally, in laying out the potential defects of magistrates as sitting judges, the Athenian clarifies the psychology of wrongdoers when they are exercising roles that seem to shield them from scrutiny by others. The very role of judge and magistrate might encourage *hubris* among those with defective characters—a strong sense that they are superior to others and therefore that they can abuse the judicial system for their own benefit, without

---

27. On this difficult sentence, see Morrow 1960: 250–51; Schöpsdau 2003: 413.

28. Morrow 1960: 263.

29. Cf. Brisson 2003, 2005, with chapter 11, "The Rule of *Nous*."

any repercussions. This worry, too, will resurface in the Athenian's extended consideration of how proceedings can go awry among magistrates sitting as jurors.[30]

Participation in local and even makeshift courts makes demands on the citizens' rational, reflective faculties. Although local jurors will not be subject to the "scrutiny" (*dokimasia*) essential to higher courts (e.g., 767d), they will be subject to accountability in the form of appeal, either to tribal courts (which are themselves selected by lot: 768b)[31] or to the Select Court (767c, 768c). Despite the possibility of appeal, of course, all jurors (even the most humble) are, in a sense, public officials or "rulers" when they render verdicts (767a). Conversely, the Athenian says, "every magistrate must necessarily be a judge of some matters" (767a)—which implies that the city's public officials, in conducting surveillance and so on, are constantly exercising rational judgment. Rational judgment informs the activities of all citizens who play a role, as expected, in maintaining the community's standards, which are embodied in the law.[32]

The Ascent to Judicial Complexity: Book 9

It is in Book 9, above all, that the Athenian explores the exacting demands, both psychologically and intellectually, placed on those who strive to judge with integrity, especially in more complex and high-stakes cases. The capital courts, in particular, are staffed by the Guardians of the Laws in addition to the Select Judges (855c)—in other words, by the city's top officials. Their proceedings provide a paradigm of the courtroom (855c–856a). As in the Select Court, any otherwise unoccupied citizens should be present in order to "listen seriously to such cases" (855d).[33] The very

---

30. One may compare, for example, the hubristic behavior of citizen-judges described by Philocleon in Aristophanes' *Wasps*.

31. On the composition of these courts, see Morrow 1960: 258–61.

32. For additional reflections on the necessity of contextual judgment and discretion, see 875d–876a; 934a–c; cf. 880c, 928c–d, 941a–b, with Stalley 1983: 147. For the use of judgment by magistrates who enforce honor, see 847a. Saunders 2001: 88 is correct, however, to point out that even though discretion calls upon and helps to develop the jurors' rational judgment, the legislator relies on it *faute de mieux*; if he could legislate for every last detail, then he would.

33. This passage explains the Athenian's provision that all citizens are invited to observe the proceedings of the Select Court (767e), on which see also Morrow 1960: 261–64. Ordinary citizens are to learn how to make good judgments by watching the city's highest and most competent officials at work. Further possibilities of discussion, and teaching and learning, as well as

activity of these judges is an education to the city.[34] After speeches by the accuser and the defendant, the judges will, in turn, conduct an "adequate examination" (*skepsin hikanên*, 855e3) of the things said.[35] (This provision looks ahead to the Athenian's emphasis on "examination" (*skepsis*) in his restatement of the "free doctor" analogy [859b–c]). For three days in a row, the judges will be tasked with arriving at a consensus on the points that they find most relevant and true. Each day, moreover, they will all sign their names to a written record of such points, to be deposited on the altar of Hestia.

Understandably, scholars have interpreted this section as remedying flaws such as those that led to Socrates' conviction. The Athenian's point, however, is much broader. At least in the most important cases, jurors will be called upon to think carefully through the evidence and arguments, to discuss the issues in the presence of their peers, and to reconsider all the relevant questions over several days. They will publicize the progress of the trial, presumably so that the entire citizenry can both learn from their proceedings and hold them accountable for their judgments. (An added advantage of publicity is that further evidence can be produced if any citizen discovers additional relevant facts or information.) Other citizens, apart from the magistrates sitting as judges, will be present in order to learn from the proceedings. It is in this context that the Athenian's wider reflections on guilt and responsibility—discussed at length in the middle of Book 9—will take effect. The basis of the court's judgments will, of course, be the law, which has to be understood, recalled, and interpreted correctly in each particular case. The demands on the top jurors are significant.[36]

At one level, ordinary courts—and their juries of ordinary citizens from the neighborhood—operate in the same way as the high courts. In both types

---

additional measures of accountability, are provided by the provision that the council members and magistrates who had elected these judges are also required to attend.

34. This idea obviously has parallels in democratic Athens (cf. Ober 1989; Lanni 2012), but here the point is that the city's teachers are not simply juries of ordinary citizens, but rather juries of philosophically trained officials, including both retired younger associates and current members of the Nocturnal Council (such as the Guardians of the Laws, the Supervisor of Education, and whichever Auditor or former Auditors are members of the Select Court).

35. Notice once again the use of the keyword "adequate" (*hikanos*) to allude to the philosophical members of the city.

36. Such is the point of the Athenian's emphasis on the lawgiver's wide-ranging writings, beyond the laws and preludes themselves, in his re-presentation of the free doctor analogy (858d–e).

of court, the Athenian stresses the need to allow due time for the proceedings, in order to enable judges to clarify disputes through meticulous, frequent questioning (766e, 855d–e). In that sense, ordinary citizens behave in similar ways to the city's highest officials. At the same time, the Athenian draws a key distinction between ordinary courts and the higher courts. All citizens are encouraged, whenever possible, to attend the proceedings of the city's two premier courts (the Select Court: 767e and capital courts: 855d). Those courts provide an education to the other citizens—an education in the city's norms of honor and dishonor, virtue and lawlessness. This education will be useful to them in their watchfulness over other citizens and in their own activities as judges.

The idea that courts provide an education to the citizenry is adapted from Athenian democratic ideology.[37] In Magnesia, though, norms of honor are produced and communicated not by ordinary citizens acting on jury-panels, but rather by leading political officials. They provide paradigms for other citizens to internalize. This point becomes more profound as the Athenian gradually reveals the identities and intellectual (i.e., philosophical) backgrounds of those officials. The city's top officials and judges exercise the highest virtues in hearing the city's most important cases, while ordinary citizens learn from them how to use good judgment in local, less important cases. Those ordinary citizens also learn to honor these officials for their capacity to apply the lawgiver's ideas effectively in particular cases.

As Book 9 reaches its climax, readers will be led to wonder, once again, how the staff of judges in "quasi-regal" courts—that is, the city's leading magistrates—will acquire an understanding that is adequate to the tasks set for them. Not only do they, qua judges, play a role similar to that of the Supervisor of Education. Moreover, the Athenian eventually reintroduces the Socratic paradox and places it at the heart of his judicial system. While he sometimes appears to ignore the force of that paradox, he also digresses in an important section in order to amplify its complexity, with uncertain implications for judicial practice. By reintroducing the Socratic paradox, he leaves unclear the status of guilt, responsibility, and punishment, in such a way as to suggest that only those with philosophical training can apply these difficult concepts intelligently and justly.

---

37. Ober 1989; Lanni 2012.

Revisiting the "Free Doctor"

Suggestively, the Athenian's restatement of the Socratic paradox (starting at 860d) is immediately preceded by his revision of the free and slave doctors (857b–e). Readers are invited to explore the sequence of ideas in the entire section. The Athenian unconventionally proposes that all thefts, great or small, should meet with the same punishment, i.e., a repayment that is double the cost of the stolen property (857a–b). Kleinias understandably objects, on the grounds that the punishment should vary according to the size of the property, its sacred or profane provenance, and other factors (857b). The Athenian is being intentionally provocative, or perhaps he has not finished his thought. Either way, in light of his later, developed penal code, he should express worries about the state of character of the thief. Yet he does not immediately do so.

Instead, he makes a general statement about existing law codes and their attitudes toward citizens. Previous legislation is incorrect. Citizens of hitherto existing cities have always been like slaves being treated by slave doctors (857c). The slave doctor ridicules the free doctor for discussing the free man's disease with him, seeking out its source in the nature of bodies. The slave doctor says, accusingly: "You fool, you are not doctoring your sick patient but rather almost educating him, as though he wanted to become a doctor rather than healthy" (857d–e). The Athenian and Kleinias agree that, like the free doctor, they are going through laws at their leisure, in an attempt to educate rather than to legislate (857e), because that process will yield an exploration of the laws that is more in accordance with nature (858c).

In unfolding this analogy, the Athenian himself recalls the analogy of free and slave doctors from Book 4 (857c). Hence, readers have often read the two passages together. Even so, it is essential to inquire into the significance of this passage in the present context, because this restatement of the analogy differs in critical respects from the earlier one.[38]

Why did Kleinias' objection to the Athenian's treatment of theft remind the Athenian of the free and slave doctors? Scholars have usually ignored this question. Kleinias believes, with traditional lawgivers, that theft on a grand scale should be punished more harshly than small-time theft—not only monetarily, of course, but also through dishonors, imprisonment, and even exile. Apparently, the Athenian finds that Kleinias' approach to punishing thieves is

---

38. Although most scholars do not take note of the differences, Laks 2001: 112–13 is an exception (cf. Laks 2000: 289, by contrast). Strauss 1975: 128–29 also focuses on the differences, with, however, a different emphasis; cf. also Lane 2011.

reminiscent of the slave doctor, while the approach that he plans to elaborate corresponds to the free doctor. How can we make sense of that connection?

Observe, first, the contrasts between the two versions of the analogy. By contrast with Book 4, the Athenian is now concerned with legislation for crime and punishment rather than the legislative code as a whole. In Book 9, the analogy concerns the doctors and their activities more than the patients and their recovery. The Athenian imagines the situation from the perspective of the slave doctor ("if a slave doctor should encounter a free doctor, here is what he would say"). He quotes the slave doctor, who taunts the free doctor and dares him to explain himself. In Book 4, the exposition was presented, supposedly, as even-handed and quasi-objective: the Athenian was simply asking Kleinias which doctor, i.e., which method of legislation, seemed better. Neither doctor spoke in his own voice, and there were no taunts, no challenges, and no contests. The Athenian's focus was on the patient (and his friends and family). In Book 9, Kleinias identifies with the slave doctor: he thinks that the slave doctor has a point (857e), whereas in Book 4, he had agreed readily that the free doctor's method was superior (720e).

These contrasts can be explained by the judicial context of Book 9. Whereas in Book 4, the Athenian was trying to explain the usefulness of persuasive preambles, in Book 9 his focus is rather on "treating" citizens in a judicial context. In the judicial context, the sick patient is the criminal whom the legal system is designed to heal or educate. (This point is confirmed by the Athenian's statement, in the next section, that injustice is a disease of the soul: 862c6–9). Both doctors are presumed to aim at the health of their patients. The slave doctor, though, wonders why simple health isn't enough for the free doctor. Why does the free doctor find it necessary to go beyond health to education? The patient's (the criminal's) return to health is equivalent to conformity to the law. The slave doctor believes that a doctor's goal should be to make criminals conform to the law, through whatever means necessary—fines, imprisonment, or the infliction of suffering. The greater the crime, in an ordinary sense, the greater the punishment. In thinking along those lines, Kleinias misses something that matters more deeply than mere obedience or conformity—namely, the criminal's state of soul, his "mental health." That is precisely what Kleinias had missed in the preceding exchange about theft, and what the Athenian had not yet had a chance to make clear.

Kleinias and the slave doctor assume that the criminal should be browbeaten and punished simply on the basis of the facts of the case, whether it is a greater or lesser theft. By contrast, the free doctor, along with the Athenian qua legislator, is engaged in a quasi-philosophical project. The

Athenian describes the free doctor sympathetically: he is "using arguments that come close to philosophizing, grasping the disease from its source, and going back up to the whole nature of bodies" (857d2–4, tr. Pangle 1980). The lawgiver meets the criminal as his judge within the court system. The Athenian is, then, explaining how true judges ought to behave. Judges should discuss each outlaw's actions with him, in order to arrive at a deeper interpretation of the motivations that led to his criminal behavior. The true judge wants to make citizens not only "healthy," i.e., obedient to a punitive, tyrannical law, but also well-educated, i.e., motivated to obey the law by a reasoned understanding of its goodness. The Athenian expects that those rendering justice—above all, the judges of the city's highest courts—will conduct just such a quasi-philosophical, psychological examination of the citizens' souls, in order to grapple with deeper questions about their responsibility and guilt, as well as their psychological health. His emphasis on adequate time and lengthy, detailed questioning (855e) makes best sense in light of this conception of the judge's duties. If Kleinias' traditionalist conception of the judge were appropriate, then such a deep probing of the case would hardly be necessary.

How do judges come to understand the law and its applications? Cities are a repository of many different sorts of writings, from poets and prose writers for example, all of whom offer "advice about life" (*sumboulên peri biou*) (858d). It is above all the lawgiver, though, who ought "to give counsel about the noble, the good, and the just" (*peri kalôn kai agathôn kai dikaiôn sumbouleuein*, 858d). The lawgiver's writings provide an education to the true judge; working to understand those writings is itself a philosophical education. Those writings are characterized by care for the citizens—resembling the care of a parent—and by intelligence, rather than by a threatening or despotic attitude (859a). The free doctor, by contrast with the slave doctor or tyrant, should manifest both philosophical understanding and care. He should use his intelligence to understand each case deeply, so as to benefit his patient according to nature. The free doctor, i.e., the true lawgiver, becomes the true judge in Book 9. The Athenian's conception of the true judge makes best sense if the city's paramount judges, who are also its top magistrates, are philosophers such as himself.

The Athenian's references to the lawgiver's writings call to mind his remark that the most honored citizen will be the one who does most honor to the lawgiver's writings (922a). They also call to mind his description of the Supervisor of Education, who compares existing literature with the lawgiver's writings in order to educate other citizens (811c–812a; cf. 822e–823a). The city's top magistrates—its judges in Book 9—assume the mantle of the lawgiver in striving to educate whichever citizens have become "sick" in their criminality. In the meantime, their "philosophizing" with those sick criminals will also serve to educate other citizens, bystanders and onlookers at the trials, who should internalize their lines of thought and thereby improve their own capacities for judgment.

The Athenian now illustrates, or indeed models, the process that is required. He first emphasizes the necessity of inquiring precisely (*diaskepteon . . . akribôs*) into temple robbing, stealing, and all injustice (859b). This reference to "precise" inquiry recalls the "precise" education required of certain leading citizens; it suggests nothing less than a philosophical investigation of the psychology of injustice. Conducting such an investigation, in itself, requires epistemological modesty: the Athenian emphasizes that he and his interlocutors are not "knowers" but rather "searchers," who have "established some things and are inquiring further into others" (859c, tr. Pangle 1980). That Socratic attitude encourages him to re-emphasize the need for "inquiry" (*diaskopoumen*, 859c1–2; *skopeisthai, skopômetha*, 859c4) into the subjects they are now discussing. This type of inquiry—surprisingly to Kleinias, at least—itself requires, not further collection of forensic evidence or anything of that sort, but rather, self-examination. The Athenian says that "with regard to the noble and just things" (*peri dê kalôn kai dikaiôn*), we have to examine our own souls in order to see whether we agree or disagree with ourselves (859c, cf. 861a–b). The Athenian thereby calls to mind a peculiarly Socratic project of self-auditing: Are our beliefs about what Socrates would call "the greatest things" consistent with one another? We want to be superior to others, but, the Athenian implicitly asks, are we well positioned to judge others if we lack self-consistency, like the many (859c–d)?

The Athenian is raising a critical set of issues in reflecting on how the city is to handle its criminals. If the city's goal is freedom, and if it seeks justice, then no doubt it will need to approach alleged wrongdoers in the right spirit—not only "eagerly," as the Athenian often indicates, but also with intelligence and care (859a) and an openness to inquiry. That openness implies both epistemological modesty and a willingness to examine oneself, in order to clarify one's own self-contradictions and potentially obscure motivations or blind spots. Strikingly, in referring twice in this section to what is "noble and good and just," the Athenian recalls the general prelude, in which "self-love" makes us poor judges of precisely the "just and good and noble" (731e). The individual afflicted by "self-love" is a poor judge of these "greatest things" because he lacks epistemological modesty, believing that his ignorance is wisdom (732a): "though we know (so to speak) nothing, we suppose that we

know everything" (732a; cf. 863c). The individual characterized by self-love
is unwilling to examine himself, unwilling to accept that his understanding
is limited and may be entirely defective; all these and related problems arise
because of his excessive partiality. These are the failures of character and intellect against which the Athenian intends to make provision, by encouraging
careful inquiry into both criminal cases and one's own soul, whether one is
legislator, magistrate, or judge.

The Athenian himself models the virtues of character and intellect required for true legislation and true judgment. Although he speaks as legislator,
he intends the city's magistrates and jurors, ideally, to integrate these virtues
into their own conduct of surveillance and provision of justice.[39] He asks
whether the just coincides with the noble, seeing that the just punishments
recently described might also be considered shameful (859d–860b). This apparent contradiction leads "the many" to distinguish sharply between the just
and the noble (860c), but it is important for us—legislators and citizens of a
superior city—to resolve the puzzles involved in this relationship, which the
Athenian now proposes to do based on his reconsideration of the Socratic
paradox (860c–d). Kleinias is bewildered by his entire train of thought;
readers, however, are on the ascent to the Athenian's ideal of a philosophical magistrate and judge. In his service in Magnesia's courts, the true judge
will have to bear in mind a range of genuinely unsettling questions. His own
thumoeidetic responses are being calibrated to seek a balance between anger
and gentleness, but this process of calibration also represents an ascent for
thumos, as the judgment informing it is being educated in an ever richer and
more conceptually differentiated way. The ascent is impossible for Kleinias
and other ordinary, nonphilosophical citizens; rather, it is the psychological
and philosophical ascent of the city's highest magistrates.

Revisiting the Socratic Paradox

Although the Athenian explicitly calls this section (860d–864c) on the
Socratic paradox a "digression" (864c), it is more closely integrated in the current discussion than many scholars have supposed.[40] This is so for two reasons.

---

39. It was standard for jurors to consider themselves agents of and substitutes for the "ancient
lawgiver" in democratic courts in Athens: see Gagarin 2020.

40. Schöpsdau 2011: 278, for example, finds that the connection between this section and
Kleinias' question about theft is hopelessly unclear and that the section is only loosely related
to the surrounding discussion. Morrow 1960 entirely ignores this section.

First, it develops our understanding of the complexities and ambiguities involved in the judge's role. Top-tier judges in the city will have to cultivate a rich philosophical understanding of the psychology of wrongdoers. Second, the Athenian uses this section to look ahead to his presentation of the "sociology of the impious." As we will discover in the next chapter, the category of the "impious" is internally diverse. The motivations and psychology of different types of impious individuals have to be carefully elucidated. The Athenian gives readers the tools for appropriate reflection on these topics in the present section.

What is the larger question to which the Athenian's discussion is a response? The question is whether the just and the noble coincide; that is, Can a criminal justice code, including punishment, fit coherently into the city's system of "noble" laws? In other words: Does this section fit coherently into the dialogue as a whole? It is a reasonable question: the Athenian has been struggling with justice, retribution, and nobility since the general prelude in Book 5 (728b–c), which is one indication of this section's integration in the dialogue as a whole.[41]

As we will discover, one of this section's key implications is that doing justice to criminals is formidably difficult and requires, at the highest levels, philosophical education and thought. While ordinary citizens acquire an education in judgment through their own civic activities, those activities are merely a shadow of the intellectually difficult tasks set by the Athenian for the highest judges. For the city to function well, philosophical guidance, leadership, and supervision are essential; only then can the just truly coincide with the noble. In brief: philosophers must oversee punishment in order to make its purposes continuous with those of the law code, so that they will not be simply punitive or angry or subservient to only the city's political exigencies.

To be more specific, the Athenian is working through the many difficulties associated with judging alleged wrongdoers, when judges themselves are afflicted by the limitations of human nature and forced to operate within the constraints of their own factual and ethical ignorance. The particular difficulty exposed in this section is one of the deepest of all in criminal judgment—namely, the question of the criminal's responsibility for his behavior and even for his character. The Athenian says that his own views on justice and nobility, as well as voluntary and involuntary action, are embroiled in confusion and even self-contradiction. He holds that everyone who behaves

---

41. L. S. Pangle 2014: 221–22.

unjustly does so involuntarily (860d, 861d). If one accepts this "Socratic paradox," however, then how will a criminal code, and in particular punishment, be possible (860e5–7)? (How, one might equally ask, will the achievement of justice be possible if legislators do not take into account Socrates' paradoxical insights?) The Athenian remarks that recognition of their own confusion is admirable (861a). It would be wrong to legislate without first questioning themselves more deeply and (one may hope) sorting out their confusions. To legislate without achieving clarity on these matters would constitute high-handed and arrogant behavior, which the Athenian has just foresworn.[42] In any event, the Athenian says that this philosophical reconsideration of the underpinnings of the judicial system should not prevent legislation (860e), but he recognizes that he must still clarify for judges and citizens how his un-traditional (to use a charitable term) beliefs about justice will fit within the penal system.[43]

How, then, does the Athenian propose to revise the traditional distinction between voluntary and involuntary injustice?[44] The starting point, he argues, is to distinguish between injury (*blabê*) and injustice (*adikia*, 861e–862a). It is necessary to redress injuries, for example, monetarily, in order to promote friendship (862b–c). Compensation is owed to those who suffer at the hands of another, however that person's actions may be motivated, and whether those actions are voluntary or not (862b–c). The lawgiver cares for the in-jured, in the first instance, without reference to the psychology of the law-breaker, and in doing so he promotes the city's welfare. The goal is to restore friendship within the city.[45]

The Athenian's first moves, though, also carry an important implication for our understanding of supposed criminals. He says that he would change

---

42. Compare 861b6–c1 with 859a4–6.

43. It is essential that the legislator himself should strive to be clear so that when judges im-pose sentences, all the citizens may follow the arguments and "somehow or other" judge the soundness of a decision (861c). This way of formulating the noble aspiration to transparency, however, implies that citizens may or may not be able to follow these arguments clearly, a nod to the difficulty, and perhaps even incoherence, of the Athenian's positions on the theory and practice of punishment. *Contra* Saunders 1991: 140–41, who optimistically regards "Plato's pe-nology" as a "single publicly understood and publicly adopted policy, built into the penal code and applied by every citizen in his capacity as a juror."

44. Illuminating recent treatments include Lutz 2012: 158–63; L. S. Pangle 2014; Weiss 2006; Saunders 1991: 139–50 (building on previous articles); and Roberts 1987, which is closely followed by Schofield 2012; Stalley 1983: 151–65.

45. Zuckert 2009: 113–19 helpfully emphasizes the saliency of this point throughout the Athenian's account of his theory of punishment.

the conventional vocabulary so that involuntary injuries should not be called involuntary injustices; such injuries are not injustices at all (862a).[46] This move is a key moment in the Athenian's account, because it shifts the judge's attention away from the supposed criminal's actions and toward his state of soul. The Athenian builds on this point with surprising consequences. He draws attention away from action and toward psychology: Does a person employ a "just disposition and character" (*êthei kai dikaiôi tropôi*) when he injures or benefits someone else (862b; cf. 862c)? Or is he infected by injustice in so acting and, if so, is the infection irreparable? While injuries and benefits are not insignificant in themselves, the Athenian focuses on the necessity of exploring the state of soul of the accused.[47] Any such psychological inquiry will obviously be more complex than the straightforward assessment of the damages suffered by a victim. On the basis of such an inquiry, the city should attempt to cure whichever unjust individuals can be cured, since injustice is a disease in the soul (862c6–9).[48] There is no question of simple retribution. As the Athenian points out elsewhere, his approach is forward-looking rather than retrospective (934a–b).

The Athenian's proposed "cure" involves bringing the criminal to embrace justice in his soul: "Either by deeds or words, with pleasure or pain, honor or dishonor, monetary fines or rewards, or in general by whatever means one can use to bring about hatred of injustice and love (or at least not hatred) of justice, this is the very function of the finest laws" (862d). The central purpose of punishment is to inspire in the criminal a love of justice; punishment is ideally continuous with the motives of the lawgiver altogether. Hence, in answer to his own self-questioning about justice and nobility, the Athenian's reinterpretation of punishment as educational suggests that even "punitive" justice in this sense is, after all, noble. Understood in this way, punishment can fit coherently within the city's law code. The Athenian's description of the "cure" is reminiscent of earlier statements about the "educational" means used in general to cultivate a love of virtue among all citizens (cf. 770c–d).

---

46. Names and vocabulary matter, as we saw in the case of the judgments of courage and cowardice in the previous chapter; cf. 944b–c.

47. Weiss 2006: 188–90 and Catherine Zuckert 2013 both provide rich and helpful (albeit contrasting) recent accounts of this passage.

48. The Athenian makes explicit the connection with the free doctor in this sentence; in general, the idea of criminality as illness, introduced in the "free doctor" passage, helps to make sense of the Socratic paradox. Just as no one wants to be ill, so too, no one wants to be unjust. Hence, criminals should be cured when possible.

Notably, these means are based on praise and blame or the manipulation of pleasure and other desires. They are suited to address faults based on the passions rather than on ignorance per se, which requires a different, cognitively richer "cure."

Rationality, however, still plays a central role in the process of judging, albeit in a way that recent treatments have tended to obscure. Though relying on praise and blame, and even manipulation, these diverse responses to injustice do not imply that either the lawgiver himself or the city's highest judges will abstain from developing, at least for their own sakes, their own rational and articulate accounts of each criminal's psychology and the corresponding punishment. If they are audited, for example, then they must be able to "give an account," as the city's representatives and agents; and for the sake of their own integrity, they ought to be able to articulate such accounts for themselves, in any event.[49] They have to be clear and oriented to justice in their own minds. The only question is, Which citizens are capable of doing so in the highest-stakes cases? In the event, the Athenian reserves the top judicial positions for those who have been specially trained, in a more "precise" way— that is, for philosophers.

Only now does the Athenian refine his earlier injunctions concerning the incurable. They are still punished for exemplary or expressive reasons, and for the reason that they liberate the city from bad men (862e–863a; cf. 934a–b). To that extent the Athenian still goes beyond what justice to the individual demands or even allows. At least partly, though, he endeavors to ameliorate the conflict between individual and city by suggesting that a death sentence is better than life itself in the case of the incurably unjust (862e; cf. 661b–c). Although he limits the death penalty to such cases (863a), the Athenian leaves in place his encouragement of anger toward incurable criminals, when compassion (even combined, if necessary, with the ultimate penalty) would be more appropriate to the framework of the Socratic paradox.

Kleinias is sympathetic to the Athenian's theory. Understandably, however, he wants an explanation of how the distinction between injustice and injury has been mixed up with the difference between the voluntary and the involuntary (863a). The Athenian has done nothing, at least up till this point in the discussion, to dispel the notion that unjust actions can be voluntary; he

---

49. Compare the Athenian's Socratic remarks on clarifying his own inconsistencies and confusions, at least, whether or not all citizens may follow his reasoning in every particular: 859c–d.

continues, in fact, to speak of certain unjust actions as voluntary (862d).[50] In response to Kleinias' query, then, the Athenian drills down into the presumptively curable criminal's psychology: What are his motivations, and what is his character? Do we understand it well enough to punish or even execute a fellow citizen?

The Athenian's ensuing psychological account is designed only to sketch the inner psychology of criminals, for the sake of high-functioning judges. He refers to three causes of "faults" (*tôn hamartêmatôn*, 863c1, cf. 864b1).[51] They are "spirit" (*thumos*, 863b3), "pleasure" (*hêdonê*, 863b6), and "ignorance" (*agnoia*, 863c1)—apparently the faults caused by the three different parts of the soul, as anatomized in Plato's *Republic*.[52] Spirit and pleasure often give rise to *akrasia*; despite knowing what is best, we are somehow overpowered by them or corrupted by them (863d).[53] Ignorance does not result in *akrasia* (863d), presumably because it does not contest our "intention" (*boulêsis*, 863e3) directly, like the passions; the language of self-mastery is inapplicable to the case of ignorance. This vocabulary makes a return in the Athenian's presentation of the impious in Book 10.

In view of his curative purposes, then, the sitting judge will want to know: How do these three types of fault corrupt the soul? Perhaps surprisingly, the Athenian first assimilates them to one another. Both ignorance and the passions, he says, pull us in a direction opposite to our "intention" (*boulêsis*). Since our "faults" turn us away from our intention, we may hypothesize that the Athenian is working with a Socratic conception of "intention" according to which "intention" naturally seeks only the "good" or flourishing of the individual. If this hypothesis is correct, then it shows that the judge should approach each criminal as an individual whose basic "intention" (*boulêsis*, i.e., wish, desire, purpose, 863e3) is sound and reliable; it is directed toward what is good. Reforming efforts should then be directed toward the failings of desire, spirit, or intellect that have somehow corrupted that basically sound inner principle. Being turned in a direction opposite to

---

50. Schofield 2012: 109–10; Lutz 2012: 158–60; Stalley 1983: 154–56. Stalley 1983: 156 argues plausibly that the Athenian should have distinguished between two senses of "voluntary" in order to uphold his theory; cf. Schofield 2012: 106–12.

51. *Contra* Stalley 1983: 157 and others, it is important that these causes of "faults" are not said to be causes of "injustice." The distinction is further clarified at 863e–864a.

52. Lewis 2012: 20; Stalley 1983: 157; Saunders 1991: 148.

53. By accepting *akrasia*, of course, the Athenian rejects the Socratic paradox in its original form.

our deepest intention to seek what is good would seem to be the very definition of "involuntary."[54]

On the other hand, the Athenian also holds fast to the distinction between the passions and ignorance when he re-emphasizes the underlying basis
of his theory: injustice is a state of soul, whether the unjust person injures another or not (863e–864a). It is the state of being tyrannized by spirit, fear,
pleasure, and so on, independent of any actions that may issue from these
psychological diseases.[55] (One implication is that throughout history most
people, most of the time, have been unjust.) The Athenian's discussion of injustice, i.e., the tyranny of the soul by passion, however, does not directly raise
the question of ignorance. Ignorance is a different sort of fault. What role
does it play?

Reworking his treatment of ignorance and the passions, the Athenian
defines justice by contrast with injustice (864a). After describing injustice as
passion's tyranny over the soul, he argues that those ruled in their souls by the
"opinion of what is best" will be considered just, even if they happen to be
mistaken in some way and, hence, to injure others (864a).[56] We had expected
him to locate ignorance somewhere in this account of injustice and justice,
but he refers instead to an "opinion of what is best." Scholars generally agree
that what this "opinion" refers to is obscure; it is at least plausible, though, to
suppose that it refers to the opinion embodied in a city's law-code.[57] If that is
correct, then, in the case of a law-abiding citizen ruled by his rationality, any
injury (*blabê*) that he may cause should not be called "involuntary injustice"

---

54. As Roberts 1987: 25 also emphasizes.

55. Consider that those with "unjust souls" who have done nothing wrong could—should—
therefore be brought into court and prosecuted for their injustice, if only the injustice of their
souls were knowable (an idea with disturbing implications, which are explored interestingly in
the film *Minority Report*, directed by Steven Spielberg, which focuses on the use of psychics
to detect crime before it is committed). Cf. 876e–877a, where the Athenian makes the point
about circumstantial luck explicit.

56. The Greek expression at 864a4 is ambiguous: *kan sphallêtai ti* could refer to "making a mistake" or to injuring others; many commentators (e.g., Schofield 2012: 113–14; Stalley 1983: 158–
59; Catherine Zuckert 2013: 187) opt for the former interpretation, but the Athenian's reference
to causing injury (*blabê*) to others at 864a8 may imply the latter (either alone or in addition
to the former). See Weiss 2006: 191–95 and Schöpsdau 2011: 304 for further discussion of this
important point.

57. For reflection on this interpretation, see Lewis 2012: 22; Strauss 1975: 132. Needless to say,
the Athenian's meditation on psychological dissonance and harmony in this section should be
read together with his reflections on "ignorance" at 689a–d, which prepare the ground for this
discussion.

(864a), because it is not injustice at all; in that sense, it is like the unintentional injuries the Athenian had considered earlier (862a). The Athenian is willing to designate as "just" at least some of those who injure others or commit faults through ignorance and thus involuntarily; these are self-ruling individuals whose rationality and respect for law are not contaminated or overwhelmed by their own passions or desires. (Note that the category of the "ignorant" is therefore diverse: at 863c–d, the Athenian shows that other types of ignorant individuals, especially those guilty of "double ignorance," will commit injustice.) In this presentation, after all, ignorance is the cause of certain "faults" and "injuries" but not the source of injustice; injustice is the tyranny in the soul of passion.[58] Obedience to the law must be declared just, even when, as often, obedient citizens will fall short of knowledge.[59] These points play an important role in the Athenian's subsequent presentation of the impious in Book 10.[60]

If we think of this digression as a thought-piece designed to educate high-ranking jurors and magistrates, then the Athenian will be educating them, in broad terms, in how to approach three different kinds of motivation for wrongdoing. First, law-abiding citizens who are honestly ignorant, perhaps like certain just-hearted "young atheists," are still to be praised as just and

---

58. Hence, ignorance should be faulted, and it should be corrected; it would go too far to say that what is done in ignorance should not be blamed (cf. L. S. Pangle 2014: 231).

59. Lewis 2012: 21–22 offers a helpful reconstruction of this section, with which my account shares elements. When the Athenian returns to ignorance at 864b6–7, he describes it, intriguingly, as "striving" (*ephesis*, 864b7) for "true opinion about what is best." Somehow that "striving" is equivalent to ignorance; the Athenian, surprisingly, substitutes that "striving" for ignorance as the third cause of all "faults" (cf. 864b1–7 with 863c1–2). He implies that an individual's or city's attempt to acquire knowledge often fails. That failure is ignorance, but it may possibly not be rooted in an unjust character.

60. As Roberts 1987: 28–29 (to which my discussion here is indebted) argues, the Athenian's conception of ignorance, as opposed to injustice, explains how "impiety, construed as an isolated failure of the intellect, can be compatible with justice (908b4–c1)"—a point that, again, plays a role in the Athenian's presentation of Book 10's "young atheist" (cf. on the contrary, Saunders 1991: 149–50); L.S. Pangle 2014: 232 similarly appreciates the connection with Book 10 and its distinctions between sincere but just-hearted "doubters" and criminals motivated by unruly passions. Lewis 2012: 23–25 also interprets this section as intimately connected with the Athenian's presentation of the young atheist. Lewis argues correctly that the ignorance of skeptics is criminal, i.e., a cause of injustice, not simply by virtue of its existence (i.e., by virtue of their ignorantly skeptical beliefs). Rather, strictly speaking, that ignorance becomes criminal only when it leads the young atheists or others to disrespect the law. That is why, I would add, the Athenian emphasizes to the "young atheist" that he should explore his questions further and, in the meantime, avoid impious behavior or any wrongdoing "concerning the gods" (888c–d); cf. further Zuckert 2009: 128.

good.[61] Their mistakes can be corrected through education: their faults are "light" (863c), their ignorance "simple" (863c). They are not even unjust. Others, by contrast, are infected by an ignorance that is "double" (863c) in that they are not only mistaken but also believe that they are wise when they are not. Their openness to change is limited, especially if their self-certitude is strengthened by (for example) political power (863c–d). Others, again, who are tyrannized in their souls by spirit or desire are unjust, but they may be curable by the diverse means the Athenian has outlined (862d). Theoretically, at least, all of these people deserve compassion, because none of them is voluntarily ruled by the passions or by ignorance; in other words, none of them has knowingly chosen to harm what is properly understood as the greatest human possession, the soul.

Like their citizen counterparts in the text, readers are left, after all, with several complexities to ponder. First, has the Athenian shed light on the relationship between the noble and the just, which originally motivated the inquiry (cf. 860c)? Arguably, yes. The Athenian has provided an explanation of the nobility of just punishment. Punishment is noble when it is educational for the criminal, in the broad sense of educating both his passions and his intellect, as each case may require (cf. 854d, 862d–e, 933e–934c).[62] This conception of punishment requires sensitive, high-functioning judges who can follow the Athenian's reasoning. If we can imagine such judges, who will be models for ordinary jurors in Magnesia, then the Athenian has explained how, at least ideally, the criminal code fits closely within, and is continuous with, the city's noble laws altogether. On the other hand, as we have seen, the Athenian's references to exemplary punishment suggest that though certain punishments may be educational for other citizens, they do not live up to the ideal purpose of educating criminals. To that extent the penal code fails to embody the desirable coincidence of the just and the noble.

Second, although the Athenian reasons that *akrasia* itself (that is, the tyranny of the passions in the soul) is involuntary, he has not explored in any depth the question of responsibility for character (cf. 731d). Are individuals responsible, and to what extent, for their own susceptibility to the passions,

---

61. For a traditional reading, see Stalley 1983: 157–59; is it possible, though, that the honestly ignorant are the good-natured young atheists, who have a naturally just character, whom we will meet in the next chapter?

62. Cf. Stalley 1983: 141–43 and Strauss 1975: 133, who holds that the Athenian has not shown that all punishment is educational, on the grounds that he has not shown that virtue is knowledge or that vice is ignorance. This objection can be answered, though, if we think of education in a broader sense, as possibly involving (for example) an education of the emotions.

which are the source of injustice or tyranny in their souls? Even if the Athenian's account is brief and inadequate, his survey tends toward a gentler treatment of whichever criminals, tyrannized by anger or desire, or simply ignorant, are designated as curable.[63]

Third, does the Athenian have the means to distinguish between innocent ignorance and culpable ignorance? How, if at all, does this contrast map onto his stated contrast between "simple" and "double" ignorance? Perhaps individuals are innocently ignorant if they follow the city's laws honestly, even if they go wrong somehow either through misinterpreting the laws or through following laws that are themselves unjust. They are culpably ignorant, on the other hand, if they fail to respect the law through believing that they know better. This distinction would enable the Athenian to cultivate compassion for ignorant but well-intentioned transgressors of the law, on the grounds that they are not committing "injustice" at all (cf. 864a). It would also encourage harsh punishment for those presumable "incurables" who arrogantly believe themselves to be better than the law.

Against the backdrop of the dialogue as a whole, this section moderates the thumoeidetic impulses of jurors, whether high or low, by impressing on them, at the very least, the obscurities of the criminal's personal responsibility. If citizens take these points seriously, then they will be more moderate in dedicating themselves to justice by punishing lawbreakers (730d). This "digression" also suggests, however, that the city's highest judges will be called upon, in the name of justice, to puzzle over the mysteries of personal responsibility in ways that will not be transparent to ordinary citizens and lesser courts. By placing this difficult philosophical section at the heart of his penal theory, the Athenian invites readers to wonder to what extent ordinary courts will actually achieve justice—and which kinds of educational background will be required if courts, whether high or low, are to apply the Athenian's theories correctly.

The Socratic Paradox and Magnesia's Penal Code

Amid all the obscurities in the Athenian's presentation, readers can infer that magistrates and judges will require both significant philosophical training and first-rate intellects if they are to succeed in applying the Athenian's difficult ideas of responsibility to the city's concrete practices of justice. While

---

63. L. S. Pangle 2014.

scholars have often found this "digression" to be only loosely connected with the surrounding discussion, it is possible to connect it more closely to the Athenian's general presentation of the criminal code. Throughout Book 9, he is concerned not only to outline the city's criminal code, but also to reflect on the psychology and practical rationality required of the city's judges. Hence, he interrupts his presentation of criminal law to discuss the appropriate conduct of judges during trials (855d–856a). He revisits the "free doctor" analogy in order to reflect on his ideally intelligent, wise, and caring approach to criminals (857c–e). In immediate proximity to these discussions, he models for judges an appropriately modest epistemological stance, after which he expounds a theory of criminal responsibility likely to inspire both questioning and awe among those faced with the task of judging others. However harsh and frightening his criminal code may at times be, the Athenian also emphasizes the difficulty of the judge's task. The Athenian is gradually, and obscurely, bringing readers around to the idea that acting as a true judge presumes prior philosophical training.

Is the Athenian's excursus on the Socratic paradox a viable basis of the penal code? Does the Athenian always respect the analysis of injury, injustice, voluntary action, and responsibility offered in this digression? The answer to these questions is complex. Scholars have doubtless noted gaps in the Athenian's presentation of the penal code.[64] Stalley points out the unusual provision, for example, that the murderer of a parent out of rage will suffer death unless the parent absolves him before dying—in which case he will simply be exiled, like others who murder in anger (869a–c).[65] As Thomas Pangle argues, moreover, it is difficult to see a rehabilitative impetus (rather than a concession to punitive anger) in the Athenian's proposal to punish beasts and stones that are "convicted of 'murdering' a citizen (873e–874a)."[66] In other cases, vengeance or retribution takes priority over an educative "cure." In the case of "wholly unjust" murder, for example, the Athenian offers a frightening argument that such murderers will face vengeance in Hades, as well as, in their return to life on earth, the vengeance of suffering precisely the fate they inflicted on their victims (870d–e); such murderers will, moreover, lack a burial, to indicate

---

64. E.g., Pangle 1980: 499–500; Lewis 2012: 26–28. Saunders 1991: 212–348 considers this question in detail; he sees a tendency for disjunction between the official, theoretical penology and the penal code itself (194).

65. Stalley 1983: 147.

66. Pangle 1980: 499–500; cf. Lutz 2012: 157–63.

that they are unforgiven (871d).[67] The Athenian makes these provisions despite otherwise distancing himself from vengeance.[68] The Athenian appears to establish these provisions for expressive or deterrent, rather than curative, reasons.

The Athenian's code is, in fact, shot through with deterrence and exemplary punishment, which fits badly with his stated theory. In examining parricides who act out of anger, for example, the Athenian ignores the Socratic paradox and even disregards the question of curative penalties: he says simply that such a person must die, and even that he would justly die many times if it were possible (869b–c). The same points hold, all the more intensely, in cases of "voluntary and wholly unjust murders of kinsmen," who are, according to the "ancient priests," subject to a spooky *lex talionis* that involves suffering similar assaults at the hands of their children or other relatives (872c–873c). It seems impossible to square these harshly retributive (not to mention disturbingly magical) punishments with an emphasis on showing mercy to criminals via the Socratic paradox and its associated questions about responsibility. In these particular cases, moreover, the Athenian refers very little to questions about whether or how these criminals can be cured. Finally, the Athenian occasionally conjures up seemingly inappropriate notions of inherited guilt: temple robbers are driven by a "gadfly" that grows in human beings because of inherited injustices—motivations for which those individuals are obviously not responsible. These individuals are encouraged to seek death if their drives are not calmed by supplicating the gods and fleeing the company of wrongdoers (854b–c; on inherited guilt, cf. also 856d). The Athenian does not even discuss the complications of his "curative" theory in his proposal of the death penalty for insurrection (856b–c) or accepting bribes (955c–d).[69]

This conclusion raises the question of the Athenian's point in the "digression" altogether. Perhaps these gaps exist either because the citizen judges are not up to the task of applying the Athenian's principles or because Magnesia's

---

67. Cf. the same practice at 873b, on murders of kinsmen, with the addition of the magistrates throwing stones at the corpse's head; 874a–b, on murderers who go undetected.

68. Cf. Stalley 1983: 148; Lewis 2012: 26–28. The Athenian is also harsh and unsympathetic to suicides, failing even to inquire into the psychological logic of their actions (873c–d).

69. Cf. Stalley 1983: 148. Nor does he explain why his theory of punishment does not seem to apply to slaves or foreigners. Is it not unjust of the city to ignore the complexities of voluntary and involuntary action with respect to noncitizens? Note the surplus harshness applied to slave criminals at 872b–c: whipping, to be followed by execution. Why not just execution, as though that were not harsh enough? Saunders 1973: 235 aptly points out that most of the city's "curative" measures involve the "infliction of suffering."

criminals are often incurable, or even because, in the Athenian's view, the angry and punitive impulses of Magnesia's citizens often need to be satisfied through barbaric punishments, however crude or even cruel. Any combination of these factors—or all of them—may play a role. These contradictions indicate that the Athenian's pursuit of unalloyed "nobility" in the criminal justice system is destined to fail, given the frailties and imperfections of our "mortal nature," even despite the Athenian's success in bringing together "the just" and "the noble" in theory.

Even despite these inconsistencies and contradictions, however, the Athenian himself believes that his theory might provide the basis of Magnesia's penal code (860e). Closer examination reveals that the Athenian often does, after all, inform the actual penal code with the gentler and more compassionate principles implied by his theory. In doing so, he presents a more coherent picture than initial appearances may suggest—one with far-reaching consequences for our understanding of the education of *thumos* and the associated faculty of judgment. To take one example, the Athenian's laws on homicide committed in anger (866d–869e) suggest a subtle examination of voluntary and involuntary action (esp. 866d–867d): Has the murderer acted impulsively or with prior deliberation? Does he feel regret afterward? The Athenian leaves the case murky because he is concerned with justice: "It would be most accurate to say that they are somewhere between the voluntary and the involuntary" (867a). He explicitly acknowledges the difficulty of determining the level of voluntariness involved in each case (867b), arguing that it is "best and truest" to say that each case is an "image" (*eikôn*, 867b3) of the voluntary or involuntary. No particular case, as empirically found, matches the ideal prototype. Although the deliberate murderer is harsher and requires harsher treatment (867b), the Athenian again points out that cases can be complex and require sensitive attunement to individual psychology:

> It is difficult to legislate for this matter with great precision. For there are times when the "harsher" of the two according to the law may be gentler, and the "gentler" may be harsher, having committed the murder more savagely, while the former was less violent (867d–e).

The acts themselves do not always directly correspond to the defendants' characters. Hence, the Athenian emphasizes that his Socratically inspired penal code will require further interpretation and future acts of judgment when judges face actual defendants in the city's courts. Strikingly, even after convicts have spent time in exile, as the law requires, the *nomophulakes* will send twelve of their number, who have looked into their cases even more carefully, who will act as judges on the city's borders, tasked with considering the question of their return (867e). The Athenian not only strives to do justice to criminals, but also demands that his magisterial judges in these cases produce carefully wrought judgments, in accordance with the laws and with justice, that offer the best and truest account of each criminal's just deserts. In light of the Athenian's complex and obscure penal theory, this task is not trivial.

The Athenian combines care for the alleged criminal with an impressive education of judgment, both among the top-notch judges in the city's highest courts, and among those citizens who attend the courts and learn from the judges' questions, their legal reasoning, and their eventual decisions. Magnesia's judges will be carrying out tasks that, to be sure, draw on their thumoeidetic nature—tasks that require a sense of honor in relation to the city and its law, appropriate compassion and anger in relation to criminal activity, and a willingness to hold themselves up to appropriate standards of legal integrity. These tasks also require judges to exercise and develop their practical intelligence in significant ways. To that extent, and despite the code's occasionally vindictive appearance, the Athenian's education of citizens in their capacity as judges tends to humanize or to mollify the system of punishment.[70] Jurors are supposed to be less angry or harsh if they genuinely grasp that no one, not even an apparently repugnant criminal, desires to possess an unjust or tyrannized soul. Such are the consequences of the Athenian's exploration of the Socratic paradox in the context of the legal code.

Conclusion: Citizens and the Lawgiver

Plato, the author, continually emphasizes the gap between the Athenian and his Dorian interlocutors. Their differences shine through already during their initial exchanges in Book 1, where the Athenian establishes leadership, not to say dominance, in the subsequent conversation. This hierarchy becomes further entrenched when the Athenian develops the civil religion that first appears in Book 2. The Athenian builds on his efforts to teach the elderly Dorians in Book 3, when he leads them ever farther from their initial patriotism and dedication to warfare, to an understanding that pleonectic imperialism,

---

70. Cf. L. S. Pangle 2014 and compare to Strauss 1975: 133. Stalley 1983: 149–50 offers helpful observations on the dangers of "forward-looking views of punishment," on the grounds that they instrumentalize individual criminals; for a similar critique, see Balot 2021, with reference to Hegel's theory of punishment.

and tyrannical overreach, are the key political failings of all previous human history—as exemplified, above all, by the history of early Lacedaimonia. In founding the new city early in Book 4, the Athenian convinced Kleinias and Megillus that a god was truly in charge; it turned out that he himself, using his own intelligence, and his understanding of human nature and nature at large, constructed a regime of law that would address humanity's central political failings. To the Dorians' continual surprise, the Athenian thereby set the city on a course of political activity that was as unconventional as it was ambitious: its ambitions were precisely to liberate Magnesia's citizens from ordinary, harmful ways of understanding themselves and their ends as human beings. In the process, the Athenian provided healthier political institutions and norms that would govern their lives.

In light of the Athenian's relationship with the Dorians, it is striking that ordinary citizens perform civic duties that require discretion and good judgment. They are envisioned as citizens rather than as warriors. Although they exercise discretion and show signs of prudence, however, the Athenian will always offer outlines, sketches, and models to keep them within the bounds of justice, as (he points out) he has often said in legislating throughout the dialogue (876d–e). His belief, apparently, is that ordinary citizens cannot fully do justice to their roles without his guidance or the supervision of the highest magistrates.

Correspondingly, the Athenian emphasizes the role of the city's highest magistrates and judges. His characterization of their activity raises questions about their identity and training. They often appear to require greater understanding of complex philosophical issues than would normally be available to even intelligent, high-ranking practical citizens. The reflective judgments that he himself offers—for example, about the considerations involved in designating a homicide "voluntary" or "involuntary," or something between the two (867a–b)—are precisely the ones that he expects them to offer in his absence. He stresses that the city's highest officials will be "lawgivers as well as Guardians of the Laws" (770a). The Athenian's presentation of these officials raises unsettling questions about their need for a philosophical education—questions that are clarified only at the end of the dialogue.

Altogether, the Athenian's education of *thumos* not only moderates angry or aggressive impulses, but also elevates the elderly Dorians' punitive and patriotic drives. If the process works as planned, then Magnesia's ordinary citizens will be thoughtful and reflective, whenever practical matters of the city come to their attention. They will imitate the Athenian. Though scholars have debated Plato's involvement in practical politics, his presentation of a detailed law-code, with detailed specifications, judgments, and corresponding rationales, is his most complete effort to describe the education of ordinary citizens. At the same time, the author never allows his readers to ignore the contrast between philosophers and nonphilosophers—and even the necessity of philosophers for enabling the city to function well.

9

The Athenian's Theology, Part I

BOOK 10 PICKS up immediately from the Athenian's discussion of the penal code in Book 9. Having addressed assault (*aikia*), he briefly legislates concerning violence (*biaiôn peri*) altogether, before turning to the "self-indulgence and *hubris*" (*akolasiai te kai hubreis*) of the young (884a). It is *hubris* toward the gods, in word or deed, that he then takes up in the dialogue's longest persuasive preamble (885b). He says that no one has ever done an impious deed or spoken an unlawful word unless he is an atheist or holds that the gods do not care about human beings or believes that they can be easily persuaded by sacrifice or prayer (885b). For the sake of convenience, I will call these three groups the "atheists," the "deists," and the "bribers."[1] In response, the Athenian offers three arguments: first, that the universe is governed by rationally ordered and intelligent "soul" rather than pervaded by random matter in disorderly motion; second, that the gods providentially supervise the cosmos and deliver justice to human beings in the afterlife, while conducting surveillance over people during their lives; third, that, as providential shepherds guarding just human beings, the gods have too much integrity to take bribes. With just human beings as their allies, in fact, the gods punish the unjust. After making these arguments, the Athenian pronounces the law on impiety.

Why does he call forth, seemingly unnecessarily, the challenge posed by the young atheist? Why not simply forgo potential difficulties with

---

1. I use the term "deist" *faute de mieux*, since deism is a complex (and internally diverse) position; I intend the term to refer only to the belief that the gods are remote from human existence and lack care for human beings.

Tragedy, Philosophy, and Political Education in Plato's Laws. Ryan K. Balot, Oxford University Press.
© Ryan K. Balot 2024. DOI: 10.1093/oso/9780197647226.003.0009

Magnesia's civil religion?[2] I see three principal reasons. First, the discussion enables the Athenian to persuade Kleinias of the necessity of the Nocturnal Council. Second, it helps him to assign an important role to Kleinias as a "manly" defender of justice and law in the city. Finally, it provides him with a surreptitious method of recruiting talented young people to study philosophy in Magnesia. This final reason depends on the intriguing surprise with which the Athenian concludes Book 10. Specifically, readers learn, the Athenian bifurcates the three groups (the atheists, the deists, and the bribers) according to their characters. He thereby creates, he says, "six kinds of faults worth distinguishing" (908b2–3). This clarification enables us, as readers, to rethink his presentation of the "sociology of the impious" altogether.

The Athenian's Introduction Raises Unsettling Questions

The Athenian begins the preamble on impiety by conjuring up a contemptuous speaker in order to explain why certain people question the city's theology. The speaker asks that the lawgiver refrain from using threats, out of consistency, and instead to "persuade and teach" him that the gods exist and that they are not susceptible to bribes (885c–d; cf. 885e). Although he refers to others who believe the gods to be "such as" the Athenian has said (885c), the speaker omits discussion of the deists and focuses only on the atheists and the bribers. The bribers constitute "most of us" (*hoi pleistoi*), while by implication the atheists are a small subgroup (885d–e). The atheists and bribers have received their views from many sources, including "those considered best among the poets, orators, diviners, priests, and thousands upon thousands of others" (885d), the conventional city's conventional authorities.

For his part, Kleinias rejects these impious ideas on the merits. Having forgotten his earlier statements about the planets' wandering motions (821c),[3] and having forgotten the inconclusiveness of the astronomical discussion in Book 7 (822b–c), he now asserts the straightforwardness of demonstrating that gods exist based on the heavenly bodies and the order of the seasons, as well as the universal belief among both Greeks and non-Greeks that gods exist (886a). What is striking is that the Athenian declines to build on Kleinias'

---

2. For different approaches to these questions, see Pangle 1976, 1980; Bobonich 1996, 2002: 99–105; Lewis 2009b: 87–91; Laks 2000: 290.

3. Cf. Zuckert 2009: 121, who also observes that the dialogue's initial exchanges may hint at Kleinias's own doubts about the "divine origin of Crete's laws."

apparently firm theological beliefs. Instead, he explains that Kleinias fails to understand the mentality of the contemptuous speaker. Kleinias assumes that those who reject the gods must be motivated by the tyranny of the passions (886a–b)—which the Athenian had offered in Book 9 as the very definition of "injustice" (863e). Kleinias assumes, in other words, that the city's chief concern should be those driven by lawless desires. According to the Athenian, by contrast, the impious individual is not (or not only) motivated by a lack of self-mastery (*akrateiai*) regarding pleasure and desire, but rather (or also) by "grievous ignorance seeming to be the greatest prudence" (886a–b). Readers will appreciate the echoes with Socrates' tripartition of the soul described in Plato's *Republic*, as well as with the three sources of "faults" in Book 9 (863b–864b).[4] These different sources of motivation shape the ensuing account of impiety. Readers will come to understand that the key distinction is between those whose skepticism is rooted in the passions (and who therefore require the reformation of character) and those whose skepticism is based on ignorance pure and simple (who, when good-hearted, deserve an intellectual cure but not the reformation of character).

Why isn't the Athenian concerned, like Kleinias, simply to quash impiety, whatever its source? If his goal is to quash impiety, then is it necessary for the Athenian to dig down to a rich philosophical discussion instead of basing his prelude on the second and third arguments alone?[5] As he points out, they have legislated on the assumption that gods exist (*hôs ontôn theôn*, 887a1–2), an assumption that Kleinias and the Magnesians will generally share. Practically speaking, the second and third arguments would have provided more than adequate theological support to the city's religiously informed

---

4. This passage contains many echoes of the Athenian's discussion of responsibility in Book 9 and should be read in concert with it; for helpful remarks, see Lutz 2012: 154–58; Lewis 2012. While *akrateia* accounts for the first two "faults" the Athenian mentioned in his theoretical statement on responsibility and punishment, ignorance is the third of the three causes of "faults" (863b–e).

5. To repeat the central question: What is the benefit of raising these issues, when they would never have arisen otherwise—as opposed to simply "re-educating" the epithumetically driven "impious" through punishment, praise and blame, or fear of the afterlife? See Pangle 1976 for a forceful statement of the problem, along with Benardete 2000: 285; cf. also Bobonich 1996 and 2002 for helpful reflections. Why does the Athenian go out of his way to focus attention specifically on the first, more philosophical argument, instead of relying on, as his tool of "re-education," the more rhetorically straightforward second and third arguments? Laks 2000: 290 strikingly maintains that "recourse to such an argument is imposed on him [the Athenian], against his will"—which is precisely contrary to the text; cf. also Mayhew 2008: 8, which equally assumes the necessity of the argument, seeing Book 10 as "Plato's fullest and final discussion of the existence and nature of the gods."

legal code, particularly among such unsophisticated settlers.[6] Omitting the first argument, in fact, would have made the prelude on impiety similar to other preludes, because, like them, the second and third arguments serve principally rhetorical purposes rather than philosophical ones. Few colonists, at all events, will understand the first argument (890e, 900c).

Along these lines, in fact, the Athenian had a variety of options at his disposal. He could have cultivated the Dorians' reverence for the gods by praising the gods' goodness and referring to well-known manifestations of their power (such as dreams or visions, as in Herodotus). Or he could have discussed traditional narratives of the gods' momentous interventions in human history, suitably purified, no doubt, with a view to strengthening his presentation of the gods' providential concern for humanity. He could have narrated those stories (per the account in *Republic* 2–3) in such a way as to emphasize not only the gods' power and goodness, but also the just man's inevitable happiness.

Instead of following a more obvious path, however, the Athenian self-consciously draws attention to philosophical discussions of theology, of which Kleinias would otherwise have been innocent. As he says (886c), it is only "among us," the Athenians, that writings exist concerning the heavens and the origins of the gods—that is, "theogonies," which, he wryly notes, tend to undermine parental authority (886c–d). Such stories are neither beneficial nor true, he asserts, but he refrains from discussing them, presumably because the city's own narratives will tell a genuinely beneficial story. Instead, he pinpoints a particular enemy or threat to the city: our more recent "wise men," he says, have to be accused and held responsible for the "bad things" they cause (886d). He emphasizes their responsibility and the need to hold them to account (cf. *aitiathêtô, aitia*, 886d3–4; cf. 887d1). They hold that the heavenly bodies are inanimate objects composed of earth and stone and hence incapable of caring for humanity.

What are the great evils these "wise men" cause? Supposedly, they are responsible for nothing less than the breakdown of social order. Their philosophical materialism leads to, or apparently licenses or is otherwise tied to, their acquisitive "materialism."[7] The Athenian explains that in their view, everything has come to be through nature, art, and chance (888e). The material

---

6. Pangle 1980: 502 and Strauss 1975, among others, have correctly noted the religious foundations of much of the legal code.

7. As we will discover, it is important to wrestle with the precise connection; contrast Mayhew 2008: 90, who writes, "Clearly, Plato believes that atheism leads to moral relativism, which in turn leads to the sophistic conception of justice, which finally leads to 'the impieties that afflict young people' (890a4–5)."

elements exist by nature, without soul, and combine randomly to produce the heavenly bodies, animals, plants, and so on. The human arts, including the political art, arise later and have little power; legislation itself, "whose enactments are not true, is not by nature but by art" (889e, tr. Pangle 1980, adapted). Even the gods do not exist by nature but, rather, by convention (889e). These beliefs give rise, the Athenian says, to quasi-Calliclean drives and arguments:

> They assert, moreover, that what is noble according to nature is different from what is noble according to convention, and that justice does not exist at all by nature, but that people are constantly arguing with one another and always changing these things; and whatever changes they make at a certain time have authority at that particular time, though coming into existence by means of art and laws but not, indeed, by any nature. All these ideas, friends, prevail among the young, who learn them from wise men, both ordinary people and poets, who say that what is most just is whatever anyone wins by force. This is the source of the impieties that befall young people, who hold that the gods are not such as the law commands us to conceive them; and because of this, civil conflict arises when they draw people toward the life that is correct according to nature, which is in truth to live as master over others and not to be their slave under the law. (889e–890a)

The Athenian closely connects materialistic natural philosophy with a Calliclean-style "immoralism." More important for the drama of Plato's *Laws*, he is offering a philosophically informed elaboration of the psychology, ethics, and politics underlying the views expressed by Kleinias at the beginning of the dialogue.[8] The Athenian's vision of societal breakdown—led by epithumetic and thumoeidetic desires and deepened by atheism—agitates Kleinias and inspires in him a desire to defend the city from these evident threats (887b–c, 890b, 890d–e).

Speaking of defending the city, in fact, the Athenian imagines the three old men offering a speech in self-defense (*apologêsômetha*, 886e). Certain "impious human beings" allege that they are doing "terrible things" (*deina*) by

---

8. Cf. Zuckert 2009: 126: "The notion that everything in the cosmos exists in opposition or strife characteristic of pre-Socratic philosophy is compatible with Clinias' initial belief that human beings are always at war. The suspicion arises, therefore, that the Athenian's argument to show that the gods exist is ad hominem."

legislating based on the assumption that the gods exist (886e–887a). Readers (though not the old Dorians) will understand that the Athenian's pointed language alludes to Socrates' speech in self-defense (*apologia*). The Athenian's evocation of Socrates' trial is complex. Like the Athenian, Socrates presents himself as being on the defensive and describes both older accusers and more recent ones (*Ap.* 18a–e). To the Athenian, though, the theogonic poets and materialist philosophers are corrupters of the citizens and their shared ethos, against whom he must defend Magnesia; in Plato's *Apology*, by contrast, the two sets of accusers (that is, the older ones, such as Aristophanes, and the more recent ones, such as Meletus) acted in concert with the city in accusing Socrates. Socrates was accused of speculating in natural philosophy, of failing to observe the city's religion, and of corrupting the young. By contrast, the Athenian argues in support of his own city's religion and conventions, while being attacked by others (virtually the rest of the world, in the atheist's presentation: 885d–e) who object to religiously informed legislation. His rivals are those who, like Socrates in the minds of his own accusers, espouse irreligious philosophical views that corrupt the young. In the first instance, then, the Athenian positions himself as an antitype to Socrates—one who is prepared to offer a defense, even a justification, of Magnesia, from the perspective of the theology that underwrites its entire law code. He stresses in this section that the law code, indeed the laws, rituals, and norms of the entire city, are based on piety (887d; cf. 890a), a point he has emphasized throughout the dialogue (713a, 762e, 799a–b, 803c–804b).[9]

Persuading Kleinias That Magnesia Needs Philosophers

The Athenian's peculiar introduction of Book 10 helps to call forth the Nocturnal Council as the city's defender.[10] He intensifies Kleinias' worry that the city requires safeguarding or defense and suggests that only philosophers can successfully defend the city. The city's religious order requires the active presence of philosophy, which alone is capable of guarding it against possible incursions from an "atheist underground."[11] If he had introduced the Nocturnal Council earlier, then this gambit would have been impossible.

---

9. Cf. Pangle 1980: 502; Lewis 2009b: 87; Lewis 2010.

10. My analysis builds on that of Pangle 1976, 1980: 503–4, 510.

11. Sedley 2013.

Now, however, both readers and the elderly Dorians will know that a philosophical council is in the offing—one that underwrites Magnesia's civil religion. It is striking that the Athenian keeps both readers and his interlocutors in suspense about the nature of that council until the very end, a point that scholars have ignored at their peril.

By persuading Kleinias that the Nocturnal Council is necessary for the city's defense, the Athenian will have succeeded in doing what Socrates' own *apologia* did not accomplish: he will have provided a self-defense of philosophy itself, by convincing all the citizens of philosophy's capacity to contribute to the city's security and well-being. He will have done so, again unlike Socrates, while keeping the city's religion intact—indeed, precisely *by* keeping the city's religion intact. A question remains, however, as to the quality of the Athenian's *apologia* for philosophy. Does his speech defend philosophy on merely instrumental grounds, by arguing that philosophy defends the city from attack and justifies the piety that underlies its law code? Or does his speech, in addition, defend philosophy on intrinsic grounds, on the grounds that the philosophical life is the best and most fulfilling human life—that philosophy is the highest human vocation? The defense of philosophy on intrinsic grounds is, after all, another unfulfilled promise of Socrates' own *apologia* before the Athenians—one that he had little time to offer, and one that his audience was incapable of grasping (*Ap.* 38a–b). We will have to wait for an answer to this important question.

Assigning a Role to Kleinias

Although Kleinias' own arguments for the existence and goodness of the gods are weak, he quickly comes to see that the Athenian has embarked on the "most beautiful and best prelude" (*kalliston te kai ariston prooimion*) for the entire law-code (887b–c).[12] In keeping with the Athenian's allegory of the free and slave doctors, he genuinely wants to persuade citizens (887b–c, 890d), instead of simply forcing them to obey. He is zealous, eager, anxious (887c, 890e). The lawgiver, Kleinias urges, should not "grow weary"; he should become an "ally" (*epikouron*) of the law and "take the field" (*boêthêsai*) on behalf

---

12. Note the linguistic resonance of this phrase with the Athenian's declaration on the "truest tragedy" at 817b4 (a "mimesis of the most beautiful and best life"). This linguistic echo is one indication among many that the Athenian's reference to the "truest tragedy" should be read in concert with his civil religion of Book 10: we will explore the "truest tragedy," and the significance of this connection, in chapter 12.

of law and art (890d). Kleinias "trusts" or "puts his faith in" the Athenian as he makes these arguments (*egô soi pisteuô ta nun*, 890d). He and others may be "slow at learning" (*dusmathei*), but whoever fails to understand at first can examine the written arguments frequently (891a). In language that develops the militaristic and "manly" overtones of this passage, Kleinias concludes: "Even if they are lengthy, if the arguments are beneficial, it doesn't appear to me, at least, to be at all reasonable or pious for any man (*panta andra*) to fail, on this account, to come to the aid (*boêthein*) of these arguments as best he can" (891a, tr. Pangle 1980).

Whatever his other purposes, the Athenian uses this section of the dialogue to define a role for Kleinias, to which Kleinias willingly adheres. Kleinias eagerly positions himself as an ally of the Athenian, a helper whose functions he describes in military language. He now displays a character well suited to such a role. The Athenian warns against excessive harshness or hatred (888a); interestingly, Kleinias is eager to fight for justice, but is not manifestly angry in doing so.[13] His thumoeidetic response is well calibrated, despite his "manly," militaristic vocabulary. He has learned from the Athenian, already, how to serve as a solid citizen, who can reliably but moderately defend the city's pieties and laws; one thinks of the better citizens who defend the city against injustice and even punish wrongdoers (730d–e).

All the same, Kleinias is aware of his need to rely on the Athenian himself for the substance of the arguments. Even if he will consult the lawgiver's writings and try to understand, he is forced to "trust" or to "put his faith in" the Athenian to defend the city at a deeper level. In other words: the Athenian has fashioned Kleinias into a figure resembling the unphilosophical guardians or warriors of Socrates' Callipolis. They are given true beliefs by the city's philosophers, but they accept those beliefs as dogma (i.e., incontrovertible *doxa*), without being able to give a rational account of them. Because they trust the philosophers, however, they are willing to defend those beliefs. In the *Laws*, Kleinias' dogma is explicitly religious, and his defense of the city a matter of piety (891a).[14]

---

13. As Mayhew 2008: 70 correctly observes. Intriguingly, it is the Athenian rather than Kleinias who is supposedly angry (cf. 888a3–5, 907b–c); as I will argue, the Athenian represents himself in this way in order to distance himself publicly from the young atheist, whom he is in reality trying to recruit.

14. Jouët-Pastré 2001 argues that the *Laws* reassesses the written word, and written laws, and gives them a newfound position of respect, as compared to the *Phaedrus*. Jouët-Pastré 2001: 39–40 suggests that written legislation helps to assure the laws' fixity, efficaciousness, and longevity in history, which is supposedly desirable because the written laws are based on the

This point is significant, in part because scholars have argued that the Athenian's purpose is to enlighten the citizenry more broadly.[15] In a minor way, that interpretation is undoubtedly correct: it would be better for ordinary citizens, and men like Kleinias, to understand more deeply the theological foundations of the city's law-code. They should indeed be persuaded rather than forced to obey, in keeping with the city's approach to legislation. Indeed, they must understand *something* of the city's theology if they are to fight eagerly to protect it.

Troublingly, however, most citizens lack the capacity to achieve any significant understanding. The Athenian is clear about the first argument's unintelligibility to ordinary people. Before embarking on it, he proposes to leave the Dorians on one side of a swirling, eddying river, while he continues the argument, with the young atheist, whose role he also plays, on the other side (892d–893a).[16] His concern is that the river might make them dizzy and "give rise to an unpleasant and nauseating awkwardness (*aschêmosunên*)" (893a). Engaging in this argument might discombobulate the carefully formed internal make-up of the Dorians—the "puppets" whose intractable strings are likely to revert at any moment to anarchy.[17] The Athenian claims not to know whether the argument is too difficult for the Dorians to understand (892e–893a), but they do not follow the Athenian's reasoning as the argument unfolds (e.g., 894b).[18] They are not appropriate candidates for philosophical discussion; rather, they are appropriate candidates for believing dogmatically in the conclusions of such discussions, as Kleinias is shown doing at the

---

Athenian's grasp of what is naturally beautiful and just; see Balot 2020b for a more complex view of legislative fixity and change in the dialogue.

15. Bobonich 1996: 268; 2002; Mayhew 2008.

16. Cf. Mayhew 2008 for helpful remarks about the Dorians' perplexity and incomprehension of the first argument. Oddly, though, he concludes by writing: "Plato would likely claim that Kleinias and Megillus were persuaded by the Athenian's arguments for the existence of the gods and thus the falsehood of atheism, but, again, it is an impoverished conception of persuasion." (Mayhew 2008: 106).

17. Cf. Bobonich 1996: 266–67 for a compatible reading of this passage.

18. Their lack of understanding explains why, in the image of the river, the Athenian imagines that he and the young atheist will be out of the range of hearing of the city's elders and sober lawgivers. The Athenian is referring, surreptitiously, as he must, to the recruitment of a ruling philosophical class. The young atheist, who is given the individualized education the Athenian finds lacking in Dorian cities (666e–667a), will become "not only a good soldier but even a man able to manage a city and its towns" (666e–667a). The young atheists will become the city's homegrown philosophers.

end of the first argument (899b–d).[19] Later, in Book 12, as if in confirmation of these points, Kleinias reveals that he has failed to grasp the Athenian's arguments—specifically, argument 1 (966d–967d). He even says explicitly that those who lack capacity should be kept separate from the "noble" people who genuinely understand these questions (966d)—people the Athenian has just called "divine" (*theion*) because they have "labored through and through" (*diapeponêkota*) over such things (966d).

We are left with an image of Kleinias as a trustworthy, energetic defender of the city's pieties—a citizen content to rely on the Athenian to argue the city's case at the deepest level. The Athenian has successfully harnessed Kleinias' warlike impulses on behalf of the city. In the process, however, he has inspired in Kleinias a great deal of respect, and even admiration, for the philosopher who can provide a firmly pious foundation for the law-code. He appreciates that the Athenian is about to offer the "most beautiful and best" prelude for the entire law-code (887b–c).[20] By the end of argument 1, Kleinias is firmly convinced by the Athenian's arguments (899d)—much more so than the Athenian himself, who remains tentative (899d).[21] The city relies on the Nocturnal Council to understand the "proofs" (*pisteis*) of the existence of the gods; its philosophers understand, as Kleinias does not, that the Athenian's arguments are not definitive (966c–d, with chapter 11, "The Rule of *Nous*").

To this extent at least, the Athenian's three arguments are performative: he has impressed Kleinias with the necessity, even the beauty, of providing a philosophical defense of the city. He has awakened in Kleinias a new appreciation for the magnificence of philosophy as the city's most robust defender. If we now recall Kleinias' starting points, and his anxious belief that his own lawgiver established his entire society with a view to defending the city's "good things" against invasion, and even expanding its power and wealth, then we

---

19. What is dramatized, among other things, is that Kleinias is willing to "outsource" philosophical understanding of theology to the Athenian, so that he can return to the work of politics as ordinarily interpreted. This dramatization depends on his persistent tendency to progress from a superficial acknowledgment that deep and controversial issues have *not* been settled, to a self-satisfied certainty about matters that the Athenian considers to be highly provisional and uncertain (cf. 820d–e, 822c–d, 899c–d).

20. As we have seen, Kleinias agrees that the discussion is necessary—it is even the "most beautiful and best preamble" (*kalliston te kai ariston prooimion*, 887c1–2), he says, a phrase that implicitly links this section to the Athenian's discussion of the "tragedy that is the most beautiful and the best" and the way of life that is "most beautiful and best" (817b). Other connections between Book 7 and 10 include, above all, the higher study of astronomy outlined in Book 7 (817e–818a) and the Athenian's disquisition on cosmology in Book 10.

21. Cf. Lewis 2009b: 88–89; Lewis 2010: 42–44.

can understand that the Athenian has now, for the benefit of Kleinias, displaced the traditional, militaristic lawgiver with a newly philosophical protector of that which genuinely matters most to citizens, and indeed to human beings as such: Magnesia's newly understood "good things."

A New "Sociology of the Impious"

It could be that the Athenian's introduction of philosophical discussion is exhaustively explained by his desire to summon forth the Nocturnal Council and to designate Kleinias the law code's loyal, thumoeidetic ally.[22] He may think, for example, that the risks of publicizing the philosophical debate are worth running, on balance, because he can thereby persuade Kleinias of the existence of a mortal threat to the city, which only the Nocturnal Council can ward off. Is it somehow possible, though, that the Athenian is not only not anxious to balance risks, but also *unconcerned* about the corrupting power of atheistic arguments? After all, his willingness to broadcast these ideas suggests, almost paradoxically, that he is not anxious that such arguments will be "scattered everywhere," with a corrupting force, in the city. How can we make sense of this puzzle?

Even though our standard interpretive practice is to work consecutively through the text, there are advantages, right now, to looking ahead briefly to the end of Book 10. The initial hypothesis of the Athenian's account involves three basic categories, the young atheists (YA), the deists (D), and the bribers (B). The larger, nonatheistic (885d–e) group of the "impious" should be disaggregated; in fact, each of the three subcategories is psychologically and intellectually distinct. Intriguingly, despite the existence of the three basic groups, the impious introduce themselves by referring to only two meaningful subgroups. They ask to be persuaded of only two things: that the gods exist and that they have too much integrity to be bribed. A certain portion

---

22. Kleinias and the Athenian now turn, once again, to working out ways to respond to these corrupters of the young (cf. 890b), who, the Athenian says, have been "getting ready for a long time now" (890b4). A very strange ground has been prepared, as though Sedley's "atheistic underground" has somehow turned up in Magnesia, like an alien invasion, and begun to corrupt the youth, Socrates-style. For readers, needless to say, the Athenian's provisions throughout the work imply that what is required for the stable rule of law is the ostracism of Socrates from the city (cf. Rowe 2003). Free speech about philosophical topics cannot exist in its promiscuously Socratic form; rather, if philosophy is to exist in Magnesia at all, then it has to become an activity (reminiscent of questioning the law, or the third Dionysiac chorus) that takes place far from public view. Strangely, however, the Athenian publicizes the debate and thereby makes impious views available, in the prelude itself, to the entire city.

of the larger impious group, they say, having listened to the learned poets and leaders of the city, habitually decides to violate the laws in the belief that "we" can make amends afterward (885d). These "others" are opposed to the young atheists, and they are "most of us" (*hoi pleistoi*, 885d). Seemingly, then, we are first confronted with the atheists and the bribers; mysteriously, the deists do not figure in this self-presentation and do not seem important, even though the Athenian had just mentioned them (885b). Either way, according to this initial account,[23] most of the impious are bribers who, having listened to traditional accounts of the gods, seek unjust gain but want to avoid punishment in the afterlife. Hence, the "B" category is larger than the other two, even larger than the other two combined; B is equivalent to "most of us," and must therefore be greater than YA + D, perhaps by a great distance.

In his first address to the three groups (888a–d), the Athenian, too, subdivides the group of the impious in a way that adds a new idea. He sees that the atheistic "faction" is younger and more curious than the others: while many young people have been tempted by atheism in adolescence, he says, no one remains an atheist during senescence. By contrast, the deists and the bribers could conceivably be older people as well as younger people, since the beliefs of deists and bribers do survive into old age (888a–c). The deists, in fact, seem generally to be older, because they are depicted as looking back over their lives as a whole, and (for example) at others' grandchildren, and growing indignant at the worldly success of the unjust (899e–900b). When compared to the young atheists, therefore, the deists and the bribers hold qualitatively different sorts of beliefs and deserve a different response from the Athenian. The atheists are a small group of young people genuinely interested in the abstract philosophical issues they raise; the others, by contrast, have no philosophical interests. They preoccupy themselves with the apparent injustice of worldly success and failure or with satisfying their materialistic greed or other worldly desires. In accordance with the Athenian's discussion of the causes of faults in Book 9 (863b–864c), these three groups would seem to fall into two different categories of motivation defined by either "ignorance" (in the case of the young atheists) or (chiefly "epithumetic," but also "thumoeidetic") "passion" (in the case of the deists and bribers).[24]

---

23. Note that this initial account is presented by the young atheist, not by the other two types. The bribers, in particular, have no desire to be persuaded.

24. Insofar as the deists are indignant or angry, of course, they may also be characterized as thumoeidetic.

The Athenian further complicates matters, however, toward the end of Book 10. He suggests that while there are three "causes" (*aitiais . . . trisin*) of crimes of impiety, each cause gives rise to two kinds (908a–b, cf. 908e). As a result, it is worth distinguishing six types of "faults" (cf. *examartanontôn*, 908b3; cf. 908e and the similar vocabulary at 863c, 864b); the Athenian bifurcates the three initial categories of "the impious."[25]

The Athenian elaborates this bifurcation in detail only with reference to the young atheists (908b–908e), adding only as an afterthought that it is possible, likewise, to divide the deists and the bribers into two subcategories apiece (908e). Within the category of the young atheists, he explains, one part is characterized by frank speech, has a naturally just character, and is educable (let us call him YA[1]), while the other part is deceptive, beastly, tyrannical, and ineducable (let us call him YA[2]; 908b–e, 909a–b; the chart illustrates the Athenian's bifurcation of young atheists, deists, and bribers).[26]

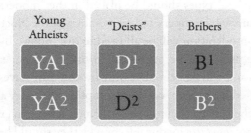

In exploring the crime of impiety, the Athenian initially hypothesizes three basic categories of lawbreaker, whom I call atheists, deists, and bribers (see pp. 243). Late in Book 10 (908a-e), however, the Athenian bifurcates these three categories. Within the category of the young atheists, he explains, one part is characterized by frank speech, has a naturally just character, and is educable (I call him YA[1]), while the other part is deceptive, beastly, tyrannical, and ineducable (I call him YA[2]; 908b-e, 909a-b). The Athenian's description shows that B[1] and D[2] probably do not exist; YA[1] is the tiny group of naturally just "young atheists" or future philosophers; and B[2] represents the large group of bribers (885d-e; see pp. 243–44). The members of YA[2] are defined more by their bad characters than by their theological beliefs. Hence, in short:

Superscript 1 = naturally just
Superscript 2 = tyrannical types, sophists, connivers
B[1] and D[2] = probably do not exist
B[2] = very large
YA[1] = very small

25. Lewis 1998: 4 is one of the few discussions of this important passage, but Lewis's conclusions differ from mine; cf. also Stalley 1983: 177–78; Zuckert 2009: 128–29; Strauss 1975: 155–56; Benardete 2000: 311–12; Saunders 1991: 306–9.

26. By contrast, for example, Schofield 2006: 323, while recognizing three different possible views, argues that the "primary audience" of the Athenian's arguments is "young people." Bobonich 2002: 102–4 and Mayhew 2010: 59–61 (though compare the fuller treatment in

The Athenian sheds light on this bifurcation in the course of specifying the punishments appropriate to each: certain atheists become criminals, he says, because of "ignorance" (*anoias*), without "a harshly angry character" (*aneu kakês orgês te kai êthous*, 908e7), while others become "beastly" (*thêriôdeis*) out of greed, acting "for the sake of money" (*chrêmatôn charin*, 909a–b), or, as the Athenian had said, "afflicted by self-indulgence in regard to pleasures and pains" (908c). These twin motivations—ignorance and materialistic self-indulgence—were the twin motivations examined in the Athenian's initial presentation of the motivations of the impious (886a–b). Here, at least, the Athenian says clearly that certain atheists are motivated by ignorance alone, without destructive and antisocial passions, while others are motivated by unrestrained materialistic desires.[27] Attentive readers have been prepared for this distinction, along with its important consequences, since the Athenian's discussion of the Socratic paradox and the three causes of faults in Book 9.

These two different types deserve different punishments, based on their educability. The "naturally just" types should be placed in the "moderation-tank," the Athenian says, and will be supervised by members of the Nocturnal Council. Those who learn moderation will be allowed to live (909a). By contrast, the "beastly" will be placed in the prison called *timôria* ("vengeance," 908a), out in the country, and will be kept alive only by domestic slaves. The city will not attempt to re-educate them, on the assumption that they are ineducable (909a–c). As in the general prelude, the Athenian refuses to explain why those ruled by desire are *ipso facto* ineducable, or why they should be held responsible for psychological evils that they did not knowingly choose. They suffer serious punishment, seemingly for the sake of the city's welfare, instead of justice (909c). The Athenian does, after all, choose the harsh punishments that he associates with the tyrannical legislator of Book 5, in order to cull the "hard nuts" from his citizenry.

One key question, mostly ignored by scholars, is the following: Why does the Athenian wait so long to introduce this refinement in his conception of the three categories? Why does he mention this seemingly critical division among criminals so casually and so briefly, without returning to it, or even

---

Mayhew 2008), tend to ignore the different characters of these subgroups and assimilate them all to the "young atheist."

27. He does not comment on whether unrestrained materialistic desires should themselves be considered an outgrowth, or a form, of ignorance, but those who act on such desires will not, at all events, be characterized by a principled and "naturally just" ignorance. The Athenian's vocabulary of "cause," "fault," "ignorance," and "character" again precisely matches that of the official account of justice and responsibility in Book 9.

making much of it? Moreover, why does the Athenian emphasize the subdivision of the young atheists' group? Why does he virtually ignore that of the deists and bribers?[28]

Earlier, the Athenian had presented YA ambiguously. YA had come to sight as a group of mocking critics of the city's civic religion (885c). Yet they sincerely wanted to hear the truth from the Athenian (885e) and lawfully insisted that they should be persuaded rather than commanded by the lawgiver (885d). It is as though they had carefully internalized the Athenian's lessons about the free and slave doctors. Even so, at 888a, the Athenian mentions that it wouldn't be right for both the young atheists and the legislators to be "mad" (*manênai*) at the same time, some out of "gluttony for pleasure" (*hupo laimargias hêdonês*) and some from anger at them. At that early stage of the discussion, the young atheists seem to be both frank-speaking and intellectually curious and yet also (at least in certain cases) motivated by a "gluttony for pleasure."

According to the later bifurcation, however, these ambiguities are resolved. Certain young atheists are frank-speaking and just by nature. They "hate injustice," "will not be drawn into doing such deeds," "flee whichever human beings are unjust" and "love just men" (908b–c). By extension, they will *not* be driven by "gluttony for pleasure"—which is, as we saw, the very definition of injustice according to the Athenian (863e). They have genuine intellectual interests; they are not deceptive but, rather, honest; they allow their doubts to show and do not concern themselves with cultivating a fraudulent reputation for good character, if it involves a loss of their own intellectual integrity. It is this frank-speaking, curious subgroup of young atheists that launches the original line of questioning at the beginning of Book 10.

Others, by contrast, lack self-mastery specifically with regard to pleasure and pain (908c); they *are* afflicted by "gluttony for pleasure." The honest atheists ridicule others, while one of the chief characteristics of the dishonest atheists is their deceptiveness, which makes them even more harmful to others (908c–d). The Athenian says that they are connivers, full of tricks: "From this type come many seers and experts in every kind of magic, and sometimes tyrants, demagogues, and generals, and conspirators with their own private mystery-rites, and the contrivances of those called sophists" (908d). They also manipulate the people's religious beliefs for the sake of their private gain (908d, 909b). They are not intellectually curious but, rather, greedy and

---

28. It is an interesting question—which I will leave to one side—why scholars have tended to ignore this passage or, when they take note of it, to refrain from pursuing its numerous implications.

ambitious. They are insincere enough to manipulate others' belief in the gods, even though they are atheists, in order to pursue material gain, status, and power. This subgroup consists of adults; they are no longer "young" atheists, but rather, fully grown men who lack intellectual curiosity and whose formidable intellects are put to entirely instrumental purposes, such as acquiring wealth, deceiving others, and obtaining political power. They are not—and perhaps have never been—characterized by curiosity, honest intellectual interest, and openness to argumentation. At least by the time they have reached adulthood, they would not have openly expressed the philosophical questions raised by the young atheists at the beginning of Book 10, because they are deceptive and lack curiosity. They want to remain hidden from the law. They are beastly types driven by their exaggerated desires; they embody "injustice" according to the Athenian's discussion of the penal code in Book 9 (863e–864a).

Without stating his point explicitly, the Athenian is alluding to Plato's *Republic* in these passages. As readers of the *Republic* are aware, Socrates expresses concern over the city's corruption of young philosophical natures; those with philosophical natures and talents can be drawn to philosophy, as one hopes, or led astray, like Alcibiades and others, into the conventional ambitions of the city (494c–495c). In the *Laws*, the young, philosophical natures—who differ from the other two subtypes by virtue of their intellectual curiosity, along with their "powerful memories and sharp capacities to learn" (*mnêmai te ischurai kai mathêseis oxeiai*, 908c)—arrive at a fork in the road when they are adolescents that is similar to the one described in Plato's *Republic*.[29] Either they will be well educated or they will be "afflicted" by *akrasia* regarding pleasure and pain; they become either philosophers or tyrants. Obviously, young atheists who become tyrants, demagogues,

---

29. As we will see further in chapter 11, this description links the young atheists to the young, budding philosophers of the *Republic*, and to the younger associates of the Nocturnal Council. On the younger associates' "sharpness" of soul (*oxutêtas . . . echontas*) in particular, compare *Laws* 964e3–4 with *Republic* 503b–c, where Socrates discusses "keenness" along with good memory and facility in learning (the young philosophers are *eumatheis kai mnêmones kai anchinoi kai oxeis*, 503c2). Note also that the Athenian stresses the younger associates' strong memories (964e–965a). As we saw in our exploration of Book 4, moreover, the true lawgiver wisely (we are told) prays for a "tyrannized city" and a young tyrant with a "tyrannized soul," who has a strong memory, is quick to learn, and is courageous and magnificent by nature, as well as "moderate" (709e–710c). These passages are clearly linked, through these verbal echoes, to the description of the naturally just young atheist. Benardete 2000: 311 is the only interpreter I have seen who points (albeit briefly and allusively) to this connection, in writing that "the virtuous atheist seems to be one of the junior members of the nocturnal council."

and sophists become old atheists—but the Athenian is no longer interested in them, because their salient characteristic is no longer atheism, but "beastliness."[30]

On these grounds, we can make certain inferences about the young atheists. First, the young atheist who is hypothetically speaking at 885c falls logically into the frank-speaking category (YA^1); or else why would he, as a conniver, risk challenging the Athenian to an open discussion about materialism and the gods? Second, the atheism of the other members of the YA category (that is, YA^2) is much less important than their bad character. The members of YA^2 are more similar to the members of B^2 than to those of YA^1, in that citizens who belong to category YA^2 also develop an instrumental relationship to religion; they distort others' religious beliefs so as to serve their own exaggerated and harmful desires. Third, YA^1 will hate YA^2 as soon as they perceive the nature of their character; the young atheists "hate injustice." Finally, the "young atheists" to whom the Athenian addresses the first argument belong to YA^1. No one else would care about it. Since the other atheists are not motivated by atheism per se but rather by *pleonexia*, they have little reason to listen to the first argument, nor would they be persuaded, somehow, to give up their self-indulgence by such an argument. Conversely, from the Athenian's perspective, since they are "beastly" types already, there is no hope of converting them to theism, after all. They belong in *timôria*.

Recruiting the Young Atheists

Why did the Athenian introduce these apparently significant distinctions only at the end of Book 10?[31] Certainly, it would have been clearer and more intelligible if he had explained at the outset that certain young atheists (YA^1) were actually honest, just, and good-natured. He could have said clearly that he was really aiming at those tyrannically minded citizens who either hope to bribe the gods or misuse religion to satisfy their own desires for pleasure. The Athenian confused these issues, however, and deliberately encouraged Kleinias, and even readers, to conflate the two types of "materialism"

---

30. There are, of course, old atheists: the traditional poets, the conventional wise men and sages, and so on; cf. also 889e–890a: there are teachers who lead the youth astray. They appear to have been working their "magic" for a long time (890b). The Athenian has obviously had many conversations with such "teachers" and "wise men," as his learned argument in Book 10 amply reveals (and as he himself indicates at the dialogue's conclusion: 968b).

31. This section develops suggestions by Pangle 1980: 503–4 and Lewis 1998: 4–5, but I take the material in a different direction.

(philosophical and pleonectic) along with the different motivations for impiety. Many scholars have ignored the Athenian's refinement of the central categories at the end of Book 10; a better approach is to seek an explanation for these oddities and obscurities.

Where could a young atheist have steeped himself in sophistical, materialist theories within the confines of Magnesia? How he could have adopted views about nature and force resembling those of figures such as Callicles and Thrasymachus? Did he go to the library to read Plato's dialogues? No. The only possible answer is that the hypothetical young atheist—or any potential young atheist who might appear in the future Magnesia—was exposed to such ideas only by the Athenian himself, in this very conversation. In the future, let us say, a young, intellectually curious Magnesian might be inspired by this hypothetical conversation to investigate scientific and philosophical questions for himself, in ways that manifestly contradict the city's teachings (readers will recall, of course, that the Athenian has specified that educators will use this very conversation as a teaching tool: 811c–e). The Athenian is relying on the probability that most citizens will not understand or be interested in such discussions. Most ordinary citizens will be either already convinced, like Kleinias, or willing to accept the written laws as the final and authoritative word on the issue, since this prelude is, in Kleinias' mind, and as he says, not only wholly adequate (899d), but also "wholly fixed" (891a).

Readers will bear in mind that the Athenian is merely offering a prelude to the law on impiety; he is not actually setting off, in a spirit of urgency, to round up young atheists in order to imprison and indoctrinate them. In offering his prelude, he dramatizes certain conversations with this "young atheist." He emphasizes that until the young atheist understands things more clearly, he should not dare in the meantime "to commit any impiety concerning the gods" (888d). In the drama that the Athenian stages, to be sure, the hypothetical young atheist has already publicly raised questions about the city's religion. Readers should, however, imagine what the prelude, with its emotionally charged drama, would be communicating to future Magnesian citizens. We already know what it communicates to citizens with philosophical "talents" that match those of Kleinias. By contrast, the Athenian is emphasizing to talented adolescents with nascent philosophical interests the necessity of refraining from publicly diminishing the city's religiously informed law code. What should they do instead? The Athenian says that they should "examine (*anaskopôn*) whether things are this way or otherwise, learning by inquiry both from others and in particular from the lawgiver; and during this time, do not dare to commit any impiety concerning the gods. For the one who is legislating for you must try, now and in the future, to teach you how these very things stand (888c–d; on the important "philosophical" term *skepsis*, see also 968b: the Athenian is a veteran of many such discussions). Instead of going to prison in order to receive a philosophical education, they are encouraged to raise questions with the "lawgiver." Absent the actual lawgiver, the young philosopher will need, privately of course, to consult the lawgiver's surrogates—namely, the philosophers of the Nocturnal Council.

How will such an education come about in the regimented environment of Magnesia? The Athenian intentionally likens his speech to Socrates' own *apologia*, as represented by Plato (886e–887a). He strengthens the comparison by referring to a dialogue with the young atheist, within his *apologia* (888a). Unlike Meletus in Plato's *Apology*, however, the young atheist does not respond in Book 10. At the end of the first argument, he is hypothetically invited to respond, but he is not given the chance to do so; Kleinias intervenes in order to declare that the argument is finished (899c–d). As in Book 7 (see chapter 12, "The 'Truest Tragedy'"), the Athenian indicates the provisionality of his own arguments and invites the possibility of further conversation about them (899c–d), whereas Kleinias accepts his arguments as a final and definitive statement of the truth. The conversation with the young atheist will have to take place elsewhere, in Kleinias' absence. The Athenian had mentioned the difficulty of following such arguments when they are spoken to "crowds" (*eis plêthê*, 890e).[32]

Intriguingly, if we allow ourselves to imagine that the Athenian is not anxiously and angrily condemning the "young atheists," but rather, cultivating them,[33] then we can see that he also depicts such a conversation happening in private. Right before the reader's eyes, the Athenian is speaking to those with unconventional ideas. He is speaking among "the impious" (886e)—a conceit that readers should take literally. He provides cover for his conversation with them by adopting a stance of vehement indignation. He persuades the elderly Dorians that he will hold his conversation across the "river," so that those nonphilosophical old men can remain in safety (892d–893a). Imagine the Athenian leading a youth astray, alone, across the river where the Dorians

---

32. Here is an obvious allusion to an important point made by Socrates in Plato's *Gorgias*: cf. *Gorgias* 452e, 455a, 459a–c, 471e–472c.

33. He does so in a highly particular, not to say peculiar, way, by provoking us to think of the atheistic challenge as a homeopathic cure for atheism (885c–e; cf. Benardete 2000: 285: "The inoculation against atheism has to incorporate the virus of atheism"; cf. Pangle 1976: 1065 for their "common ground" with the Athenian).

cannot hear the ensuing conversation. The Athenian says, indeed, that the argument itself is the river (892e). Even when it is spoken openly before them, the Dorians cannot handle it or understand it, because it is so dizzying and unfamiliar; they should be left in safety, while the Athenian conducts the questioning, apart from them (893a). He is displaying how a private philosophical conversation can take place, even in Magnesia, between a lawgiver and a young person of philosophical ability and interest, in the absence of, or over the heads of, his well-meaning, dogmatic, fearful, touchy, and thumoeidetic fellow citizens. The Athenian's way of stage-managing the conversation provides a protective carapace for the philosophical discussion that links it tightly to the city's purposes and beliefs. He thereby convinces Kleinias and Megillus that any philosophical threats to the city will be contained. In the process he teaches the young atheist how an argument in support of the gods and against the materialists can be mobilized so as to benefit the city without endangering the possibility of philosophy within it.

Implicitly, at least, the Athenian thereby pinpoints a special feature of Magnesian social life, one that is absent from the "virtuously ignorant" Dorian regimes. Early in the work, the Athenian had criticized the Dorians for treating all their young alike, "like a herd of grazing colts. None of you takes his own colt and drags him apart from his fellow grazers, despite his anger and vexation" (666e). The Athenian perceives a need, unmet by the Dorian lawgivers, to educate certain young individuals in private: "You don't give him a private groom or train him by rubbing him down and soothing (*hêmerôn*) him, giving him everything that is fitting for child rearing" (666e).[34] The consequences of this failure are enormous, because only such a private grooming will make the young man "not only a good soldier but even a man able to manage a city and its towns" (666e–667a). Early in the work, the image of the wild, complaining colt is hardly explained; in Book 10, however, its meaning becomes clearer. The colt is the young atheist. The Athenian takes him apart in order to offer him a special education—one that will turn him into a complete human being, "soothing" or "taming" him appropriately (cf. 890c), and developing his capacities, so that he will understand the appropriate order of the virtues (667a), both in the individual and the city. He has to be taught, not only how to do philosophy well, but also how to speak moderately with other, nonphilosophical citizens, who will remain soldiers, just as the Athenian Stranger is doing in the text itself. The Athenian has found a

---

34. On "soothing" the colt, compare the Athenian's linguistically connected desire to "soothe" or "tame" (*hêmeroun*) the young atheist at 890c8; see also the similar language of the "free doctor" passage at 718d, 720d.

way to "corrupt" the youth without destabilizing the city—indeed, in a way that is positively agreeable to the city.[35]

At the same time, if we understand the character of the young atheists as the Athenian does, and if we keep in mind the provisionality of his conclusions, then his way of presenting the discussion is also designed, implicitly and even surreptitiously, to elaborate the possibility that a Socratic way of life may—despite appearances to the contrary—still be possible within Magnesia itself, among the philosophical elite of the Nocturnal Council. The Athenian has recognized, as the Platonic Socrates often did not, that convincing ordinary citizens of the goodness, or even greatness, of the philosophical life requires, not an intellectual argument or dialectical exchange, but instead the more delicate and oblique, and nonphilosophical, approach that he (successfully: e.g., 969c–d) adopts with Kleinias and Megillus. It is possible, after all, to recruit and cultivate young philosophers without distressing their parents or the city's authorities.

This interpretation, though unconventional, helps to resolve another long-standing problem in the interpretation of the dialogue's final books. As we have seen, the Athenian does not explain how philosophers—those of the Nocturnal Council, for example—are to be chosen and trained. Late in Book 12 (968b), the Athenian says merely that a roster of candidates for philosophical education will have to be drawn up. We now have an explanation of how they will be recruited. They will be "tested" (cf. 735a with 751c) by their attraction to this very conversation and by their courageous willingness to persist in questioning the authorities. Once Magnesia has reached its fully developed form, readers are encouraged to imagine, the senior members of the Nocturnal Council will draw on these naturally just young atheists in order to recruit them, at the appropriate age, as the "younger associates" of the Nocturnal Council (951e, 961a–b); that is the significance of the verbal echoes that we have discussed, among varying texts and passages (Plato's *Republic*, along with *Laws* Books 4, 10, and 12). Perhaps, by recruiting younger citizens of talent and philosophical interest, the Athenian has devised a way not only to avoid distressing their parents, but also even to make them proud: the younger associates of the Nocturnal Council are especially honored by the city (952a–b). They are, moreover, on track to become the city's magistrates

---

35. The Athenian's supposed *thumos* toward the young atheist is therefore the ally of reason (as seasoned interpreters of Plato's *Republic* will recognize). In the drama with the young atheist, his presumed anger exists in order to produce order and to defend the city, its theology, and the philosophers.

and leaders. As we saw in elaborating the image of the "colt," the young atheist will become "not only a good soldier but even a man able to manage a city and its towns" (666e–667a). In developing the figure of the "young atheist," and in providing for the appropriate education of him, the Athenian is referring, surreptitiously of course, to the creation of a ruling philosophical class.

Conclusion: Deists and Bribers in Book 10

The Athenian's eventual refinement of his categories has a substantial impact on our understanding of the deists and the bribers, too. He offers certain clues about the provenance and character of the deists at the beginning of his second argument (899d–900c). He represents them sympathetically, as individuals possessed of a certain kinship to the divine. That kinship encourages them to believe in the gods' existence as such, whatever else they might hear or experience (the Athenian makes no such statement about the bribers, even though they, too, *ex hypothesi*, believe in the gods' existence). They want to believe in the gods; they want to believe, per the city's religion, that the just will be rewarded and criminals justly punished. The deists have become disaffected when they observe the good fortune of unjust people. Particularly disheartening is the spectacle of those unjust yet successful people who come to the end of life and leave behind children who enjoy high status (899d–e). Instead of questioning the existence of the gods or holding the gods responsible for injustice, however, the disappointed deists conclude that the gods neglect human beings as a matter of course. When they fail to reconcile their observations with the city's public teachings, their experience weighs more heavily in the balance than what conventional, misguided poets may have taught them. Even though the deists sound like old, sad individuals, the Athenian is still addressing a young man, he says (900c, 904e). Nonetheless, this young man is not a radical or curious individual; and the Athenian could equally be addressing an older man, since deistic opinions survive, as he has said (888c), into old age. Such opinions do not derive from a questioning spirit, but rather from a soul that has imbibed the city's teachings willingly and then become disillusioned when those teachings fail, on observation, to match up correctly to the varying earthly fortunes of the just and the unjust.

Perhaps the deist resembles Adeimantus or the characters that Adeimantus conjures up, who are tempted by the thought that the gods neglect humanity (*Rep.* 365d). These people are confused and ultimately disappointed by the ambiguities of the accounts offered by poets, priests, and the city's other authorities (*Rep.* 366a–d). Unlike Adeimantus' hypothetical figures in the

Republic, however, the deists are not driven by a frenzy of desires. They actually want to believe in the gods. As ordinary, disaffected citizens of Magnesia itself, the deists tend to be disappointed, and perhaps indignant, rather than pleonectic or tyrannical. That is why, I would suggest, they seem to have dropped out of the impious men's initial presentation (885d–e), which stresses unjust, acquisitive activities. The Athenian simply wants to help them avoid deteriorating into a more dangerous condition of impiety (900b). It is the possibility of unjust, tyrannical drives that truly riles up Kleinias, who perceives such drives to be the underlying motivation for all the beliefs of the impious (886a–b). Except for a vanishingly small number, then, D^2 (the category of greedy, tyrannically minded deists) will not exist, since its presumptive members do not fit the description of deists that the Athenian offers. As a result, most (if not all) deists should end up in the moderation-tank in order to receive further instruction in theodicy, in accordance with the city's religion. Since they have a nature that resembles that of the gods, most of them will have a "naturally" just character that has not thrived, nevertheless, in the course of their lives thus far. But they can perhaps be re-educated. In that case, however, does the deist need to learn moderation? Not in respect of his appetites, the Athenian indicates, but rather only in respect of his outspoken public speech, which may be based on indignation about the injustices he perceives. He needs to stop complaining publicly, perhaps through learning, if he can, why the just life is the happy life, despite the apparent exceptions to that principle. These complainers pose a less serious threat to the city's political stability than the others, even if they may at times encourage a lack of respect for the city's religious teachings.

In short, then, the deist is the disillusioned individual who has subscribed to the city's eudaimonism but come to see that the unjust may still enjoy conventional happiness. More than the other types, then, the deist raises questions that take us back to the central controversy of Book 2: Which life is happier, that of justice or of pleasure-seeking? He provides the Athenian with an opportunity to address that question once again, but now in a newly religious register. Perhaps, after all, the "god" will give Kleinias and the Athenian consonance in Book 10; that will be our focus in the next chapter.

The psychology of the bribers is the most straightforward of the three. Bribers are ordinary lawbreakers and acquisitive people, such as those evoked by Adeimantus in Plato's *Republic*, who uses similar language and concepts (cf. *Republic* 365c–366d). They simply want to live the materialistically blissful life of the tyrant without being punished in the afterlife. Traditional religion licenses that very possibility. They are unlikely to arrive at this position solely as an intellectual stance; they are motivated by acquisitiveness, not intellectual curiosity. They are not even atheists; they believe in gods who can be bribed. They deserve, and receive, their own argument from the Athenian—the final argument of the prelude in Book 10. They are hardly likely to care about the first argument, much less to be persuaded by it to change their behavior. They rationalize their behavior and reassure themselves that their ill-gotten gains can be used, later in life, to bribe the gods. Especially when we recognize that the bribers can be older men, too, they will remind the reader of the wealthy but superficial Cephalus, who departs the conversation of *Republic* Book 1 in order to sacrifice to the gods, in hopes of making amends for his own lack of interest in justice throughout his life, and out of fear of his impending death (*Rep.* 330d–e, 331a–b, 331d).

By describing them as he does, however, the Athenian creates the strong suspicion that most bribers will end up in *timôria*, because they are "beastly" (as Cephalus is not). In fact, despite his nominal acknowledgment of the category (908e), his description leaves vanishingly little room for B^1, that is, just and good-natured bribers. If individuals are just, good-natured, and disposed to flee the wicked, then why would they need to bribe the gods at all? Bribers, then, will tend to be outlaws, not so much because of any special beliefs about the gods, but rather, because of their lawless and riotous desires. This characterization should figure into our understanding of the Athenian's final argument in Book 10: as the harshest and most vehement of the arguments, it exists in order to frighten and dissuade the unjust, and to find a place for Kleinias in fighting injustice. The Athenian is much less interested in offering serious arguments to the effect that the gods are genuinely the caring watchdogs of humanity. The bribers need to be addressed at a different level.

The Athenian links both deists and bribers to the large themes of the work as a whole. They provide a vehicle for him to reconsider the question of justice and pleasure and to reignite Kleinias' thumoeidetic energies in fighting injustice. His characterization of both deists and bribers will remain important as we turn to consider his three substantive arguments in the next chapter.

10

The Athenian's Theology, Part II

IN BOOK 2, the Athenian elicits from Kleinias a confession of the tyrannical desires that have arisen amid the disordered legislation of traditional Greek societies. Lacking an adequate psychological and ethical understanding, Kleinias has come to believe that virtue consists in self-mastery rather than rational order. This ethical belief often inspired individuals, factions, and entire cities to seek mastery over others. So far from ameliorating these difficulties, traditional legislators intensified them: they led their citizens to embrace pleasure as the greatest good, even as they tried, quixotically, to constrain the pursuit of pleasure through laws, social sanctions (such as shame or humiliation), and punishment. They failed to resolve the potential for conflict between the individual and his community; they failed to convince their citizens that virtue is not only good for others, but also good for the virtuous individual. In effect, they taught their citizens, with Thrasymachus, that justice is "another's good."

In Book 2 the Athenian explicitly connects these ethical and political ideas with religious or metaphysical ones.[1] Understanding the depth of the impasse that he and his interlocutors confront, the Athenian suggests that they will come to an agreement if and only if the "god" gives them consonance (662b). Their agreement will be, specifically, that the "the unjust life is not only more shameful and more wicked, but also less pleasant in truth than the just and holy life" (663d). The Athenian has added piety to the arguments offered by Socrates to Glaucon and Adeimantus; unlike Socrates, of course, the Athenian does not make a philosophical case for justice.[2] With his current

---

1. Benardete 2000: 287–88 is one of the few commentators who appreciate this connection; his interpretation differs from, but is mostly compatible with, my own.

2. Strauss 1975.

Tragedy, Philosophy, and Political Education in Plato's Laws. Ryan K. Balot, Oxford University Press.
© Ryan K. Balot 2024. DOI: 10.1093/oso/9780197647226.003.0010

interlocutors, the Athenian gathers that justice cannot stand on its own, however much he himself may believe in its intrinsic goodness and self-sufficiency. The pleasures deriving from a pious life may be, for Kleinias, the source of that life's most immediate attractions; they are at least a starting point from which conventional people may be educated to see things otherwise. All the same, as the Athenian recognizes, embracing justice for the sake of its manifold pleasures is a risky strategy and one that he adopts only in the short term and for Kleinias' sake. It is a strategic distortion—though perhaps a necessary one—of his own rational eudaimonism.

The Athenian's turn to religious or metaphysical ideas is intelligible at two levels. First, he recognizes that, suitably reformulated, religion may be powerful enough to persuade Kleinias (and other conventional people) that justice does, after all, contribute to, or even (partly) constitute, the just man's flourishing. In the ordinary citizen's view, however, justice contributes to the just man's flourishing, not on its own account, but only because the gods make it so. Even that dim level of ethical understanding improves upon the quasi-immoralism with which Kleinias begins.[3] In Book 10, the Athenian makes strides in encouraging Kleinias and those like him to approximate to his own rational eudaimonism. Second, the Athenian discerns that underlying Kleinias' ethics and politics is a set of implicit assumptions about the fundamental character of the world—an ontology, so to speak, which the unphilosophical Dorian does not present explicitly or self-consciously. Kleinias assumes that motion, chaos, and disorder are the fundamental characteristics of the world—both the natural world, with its supposedly wandering planets (821b–c), and the human world, from its anarchic interstate relations down to intrapolis conflict and the warring passions of the individual soul. In order to make his first principle effective—the idea that the god rewards the just, by giving them a good life now and hereafter—the Athenian has to convince citizens that the gods themselves are part of, or even supervisors of, a cosmic order that is not susceptible to the disorderly motions or chaos assumed by Kleinias. To ordinary citizens, any whiff of the materialistic "motion thesis"

---

3. By this stage of this discussion, readers should appreciate that it is not entirely Kleinias' fault that he (and others like him) will be unable to rise higher than a dim level of ethical understanding. Mortal nature (e.g., 731e–732b), traditional communal life (as in the Dorian cities or Persia), and human history (as illustrated in Book 3) are stacked against them. Nature and the gods are not providential in this sense. It is unlikely that most human beings will flourish eudaimonistically. Even so, as human beings, we must do what we can, as the Athenian admonishes citizens (e.g., 727b–c). On these points, cf. Lutz 2012: 139–58.

would—whether the inference is logically entailed or not—appear to license lawbreaking.

Before launching into his discussion, the Athenian mentions that the three men will have to traverse unfamiliar territory. His implicit strategy is to introduce extralegal topics, such as theological arguments, in order to reinforce the elderly men's agreement on the city's law-code. Kleinias urges him on: "I gather that you think we are going outside legislation (*nomothesias ektos*) if we take hold of such arguments" (891d–e); but, he says, if there is no other way to be in consonant agreement (*sumphônêsai*) that the law speaks correctly about the gods, then we must, indeed, proceed this way (891e). He wins Kleinias' full cooperation in that project, as he had done earlier in Book 2, when he proposed that they could proceed to fashion the law-code only on the basis of the god's own gift of "consonant agreement" (*sumphônian*, 662b2). As in Book 2, the Athenian's account of the god enables him to persuade Kleinias that justice contributes, not only to the city's health, but also to his own flourishing. The Athenian turns to these theological arguments because he cannot convince Magnesia's ordinary citizens directly, and on the merits, of the intrinsic goodness of justice. While the young atheist resembles Glaucon and Adeimantus in certain respects, the Athenian's other audience—Kleinias, Megillus, and Magnesia's future citizens—differs markedly from Socrates' audience in Plato's *Republic*.

The First Argument: Questions and Difficulties

By contrast with the ethical focus of Book 2, where god is mentioned in passing alongside civic myths and lies, Book 10 addresses theological questions in the first instance. The Athenian's new rival is, not the lawbreaking tyrant with his ethics of self-aggrandizement, but rather philosophical materialists, who hold that "all things come to be, have come to be, and will come to be, by nature, by art, and by chance" (888e). Kleinias is unfamiliar with such discussions and unable to discern their significance (888e–889a). The Athenian explains that, in the materialists' view, the elements (fire, water, earth, and air) exist by nature and by chance (889b); these in turn produce the heavenly bodies, which have no souls. By means of chance and necessity, rather than intelligence or divinity, the elements are forcibly mixed together to produce not only the heavens, but also animals, plants, and the seasons of the year. The arts (*technai*), a human product, appear later and produce mostly "playthings" (*paidias*, 889d1) that contain little truth—such as painting or music. Other arts, however, such as medicine, farming, and gymnastics, work in tandem with nature to produce "serious" results. The political art shares an inkling of common ground with nature, but for the most part exists solely by means of art. In particular, the enactments of legislation (apparently a subdivision of the political art) are not true, including the gods, who exist by legislative fiat and are therefore presented diversely throughout the world.[4]

This chain of reasoning, the Athenian says, leads to disastrous political consequences. Hence, in response, he argues that the universe is governed by rationally ordered and intelligent "soul" rather than pervaded by random matter in disorderly motion. Most scholars have understood this account as a "metaphysical theology" that underwrites the city's legal code and way of life.[5] On the conventional view, the *Timaeus* provides a philosophical basis for the Athenian's theology, which is a less systematic formulation that suits the dialogue's reduced philosophical ambitions.[6] Schofield, for example, holds that the arguments of *Laws* Book 10 "embody a sense of a transcendent moral framework for political and social existence" and explicate either " 'Plato's theology' " or his "political theology—i.e. that theological system, no doubt seen by him as that true theological system," that will justify Magnesia's political order.[7] Bobonich argues that in order to undergird the city's law code, the Athenian gives in Book 10 "several elaborate

---

4. On Archelaus as the source of these ideas, see most recently Betegh 2016. Mayhew 2008 argues that it is not necessary to identify a specific source, on the grounds that "Plato" is targeting the general "atheistic" movement of natural philosophers.

5. Bobonich 2002: 108. A further step in this direction is Pierris 1998, who speaks of approaching "questions of political philosophy by operating in the field of ontology" (118); cf. also Piérart 1974: 476. Neschke-Hentschke 2001 reads "Plato" as a theorist of natural right and natural law who constitutes a predecessor of Locke, but at the cost of disregarding the Athenian's project of civil religion and of overemphasizing Locke's distance from Hobbes.

6. For a variety of conventional interpretations, see Stalley 1983: 172–75; Bobonich 2002: 101–9, 208, cf. 454–59; O'Meara 2017; Laks 2000: 290–91 argues that that Book 10 represents an "argument based on physical theory to establish the rationality of the universe" and speaks of "the theodicy of Book X." Mayhew 2008: 198 appreciates the need to examine the Book 10 account on its own terms, independent of other dialogues, but his interpretation differs from the one offered here.

7. Schofield 2006: 324–25. I propose that we regard the Athenian's theological effort not as a "political theology," but rather as a "civil religion," i.e. a use and manipulation of religion for political purposes. On civil religion, see Beiner 2010 and, with respect to Plato in particular, Strauss 2004, who illustrates the tradition of interpreting Plato as a civil religion theorist going back to Farabi and Maimonides. Zuckert 2009: 143 is correct to write: "In the Athenian's city philosophy becomes the source of a kind of natural theology that begins to look very much like what modern thinkers call 'ideology,' that is, the use of philosophically derived concepts and arguments to support a specific political order." Cf. also M. Zuckert 2013 on the "political theology" introduced in Book 4.

and philosophically sophisticated arguments for the fundamental theses of Magnesia's theology."[8]

Others see particular difficulties in the Athenian's arguments. First, for those who see *Laws* and *Timaeus* as fundamentally compatible, the Athenian's presentation arguably conflicts with Timaeus' arguments about precosmic motion and evil.[9] Second, and more important, they give rise to puzzles of their own. The Athenian's argument from the "prime mover" (894e–895b) fails to gain traction against a materialist who argues that disorderly motion has always existed.[10] Arguably, in fact, the Athenian attributes to the materialists an account of the origins of motion (889b–c) centered on the capacity of the elements to give rise to "random locomotion which is followed by combination," in which case, soul is unnecessary as an explanation of the origins of motion.[11]

We might add that the Athenian's supposed refutation of the materialists' belief in the dominance of chance and natural necessity fails to take into account the avowed hegemony of chance and necessity in the Athenian's own account of Magnesia's foundation (709a–c).[12] In fact, his presentation of the human arts (sailing, piloting, medicine) in founding Magnesia is reminiscent of the materialists' account of art (cf. 709b–c, 889c–e), in that both are centered on the effort to ameliorate humanity's condition of relative weakness by complementing natural forces in a world dominated by chance. Similarly, the Athenian's account of cosmic order also fails to do justice to his presentation in Book 3 of the dangerous necessities, destruction, and natural disorder with which early humanity was forced to contend.[13] Even beyond the

---

8. Bobonich 2002: 102. Bobonich 2002: 94 argues that in Book 10 "Plato offers a refutation of certain atheists." The basis of this refutation is his conviction that "at the level of the kosmos, god perfectly instantiates reason and orders both bodies and souls so that, as far as possible, their best condition is attained" (Bobonich 2002: 95). Are the second and third arguments also part of the Athenian's "metaphysical theology"? Although they have mostly dropped out of recent discussion, Mayhew 2008: 212 holds that "The gods hear our prayers and generally wish us well." For a helpful critique of these interpretations, see Lutz 2012: 144–58; Zuckert 2009: 125–28. Cf. also Klosko 2006: 247–48, who adds that "Plato's arguments throughout this section are weak and beg various questions at issue" (248); and Stalley 1983: 28–31, 33–34.

9. For discussion and bibliography, see Nightingale 1996.

10. Mohr 1985: 165–70; Pangle 1976: 1074.

11. Parry 2003: 275. For further criticisms, see Strauss 1975: 148–49.

12. Nightingale 1999a reads the two accounts as complementary (though cf. Nightingale 1999a: 319 for acknowledgment of certain tensions or conflicts); whereas I read them as deliberately at odds with one another.

13. Halper 2003, cf. Nightingale 1999a.

question of simple order is that of the gods' care for humanity, the subject of the Athenian's second argument: neither the natural world nor human history, as recounted in Book 3, manifests the providential care attributed by the Athenian to the gods.[14]

Apart from these difficulties, the Athenian also creates doubts about even his more successful arguments. The young atheist, or a reader, might at least wonder, for example, about the soundness of the Athenian's quick inference from the supposedly circular motions of Intelligence to the god's governance of the beautiful revolutions of the heavens (897c–898c). Their doubts may be intensified when the Athenian for the second time poses the question (898c) of which type of soul—the best or its opposite—supervises the heavens, to which Kleinias responds that piety permits only one answer (898c). If we imagine a young atheist listening to the arguments, then we can also imagine him raising his own questions—which, in the first, most philosophically rich argument, Kleinias' aggressive piety prevents him from doing, even when the Athenian invites the young atheist's questions (899b–d). At a minimum, this sequence of exchanges may inspire doubts about whether a preexisting, unjustified piety can possibly legitimate the final, central inference to divine management of the heavenly bodies.[15]

On the other hand, the Athenian's argument is far from daft; indeed, it *has* to be successful enough to intrigue the young atheist, and even to form the basis of a philosophically exciting conversation with him.[16] If the young atheist is one of the Athenian's audiences in Book 10, then the Athenian wants to suggest that philosophical discussion is exciting and worth pursuing. He is a hunter of young people by means of philosophical

---

14. In an interpretation that complements my own, Halper 2003: 258–63 also offers several reasons for eschewing a literal reading of the Athenian's three arguments. He focuses on the difficulties raised by the Athenian's particular characterization of soul as self-moving motion, which, in the context of an exhaustive list of types of motion, arguably implies that "soul cannot be moved by another" (259). Hence, Halper asks, how can the gods be thought to provide care, reward, or punishment to souls that cannot be moved by another? How can the gods (as souls) be moved by either our gifts or our virtue? If the gods genuinely care for humanity, then why do certain individuals still question their existence?

15. It is striking that recent scholars of the dialogue, such as Bobonich 2002 and Schofield 2006, have paid so little attention to the actual arguments of Book 10, their progression, and their interconnections; Brisson 1998; Mayhew 2008, 2010; Benardete 2000; and Lutz 2012 are exceptions.

16. Pangle 1976 helps to make clear the twofold audience of Book 10—concerned citizens and potential philosophers—the latter of whom will be curious about the gaps and ambiguities in his argument and presumably wish to follow them up in further philosophical discussion.

friendship (cf. 823b). If significant philosophical difficulties hamper the Athenian's discussion, however, then how would his seduction of the young atheist take place?

Conceivably, at least, behind the Athenian's presentation may lie a Eudoxan, mathematical theory of the circular revolution of the heavens, an idea that pervades other Platonic dialogues.[17] Indeed, perhaps alluding to this idea, the Athenian later refers to the exquisite ordering of the heavens, which can be understood mathematically (967b). Although he does not initially confront the young atheist with those further arguments, the young person may well inquire into the deeper basis of the philosopher's apparent convictions about heavenly motion. Then, if he encounters these additional speculations, he may recall the Athenian's provocative discussion of incommensurable magnitudes (819c–820d). That mathematical difficulty appears to cast doubt on any simplistic belief in the proportionate, beautiful, and readily intelligible mathematical order that supposedly pervades the heavens (see Pesic 2003). If the Eudoxan theory gives evidence of a rationality that penetrates nature, then does the discovery of incommensurable magnitudes give evidence to the contrary—that irrationality, after all, is the ultimate driver of nature's workings?

However the case may stand, the Athenian has not banished doubt about the existence of rational or providential gods. To the contrary, his arguments have also created further reasons for doubt, inquiry, and speculation on such matters.[18] To be sure, his attempt to prove the existence of god is ambitious,

---

17. Morrow 1960: 482; Bobonich 2002: 108–9.

18. A young atheist may have in mind many other questions that grow out of the Athenian's account. For example, why does the Athenian believe it necessary to argue (896e) for the existence of at least two souls, embodiments of good and evil, rather than, like Augustine and many others, for one God, and why does he refuse to explain the existence of evil otherwise, for example as a deficiency of goodness (cf. Pangle 1976: 1076)? Why is evil not, as in the *Timaeus*, the result of "spontaneously moving matter" (Halper 2003: 259–60n5)? Does the Athenian believe that soul is responsible for the very existence of matter since it is the cause of all things (896d)? But how can soul exist or act in a nonembodied form (cf. Halper 2003: 259n.3; Stalley 1983)? Why is soul incapable of being moved by other things—for example, bodies, as the Athenian often stresses throughout the dialogue in the case of human souls? Finally, as Cleary 2001: 130 (cf. 132) has pointed out, the Athenian introduces confusion in the ordering of the ten types of motion, since "the first motion enumerated (i.e. circular motion around a fixed centre) turns out to be an image of the motion of *Nous*, which itself is prior to soul." What is the significance of that motion's priority to soul's own motion? For further criticism, see Lutz 2012: 145–46; Pangle 1976; Strauss 1975; Mayhew 2008; Stalley 1983: 169–74; Benardete 2000: 299–306.

and any such attempt is liable to be deficient.[19] The Athenian's effort is neither trivial nor hopeless. Rather, the understandable persistence of doubt invites further philosophical discussion between the legislator and the young atheist. Meanwhile, the Athenian's other audience, of Kleinias, Megillus, and Magnesia's ordinary citizens, will be unaware of such doubts. As Kleinias' pious reaction illustrates, ordinary, nonphilosophical citizens will find the Athenian's arguments unquestionably convincing.[20] Hence, while continuing to intrigue talented young people, the Athenian also demonstratively "proves" to the ordinary citizenry that the gods are rational, just, and caring. The city's demonstrably sound belief in such gods can be irrefutably defended, after all, by its own philosophers, i.e., the Nocturnal Council.

Does the Athenian accept his own conclusions as personal articles of theological belief? Most scholars have assumed so. It is less prejudicial, though, to take a minimalist approach. A philosopher of his stature and self-consciousness would be aware of reasons for doubt as well as belief, of arguments for and against his stated position, and of the need to carry on the conversation in the future. He has obviously carried on many such conversations in the past. Even if the Athenian cultivates dogmatic citizens, there is no reason to imagine that he himself is a dogmatist.

Allegorical and Educational Interpretations: The Argument's Impact on Kleinias

In part, at least, the first argument is intended to provide a philosophical invitation, if not education, to the young atheists. To understand the Athenian's purposes in relation to ordinary citizens, though, it is essential to forgo a contentious philosophical interrogation of his position. Instead, we should focus on the argument's impact on Kleinias.[21] He is less attuned to the argument's philosophical strengths and weaknesses, but perhaps correspondingly more sensitive to its symbolic thrust. Even if Kleinias himself cannot (like the

---

19. As Mayhew 2008, 2010 rightly points out. But what is important is to understand why its deficiencies take the shape they do and how the Athenian's particular construction of this argument is responsive to other major themes of the work.

20. Another important question, unasked by Klenias of course, is how the Athenian's astral gods are connected to the traditional gods of the city, on which see Lewis 2010; Abolafia 2015.

21. Lutz 2012: 7 helpfully interprets the Athenian's effort as one of finding "common ground" with Kleinias, in respect of living a virtuous human life.

young atheist) understand the argument clearly, his mind can be changed at
another level by the Athenian's images and general ideas.

Pangle's analysis exemplifies this approach. He interprets the Athenian's
first argument as an allegory of *thumos*. According to Pangle, the Athenian
obscures body's capacity to act upon soul, and thereby emphasizes each
individual's complete responsibility for himself. The Athenian's exhaustive,
quasi-Manichean division of soul into good and evil types then "creates a
cosmos filled with, and moved by, responsible beings engaged in the mighty
moral drama of a universal contest between active good and active evil."[22]
The Athenian's drama of *thumos* encourages thumoeidetic Dorians such as
Kleinias and Megillus to take pride in enforcing the just laws of their city. This
analysis illustrates the first argument's capacity to convey a nonphilosophical
point to Kleinias.

Another interpretation stresses the Athenian's ethical purposes. As Halper
suggests, "The message [of the first argument] is no less clear from being unstated: to the extent possible, we ought to act like the gods and this *imitatio
dei* is possible to us because our souls, like the divine souls, are self-moved and
because they contain the principle of rationality."[23] According to Halper, the
Athenian is arguing for the "dignity of the soul."[24] Soul is independent and
self-determining. In particular, it cannot be forced into motion by the body.
Individuals who acknowledge soul's priority will thereby possess a basis for
making ethical decisions—for example, in prioritizing the soul's good over
corporeal goods.[25]

Both these interpretations help us to see that the Athenian's argument
amplifies points he has been registering throughout the dialogue. On the
one hand, he will be reorienting *thumos* in a less militaristic, more political
direction—a direction oriented to justice and useful to the city. On the other
hand, his emphasis on the priority of soul elaborates his attention to properly honoring, or caring for, the soul. He had stressed that the soul should be
honored above the body and material possessions, since the soul is the possession "that is most one's own (*oikeiotaton*)" (726a–727a). The first argument

---

22. Pangle 1976: 1076.

23. Halper 2003: 264. Cf. also Brill 2013, which, intriguingly, focuses on the therapeutic force
of the Athenian's presentation. Brill 2013: 202 helpfully points out that the "clinical context of
Book 10's account of soul (its occurrence as a prelude and thus as a form of treatment) advises
against assuming that it represents what Plato takes to be true about the soul."

24. Halper 2003: 264.

25. Cleary 2001: 131 anticipates Halper on this point.

of Book 10 deepens the citizens' sense of the priority of soul, by showing that soul comes before body and is its natural ruler. Honoring the soul is essential to living a life that is truly according to nature—a life that will, moreover, enable individuals to find favor with the god by assimilating themselves to him (716c–d).[26]

It is illuminating to interpret the first argument at a mythopoetic level. It inspires the citizens to see things differently, without assuming that they would benefit from a cognitively rich exposition. What the second, ethical approach in particular misses, at least in its current formulation, is an explanation of the context of its central idea, that of *imitatio dei*. In order to make sense of this idea, we have to explore the argument's evolution from materialism to the god's rational ordering of the heavens. Why does the Athenian begin with a debate over materialism and antiquity, only then to move on to an argument for soul as independent and self-moving? What is the significance, in this light, of the culminating idea that human beings should strive to imitate the gods? It is only by appreciating the significance of these questions that we can uncover the full ethical import of the Athenian's presentation of Magnesia's theology.

The Progression from Materialism to Teleology: "First Things" and "Nature"

My own answer to these questions emphasizes the argument's progression from materialism to a teleological understanding of the soul that supports the Athenian's rational eudaimonism. This progression is designed to make manifest, and to contribute to, the ethical and psychological evolution that Kleinias undergoes in the course of the dialogue.[27] Specifically, the Athenian wants to hack away at the "motion thesis," which seems to license injustice and encourage tyrannical aspirations. He aspires to replace that thesis with a teleological conception of the soul that gives a privileged place to *nous* and the ethical virtues as the soul's good, as the realization of its true essence. This progression is the culmination of a project initiated by the Athenian in Books 1–3. From the outset, the Athenian strove to persuade Kleinias to abandon his "materialist" conception of states and souls in favor of an implicitly

---

26. Cf. Halper 2003: 265.

27. Whereas Halper 2003 views it as an education for thoughtful people in general, I see it as much more closely tied to Kleinias' character and development throughout the dialogue.

teleological conception. In Book 10, the Athenian both consolidates and furthers his education of Kleinias along these lines.

While the Athenian offers, in general, an exciting and appealing philosophical argument, his vocabulary, images, and rhetorical strategies also speak directly to Kleinias' own presuppositions. In Book 10 the Athenian's sensitivity to Kleinias' starting points takes the form of a decided focus on antiquity. From the outset of the dialogue, the Athenian builds on his interlocutors' own belief in the significance of antiquity, even though he himself thinks it a great error to equate antiquity with wisdom, goodness, or authority.[28] Reverence for antiquity, all by itself, signifies nothing more than obedience to a frequently mindless tradition. In Book 10, though, the Athenian reverts to his appeal to antiquity because he anticipates that old age will elicit his interlocutors' reflexive respect. He relies on their deep-seated intuitions about antiquity in the present situation, in particular, because he understands how alien and unfamiliar they find theological arguments (891e, 892d–893a).

In focusing the opening stages of his argument on antiquity, the Athenian not only appeals to Kleinias' presuppositions but also implicitly accepts a fundamental premise of his materialist rivals. An important assumption of the materialists' account is that antiquity alone provides a just claim to priority in nature. The appeal to antiquity leads, therefore, to the argument's deepest question—that of the true character of nature. All along, Kleinias has understood that the crux of the argument concerns the status of "nature." He appreciates that somehow the Athenian has to show that law itself either exists by nature or that it is not inferior to nature, as the product of intelligence (890d). The materialists argue that the antiquity of matter gives evidence of its having priority by nature—that it "is by nature" (892b). Their identification of "nature" with what is chronologically first has the consequence that, in their view, nature, in a wider, normative sense, is constituted by the disordered motions of matter. This belief, in turn, appears to license the ruinous normative conclusions drawn by Callicles and others, that the rule of force is our natural destiny, that justice is merely conventional, and that law is nothing more than a mutable product of feckless human arts.

The Athenian takes his stand on precisely the ground that Kleinias shares with the materialists. He argues from the chronological priority of soul to soul's preeminence in nature. Soul, he argues, is "one of the first things,"

---

28. The principle of building on the Dorians' presuppositions is by now well established in interpretation of the dialogue—e.g., Annas 2017, most recently, but the idea is also significant in Pangle 1980; Strauss 1975; and Morrow 1960.

came into being "before all bodies," and "is the ruling cause" (*archei*) of every change and subsequent modification (892a). Hence, according to the argument he will present, "it would be almost completely correct to say that it [soul] is especially by nature" (*schedon orthotata legoit' an einai diapherontôs phusei*, 892c, tr. Pangle 1980, modified). After enumerating the ten types of motion, supposedly an exhaustive list, the Athenian asks which type is "strongest" and "active in a superior way" (894d)—and Kleinias responds that self-moving motion is superior in power "by a very long way" (*muriôi*) and the others are all "later" (*husteras*, 894d). The possibility of construing soul as the *archê* of motion enables the Athenian to equivocate fruitfully on the notions of "beginning" and "rule," so that the eldest "being" can be acknowledged, by virtue of its antiquity alone, as a natural ruler. All the attributes of soul (opinion, intelligence, art, law) are therefore prior to material things, the Athenian argues, with the result that art (*technê*) and intelligence (*nous*) rule over bodies (892b). The Athenian liberally exploits the ambiguities of priority in time, priority in power, and priority in rank throughout the passage, because antiquity already has a claim (whether justified or not) to the elderly Dorians' respect.[29]

If readers were inclined to dispute the Athenian's argument on its own terms, then they might extend the Athenian's own express doubts about antiquity to his initial arguments for the superiority of soul. They might ask, for example, why antiquity, and nothing more, should give normative status to self-moving motion. Indeed, why should even the presumed *power* of self-moving motion give any privileged status to "soul"? Is it true, after all, that soul's "might" somehow grants it the "right" to rule? Moreover, why do the first beginnings of the "beings" constitute the primary basis from which to judge their natures? Why should "nature" in a normative sense derive from beginnings or origins rather than "ends"—that is, the teleological fulfillment of things, which disclose their natures only when they are fully developed?

Even despite these problematic features, however, the Athenian pursues his focus on antiquity. He believes that this argumentative strategy, while philosophically defective, has the best chance of persuading Kleinias to abandon any remaining allegiance, witting or unwitting, to the materialistic outlook. An emphasis on soul's antiquity is likelier than other possible arguments, even philosophically stronger ones, to persuade Kleinias of the natural "priority" of soul. It is striking to observe how much space is taken up by the Athenian's

---

29. On several equivocations in this argument, see Benardete 2000: 299.

arguments to this effect. His argument from antiquity runs from 892a to 896c; his explanation of soul's characteristics and the character of divine soul is considerably shorter (896d–898c), as are his aporetic comments on the sun's motion (898d–899a). He spends a great deal of time leading up to the following preliminary (though highly emphatic) conclusion:

> We would have spoken correctly and authoritatively, then, and in the truest and most complete way, when we said that in our view soul came into existence prior to body, and that body is secondary and later, and that soul rules, while body is ruled, according to nature. (896b–c)

In addition to the argument's length, the proliferation of laudatory adverbs in this conclusion suggests that it is very important that Kleinias should accept the chronological priority of soul and, correspondingly, its priority in other senses. The Athenian is willing to allow Kleinias to conflate chronological priority with priority in rank or authority, because he deems that conflation to be his best hope of convincing Kleinias to abandon materialism and to accept that soul is a naturally ruling power.

Kleinias and the Materialists

Whether self-consciously or not, Kleinias subscribes to the materialists' conception of nature. The starting point is their shared belief in the normative status of chronological priority, of "what comes first." More importantly, though, they emphasize "efficient" causation, the random "pushes" of matter in combination, growth, and dissolution. Whether among the elements or human social groupings, anarchic forces result in combination and dissolution. The only possible "ruling cause of things" is a preponderance of force in nature, which is the equivalent of "power" in the human, social world.

These ideas manifest themselves with evident clarity in Kleinias' understanding of ethics, politics, and interstate relations. The elderly Dorian's ethical and political views originate in the belief that the world, from high to low, from large to small, among states, and within individuals, is constituted by disorder, instability, and even chaos. The world's anarchic character, as Kleinias imagines it, is confirmed by the human history of Book 3. Empirically speaking, the rule of force prevails. This empirical "finding" was transformed into a norm, encapsulated in what the Athenian had called the "fifth title to rule": that "the stronger should rule and the weaker be ruled" (690b4–5). This norm is widespread throughout the animal world and "according to nature, as the Theban Pindar once said" (690b7–8). Kleinias' conception of nature is remarkably compatible with that of the materialists.

At a general level, in fact, Kleinias, the young atheists, and the materialist philosophers all subscribe to a unified world view that extends from politics to ethics and psychology to the "particle physics" of which the cosmos itself is composed. Whether he knows it or not, these are the ideas that Kleinias, as well as the young atheist, has absorbed from "those considered best among the poets, orators, diviners, priests, and thousands upon thousands of others" (885d). It is no wonder that this unified theory should come to seem "compellingly necessary" (690b) to those who live within it, at whatever level of comprehension they can muster. How can these ideas—which are both descriptive and normative, in interlocking ways that are not necessarily logical –be transformed into a healthier approach to ethics and politics (not to mention cosmic or theological speculation)?

The Teleological Character of Divine Soul

Starting in Book 1, the Athenian's ambition is to replace Kleinias' self-destructive ideas with the belief that both soul and city are naturally characterized by governing purposes or ends. Ideally, human beings should aim to uncover natural ends that fulfill the inborn faculties of both cities and souls. Understood properly, these characteristics are not naturally disordered or ranged in violent conflict; rather, they are ranked according to a natural hierarchy. Humanity's teleological fulfillment lies in the achievement of rational order and its associated ethical virtues. In Book 10, the Athenian symbolically represents this rational order by providing images of the naturally beautiful motions of divine soul.

Having successfully led Kleinias to abandon his allegiance to materialism (896c), the Athenian outlines soul's faculties and activity, including its dispositions, wishes, opinions, calculations, memories, and so on (896d). The question is how to set the soul in order: how should its "cords," its many impulses, faculties, and powers, be arranged so as to enable it to achieve its most perfect and healthy condition? The Athenian first acknowledges the existence of two different and opposed kinds of souls (896e)—which give rise to either justice or injustice (896d). In principle, soul may be good or evil. He then persuades Kleinias that in ruling the material world, soul reaches its pinnacle when it "takes as its helper Intelligence (*nous*)—god, in the true sense, for the gods" (*theon orthôs theois*) and "guides all things toward what is correct and happy" (*ortha kai eudaimona paidagôgei panta*, 897b, tr. Pangle

1980, modified).[30] Conversely, when it associates with "ignorance" (*anoiai*), it "produces results which are in every respect the opposite" (897b). Divine soul is "prudent and full of virtue" (897b). Still, the Athenian insists, the question remains: Which type of soul, the divine and virtuous one, or its opposite, is in control of "heaven and earth and the whole circular revolution (*ouranou kai gês kai pasês tês periodou*, 897b)"? Kleinias has little idea how to make progress on this question (897c).

It is worth pausing to consider what the Athenian has and has not demonstrated by this stage. If he has convincingly shown that *nous* is a god for the gods, that certain souls take *nous* as a helper in order to rule providentially, and that divine soul is prudent and virtuous, then he would seem to have demonstrated at a minimum, against the young atheist, that the gods exist. No atheist could accept his characterization of "divine" soul, even if it should (*per impossibile*) turn out that demented rather than rational soul rules the heavens. Rationally ordered and "divine" souls that take *nous* (the god of gods) as a helper exist. If that claim is nothing more than a widely accepted, uncontroversial premise, then the Athenian should have offered it to the young atheist at the outset. Yet he did not. Rather, he proceeds to offer a vivid presentation of the nature, character, and power of divine soul. While the argument is ostensibly about the gods' existence, it actually provides reasons for Kleinias to abandon materialism and to accept a newly teleological conception of the soul. The Athenian's purpose is to provide an attractive paradigm of soul for Kleinias, specifically through images.

The Athenian now proceeds to the question of which soul rules the heavenly bodies. Supposedly, they can resolve the conundrum by looking at the motions of those bodies. Do they move according to the revolutions and calculations of *nous*, or in a demented and disordered way (897c)? The Athenian's argument is that the motions of *nous* are circular, and therefore ordered and regular; demented souls are characterized, by contrast, by disordered and disproportionate motion (898a–b). When the Athenian asks Kleinias, then, whether heavenly bodies are moved around by *nous* or by a demented soul, he responds that the only possible, and pious, answer is that the best soul, the soul with every virtue, drives the heavenly bodies (898c). By means of the Athenian's arguments, images, and analogies, Kleinias is entirely convinced that the gods rule the heavens—even, unwittingly following Thales, that all things are full of gods (899b).

---

30. At 897b2, I follow the manuscripts and Burnet in reading *theon orthôs theois*, as opposed to the Budé editor.

The Athenian's account suggests—certainly without proving—three conclusions. First, he is offering an avowedly teleological conception of the soul, in which the soul (including divine soul) achieves its flourishing condition through following the leadership of *nous* and cultivating the other virtues in its light. As a result, he does offer a response of sorts to those who wondered where "nature" lies: is it in the origins of things or in their ends, their fulfillment as flourishing beings? The nature of soul is revealed only when we consider its fully cultivated condition, a condition that emerges when it takes "intelligence" as its leader and develops its own proper excellences. In other words: its nature surfaces only when we grasp its *telos*.

Second, only souls governed by "intelligence"—not just any souls, to be sure, since souls are often insane, ignorant, or evil, according to the Athenian—can govern well. Hence, only virtuous souls are entitled to rule, because of their ability to make things flourish—not because of their antiquity, in other words, but because of their comprehension of, and contribution to, the teleological growth and development of whatever they supervise. The Athenian creates a remarkable verbal echo between the Cretan laws (in his fantastical re-envisioning of them) that are "correct and make those who use them happy (*echousin gar orthôs, tous autois chrômenous eudaimonas apotelountes*)" (631b), on the one hand, and divine *nous*, which "guides all things toward what is correct and happy" (*ortha kai eudaimona paidagôgei panta*) (897b, tr. Pangle 1980). Accordingly, the culmination of the Athenian's first theological argument has profound political implications. It explains in a clear way the basis for evaluating the best "title to rule" among the seven considered by the elderly speakers. The winner is not Pindar's law of force, but rather, the sixth law, endorsed by the Athenian himself, which orders the ignorant to obey and the prudent to rule (690b). The reason is that *nous* enables the prudent to lead and rule for the welfare—the flourishing—of citizens.

Finally, the Athenian is conveying a message to Kleinias: that the soul is not a battleground of overwhelming forces locked in violent conflict. Rather, the soul is under the control of the individual. Kleinias' own soul, indeed, can be beautifully ordered and harmonious, and that is its good. That is the meaning of "imitation of the god" (*imitatio dei*). The Athenian makes this point by unfolding the argument strategically, in a way suited to appeal to Kleinias. In arguing for the "priority" of the soul, the Athenian gradually develops his idea that the independent, self-moving soul is the quintessence of "the self." The first part of the Athenian's argument shows that, as human beings with soul, we are the products of our own choices. Soul is not moved by anything other than itself, including, apparently, the passions stemming from bodily desire.[31] If our souls are our "selves," our "ownmost" thing, then we both can and must take responsibility for ourselves and, especially, for our own ethical development. Accordingly, the goods of the soul—the virtues, led by *nous*—should be every citizen's greatest object of care.

The Athenian's particular representation of divine soul explains what is involved in such care. The appropriate care of the soul will naturally prioritize intelligence, moderation, justice, and courage, in that order, as the chief goals of self-cultivation. *Nous* itself is characterized by beautiful, orderly, and proportionate motion (898a–b), as are the souls that it leads, above all, the divine soul, which is "best" and has "every virtue" (898b–c). Now, by analogy, Kleinias can see, if he ever will, that his own flourishing lies precisely in caring for his soul in this way. By virtue of its wise leadership, *nous* enables the soul to arrange matter into a harmonious order, rather than ruling it through force: it "guides all things toward what is correct and happy" (897b). Virtue is no longer a constraint upon the soul, much less a source of the soul's contradictions—as it was for the citizens of the traditional lawgiver of Book 2. Rather, virtue is the appropriate natural target of all souls that wish to be "correct and happy." The soul's own good lies in the cultivation of virtue.[32] As the Athenian had predicted in Book 2 (662b), the god has finally—and dramatically—given the Athenian and Kleinias consonance on this point.

This argument in Book 10 is one significant element of the gradual education of Kleinias. As the argument moves from materialism and a respect for antiquity to a teleological grasp of soul, so too does Kleinias himself move from a materialistic grasp of the world, in Books 1–3, to an understanding—based in images—of the soul's teleological character, in Book 10. The Athenian's presentation leads Kleinias to a deeper consciousness of his own soul's movement over the course of the work and thereby cements his dedication to a teleological understanding of his own soul and the souls of Magnesians. The argument therefore operates as an allegory, and a culmination, of Kleinias' ethical

---

31. Halper 2003: 264–65. The Athenian had raised this point in the general prelude (727b), as part of his exhortation to all citizens to honor their souls by accepting responsibility for themselves. While the Athenian had apparently disowned this strong sense of self-ownership in his theory of punishment and responsibility in Book 9, he also powerfully asserts the principle that human beings have agency—that they choose their own destinies precisely by choosing their own characters. On this tension in the Athenian's presentation, see Lutz 2012: 154–56.

32. Notice that there is no longer a question of seeking divine favor; this is the soul's natural development. It is independent of the gods. We are not the playthings of chance or of the god, at least in the sense that we can improve the condition of our souls all by ourselves, to different degrees depending on our natural talents.

transformation. To be more precise: does the argument of Book 10 simply manifest a transformation that the Athenian has already effected, does it consolidate the Athenian's gains, or does it contribute to Kleinias' education? I would suggest that it does all three things, which are, in fact, interconnected. The Athenian's argument helps readers and the young atheist understand the transformation of Kleinias that the Athenian has sought to effect throughout. By the time we reach Book 10, Kleinias is ripe for accepting and internalizing the Athenian's presentation of divine soul, because the Athenian has already prepared the ground. As a result, the argument contributes to and cements Kleinias' education by inscribing a particular vision of teleological soul in the heavens. It lodges the idea firmly in Kleinias' mind.

How Does Kleinias Understand the First Argument?

What is the nature of Kleinias' new understanding? What is the character of the transformation effected by the Athenian? Consider Halper: "The message [of the first argument] is no less clear from being unstated: to the extent possible, we ought to act like the gods and this *imitatio dei* is possible to us because our souls, like the divine souls, are self-moved and because they contain the principle of rationality."[33] I agree that this "message" (and the others that we have excavated) is "unstated," but can we clarify more precisely how the Athenian's central points are conveyed? In what sense are they stated and in what sense unstated?

In the preceding account, I have referred to the Athenian's education of Kleinias in Book 10 as symbolic, imagistic, mythopoetic, and allegorical. Obviously, the Athenian is offering materialists an argument for the existence of a god or gods, whatever its defects and open questions. On the other hand, the Athenian is also encouraging Kleinias to abandon any ground he shares with the materialists and their Calliclean offspring. To replace their unhealthy ideas, he offers Kleinias a vivid image of the divine soul as beautiful and rationally ordered, as a goal to which he can himself aspire. A thoroughly convinced atheist could find many reasons to dispute the Athenian's argument, but Kleinias is less concerned with and even aware of any high-powered philosophical disputations. He is more open, or susceptible, to the Athenian's general symbolic forms of communication.

---

33. Halper 2003: 264. For further reflections on *imitatio dei*, see Rutenber 1946, Sedley 1999.

In the first argument, the Athenian uses a variety of images and analogies to convince Kleinias that nature, in its inner principles and deepest essence, is beautiful, harmonious, rationally ordered, and intelligible to human beings. The Athenian wants Kleinias to develop a certain general sensibility about how things naturally stand in the world. He wants to cultivate Kleinias' "intuitions," his judgment as what "feels right" or "makes sense." He does so by replacing a sensibility of disorder and conflict with one of harmony and beauty, in which all things are full of (rational and caring) gods. Kleinias emerges with a set of suggestive images. Needless to say, this interpretation conflicts sharply with those which suggest that the Athenian uses the first argument in order to ascend to the summit of philosophical reflection, with a view to providing a philosophical background for ordinary citizens.

Socrates, the Athenian, and the Sun

In characterizing soul's rule over the heavens, the Athenian first examines how *nous* moves according to nature. Since the question is so difficult, he suggests that "therefore it's just, at this point, for you to take me as a helper in answering (*dio dê kai eme tês apokriseôs humin dikaion ta nun proslambanein*)" (897d, tr. Pangle 1980, modified). In this statement, the Athenian already communicates an important point to Kleinias. He does so by means of a verbal echo, which readers will find it impossible to miss. Soul, just seconds earlier, makes things correct and happy, the Athenian says, when it "takes as its helper Intelligence (*nous*)—god, in the true sense, for the gods" (*noun men proslabousa aei theon orthôs theois*, 897b). (Divine) soul takes *nous* as a helper; the Dorians should take the Athenian as their helper. The Athenian embodies *nous* for the Dorians. He is their natural leader, by virtue of his intelligence. Their relationship exemplifies the sixth "title to rule," "the one bidding the ignorant to follow and the prudent to lead and rule" (690b–c). He stands in for their god. Readers recognize the verbal jingle; does Kleinias? It is impossible to say with certainty, but the Athenian is trying to "naturalize" his own leadership of the Dorians, by creating an obvious parallel between himself and divine *nous*. Noncognitive education often works the same way, the assumption being that communication along such analogical and symbolic lines is effective even if not stated explicitly.

What help, then, does this mortal god provide to his elderly interlocutors? The Athenian offers a series of pregnant images to persuade Kleinias. In the process he also conveys important points to readers. He remarks on the advisability of examining an "image" (*eikona*, 897e1, cf. 897e5) of *nous*, because it is impossible to "look upon *nous* with mortal eyes and thereby know it adequately" (897d–e). Trying to look upon *nous* directly would be a blinding experience, equivalent to looking straight at the sun (897d). Whereas Socrates in *Republic* Book 5 had offered the sun as an image (literally the "offspring": 506d–507a) of the Good, the Athenian recommends avoiding the sun or *nous* and examining whichever of the ten motions *nous* resembles. By contrast, again, at *Republic* 516b–c, Socrates mentions that those who leave the Cave will look directly at the Sun in order to study it; they would then infer that the Sun "governs everything in the visible world" (tr. Grube, rev. Reeve 1997). By alluding to the *Republic* in this passage, the Athenian indicates to his readers that this discussion is farther removed from the Good even than Socrates' discussion, which is avowedly based on a simile. In fact, the density of the Athenian's references to "images" in this passage points knowledgeable readers to the lowest portion of the Socrates' divided line, the realm of "imagination" (*eikasia*: 509e1–510a3: *eikones, eikonas*), which involves "shadows, then reflections in water and in all close-packed, smooth, and shiny materials, and everything of that sort" (510a1–3, tr. Grube, rev. Reeve 1997).[34]

Kleinias—and the future Magnesians—will comprehend the motions of intelligence itself, not to mention the Good, only dimly, that is, by means of images, e.g. the physical motions of the heavenly bodies themselves. They are receiving, at most, an imagistic education in the nature of the divine soul and its teleological order.[35] The Athenian emphasizes this very point as he elaborates upon his description of intelligence as being reflected in circular motion. He "likens" the motions of intelligence to "the motions of a sphere turned on a lathe" (*sphairas entornou apeikasmena phorais*, 898b). He remarks that the three old men are excellent "craftsmen of beautiful images in speech" (*dēmiourgoi logôi kalôn eikonôn*, 898b, tr. Pangle 1980, with Pangle 1976). Readers will understand, by contrast, that the philosophers of the Nocturnal Council possess an understanding of an entirely different order. As the Athenian later says, they will grasp not only the priority of soul but also that "intelligence (*noun*) controls what exists in the stars" (967d–e). They will be "able to give an account (*dounai ton logon*) of as many of these things as have a reason (*hosa te logon echei*)" (967e–968a). The philosophers will be able to give a rational and articulate account of these all-important matters,

---

34. On *eikasia* in relation to religion in Plato's *Laws*, cf. Dodds 1951 234 n.89, quoted in Schofield 2006: 316.

35. For a more positive, and in my view excessively optimistic, reconstruction of the Athenian's argument at this point, see Brisson 1998: 195–96.

whereas ordinary citizens must, and do, rest content with a comparatively impoverished, imagistic grasp of them.[36] As the embodiment of *nous*—the highest portion of the Divided Line—the Athenian has created beautiful images in order to convince Kleinias and the Magnesians that fully virtuous divine soul rules the heavenly bodies. He gives them at most an "eikastic" or imagistic understanding.

This analysis is confirmed by the Athenian's ensuing account of the sun's motion. The sun retains its allusive character as the Athenian brings his first argument to a conclusion. (Ask yourself why the Athenian chose the sun instead of the moon or the planets in order to illustrate the final stage of this argument.)[37] How, then, does soul move the sun around the heavens? In the case of the sun and all living things, he says, human beings can perceive their bodies with their senses, by seeing them. Their souls, however, along with "soul" as a class of things in general, grow up all around us, but they cannot be perceived by any of the body's senses (898d–e). The class (*genos*) of soul is "imperceptible" (*anaisthêton*) but "intelligible" (*noêton*) (898e). Hence, the Athenian suggests that they will have to comprehend the sun's movements, after all, by means of "*nous* alone" (*nôi monôi*) (898e). After convincing Kleinias of the divine supervision of the heavens by "eikastic" and poetic means, it is striking that the Athenian shifts so profoundly, in order to emphasize the need for purely "noetic" comprehension of the heavens' movements. His references to the Divided Line could not be clearer.

Does this shift suggest, however, that somehow Kleinias has instantly become capable of the noetic comprehension of the movements of intelligence, which the Athenian now brings to the fore? Hardly. By contrast with his emphatically pious subscription to the Athenian's earlier argument for divine revolutions in the heavens (898c), Kleinias now, once again, finds himself at a loss: What? How does soul drive the sun around the sky? (898e). The Athenian offers the following possibilities: either soul is in the sun, or it pushes the sun with external force, or it moves the sun with "some other surpassingly wondrous powers" (*dunameis allas tinas huperballousas thaumati*, 899a). However it all works, the Athenian assures him, the god is in control

---

36. The "intelligence of the beings" is merely "said" to be in the stars: presumably, this is an open question, and, moreover, presumably intelligence has its own motions and character, which must be understood by *nous* alone. Astronomical movement is a poor and inadequate model of that perfect movement. Such movement, however, is the highest level of the Magnesians' understanding. Cf. the discussion at *Republic* 528e–30c.

37. On the allusion to the *Republic*, cf. Lewis 2009b: 89.

of the process. Kleinias acquiesces in this description, even announcing, in a dramatic way, that everything that the Athenian has said makes sense to "anyone, at least, who has not reached the furthest limit of insanity" (*ton ge pou mē epi to eschaton aphigmenon anoias,* 899b). The god is firmly in control of the heavenly bodies, and so *a fortiori* gods exist—and are everywhere (899b). (Imagine the usefulness of this point for surveillance of the Magnesians.) As everyone now agrees, the argument is over.

What is most striking about this final section of the first argument is its existence. The Athenian refrains from exploring the possible causes of the sun's motion, beyond attributing it to soul. He offers neither proofs nor demonstrations of any of the possibilities he mentions. He does not clarify what those possibilities involve. He does not even stop to consider the probabilities that one might assign to the three different options. In light of his apparent incuriosity, in fact, readers should wonder why he raises the issue of the sun's motion at all. The question becomes even more perplexing when we recognize that the conclusion of this final appendix adds nothing to the Athenian's previous, apparently irrefutable demonstration that gods rule the heavens in a rational, orderly fashion (cf. 899b–c with 898c)—and therefore, again *a fortiori*, that gods exist. What would the Athenian have lost, in those terms, by forgoing this appendix, by ending the first argument at 898c?

These reflections invite us to consider another possible interpretation of the passage. The argument was long over, even before the appendix, in that it had already convinced Kleinias and the future Magnesians of the god's existence and his rational governance of the cosmos. If that is so, then the point of the appendix (which returns to noetic investigation from Kleinias' dim, eikastic comprehension of the sun) is to reveal to readers that a properly noetic inquiry, or grasp, of these questions is unnecessary for the civic purposes to which the first argument is put. Kleinias is incapable of going further, in any event, because he is incapable of noetic appreciation of such arguments. His understanding is merely eikastic. In illustrating Kleinias' limits, though, the argument also invites further noetic speculation among the young atheists. If the young atheist is interested in pursuing the three possibilities further, and in learning to advocate for one or the other explanation of the sun's movement, or even to construct his own independent hypotheses, then he will need to do so across the river from Kleinias. Kleinias shuts down the inquiry because he is pious and convinced. By contrast with the young atheists, he will only ever possess the dimmest appreciation of the Sun. The Athenian, on the other hand, is nondogmatic and open to further arguments on these philosophically interesting topics.[38] The argument's loose ends constitute an invitation to more philosophically inclined listeners, such as the young atheist, to pursue these questions further.[39]

Argument 2: Responding to the "Deists"

Ostensibly, the Athenian's second argument is designed to show that the gods govern the world, including the human world, justly and with care. As a result, they deliver rewards to the just and punish wrongdoers. Making a successful argument to this effect would be one method of giving Kleinias and the Athenian consonance. This type of argument would show that, through the gods' active agency, the just life gives the individual happiness, success, and prosperity—as opposed the unjust life, even in its most successful, tyrannical form. *Ipso facto* the just life would be worthy of choice by individuals like Kleinias, who are (as he reveals in Book 2) ambitious to achieve worldly success and all its concomitant material pleasures. If the Athenian could make this case successfully, then the internal conflict produced by the traditional lawgiver would be resolved—at least at one level.

Even if the Athenian were successful in making this argument, however, an important difficulty would remain. Individuals persuaded by such an argument would embrace the life of justice for exclusively instrumental reasons. They might be led to believe, for example, that the gods' providential concern for the just would assure human beings (if only they should choose justice) of possessing material wealth, social status, and power. In that case, though, they would fail to choose justice for its own sake. Their "mercenary" or instrumentalized "life of justice" would lack the internal goods that a noninstrumental life of virtue, pursued for its own sake, alone makes possible. More broadly, their choice would be based on a defective conception of "happiness," which prizes power and material joys rather than the soul's health.

These difficulties encourage readers to pose a number of questions. Will the Athenian rest content with trying to persuade the Magnesians to choose the life of virtue on such grounds? Or will he, to the contrary, take this opportunity to reach to the ground of his interlocutors' beliefs—all the way to their potentially misguided conceptions of happiness or flourishing? If

---

38. Lewis 2010: 42–44 similarly notes the Athenian's tentativeness, his lack of dogmatism about his own arguments; cf. Lewis 2012: 24. Cherry 2013: 56–57 also stresses the uncertainty of theological understanding, pointing to 966c. Cf. Strauss 1975: 147–48.

39. On the "invitation," cf. Lewis 2010: 44.

so, then how will his efforts fare? And, if he chooses instead to allow the instrumental conception of justice to remain intact, then why would he do so?
Seen in this light, the second argument is of great significance, not only for
persuading those who harbor doubts about the gods' providential care, but
also for informing readers about the depth of the Athenian's commitment to
cultivate in citizens a love of justice for its own sake.

Refining Our Picture of the Deists

The targets of the second argument are those who affirm the gods' existence
but deny their concern for humanity. Although their kinship with the gods
draws them to the divine, their interpretation of good and bad fortune leads
them to impiety:

> But the private and public fortunes (*tuchai*) of bad, unjust people
> lead you toward impiety—people who are not truly flourishing
> (*eudaimones*), but are considered happy in popular opinion, exces-
> sively but misguidedly, since they are incorrectly celebrated in poetry
> and in every kind of discourse (899d–e).

Why do the gods allow unjust human beings to "flourish" (as flourishing is
conventionally understood)? In describing the deists' position, the Athenian
highlights their ignorance of genuine happiness. Witnessing the apparent
"success" of the unjust, they experience disappointment and indignation. As
the Athenian emphasizes, their reactions are rooted in their misguided acceptance of conventional views about material flourishing and worldly status.
In that sense he rejects their question altogether: unjust human beings do not
flourish in the only true, meaningful sense.

The deists appear to be driven by both indignation and ignorance.[40]
Having taken over certain misguided opinions from traditional poetry and
other sources in ordinary Greek culture, they are angry about the injustice
of worldly success. Despite their education in Magnesia, the deists still subscribe to the conventional understanding of what is good and bad. They have
not been persuaded by the Athenian's arguments throughout the work. Their
"condition" (*pathos*) involves a failure of reason (*agomenos . . . hupo . . . alogias*)

---

40. Lewis 2012: 23–25 once again helpfully connects these questions to the Athenian's presentation of the motivations for injustice and punishment in Book 9. For helpful commentary on
the entire section, see Lutz 2012: 148–52.

rather than a specific vexation with or aversion to the gods (900a–b). As in the first argument, therefore, the Athenian must dig down to the roots of these misconceptions, because they have distorted citizens' souls to such an extent.[41]

To take a prototypical example, deists might learn that an acquaintance's grandchild has risen from humble origins to the pinnacle of worldly success, i.e. tyranny (*ek smikrôn eis turannidas te kai ta megista aphikomenous*), by means of impiety itself (899e–900a). The grandchild is a Machiavellian hero. The Athenian's particular formulation links the present discussion to his key disputation with Kleinias in Book 2, who also admires and longs for tyranny.[42] Like the traditional citizens of Book 2, including Kleinias, the deists experience significant psychological turmoil.[43] Despite their natural kinship to the gods, and despite their aversion to injustice, the deists nevertheless, in conflict with themselves, admire and even envy the successful tyrant. It is as though they expect the gods to intervene in order, paradoxically, to give tyrannies to the just as a reward for their justice! As the Athenian has often stressed, psychological dissonance is the greatest ignorance (689a–c). It is the obvious result, however, of leaving ordinary conceptions of happiness intact, while imposing justice as a constraint; that is, it is the predictable outcome of a failure to understand that and why justice is of intrinsic benefit to its possessor.[44]

Because of these connections with Book 2, we are entitled to infer that the deists illuminate one facet of Kleinias' character, a disturbed and

---

41. Precisely how the distortion has occurred is not explained.

42. As we saw in Book 2, Kleinias' own position resembles that of Polus in Plato's *Gorgias*. This connection is intriguing in the present context, because Polus himself offers as an example of exceptional happiness the successful tyrant Archelaus of Macedon. King Archelaus was originally a slave of the previous king's brother, who became tyrant through committing heinous crimes. His biography conforms closely to the details of the success story that worries the deists. Like the Athenian, Socrates recognizes that Polus' admiration for Archelaus is shared by the many, but he is undeterred, of course, by the view's conventional appeal (*Gorg.* 471a–72c).

43. In that respect they are like Polus who, as Socrates reveals, longs for tyranny despite viewing it as shameful. They also resemble the citizens educated by the traditional lawgiver; these citizens subscribe to law and justice, while also, incoherently, prioritizing private pleasures and ambitions.

44. On this point in general, see MacIntyre 1984. We may think of the deists as envious and resentful: "Why do other people's grandchildren enjoy so much wealth, status, and power? I have lived justly, so why is my life so empty, so lacking in these goods?" As just people, their admiration of tyrants is self-contradictory, but it has a hold on them nonetheless. It makes them unhappy or dissatisfied. It even tempts them, as the Athenian suggests, to possibly graver impiety (900b), if their doubt and disappointment should lead them to entertain atheism.

unsatisfied tendency in his soul. What Kleinias shares with these deists is the self-contradiction he has inherited from his traditional lawgiver. Like the deists, Kleinias is a law-abiding citizen, but underneath his patriotic allegiance to law lies an unsatisfied desire for tyranny. Citizens thrown into this situation through a defective education—promoted by an ignorant lawgiver—will tend, at least in certain moments, to feel the point of the deists' disappointed questions about the gods. If the gods are good and genuinely care about virtue, then why does evil flourish? It is this indignant question that primarily concerns the deists; they are, in actuality, less concerned with receiving "rewards" for their justice than angry over the spectacle of the success of the unjust. Their conception of rewards is limited to the unjust acquisition of "goods" such as tyranny, which are not intelligible as the rewards of justice (of all things).

If the deists illuminate one significant element of Kleinias' character, then the Athenian will be aligning the second argument of Book 10 with the first. In the first argument of Book 10, the Athenian brought out the similarities between Kleinias and the young atheist. He thereby helped Kleinias to abandon his attachment to a materialistic framework. In the second argument, the Athenian conjures up deists who also, in a certain respect, resemble Kleinias. In both cases, the Athenian's arguments in Book 10 constitute the education of Kleinias, who, as always, stands in for Dorian citizens in general and for the future citizens of Magnesia.

The First Movement in Argument 2 (900c–903b): Persuasion through Logos

The deists' questions can be seen to grow out of the Athenian's general prelude. According to the Athenian, avenging Justice follows the god in order to punish the rich, powerful, and arrogant—a wrongdoer who "seems to be someone important in the eyes of many people" (716b), such as the deists. The Magnesians are encouraged to believe that such wrongdoers will be punished, in this life and "through the blameless vengeance of Justice," by "bringing complete ruin to himself and his household and city as well" (716b, tr. Pangle 1980). In Magnesia, of course, the city itself punishes outlaws in this life and works hard to prevent any citizen's revolutionary activity or rise to tyranny. Encouraged by the Athenian, then, citizens may believe, initially at least, that the gods support the city in punishing criminals; in fact, though, in Book 9 and elsewhere the gods play a vanishingly small role in conducting surveillance or punishing wrongdoers. Taken as a whole, the second argument of

Book 10 is designed to straighten out these points—to clarify for Kleinias and the Magnesians, not to mention readers, precisely how Magnesia will deliver justice to criminals. Echoing the dialogue's very first line—was it a god or a man who laid down laws?—this argument shows that it is a (god-like) human being like the Athenian Stranger who does for the Magnesians what they hope a god will do.

The deists' questions and doubts, however, are inspired not by the circumstances of Magnesia, but by the ordinary framework of Greek political life. In a conventional context, tyranny is an important political threat; it would make sense that a deist could look around at his neighbors and find that their offspring had, indeed, been impiously successful in worldly terms. Such is the case that the Athenian obviously has in mind. In that context, though, the evidence of the deists' own experience shows that the Athenian's religious pronouncements in the general prelude are simply false. Outside Magnesia, evidently, the gods do not punish injustice; inside Magnesia, injustice is punished, but not by means of divine intervention. The Athenian recognizes—as do the deists—that the gods do not punish injustice in this life, as they had expected them to do. No argument to that effect could possibly be successful, because experience shows otherwise.

The inevitable failure of such arguments, in fact, makes the Athenian's first response to the deists all the more surprising (900c–903a). Broadly and synoptically, the Athenian argues that the gods are fully virtuous and therefore exercise admirable supervisory care over all things (900d). He discusses their virtues at some length, showing that they cannot fail prey to vices such as carelessness, idleness, luxury, or ignorance—the vices that might somehow prevent them from supervising "the whole" adequately (900d–902b). Then he shifts gears: he emphasizes that all living things are the gods' possessions, but human beings are special because they are the most "god-revering" (*theosebestaton*) thing of all (902b). Like (or surely superior to: 902e) the human craftsmen, the god will neglect neither the small nor the large objects of his care (902d–903a). He is too virtuous to do so (903a). Kleinias agrees that it would be neither pious nor true to say anything to the contrary (903a). The Athenian mentions, in conclusion, that he will also need to offer the deist[45] "certain

---

45. Note that he is again said to be a young man (903a–b): cf. Mayhew 2008 for potential explanations. As Strauss 1975: 151 points out, at 901c the Athenian indicates that he is actually speaking to both the deist and the briber: "By conjuring up prematurely the man who believes that the gods care for human affairs but can be bribed, the Athenian has simplified matters greatly for the benefit of the good cause."

narratives that will enchant him" (*epôidôn . . . muthôn . . . tinôn*) in order to confirm his points (903b).

This argument is designed to reassure the deists that, after all, the gods do care for them, and that they are too virtuous to neglect humanity. Kleinias is convinced that this argument sets out the case accurately (903a). The difficulty is that this argument is not responsive to the deists' concerns. What is left unexplained is how the gods can supposedly care for humanity while allowing evil to flourish. The Athenian's argument does nothing more than restate the idea that human beings should have faith in the gods' justice and supervisory care. The deists have been told, all their lives, as in the general prelude, that the gods care for humanity. Now they are, on the surface at least, told the same thing again in a different way. How is the Athenian's restatement of the traditional pietistic view meant to assuage their feelings of disappointment and betrayal? After hearing this argument, will they now believe that the gods do, after all, punish wrongdoers and reward the just? Probably not. In fact, as in the first argument—but even more glaringly now—we are left with the impression that the Athenian's presentation makes little sense as a direct response to the deists' disappointment and turmoil. (Naturally, this difficulty flies over Kleinias' head: 903a).

Another path clearly suggests itself. Shouldn't the Athenian explain to the deists that the conventional "goods" are not good at all? As with Kleinias in Book 2, he should, apparently, now try to convince the deists that they are mistaken about the nature of happiness itself. Material goods, social status, and political power are good for good people and bad for bad people. In reality, tyrannical success is not enviable. Instead of confronting the issue directly, like Socrates in *Gorgias* and *Republic*, however, the Athenian adopts an indirect approach. He has already learned in his discussion with Kleinias that a direct, sincere expression of his own understanding will not persuade his interlocutor. The real question is which ideas the Athenian will now choose to emphasize, first in *logos* (the first movement) and then in *muthos* (the second movement). Will he try to transform the deists' misguided opinions? Frighten them into submission? Or change their perspective? Whatever his strategy, the Athenian intends to connect this argument to the previous one (900b–c), indicating that this argument descends sharply in intellectual difficulty and quality from the first (900c). He does so by concentrating first on virtue (900d–902b) and then on craftsmanship (902b–903b).

Virtue in the First Movement (900d–902b):
Justice as a State of Soul

The Athenian is addressing his ethical message to Kleinias and others like him, who can understand such messages only in an imagistic or symbolic form. In the first argument, he had emphasized the god's possession of *nous*—"intelligence," the leader of the virtues (897b–898b). He had also attributed "virtue" in general to the god (897c, 899b), as had Kleinias (898c), but without explaining in detail the character of the god's virtues. He now sets himself the task of remedying that defect: since the gods are "good (*agathoi*) in every excellence (*pasan aretēn*), they possess the care (*epimeleian*) of all things as their very own" (900d). The Athenian specifies that the gods possess *nous*, moderation, and courage (900d–e).

So far, so good—except for two salient features of the subsequent exposition. First, the Athenian proceeds to explain, not so much the gods' virtues, as their lack of vice. The difference, as we shall see, is subtle but significant. The gods lack any vices that would lead them to neglect humanity. Second, the Athenian omits to mention that the gods possess justice, or, if necessary, to explain why they lack justice.[46] That omission is especially surprising. Justice is (apart from *nous*, moderation, and courage) the only other remaining member of the Athenian's four "divine goods." More particularly, the deists themselves are disturbed by the gods' apparent failure to show concern for justice in particular—so why should the Athenian now leave justice, of all things, out of account? These two unusual features work together to produce an interesting result.

According to the Athenian, then, the god lacks the vices of carelessness, idleness, and luxury; these three vices are the opposites of the god's three virtues (900e–901a), as the Athenian later confirms (901e–902a). In other words, when the Athenian mentions carelessness, idleness, and luxury, he intends to call to mind the vices of ignorance, cowardice, and self-indulgence, which are the opposites of *nous*, courage, and moderation (901e–902a). His point is that the god would neglect humanity only out of ignorance, cowardice, or self-indulgence; and he lacks these vices. On this basis, the Athenian states his preliminary conclusion as follows:

---

46. Mayhew 2008: 160 expresses a lack of interest in the omission of justice, saying that "Plato surely believes the gods are just." Cf. Strauss 1975: 151–54.

> Most excellent man, should we consider you to be saying that the gods
> are ignorant and that because of their ignorance they neglect what
> they should care of, or that they know what they should do, and, as the
> worst human beings are said to do, though they know that it's better
> to behave differently, they fail to do so because they are defeated by
> pleasure or pain? (902a–b)

The answer is: of course not. The god is wise and willing and able to supervise
humanity, and he lacks the ignorance, cowardice, and self-indulgence that,
as we all know, he says, tend to keep certain human beings from correctly
practicing their crafts (902e–903a).

What the Athenian is saying, in an indirect way, is that the god lacks any
of the vices of soul, any of the passions or ignorance itself, that would cause
souls to become unjust. His mention of ignorance and *akrasia* in the quoted
passage alludes strikingly, and surprisingly, once again, to his earlier discussion of injustice and responsibility in Book 9. According to the Athenian in
Book 9, there are three causes of "faults" in souls: spirit, pleasure, and ignorance (863b–c), revised as pain, pleasure, and ignorance (864b). These factors
operate in the soul either when the soul is akratic (863d) or simply ignorant
(863d). Injustice is the tyranny in the soul of passion that overpowers our
boulêsis, our rational wish to lead flourishing lives (863d–e). The Athenian
emphasizes that the gods are neither ignorant nor akratic (902a–b), and he
reaffirms the point shortly thereafter (903a). By this means the Athenian
implies, without stating his point directly, that the gods have no injustice, no
"faults," in their souls.

In giving his argument this particular structure, the Athenian implies
that the god is not actively and energetically involved in rectifying injustice.
The gods are perfectly just and otherwise virtuous—yes. But justice is a state
of soul, best exemplified by the gods whose souls are rationally ordered, not
damaged by the vices that cause injustice. In order to appreciate the gods' justice, observers have to be aware that their justice is nothing more than this
healthy and sound condition of soul. The Athenian's gods are not the traditional Greek gods, whose souls were inflamed with sexual lust, envy of others,
and angry self-assertion. Inspired by a misguided conception of happiness and
goodness, the traditional Greek gods not only fostered injustice among their
mortal favorites, but also pursued unjust gains themselves. The Athenian is
saying: the "real" gods are nothing like the gods of the Greek tradition. To
those with a disordered conception of happiness, such as the deists, though,
the "real" gods' justice is hidden. Their justice does not manifest itself in crude

interventions in the human realm. In particular, Kleinias should not expect the gods to intervene directly in order to alter the fortunes of the just and the unjust. Why not? The reason is that doing so would show that even the gods possess a superficial and misguided conception of happiness.[47] "Real" gods know, though, that tyrants are not genuinely happy; they will not communicate, through their behavior, any contrary message. The gods care for justice by exemplifying it, not by dethroning successful tyrants. If you are genuinely interested in understanding the justice of the gods, then look no further than their souls.

As in the first argument, the Athenian communicates, nevertheless, that human beings can achieve their own good by likening themselves to the god—by rejecting the tyranny of pleasure and pain in their own souls, by cultivating understanding, and by adhering to the rule of reason. Such is not the answer that deists want, but it is the answer that they need. Contrary to the deists' opinion, the gods care admirably for justice, precisely by exemplifying it, rather than by intervening in human affairs; the gods are truly happy because they have virtuous souls; that is the meaning of true happiness. Hence, doubly contrary to the deists' opinion, human happiness, properly understood, comes through imitating the "real" gods, properly understood, not through seeking tyranny or fantasizing indignantly about divine vengeance. This answer provides the Athenian's indirect and symbolic case for justice as the healthy and desirable condition of the soul. The gods are left as a paradigm of the perfectly just soul—nothing more and nothing less.

In making this response to the deists, the Athenian freely acknowledges that the gods do not intervene in human affairs.[48] This acknowledgment is not a disadvantage of his account. Rather, it makes the Athenian's argument consistent with his representation of human affairs in Books 3 and 4, where the gods' providential care is nowhere to be found. In giving the deists (or Kleinias, to the extent that he is deistic) the answer that they need, the Athenian requires that they abandon the childish belief that the gods can and should rescue them from disasters of circumstance or of their own devising. That belief is unrealistic and therefore unworthy of the human being. It certainly will not contribute to anyone's flourishing or happiness, properly understood. Our flourishing condition is our own responsibility, and politics

---

47. St. Augustine was later to build on this type of argument in explaining why God allows the sun to shine on good and evil alike (*The City of God against the Pagans*, 1.8).

48. Notice, of course, that the Athenian himself, who is like the god, does intervene in human affairs; there is a disanalogy, then, between the god-like Athenian and the god.

is a human concern. The Athenian really is digging down and trying, in a symbolic way, to transform the misguided outlook of anyone who persists in worshipping tyrannical success. He develops these themes further as he unfolds the remainder of his response to the deists.

Craftsmanship in the First Movement (902b–903b): The Lawgiver's Supervisory Care

Perhaps, though, either Kleinias or the Magnesians, or even readers, will suppose that the gods could and should intervene in human affairs in another way—by supporting the city's effort to punish the unjust and reward the just. What role, if any, do the gods play in the city? Do they intervene in order to punish the unjust? Do they, after all, satisfy the deists' wishes for a divine savior? As most interpreters have recognized, the Athenian does not explain precisely how the gods show care for humanity or justice.[49] Arguably, the reason is that, in his presentation, they do not directly intervene in human affairs; at most, they embody or perfectly exemplify the soul's virtues.

On the surface, at least, the gods of the Athenian's second argument—fully virtuous and knowledgeable, and (supposedly) caring for humanity in every detail—are reminiscent of Kronos and his supervisory demons in Book 4 (713c–e). Understanding humanity's shortcomings, and in a spirit of care and philanthropy, Kronos established *daimones* as kings in our cities, because human beings cannot rule themselves without suffering disaster. This species (*genos*) of demons exercised supervisory care over us (*epimeloumenon hêmôn*), providing "peace, a sense of honor, law and order, and an abundance of justice (*aphthonian dikês*)" for us (713d–e). They worked things out so that the human race was not only free from conflict, but also "happy" (*eudaimona*, 713e). Seemingly, the deists expect the gods to act like Kronos' philanthropic demons. They believe that the gods or demons can and should deliver justice to human beings and thereby make them "happy." They are disappointed, even indignant, when the gods fail to do so. Their reaction is childish. Taken literally, as an object of wish fulfillment, the Kronos story represents a childish, regressive worldview: the world of Kronos is not the world in which human beings live. It does not represent the human condition of Books 3 and 4. Our world is better than that world, in fact, because in our world we are responsible for our own happiness. As in the first argument of Book 10, human

49. E.g., Halper 2003.

beings have "dignity."[50] If the deists still cling to a childish longing for Kronos' or the gods' parental care, then now is the time, at last, for them to grow up; and the Athenian will help them to do so. If the general prelude had once encouraged such longings, then the Athenian is now correcting himself.

How so? What does it mean for the deists to "grow up"? Even in Book 4, the Athenian had indicated that the age of Kronos was mythical. It was his own activity in Book 4—his own intelligent craftsmanship, not the god's— that enabled him to establish the city in a world admittedly controlled by fortune and forces capable of overpowering us (709a–d). He (not the god) is the "pilot" who navigates through hurricanes (709b–c). Throughout the dialogue, he is the individual who exercises "supervisory care" for Kleinias, Megillus, and the Magnesians. He is the "caring parent" of all citizens, who lies behind the laws (859a). He is the "free doctor" whose education of cit-izens makes their souls sounder and healthier (720a–e, 857c–e). Although Kronos and his demons are said to be philanthropic, the Athenian turns out to be the philanthropic god (albeit a mortal one) that the new founda-tion needs.

The key issue in the first movement of argument 2 is that the deists expect the gods to punish wrongdoers and to reward the just. Their concern appeared misplaced since Magnesia itself knows no successful tyrants. If readers now regard the deists as harboring childish longings for parental care of this exis-tential sort, then they should also understand that tyrants do not succeed in Magnesia for a precise and readily explicable reason. Lawbreakers meet with just punishments because of the lawgiver's own intelligence and supervisory care for the citizens. In demanding that citizens abandon their juvenile hopes, the Athenian also asks readers—if not also Kleinias and the Magnesians themselves—to recognize that it is not the gods, but the Athenian, if anyone, who delivers justice to the human beings in his care, by virtue of a suitably enacted legal system.

These points emerge, just beneath the surface, from the Athenian's anthro-pomorphic presentation of the gods and, ultimately, from his comparison of the gods to human craftsmen. In exploring the gods' virtues, the Athenian offers a decidedly anthropomorphic presentation. He attributes *nous*, moder-ation, and courage to the gods and mentions that their opposing vices can be found only in human beings (900d–e). If anyone deserves to be criticized for carelessness, laziness, and luxuriousness, then, it is not the gods, but human

---

50. Halper 2003 is not wrong to use this word, though I develop the idea somewhat differently.

beings. Human beings are the ones who achieve virtue through ordering their souls when confronted with the temptations and passions of mortal nature. To reinforce these points, the Athenian quotes Hesiod as criticizing human beings who are careless, idle, and self-indulgent, like Hesiod's brother Perses (901a). These qualities are, as the Athenian and Hesiod agree, hated by the gods (901a), but they apply more naturally to human beings than to gods (900e–901b).

Just after the preliminary conclusion concerning the gods' state of soul (902a–b), the Athenian turns explicitly toward humanity as a special object of the gods' care. Here he creates an analogy between the gods and human craftsmen. He calls to mind a doctor who exercises supervisory care over others (902d), as well as "pilots or generals or household managers" and "even certain statesmen" (902d–e). If these craftsmen are virtuous, then they will take into account small as well as large parts of their tasks (902d): "stonemasons say that large stones don't lie well without small ones" (902e). Surely, the gods cannot be worse than human craftsmen (cf. 858b–c)?

The question should make the Athenian's various audiences—readers, Kleinias, the Magnesians—wonder: In the matter of providing just punishments and rewards, are the gods superior to human craftsmen, such as "certain statesmen," certain free "doctors," certain "pilots" or stonemasons of the city? Just beneath the surface of that question, citizens might be thinking to themselves: Who, after all, has done the work of caring for Magnesia's citizens—the gods, or the Athenian? Upon only a little reflection, they should acknowledge that the Athenian has actually done, in practice, whatever the deists want the god to do, such as punishing outlaws. Magnesia's lawgiver is the virtuous statesman who answers their disturbing doubts. Magnesia has been founded in such a way as to calm the fears and anxieties of such individuals, even before they arise. Magnesia itself has already rectified all the wrongs and injustices that in other circumstances would harass the deists. No tyrants arise in Magnesia.

The Athenian is, then, making a specific point to Kleinias and the Magnesians. Stop being childish and recognize that your concern for justice has already been addressed—by the Athenian himself. (If it has not been addressed, then the only reason is that your own conception of happiness is misguided and corrupt.) Human beings have to take responsibility for themselves. The Athenian has taken responsibility as a legislator, and Kleinias and the Magnesians are called upon to help him, as he soon reveals. Meanwhile, they should take responsibility for their own lives by imitating the perfectly just soul represented in imagination by the god. If the Athenian succeeds in conveying this message to Kleinias and the Magnesians, then their abandonment of their childish hopes and longings will be complete.

The Second Movement of Argument 2 (903b–905d): The Justice of the Gods in Muthos

In the argument's second movement, the Athenian intends to offer certain "mythic incantations." He does not explain why this second movement is necessary. Even though it too relies on arguments (903b4), the second movement will somehow be more pleasant than the first.[51] A tentative explanation is that this movement will appear, at least superficially, to show the gods intervening directly in mortal affairs, by ordering the movements of the just and unjust in accordance with their deserts. Just beneath the surface, however, the Athenian's point remains constant. As human beings, we have both the capacity and the responsibility to choose our own fates.[52] If we correctly understand and follow the course of our teleologically defined development, then we will choose to live with the gods, the embodiments of every virtue, so as to flourish as human beings. If we choose otherwise, by indulging ourselves or by failing to obey the law, for example, then we will be miserable: we will "go to Hades." Either way, the gods will neither reward nor save humanity.

In his opening gambit (903b–e), the Athenian emphasizes the gods' supervisory care for the safety and virtue of the whole cosmos. In practice, their care implies that "rulers" (*archontes*) have been set the task of supervising each of the world's smallest parts, including the "wretched" or "stubborn" deist (*ô schetlie*) (903b–c). In all their complaints, the deists fail to understand that by nature the suffering and activity of each part, even the most infinitesimal, looks to the good of the whole.[53] Such is the design of "every doctor and every skilled craftsman" (*pas . . . iatros kai pas entechnos dēmiourgos*, 903c). One may compare the previous movement of the argument, in which doctors, statesmen, and other craftsmen exercise care over the smallest parts of their

---

51. Saunders 1973: 233 finds it "anaemic" but notes many ways in which it is poetic and rhetorical.

52. Lutz 2012: 154–56 helpfully shows that this line of reasoning conflicts with the Athenian's general remarks on responsibility for wrongdoing in Book 9.

53. The part is a part of a whole. This idea is very similar to what the Athenian has said about the citizen and the city. Citizens have been born not for themselves but for the city (cf. e.g., 772e–774a), but playing an appropriate role in the city is also beneficial to them as parts of the city (773a).

charges (902d). The naturalism of the human craftsman's activity lies just beneath the Athenian's theological vision.

Having established this divine framework for the argument, the Athenian now reasserts his own rational eudaimonism in a more naturalistic way. The deists, he says, do not grasp that "what is best in your case is what is good for the whole and for you, such is the power of that which brought you both into being" (903d, tr. Griffith 2016). The Athenian uses highly abstract language to suggest that his characterization of nature applies to the entire cosmos, that it is pervasive throughout all of nature.[54] His point is as follows: by nature, by the power of the very generation of wholes and their parts, an individual's active, virtuous contribution to the whole (or even his passive, justly deserved punishment) is good, not only for the whole, but also for himself as a part. To make this idea more concrete: at least initially, a virtuous individual cultivates his virtues with a view to "the whole" (the cosmos, or even the city). Over time, however, and with greater wisdom, that individual should understand that his virtuous contribution to the whole is not a "self-sacrifice" for the community; rather, it constitutes his own flourishing as the type of being that he naturally is. The Athenian's expression of his own rational eudaimonism—and its political implications—could not be clearer.

The gods have ordered nature and the cosmos in order to embody this eudaimonistic principle. The Athenian also refers, however, to the human craftsman to whom the god is likened; once again, the god serves as a projection of the human craftsman. The legislator has created a "whole," a city in other words, that commands the respect and allegiance of citizens raised within it. Those citizens should come to view the city as prior to themselves in that crucial respect: they are born for it, and not it for them. The Athenian, in fact, makes precisely this point throughout the dialogue (e.g., 772e–774a). In making this point, however, the Athenian does not intend—like the Dorian legislator, for example—to sacrifice the individual at the altar of the community. The individual's virtuous contribution to the community is also an activity that constitutes his own flourishing (cf., for example, 773a). If life within the city detracts from the individual's development of his own virtues, and thus from his flourishing condition, then the city itself must be abandoned (770c–e).

---

54. As Saunders 1973: 233–34 points out, this myth differs from other Platonic myths of the afterlife in refusing to differentiate geographically between this world and the next, and in referring to the "entire physical universe."

What role do the gods play in the Athenian's account? If the natures of parts and wholes function according to the stated principles, at a cosmic level, then very little should be left for the god to do—contrary to the deists' hopes and longings. That is precisely what the Athenian now emphasizes: human nature functions naturalistically and eudaimonistically, with very little input from the gods (in reality: none at all). Souls undergo transformations caused by themselves and other souls (for example: by means of education); "no other task is left for the draughts-player except to transfer the character that is improving to a better place, and the one that is deteriorating to a worse place, as appropriate in each case, so that it obtains the destiny that it deserves" (903d). We might imagine that transferring souls around the universe would require great efforts and struggle. Kleinias, in fact, asks the Athenian to explain in what way the gods effect these mighty transfers from one cosmic realm to another. The Athenian responds that this task actually requires extremely little of the gods (903e). It requires only "the greatest ease of supervisory care" (*rhaistônês epimeleias*, 903e).

The Athenian's startling phrase is even more startling than initial appearances suggest. It requires sensitive readers to pause. As an expression, his phrase comes dangerously close, even in its sound, to *rhathumia* (a Greek term that ranges from "recreation" and "amusement" to "indifference" and "laziness" in classical authors, and a term for which the Athenian's own word *rhaistônês* is a synonym). Arrestingly, the Athenian had worked hard to distance the gods from *rhathumia*, the vice of "idleness" or "laziness" (*rhathumia*: 901e3, 901e6–7, 903a3), in the first movement of argument 2. After all the Athenian's protestations in the first movement, it now turns out that the gods' supervision of the whole for the sake of justice is idle, carefree, and easygoing. If the world was not rationally ordered—if cold (or "ensouled"[55]) water came from fire, for example (903e)—then things would be difficult to supervise.[56] In that case, the gods would have to put in effort. As things stand (*nun d' . . .*), however, in the present dispensation, as the Athenian repeats in conclusion, there is a "wondrous and luxurious ease (*thaumastê rhaistônê*) for the one exercising care for the whole" (904a). If the Athenian could not be clearer about rational eudaimonism in his introduction to the second movement, then equally he could not be clearer that the

---

55. Cf. Saunders 1973.

56. Note that to that extent, and to that extent alone, the world has to be "ordered" in order for the Athenian's rational eudaimonism to make sense. Mares cannot give birth to hares. In this picture, however, the gods need not operate the machinery of the cosmos.

gods are, after all, idle and leisured in their supervision of the whole. There is nothing for them to do. Nature orders the whole; the lawgiver governs the city; the gods do nothing.[57]

On the other hand, human beings play an important role in crafting their own destinies. The god has assigned—so to speak—to us, in all our wishes and desires, the responsibility of determining the sorts of people we become (904b–c). We must take responsibility for ourselves. The causal principles of our own transformations lie within us (904c6–9). Once we choose our own lives, then, in consequence, we will move to the places of our natural destiny, either in the afterlife, or indeed in this life (904e). As Halper puts it: "In sum, though the Athenian's second contention is that the gods care for humanity, what really emerges is that we care for ourselves and that the activity of soul is its own reward."[58] The "reward" is either that we move to a "better place" (903d) or that we live among those who are like us, for better or worse (904d–905a). The Athenian's point remains constant. Souls are moved according to the laws of "destiny" (*tês heimarmenês*, 904c; literally: "one's allotment," "one's share"). You receive the share that you deserve, based on your justice or injustice, or, in other words, based on the state of your soul.[59] Because of this emphasis on an individual's state of soul, it was important, and hardly meaningless, that the gods of the first movement, however inactive, exemplified the virtuous perfection of soul. They implicitly made the Athenian's case for the significance of cultivating the soul's healthy condition; and now we see, if we failed to know it already, why that is important.

All the same, the Athenian adds to his presentation a note of surveillance and fear designed to shake those who still believe in divine intervention, as well as to please deists who still cling to the hope that, after all, the gods will punish the unjust. Just in case the naturalistic explanation of rewards and punishments fails to resonate, the Athenian mentions that the fearful—or people who are dreaming—describe the movements of the unjust soul as going to Hades (904d). He also quotes a line from Homer's

---

57. Cf. Saunders 1973: 234: "The whole process is ... automatic and inevitable" and Nightingale 1999a: 321–23. Saunders 1991: 206: "Old-hat mythical eschatology gives way to new-style physics, which lends a fresh sense to the fundamental truth that the good create their own heaven, the wicked their own hell."

58. Halper 2003: 265.

59. Saunders 1973: 237 rightly emphasizes this point, which reveals the close connection between penology and eschatology in the dialogue. Where human lawgivers may have failed to perceive states of soul accurately, the cosmic justice system is both surpassingly just (since it is based on an accurate appreciation of the state of each soul) and exceedingly efficient.

Odyssey (19.43): "Such is the justice of the gods who hold Olympus" (904e), transforming for his own purposes the Homeric word *dikê* ("manner") to signify "justice."[60] Intriguingly, the Athenian chooses the Homeric passage in which, with the help of Athena, Odysseus and Telemachus hide the hero's arms in the storeroom, with a view to taking vengeance on the unjust suitors. The Athenian calls to mind—for readers, clearly—the possibility of interpreting the Homeric epic as a theodicy in which the gods, above all Athena, help Odysseus to punish the lawless suitors. For all the Athenian's emphasis on naturalistic interpretation in this passage, then, he also uses the idea of divine punishment to frighten any citizens who may doubt that the gods punish the wicked. He calls up the terrors of Hades or an "even fiercer place" (*agriôteron eti . . . topon*) (905a–b).[61] He speaks of divine vengeance (905a) and even divine surveillance: no one, he says, "will boast of having gotten the better of the gods" (905a), not even those apparently successful tyrants whose punishments will contribute to the good of the whole (905b–c). The dialogue's themes of surveillance and punishment, stretching from the general prelude onward, resurface in this explicitly mythological incantation, designed to enforce justice even among those who remain unpersuaded by the remarkable force of the Athenian's previous arguments.

For other, more searching members of his audience, however, the Athenian's account of Hades and Homer will render an entirely different significance. To them he will be saying that only the fearful and anxious—those who fail to think naturalistically—refer just punishments to Hades. Hades is part of an old wives' tale. The unjust *do* suffer, but not because the gods mythically transport them to a place of damnation. They suffer because they have made bad choices; they have failed to choose a path that would fulfill their teleological natures as human beings. (The Athenian does not, at this stage, reconcile this view with his statement on responsibility for character in Book 9.) Along the same lines, he mentions the theodicy of Homer's *Odyssey*. Within a mythological framework, the gods provide direct support to just and admirable heroes in punishing wrongdoers. Homer's epic, the Athenian suggests, is a paean to the gods' justice. What the gods' justice amounts to, however, is the operation of humanity's nature, independent of divine agency or intervention.

---

60. England 1921: 2: 497.

61. At 905b1, I follow Burnet in reading *agriôteron* rather than Diès, who reads *apôteron*; both readings are based on marginal comments in the manuscripts.

Argument 3: A Place for Kleinias in the Cosmos

The third argument is directed at those who hold that the unjust can prevail on the gods by offering them bribes (905d). This brief argument is not only surprisingly crude by comparison with the other two, but also proceeds by means of an even denser array of analogies between the gods and human "rulers" or craftsmen. The Athenian begins by pointing out that if the gods manage the heavens, then they must be "rulers" (*archontas*) of some sort; but which rulers do they resemble, which rulers can we compare to them (cf. *prosphereis, apeikazousi,* 905e)? Chariot drivers, ships' pilots, generals? Perhaps doctors treating disease? Or farmers or herdsmen? They are like sheep dogs, shepherds, or the "highest masters" (906b). Unjust individuals attempt to persuade virtuous guardians that they will suffer no penalties if they accept bribes (906b–c). More appropriately, the unjust argue that the gods will forgive them if they win bribes in the process (906d). Whichever comparison we use, the gods are, in the Athenian's strategic presentation, both fully virtuous and comparable only to human experts, knowers, or rulers. A virtuous ruler or craftsman would never sell out his charges just for the sake of gifts. The gods, though, are the greatest guards and guardians of the greatest things (907a). Surely they are not inferior to sheep dogs, are they?

If the Athenian's audience has followed him to this stage of his dismissal of the traditional Greek gods, then little, if any, argument is necessary—and indeed little argument is offered. In making these crude and childish points, the Athenian has descended even further—to the level, at most, of Cephalus, another briber, who declines to listen to Socrates' argument on justice in Plato's *Republic*. Why is any argument necessary if you already agree that the gods are fully virtuous and maximally capable of guardianship? For readers who have been following the discussion carefully, none of these new arguments will make sense because the gods simply do not intervene in human affairs or exercise agency in any event.

Intriguingly, however, readers will not find in this portion of the prelude a feature that they might have anticipated: namely, the frightening dissuasion of bribers. The only dissuasion of bribers emerges in the penalty phase of Book 10, when the Athenian turns to the law on impiety (907d). If there is no dissuasion, then there is no persuasion, either: bribers will hardly care about the Athenian's silly third argument, because their unjust habits are not based on their belief in the strength of their arguments (cf. 907c). They are less interested in argument than in material acquisition, or *pleonexia* (906c1, 906c3, cf. 906b5). What, then, is the significance of the third argument—if it, too, is not what it initially appears to be?

We can best understand this argument by interpreting it as the Athenian's effort to give Kleinias a firm place in the city—even in the cosmos. If Book 10 constitutes the education of Kleinias, then it makes sense that the Athenian would try to find a place in the cosmos suitable for Kleinias—one that would reorder his understanding of nature's implicitly tyrannical implications. The Athenian's assumption, built up over the course of the work, is that Kleinias needs a new, metaphysically grounded sense of himself. Early in the dialogue, Kleinias had indicated a belief, coherent or not, that somehow his bellicose ontology sanctioned his militarism and *pleonexia*. The Athenian has strived to cleanse Kleinias of this belief at a deep level, beginning with the material-istic assumptions that he had absorbed from his culture, and working up to his own more explicit and self-conscious views on military prowess and ac-quisition. He formidably impressed upon Kleinias the view that the cosmos is a teleological whole, ruled by Nous, whose rational order gives meaning and purpose to its elements, however apparently random and antagonistic they may be. Having moved Kleinias from materialism to teleology, he now moves him from the pursuit of *pleonexia* to defense against it. Such will be his role in both cosmos and city.

Having impressively defeated the atheists, as Kleinias supposes, the Athenian is now better positioned to convince him that the natural order requires military allies, because, despite the priority of *nous*-governed soul, the world is also riven by a vast cosmic battle, a war between good and evil:

> Since we have agreed among ourselves that heaven is filled with many good things, and also of the opposite (which are greater in number), there is, we are saying, a deathless battle of this sort taking place, which needs a wondrous guard; the gods and daimones are our allies, and we are, in turn, their property. Injustice and arrogance combined with thoughtlessness destroy us, while justice and moderation, combined with prudence, save us (906a–b).

By explaining these broad points to Kleinias, the Athenian recruits his char-acteristic pugnacity to serve the justice and rational order maintained by the highest and best gods. If the gods are shepherds or guardians, then Kleinias and those like him will be guard dogs (906b), who belong to the gods (906a–b).

How can we square the Athenian's reference to a cosmic battle with his earlier arguments, in which the god ruled the heavens according to the perfect revolutions of *nous*, and in which only human (not divine) souls manifest the vices (900e)? Heaven is not supposed to be full of both many good things "and also of the opposite things" (906a). No doubt it comes as a surprise, after internalizing the Athenian's conviction that evil exists only in the sublunary part of the cosmos, to hear that there is more evil than good in the heavens (906a)![62]

The best explanation of this contradiction is that the Athenian wishes to keep alive, for Kleinias' sake, two ideas that stand in tension with one another. The universe is supposed to be characterized by rational order and managed by the god's *nous*, on the one hand, but it is also, on the other, characterized by a military conflict that requires warriors, guardians, and allies of *nous* to fight on behalf of justice.[63] As England has noted, the Athenian previously referred to the universal warfare of virtue and vice (904b), as he now refers to the medical warfare against bodily disease (905e).[64] Warfare exists by nature in order to further the establishment of peace, justice, and rational order. Kleinias' own role will be that of fighting courageously on behalf of these ideals. The situation is similar in Magnesia itself; the Athenian domesticates *thumos* but also gives it a significant role in supporting the city's system of surveillance and punishment, not to mention its military activities.

In assigning Kleinias this role, the Athenian remains true to his own rational eudaimonism. Thanks to the education he receives from the Athenian, Kleinias can self-consciously carry out his appropriate function within the cosmos construed as a teleological whole: the Athenian's transformation of Kleinias will be beneficial not only to others and to the cosmic order, but also to himself (903b–d). The Athenian has convinced him, in other words, that his own fulfillment will be ensured through carrying out his appropriate function in the cosmos (903b–d). It is healthy to think of war, not as a means to satisfy his own *pleonexia*, but rather as part of a larger project of defending justice and seeking peace.

---

62. In a footnote to their translation, Griffith and Schofield (2016: 395n.53) suggest implausibly that "By 'the heaven' here the Athenian must mean the whole universe, humans on earth included, since the motions of the heavenly bodies themselves are governed by good souls (897c–899b)." Why not say, rather, that the Athenian has shifted his idea because he now has in mind a different purpose—and Kleinias doesn't mind (as he failed to notice, for example, the contradiction between his own theological views in Book 7 and in Book 10)?

63. Zuckert 2009: 126–27 astutely notes this contradiction and argues that the vision of a "cosmic battleground" "does not provide a firm foundation for political order." Cf. Lutz 2012: 153.

64. England 1921 2: 500.

Strikingly, in describing Kleinias' new opponents, i.e. those who commit injustice and then try to bribe the gods, the Athenian explicitly links *pleonexia* to bodily disease and plague: "We believe, I suppose, that the fault just now named, the desire to take more than one's share (*tēn pleonexian*), is called disease in the flesh of bodies, pestilence in the seasons of the year and over a period of years, and this very thing, in cities and regimes, with a change of name, is injustice" (906c). The *pleonexia* apparently sanctioned by Kleinias' view of nature as internally discordant and antagonistic is seen to be a disease, against which the gods themselves fight on behalf of health (905e), and against which the Athenian fights as the free doctor who pursues illness up to its source. Now that he is able to grasp, at some level, the cosmic and teleological significance of *pleonexia*, warfare, and antagonistic motion, Kleinias' energies have been enlisted in the same project. He has internalized the Athenian's rational eudaimonism; he is the helper of not only the gods in the cosmos, but also of the Athenian himself in the city. If any ambivalence lingers in him, or any residual attraction to the life of *pleonexia*, then perhaps the Athenian will be implicitly addressing Kleinias, too, when he expresses the hope that his argument will, at last, have persuaded the recalcitrant "to hate themselves, and to desire somehow the opposite dispositions" (907c–d). Since Kleinias is still a work in progress, the Athenian still finds it useful to build on his internal dissonance in order to confirm the recruitment of Kleinias' considerable powers to the side of justice in the city. All three of the Athenian's arguments have contributed to the education of Kleinias.

II

The Rule of Nous

*The discourse which seems to wander as it lists does so in
obedience to the subtle purpose of its author.*[1]

IN THE LATTER half of Book 12, the Athenian provides an extended account of the Nocturnal Council. The character of this council is significant for
our interpretation of the dialogue altogether. As Bobonich and Meadows have
argued: "The more political authority that is assigned to the Nocturnal Council,
the more politically passive most citizens of Magnesia will be. Thus the question about the power of the Nocturnal Council has significant implications
for our evaluation of the ethical capacities of non-philosophical citizens."[2] The
council's significance, however, also extends to our view of Magnesia's regime
of law as such. What, then, is the role of the Nocturnal Council?

Given the question's importance, it is striking that the Athenian
relegates his account to the dialogue's final exchanges. He describes the
Nocturnal Council allusively, without clarifying its legal and constitutional position or its duties and responsibilities. His presentation raises a
number of questions. What is the council's legal, constitutional role? Who
are its members, and how are they related to the city's other magistrates?
Why did the Athenian refrain from describing the Nocturnal Council
along with other institutions and magistrates in Books 6 and 9? With
what conclusions does the Athenian leave readers at the end? How would
the audience's experience of reading the dialogue differ if the Nocturnal
Council were absent?

---

1. Cherniss 1953: 378.

2. Bobonich and Meadows 2020.

Tragedy, Philosophy, and Political Education in Plato's Laws. Ryan K. Balot, Oxford University Press.
© Ryan K. Balot 2024. DOI: 10.1093/oso/9780197647226.003.0011

The Athenian heightens our uncertainties in his final sentence in the dialogue:

> If this divine council comes into existence for us, O dear companions, the city must be handed over to it (*paradoteon toutôi tên polin*). No one of those who are now (so to speak) "lawgivers" has any quarrel (*amphisbêtêsis*) with this. What we touched on in our discussion a little earlier as a dream, having somehow mixed an image of the union of head and intelligence (*nou*), will really (*ontôs*) be nearly a fully complete waking reality (*hupar apotetelesmenon*), if the men are chosen precisely by us, suitably educated, and, having been educated, live on the acropolis as fully formed guardians (*phulakes*) whose like, with respect to excellence in keeping the city safe (*sôtêrias*), we have never in our previous life seen come into existence. (969b–c)

In exalted, hyperbolic language, the Athenian calls to mind nothing less than philosophical rule, i.e., the rule of men who embody *nous*—a possibility that, until the dialogue's final sentence, had been imagined, he says, only in dreams. If such guardians will—really (*ontôs*)—exist, then they will be men unlike any we have previously seen.[3] The city must obviously be "handed over" to this council. Yet how can philosopher-rulers fit within the regime of law developed throughout the dialogue?

Reconsidering the Controversy

For scholars of previous generations, the Nocturnal Council renders the dialogue incoherent.[4] The rule of law is apparently overthrown by another political paradigm—namely, the rule of reason—featured in the *Republic* and *Statesman*.[5] Klosko has emphasized the lack of

---

3. Are they men only? See Kochin 2002; Zuckert 2009: 134.

4. See, among others, Barker 1918/1947: 404–10; Brunt 1993: 250–51; Klosko 1988, 2006, 2008, 2011; Brisson 2003, 2005. Klosko has consistently held that Book 12 represents a clean break from the preceding eleven books; many of his writings, along with the writings of his critics (Bobonich 2002; Marquez 2011), are preoccupied with the question of legal fixity and change. On this important question, I offer a different interpretation, compatible with the views expressed here, in Balot 2020a.

5. Cf. Barker 1918: 406. For Brunt 1993, the philosophers of the Nocturnal Council represent a *deus ex machina* similar to the philosopher-rulers of the *Republic*. Arguably, Aristotle's account of the *Laws* supports this interpretation, because Aristotle mentions that both the *Laws* and

any institutional account that would explain the council's political role.[6] Accordingly, he has suggested that the council was meant to hold "some unspecified high political office"—which creates a "fundamental break in the argument of the *Laws*": "Presumably, had he lived to complete the work he would have integrated the two parts into a consistent discussion."[7]

For other scholars, the Nocturnal Council grows organically out of the (presumed) need to provide a philosophical foundation for the rule of law.[8] So far from breaking with or overturning his own regime of law, the Athenian all along anticipates the need for legislative successors with a philosophical grasp of the law's meaning and purpose (e.g., 632c5–6, 769d–770e).[9] He also alludes to the more precise education that certain citizens will receive, specifying, indeed, that he will discuss those citizens when they reach "the end" (*proiontes epi tôi telei*, 818a). The philosophical members of the Nocturnal Council are charged with the task of counselling those religious offenders imprisoned in the "moderation-tank" (*sôphronistêrion*, 908a, cf. 909a).[10] Moreover, these "integrationists" suggest, the regime of law can not only accommodate the Nocturnal Council; it *requires* some such body.[11] Without individuals who grasp the city's *telos* the regime will inevitably "wander" (*planasthai*, 962d3, 962d7–8). Without having any constitutional power to override the law, though, the Nocturnal Council provides nothing more than informal guidance to the city and its officials, based on philosophical understanding to which most citizens have no access.[12]

---

the *Republic* prescribe a similar education (*Pol.* 2.1265a2–7; cf. e.g., Cherniss 1953: 377). Cherry 2013: 55 argues that "philosophy . . . comes to rule in the city" by means of the Nocturnal Council.

6. Klosko 2006: 254.

7. Klosko 1988: 84–85.

8. For the view that the Nocturnal Council is well integrated and exercises only "informal" power, see Morrow 1960, followed by Bobonich 2002; Marquez 2011; Stalley 1983: 112, 133–34; Annas 2017; Lewis 1998; 2009a: 654–56; Schöpsdau 2011: 576; Samaras 2002: 285–301. Larivée 2003a notes the affinities between the Chorus of Dionysus and the Nocturnal Council in an argument along these lines; this affinity, however, is already explicated in Strauss 1975 and Pangle 1980 and does not settle the question.

9. Brisson 2001: 161.

10. Cf. Schöpsdau 2011: 576; Larivée 2003a; Lewis 1998.

11. Laks 2000: 283: that the Nocturnal Council is "indispensable . . . would seem self-evident."

12. For varying interpretations of the Council's institutional role, see Morrow 1960: 510–11, Bobonich 2002: 394; Stalley 1983: 133–34. For other attempts to reduce the gravity and friction of the Athenian's final sentence, see Schöpsdau 2011: 581; Morrow 1960: 512.

Debates over the Council's "constitutional position," however, ask the wrong question. Recall the Athenian's final sentence in the entire dialogue: "If this divine council comes into existence for us, O dear companions, the city must be handed over to it (*paradoteon toutôi tên polin*)" (969b).[13] The Athenian does not explain or justify its role; he does not identify the limits of its competence or its relation to other political bodies, such as the (ordinary) citizens' council. He does not say that it is to be held accountable by the *euthunoi*. He does not specify how its elderly philosophers become philosophers or the lengths of their terms (if any). He identifies no procedures, no modes of communicating to the city, no methods of taking votes or having discussions. Readers are intended to experience surprise when confronting the dialogue's final pages, particularly the final sentence. That sentence, in particular, is meant to leave readers uncertain about the significance of the dialogue's final exchange—perhaps uncertain about the regime of law altogether.

Imagine how different the reader's experience would be if the Athenian had introduced the Nocturnal Council in Book 6 (for example), amid his discussion of other magistrates. If he had done so, then readers would reasonably have expected the Athenian to offer a detailed explanation of the Nocturnal Council's composition, legal powers, and relationship to other official political organs. No impressionistic treatment would have sufficed. Why didn't the Athenian offer such a treatment in Book 6, if the integrationists are right? In other words: the integrationists entirely neglect the drama of the dialogue's conclusion. They ignore the quality of suspense that the Athenian has created throughout this long conversation, as he has dropped hints about philosophers who would make an appearance at the end. Readers should have been waiting for them and, all along, wondering how they would fit in.[14]

On its face, the Nocturnal Council does not fit in. Instead, it constitutes an utter reversal, a categorical transition from the rule of law to the rule of *nous*. The Athenian now seems to be saying, after all, that the city needs philosophical rule—or else its regime of law, whatever its character, will be dysfunctional. The regime of law is nothing without philosophical guidance and supervision. This bold announcement involves a dramatic downgrading of

---

13. Klosko 1988: 79: "This remark—especially considered in its immediate context—clearly implies that the council is to be the main political authority in the state."

14. Pradeau 1998: 179–80 is one of the few interpreters even to ask this important question, though his analysis, which stresses the need to order the city before the introduction of philosophy, differs sharply from my own.

the regime of law, as well as the ethical and intellectual lives of ordinary citizens that take place within that regime. A profound hierarchy separates the council's philosophical members from Magnesia's ordinary, nonphilosophical citizens.

Does this interpretation imply that the text is incoherent? Not necessarily. There is another possibility. Instead of being incoherent or implying mental imbalance, the dialogue ends on an unsettling note. It unsettles everything that has preceded. As Morrow asks: "Is it possible that on the very last page Plato [note: not the Athenian Stranger!] completely reverses himself, and repudiates not only what he has just said, but also the fundamental principles he has insisted upon in three hundred and forty-five previous pages of text?"[15] My answer is yes, the Athenian Stranger casts doubt on the dignity and worth of everything that has preceded in this extravagantly long dialogue. To be precise, the Athenian uses the rule of *nous* as a basis for forcing readers to re-think the regime of law. The Nocturnal Council (insofar as it embodies philosophical understanding or *nous*) serves as an ideal by which the Athenian implicitly criticizes the regime of law. The dialogue can be coherent even if the regime of law is revealed, albeit only at the end, to lack self-sufficiency.

To understand the council in this light would give it a clear purpose within the context of the dialogue: it would deepen readers' appreciation of the limits of the regime of law. If this were its purpose, however, then there would be no need to make the council fit coherently within the regime of law. On the contrary, revealing its lack of congruence with the regime of law would constitute a positive advantage from this perspective. The incongruence would suggest that regimes of law are characterized by a lack of philosophical depth and a correspondingly limited ability to educate their citizens or to enable their citizens to rule themselves and to live flourishing lives, altogether. They may achieve decent, not highly impressive lives, but only if they are indirectly, and even surreptitiously, ruled by philosophers.

To adopt this interpretation suggests that Magnesia is not intended as a political blueprint or as a realizable political ideal. Instead, the dialogue exists in order to educate its readers philosophically about politics. In order to convey its education, however, it need not present a coherent (much less a realizable) political regime. In fact, unsettling the coherence of the regime

---

15. Morrow 1960: 513; the question is also helpfully formulated and examined by Piérart 1974: 230–34, who does not see the Nocturnal Council as "in any way" requiring an abandonment of government by laws: "It does not question the other institutions but rather completes them" (232).

may enable the author to make a vivid educational point that could not otherwise be communicated. The dialogue is coherent as an educational text, even if the regime is not coherent. The Athenian "unloads" the Nocturnal Council like a bomb in the final few Stephanus pages of this notoriously long, complex, and at times tedious dialogue. Now we can understand why: he has no interest in rendering the council compatible with the regime of law as it had previously appeared. You had thought that the regime of law was a stable, healthy regime? Think again, the Athenian seems to say, because it is essential to hand the regime over to philosopher rulers, who will (at least hypothetically) rule by means of law, punishments, religious myths, and other teachings.

Looking Backward into the Text

Consider again the Athenian's final statement: "If this divine council comes into existence for us, O dear companions, the city must be handed over to it (*paradoteon toutôi tên polin*)" (969b). Isn't the Athenian proposing that the entire city be entrusted to the Nocturnal Council, "rule of law" be damned? As Klosko argues, "This remark—especially considered in its immediate context—clearly implies that the council is to be the main political authority in the state. Since this is the clearest indication of the council's constitutional position, it should be taken seriously."[16] The city is to be "handed over" to the Nocturnal Council.

Intriguingly, this unsettling *paradoteon* passage—apparently unbeknownst to either camp of the interpretive rivalry—echoes the earlier discussion in which the Athenian founds Magnesia as a theocracy in Book 4.[17] After reminding Kleinias of the seven titles to rule (714e, cf. 690a–d), he asks him to consider "to whom our city must be handed over (*skopei dê poterois tisin hê polis hêmin estin paradotea*)" (715a). The verbal echo with 969b3 is unmistakable. To whom should the three old men "hand over the city"? Who should be its rulers and chief magistrates? Should the city be a democracy, an oligarchy, or what? The Athenian's answer, in Book 4, is that Magnesia will be handed over to those who are the most obedient servants of the laws. The

---

16. Klosko 1988: 79.

17. This connection undermines the belief of Morrow 1960: 512–13 that this passage is single, isolated, and vague; on the contrary, it is closely connected to another critical passage in Book 4, and its importance is magnified by its being the Athenian's final statement. Lewis 1998: 11 also misses this critical connection.

end of Book 12 looks back to precisely this question: Who should rule? Now, though, the Athenian answers his own question differently. The regime is not a theocracy or a nomocracy but, rather, a noocracy. The city is handed over to philosophers. The very end of the dialogue signals the return of a philosophical lawgiver with political power, ruling outside and above the law, as though tyrannically. Seemingly, at least, this model of power had been superseded by the nomocracy established in Book 4, when the true legislator and the young tyrant had been dismissed in favor of the rule of law. At the end of the dialogue, by contrast, the true legislator with political power has been reinstated.[18]

Other verbal echoes point in the same direction. In the *paradoteon* sentence in Book 12, the Athenian also says, "no one of those who are now (so to speak) 'lawgivers' would have any quarrel (*amphisbêtêsis*) with this" (969b). The statement is obviously a swipe at current legislators. None of the present-day lawgivers are genuinely lawgivers; they are simply *called* "lawgivers." To whom is the Athenian referring? Again we find the answer in Book 4. The Athenian is referring to those who hold that the laws of existing regimes have a legitimate claim to justice. Just after he had described Magnesia's magistrates as servants of the laws and gods (713e–714a), he mentions, by contrast, tyrannies, oligarchies, and democracies who trample the laws. He asks Kleinias whether he appreciates that "some" argue that there are as many laws as there are regimes. More specifically, he says, some argue that the laws of existing regimes are legitimate insofar as they look to the preservation of those regimes, rather than virtue (714b). In that case law is simply, as Thrasymachus had declared, the advantage of the established regime (cf. 714c–d). "Do not think," the Athenian warns, "that the present controversy (*tên nun amphisbêtêsin*) is about a trivial matter (*phaulou peri*); rather it concerns the greatest matter (*peri tou megistou*)" (714b). Again the verbal echo is unmistakable. Even among these so-called lawgivers, the Thrasymachean ones, there could be no controversy about handing the city over to the Nocturnal Council; much less could there be any controversy among us, Magnesia's lawgivers. These "divine men" of the Nocturnal Council are recognizably superior to other human beings. Should they ever exist, their title to rule would be widely acknowledged.

Remarkably, vocabulary used in establishing the regime of law now reappears in an entirely different context, where the city is handed over, not to law, but to the Nocturnal Council, and where the dispute over the regime

---

18. Why does the Athenian refuse to make this point directly? The reason, as we have often noted, is that the elderly Dorians reject direct rule by other human beings as tyrannical.

is settled in an entirely new way. Readers had thought that foundational questions about the regime and its rulers were firmly resolved back in book 4, where the regime was handed over to Magnesia's magistrates, who were the servants of the laws and the gods. The verbal echoes suggest that these earlier provisions will have to be rethought. Book 12 brings to the surface, once again, the rule of *nous* that had been raised only to be suppressed during the foundation-scene in Book 4.

Burials, Bodies, and Souls

After discussing burials—an "end" in one sense—the Athenian turns to the "end" in another sense, namely, the end of their legislation (960b–c, cf. 962b). Throughout this section, we should remain alert to the "metatextual" sense of the Athenian's remarks: in this case, in addition to the end of their legislation, he is also referring to the old men's proximity to the "end" of this very long dialogue. Strikingly, and surprisingly, the Athenian emphasizes throughout these final ten Stephanus pages that the city does not (yet) have an adequate safeguard, beginning with his references to Atropos and "irreversibility" (960d). Somehow, despite the Athenian's elaborate construction of the regime, his installation of the finest laws, and his establishment of the "guardians of the law," the legislators have not built on a firm foundation (960e). They still need a "safeguard" (*sôtêria*, 960e9), an "anchor" (*ankuran*, 961c5), a "savior" (*sôtêra*, 961d1). Where, indeed, can they find an appropriate foundation for the regime, since all that has gone before is, apparently, so unexpectedly wobbly and unsound?

The Athenian addresses this question by analogy: the savior of an animal is "by nature the soul and the head, at least for the most part" (961d). Or, more precisely, it is the virtue of these two: *nous* in the soul, and sight and hearing (*opsis kai akoê*) in the head (961d). The mixture of *nous* with these senses would justly be called the safeguard (*sôtêria*) of each (961d, cf. 961e). The Athenian's comparison of the Nocturnal Council to the city's soul is telling in light of his discussion of burial. Just slightly earlier, he had emphasized that the soul is far superior to the body (959a), and that "in life itself the part that constitutes each of us is nothing other than the soul, while the body follows each of us as a semblance" (959a–b, tr. Pangle 1980, modified). The soul is "the part that really (*ontôs*) is each of us" (959b). While the body is an *eidôlon* of the dead, the soul travels in death to another realm in order to give an account (*dôsonta logon*, 959b).

Already, the implications are dramatic. The Nocturnal Council is really the city (and embodies its virtue); the rest of the city is merely the trunk

(964e). Like the body, that "trunk" is a mere "semblance" of the city itself, unable to give an account of itself (959b). In these opening remarks, the Athenian radically diminishes the worth of everything discussed in the previous books (for example, the ordinary citizens and their laws), by comparison with the Nocturnal Council.[19] The Athenian is saying not only that the Nocturnal Council will be the only adequate safeguard of the city. Moreover, and more importantly, all of Magnesia's detailed (and at times interminable) regulations, all the laws and procedures and rituals and traditions—all of it was built on sand, despite the Athenian's aspirations. The Nocturnal Council, with the younger auxiliaries (961b), is the soul of the city. Indeed: the Nocturnal Council constitutes the city itself. If we take these points seriously, then we have to wonder: what has been happening—Morrow's question—for the previous 345 pages?

Socrates redivivus

Surprises, reversals, and new directions become increasingly salient. The Athenian frequently raises the specter of Socrates in these final pages. He first makes Socratic points about the importance of the soul as opposed to the body.[20] He uses the Socratic language of "giving an account." He then turns to a standard, Socratic craft analogy in order to deepen his point. The examples of generals and doctors show that craftsmen must, above all, have knowledge of the "goal" or "target" (*skopon*, 961e) of their arts; without that knowledge, no practitioner of these arts can be said to have *nous* (962a). Similarly with a ruler or magistrate (*archôn*): he could never justly be called a "ruler" or save the city without knowing the political *skopos* (962a–b). The city would be "without *nous*" or "foolish" (*anous*, 962c), without a ruler who knows its end. To be blunt: Magnesia is foolish without the Nocturnal Council.[21] It

---

19. The discussion in Book 10 has prepared the ground for these points: soul has priority to and authority over body. *Nous* in the soul is its ruler and leader.

20. The notion that the soul is the (true) self appears, of course, in many dialogues, including *Phaedo* and *Alcibiades I*; on the *Laws* as presenting legislation that embodies Socratic "care of the soul," see Larivée 2003b.

21. It is possible to argue, with the integrationists, that the Nocturnal Council can be integrated into the city, and that the law simply needs the guidance of wisdom. Even they would have to agree, though that the city and its law-code are foolish, and therefore worthless, without the Nocturnal Council. The law itself does not embody wisdom about the pursuit of virtue. If it did, then what need would we have, in addition, of the Nocturnal Council?

lacks the "leader" of the virtues, *nous* (631c–d), until the Nocturnal Council appears at the end. As readers, we will keep in mind the numerous examples of "rulers," "knowers," and "leaders" used by the Athenian in defining his project in the first three books. No community, no group engaged in a serious project can achieve its purposes without a knowledgeable ruler or leader. The city is nothing without the Nocturnal Council—a severe diminishment of the goodness, even the viability (770c–e), of the city described in the long preceding discussion.

Strikingly, the "ruler" must know not only the city's goal and the means of its attainment, but also "who advises it [the city] well or badly, first among the laws themselves and then among human beings" (962b). The city requires a knowledgeable ruler who deserves to sit in judgment not only of Magnesia's citizens but also of its laws. Readers—if not Kleinias and Megillus—can now understand why the city has not yet found an adequate safeguard: it needs knowledgeable individuals who can judge, and potentially criticize, the laws.[22] Philosophers are the standard, the measure, by which law is judged (earlier "god" was the measure of all things: 716c). The Athenian says nothing to the effect that these knowledgeable individuals will be held accountable by the laws. Just the opposite: the laws are held to account by them. Gods are no longer the standard of anything.

As for the knowledge possessed by such rulers, the "end" of the political art would seem to be already well known from the final statement of Book 1: it is the care of souls (650b), or, more specifically, the cultivation of virtue in those souls (963a; cf. 770c–e). What more is there to say? Again in a Socratic spirit, the Athenian pursues the question of the precise content of the ruler's knowledge. As in most of Plato's short, "Socratic" dialogues, the initial responses to important questions turn out to be inadequate upon further reflection. More work, additional open-ended inquiry, is essential to making progress. That is what we see in Book 12: a reconsideration of all the certainties, all the pieties, that had made the rule of law function even as well as it had once seemed to function.

As a result, the Athenian initiates a novel reconsideration of the end of the political art and the "target" of the preceding legislation. Remarkably, the very foundations of the regime—and all the issues and difficulties that had once seemed permanently settled—are held up to critical scrutiny in an open-ended way. Although the Athenian emphasizes that the political art must

---

22. On changing the law in Magnesia, see the companion article Balot 2020a.

look to one thing, virtue, upon pain of creating legislation that will "wander" and thus undermine itself, Kleinias remarks, without irony, that they had agreed that virtue is four (963a). Kleinias is not puzzled by this apparent paradox. Indeed, the Athenian had encouraged him not to trouble himself if the lawgiver's goals seem to shift frequently—or if the city's focus on moderation, prudence, and friendship seems to point beyond a single goal.[23] Kleinias understands that *nous* is hierarchically set over the other three virtues as their leader (963a); accepting the Athenian's earlier encouragement, though, he sees no need to explain how all the virtues, in their complicated interrelations, count as one. Is it impossible, for example, that the virtues themselves should come into conflict? That possibility is suggested by the Athenian's subsequent explanation that even beasts and young children share in courage, because "a courageous soul comes into existence apart from reason (*aneu logou*) and by nature (*phusei*)" (963e), whereas, of course, *nous* could never enter a soul without *logos* (963e).[24] If courage can exist without *logos* or *nous*, then it might well manifest itself as the "toxic courage" that drives the quest for domination. The Athenian is raising, right at the end, eminently Socratic puzzles about the unity of virtue, to which the city (not to mention Kleinias and Megillus) has no answers.

Lack of clarity about such puzzles, in fact, creates conditions ripe for the re-emergence of the Thrasymachean challenge to law (962d–e), which plunges citizens of ordinary cities into relations of domination and slavery, and which had presumptively already been disposed of in Book 4. Ordinary citizens in Magnesia's regime of law—men like Kleinias—have no well-grounded, articulate conception of the foundations of the city (963c), much less of the potentially problematic uncertainties that beleaguer those foundations. As it often does, Socratic questioning serves to bring to light certain ambiguities and inconcinnities in the understandings by which nonphilosophical citizens (whatever their status in regimes of law) live their lives.

---

23. See, for example, 693b5–c5. On the goals of freedom, prudence, and friendship see 693b3–4, 693c7–8, and 693d8–e1; the Athenian offers yet another reformulation in the description of early Persia at 694b6; cf. also 701d.

24. To be sure: the Athenian himself does not believe in the adequacy of this notion of "natural courage," devoid of practical reason. In this passage, however, he raises the possibility of "natural courage" precisely in order to suggest that, at least at face value, courage is different from *nous* (the implication being that courage might come into conflict with *nous*). On the unity of virtue in this passage, see L.S. Pangle 2014: 244–46; Schöpsdau 2011: 590–92.

In a further, entertaining but revealing, step, the Athenian takes it upon himself to apply the Socratic elenchus to "political *nous*" itself (*ton de politikon* [*noun*, from 963a] *elenchontes*, 963b), as if it were a human being: "O amazing man! Where do you aim?" (963b). Can you, like the other arts, name that one thing that is your ultimate goal? When the Athenian suggests engaging in question and answer in order to make progress, Kleinias has no idea what he means (963d). He fails to understand the questions, much less any possible answers. He makes manifest the reality of the Athenian's claim that the city is "foolish" (*anous*) without the philosophers of the Nocturnal Council.[25] By contrast, the Athenian himself (like the soul) can "give an account" (note 964a) of courage and intelligence. He wants Kleinias and Megillus to give a similar account of other virtues and to ask him challenging questions about the relation of names to definitions, on pain of being charged with shameful ignorance about the greatest things (964a). In other words, he wants to carry on a Socratic conversation with other philosophers or philosophical students, but the Dorians are incapable of rising to this challenge even to the slightest degree. This exchange gives us, as readers, a powerful sense of the wide abyss that separates philosophers from Magnesia's nonphilosophical citizens.

Why does the Athenian refuse to revert to his earlier position, in Book 10, that when difficult philosophical issues arise, he should "cross the river" alone? Why shouldn't he do both the questioning and the answering, while Kleinias and Megillus merely watch from the other bank? In Book 10, he strove to build a protective carapace that kept the rule of law intact by cultivating reverence for the law among ordinary citizens.[26] In Book 12, he is exposing the contradictions, the fault lines, and the *aporiai* that characterize the project of constructing a regime of law in the first place. If we now ask, "Why would the Athenian do that? Why would he unsettle, at the very end, the regime that he has labored to construct over so many long books?" then we have to understand that question, not, with Morrow, as a deflationary one, as one that serves to eliminate the contrast between Books 10 and 12, on the grounds that such a contrast is impossible. Rather, we must understand that question as placing a special onus on the reader. Why, indeed, would the Athenian change tack in such a radical and—to the reader, but not to the Dorians—obvious way,

---

25. On the foolishness or ignorance of historical regimes, as discussed by the Athenian, see 688e–689e. Book 3 illustrates the harm that comes to cities that are dominated by ignorant leaders.

26. On the centrality of reverence in the dialogue, see Ballingall 2017, Ballingall 2023.

in the final pages of this long dialogue? The answer is that he is unveiling for readers the nomocracy's lack of viability, unless it is somehow, paradoxically, ruled by philosophers.

So far from settling these Socratic questions about virtue—as though they *could* be definitively settled—the Athenian leaves the *aporia* in place, at least for the moment.[27] The Athenian does, however, envision a Nocturnal Council that will make outstanding progress in addressing such Socratic questions. He proceeds to call to mind Magnesia's highest officials, "a lawgiver and a Guardian of the Laws, and someone who believes that he is superior to everyone else in virtue" (964b); those who have received prizes (*nikêtêria*, 964b) for their virtues, such as interpreters and teachers; those who are "guardians of the others" (*tôn allôn phulakas*, 964b). What is the character of such leaders? Won't the city's leading officials, the Athenian asks rhetorically, be "better than the others in teaching and making absolutely clear the power of vice and virtue" (964c)? The city's officials will, in particular, be superior to random poets or self-proclaimed educators in that respect (964c). Up till now, however, as the Athenian has just demonstrated for all to see, ordinary, nonphilosophical citizens, of whatever office or stature, will not be able to deliver any such explanations (cf. 964d). That is why the city requires guardians with an extensive philosophical training; without them, the city will become a miserable failure: "In a city like that, where the guardians (*phulakes*) are not adequate (*hikanoi*) in word or deed (*logôi ergôi*), with an adequate understanding of virtue (*aretês peri gignôskontes hikanôs*), is it any wonder that this city—since it lacks guardians—suffers the same things as many existing cities?" (964c–d). Is the Athenian possibly alluding to the idea that cities will have no rest from evils until philosophers rule (cf. *Rep.* 473c–e)? Will Magnesia, after all, have guardians who are adequate in word and deed to lead the city to happiness?

Philosophers and Nonphilosophers in the City

It would be hard to overstate the surprising, even shocking, quality of the Athenian's argument at this stage. He is suggesting that Magnesia should be handed over to philosophers, that the city must somehow, at the last minute, find a place of great respect for the head and senses of "prudent men" (*tôn*

---

27. Correctly noted by Schöpsdau 2011: 590. For now, at least, the Athenian preserves an important ambiguity: do the members of the Nocturnal Council know the truth about such matters, or do they remain, like Socrates, (merely) philosophical searchers?

emphronôn, 964d6). In describing philosophers as the "head" of the city, he denigrates the general run of Magnesia's citizens: the city is nothing more than the "trunk" (*tou kutous*, 964e1).[28] The image indicates clearly who will be in charge (the Nocturnal Council, the head) and why (its rationality, as opposed to the passions and desires of the trunk)—a point that is spelled out even more clearly in the ensuing discussion.

The Nocturnal Council itself, placed atop this trunk, is composed of both younger associates and older philosophers. The Athenian packs a great deal of substance into his description of these two groups. He says that the younger guardians have the "best natures" and are "keenest" in every part of their souls (964e). His emphasis on the high quality of their natures, as well as their keenness, recalls Socrates' description of the first-rate natures of young, potential philosophers in the *Republic* (cf. *Rep.* 485a–487a, 494a–b, 503b–c).[29] This allusion is strengthened when we recall that his earlier characterization of the younger associates emphasized their intellectual capacities and dedication (952a): having been carefully selected, they are expected to devote themselves with great seriousness to whatever the older members judge appropriate. The Athenian's emphasis on the younger associates' dedication to study in this passage is obvious from his repetition of the vocabulary of "learning" (*manthanein, mathêmata*: 952a2, 952a3, 952a4, 952a7). They are to be chosen on the basis of their age, "capacity to learn" (*mathêmatôn dunamesin*) and dispositions and character (968d). Moreover, the Athenian says that the younger associates must be judged "worthy in nature and upbringing" (*epaxion ... phusei kai trophêi*, 961b). If they are judged "unworthy" (952a7), presumably based on their failures of intellect (952a) or character (952b), then they bring shame on whoever invited them. These allusions to Socrates' description of the philosophical nature also pick up the same allusions in the Athenian's description of the young tyrant (709e).

By contrast, the old men are likened to *nous* (*tous de nôi apêikasmenous*) and "think about things worthy of account in a superior way" (*axia logou diapherontôs phronein*, 965a). As Schöpsdau has noted, though, the contrast between the groups is gradually eliminated, since the underlying thought is that at least some of the younger associates will ascend, eventually, to become

---

28. On the meaning of the "trunk," see Schöpsdau 2011: 594.

29. On the younger associates' "sharpness" of soul (*oxutêtas ... echontas*) in particular, compare *Laws* 964e with *Republic* 503b–c, where Socrates discusses "keenness" along with good memory and facility in learning. Note also that the Athenian stresses the younger associates' strong memories (964e–965a).

senior members.[30] In the Nocturnal Council, we find philosophers and philosophers in training (some of whom, no doubt, will not ascend to the heights of the senior members).

This assimilation of senior and junior members enables the Athenian to distinguish sharply between philosophers with a deep understanding of virtue and vice, along with their assistants in training, on the one hand, and ordinary citizens, on the other, who have little understanding of the most important things. That distinction underlies the Athenian's emphasis in the final sentence of this exchange, which contrasts those who are raised and educated with great precision, and all the rest who are not (965a). The younger associates are chosen on the basis of their nature and upbringing, which allow them to benefit, one expects, from the more "precise" education to which the Athenian has referred sporadically throughout the work (965a; cf., for example, 818a). Overall, then, the Athenian focuses attention on those leaders who have successfully acquired a philosophical education, along with the younger recruits who might, as the allusions to the *Republic* suggest, be able to become philosophers themselves. Both in common, and particularly the experienced philosophers who are likened to *nous*, will—*really*—save the city (965a). You had once believed that the law would save the city? No. The philosophers and their assistants will *really* save the city.

Finally, and accordingly, at this very late stage of the dialogue, we discover who in the city deliberates (*bouleuesthai*): the old men, the images of *nous*, deliberate, along with their younger assistants (*hupêretais*) (965a). We had previously noted that, up until this point, the city appeared to contain no deliberative body. No Assembly is said to make decisions about war and peace, about the distribution of resources, religious rituals, and so on. Where does deliberation about the city's future take place? We finally receive an answer: in the Nocturnal Council. Only philosophers are qualified to deliberate on behalf of the city.[31] The republican ideal of self-rule has been removed from consideration without any qualification. The reason is that the city will never flourish without philosophers making decisions for it from the acropolis. Those philosophers will rule by means of law.

---

30. Schöpsdau 2011: 585.

31. Commentators have paid too little attention to this crucial point; notable exceptions are Brisson 2003: 225; Brisson 2005: 107; Brunt 1993: 257–58. For a different interpretation, see Bartels 2017.

Tyrants on the Acropolis?

Strikingly, the Athenian now reveals that the combination of the "young tyrant" with the "true legislator" from Book 4 foreshadows the Athenian's description of the Nocturnal Council. In Book 4, as we have seen, the rule of reason was represented by the true lawgiver. It was suppressed in favor of the regime of law during the city's foundation. The elderly Dorians would not accept the direct rule of rationality; it was equated, in their minds, with tyranny. Now the Athenian brings back the rule of reason with precisely these tyrannical associations. He restores the rule of rationality at the end of the work and points to the possibility of a paradoxically virtuous tyranny. Just as the dialogue's final sentence reverses the decision, made in Book 4, to "hand over" the city to the law and its servants, so too does the Athenian's restoration of a virtuous philosophical tyranny reverse the suppression of the rule of reason in Book 4.

Consider first the Athenian's description of the Nocturnal Council's "younger associates." Just as the Athenian likens the older members to *nous*, so too does he liken the junior members to "sight" and "hearing" (961d). The younger associates are the "noblest senses" (961d, cf. 961e, 964d). They "survey the whole city in a circle, and as they keep watch they hand over perceptions to the memories, and report everything in the city to the elders" (964e, tr. Pangle 1980). The junior members are the old men's "eyes" and "ears," so to speak (961d), reporting everything to them (964e–965a). This reference to "eyes" and "ears" hints that the younger members will conduct surveillance on their fellow citizens, a familiar feature of life in Magnesia. In particular, suggesting that they are the council's "eyes" and "ears" calls to mind the "eyes" and "ears" of the Great King of Persia. As Balcer has argued, the Persian "eyes" and "ears" of the Great King were well known to classical Greeks (they served, in his view, as the model for the Athenian *episkopoi*, traveling imperial officials who supervised the Athenians' "allies" and then reported back to the Athenian demos).[32] The younger members of the council not only serve as philosophical students in the Nocturnal Council, but also gather information on the citizenry and report back to their superiors. They resemble, for example, the spies employed by the notorious tyrant Deioces, who walled himself in on the acropolis in order to create distance between himself and

---

32. Balcer 1977. Brisson 2005: 112 notes that these younger associates are "assimilated to the eyes and ears of the Council." For a thorough examination of the surprisingly detailed dossier of evidence concerning both domestic and foreign spies in classical Greece, see Russell 2000: 103–39.

his subjects (Hdt. 1.100.2); as Russell has shown, in fact, domestic spies were characteristically used by tyrants and monarchs to surveil their populations.[33] The overtones of the Athenian's description become increasingly menacing, not to mention distant from the respectable institution imagined by the integrationists.

These allusions should be connected to the Nocturnal Council's location on the acropolis (969c).[34] Little had been said previously about the acropolis of Magnesia, despite the Athenian's attention to the political geography of Magnesia in general (704a–707d, 745b–e, 747d–e, 778c–779d). What is the meaning of the Athenian's desire to place the Nocturnal Council on the Acropolis? To any reader acquainted with the traditional use of the acropolis as a political and religious space, this detail will be conspicuous, even striking. The Magnesian acropolis (like the Athenian Acropolis) is a religious space generally reserved for the temples, i.e., the houses, of the gods. Situated on the acropolis as perfect guardians, the philosophers of the Nocturnal Council are being assimilated to the traditional Greek gods and to the philosopher-rulers of Callipolis, who are often described in the *Republic* as divine or god-like men (e.g., 500c–d, 501b, 540b–c; cf. also *Laws* 792c–e, 666d, 945c with Lisi 2004: 15).

More directly relevant, however, is that the acropolis is also the space that ambitious men had traditionally attempted to seize when they wanted to be recognized as tyrants (e.g., the Athenian Kylon at Hdt. 5.71). Like gods, tyrants operated outside the traditional human communities governed by laws, customs, and traditions. They stood above the rule of law and set the city in order. In the archaic Greek poetic tradition, they were often represented as dealing "straight justice" to the *hubris* of their fellow citizens, as "regulators" (cf. *euthuntêr*, Theognis 40) who provide cities with *eunomia* and *kosmos* (order).[35] At the end of the dialogue, the Athenian summons up the idea of

33. On Deioces, see Balcer 1977: 256; on the use of domestic spies by tyrants and monarchs in particular, see especially Russell 2000: 107–14. If Brisson 2005: 112–16 is correct that the *agronomoi* were part of a "vast hidden process of selecting political élites," then the surveillance mentioned at 964e–965a may help to shed light on the Athenian's reference to the Spartan *krypteia* in describing the *agronomoi* (763b–c).

34. These paragraphs on the acropolis represent a revised version of a similar discussion in Balot 2020a. Few scholars have ever paid attention to the geographical location of the Nocturnal Council. Schöpsdau 2011: 606 links this passage to other Platonic dialogues in which the acropolis of the soul is its seat of rationality; Brisson 2001: 163–64 helpfully discusses its gatherings at the Sophronisterion.

35. Among many other treatments along these lines, see, for example, Nagy 1983.

a "virtuous tyrant," a philosophical ruler who rules others freely and unaccountably, not only because he possesses liberated *nous*, but also because his soul's impulses and appetites conform to the leadership of *nous* (cf. 966b with the discussion that follows).

The possibility of a virtuous tyrant is far from novel within the dialogue.[36] In Book 4, Kleinias (correctly) understands the Athenian to be arguing that the best city comes into existence "from tyranny" (*ek turannidos*, 710d), with an "eminent lawgiver" (*nomothetou . . . akrou*; cf. 710e: a "true lawgiver," *alêthês . . . nomothetês*) and an "orderly tyrant" (*turannou kosmiou*, 710d). The Athenian had imagined, no doubt hypothetically, a "true" lawgiver in possession—not of correct opinion or even a deep understanding of things— but rather of the *truth* (*ton nomothetên alêtheias echomenon*, 709c). This lawgiver wisely (we are told) prays for a "tyrannized city" and a young tyrant with a "tyrannized soul," who has a strong memory, is quick to learn, and is courageous and magnificent by nature (709e), as well as "moderate" (710a–b; cf. 710c). Like the description of the Nocturnal Council, this earlier passage alludes to Plato's *Republic*, above all, in the Athenian's description of the young tyrant's character.[37]

The Athenian had earlier elicited Kleinias' attractions to tyrannical power and immortality (661d–e). He asked Kleinias whether these things are good even if possessed by an unjust and arrogant person (*adikos . . . hubristês*, 662a, cf. 713c). Kleinias' attraction to tyranny, power, and immortality remains undisturbed, even despite these defects of soul and their accompanying shame (662a). The Athenian puts forward what is apparently his own view, however, when he says that a variety of goods, including health, beauty, wealth, sharp senses, and tyranny (tyranny! at 661b), are good for good men and bad for bad men (661a–c).[38] In other words: a good man, a philosopher, will make good use of tyrannical power, contrary to conventional abuses associated with such power. (Kleinias believes, by contrast, that these things

---

36. At two prior moments in the conversation, the Athenian had raised the possibility of philosophical tyranny, only to dismiss it—apparently—as either impossible or undesirable (709e–711e; 875b–d).

37. For further details, see the discussion of these points in chapter 4, "A New Beginning: Founding Magnesia."

38. Note the "sharp senses of seeing and hearing" at 661a and compare to the Nocturnal Council's younger associates, who are the eyes and ears of the senior members and are distinguished by "sharpness" of soul (*oxutêtas . . . echontas*) at *Laws* 964e.

are good for both good men and bad men, regardless of the defects of their character.)

The Nocturnal Council—a body of philosophical rulers on the acropolis, conducting tyrant-like surveillance by means of its "eyes" and "ears"—was foreshadowed by these references to tyranny and true lawgiving. In both earlier discussions, the Athenian had indicated that he saw the attractions of tyrannical power for the virtuous philosopher. In Book 4, though, the Athenian suppressed that possibility in favor of his foundation of the regime of law. He still illustrated the significance of rule by *nous* in his own leadership in the dialogue itself. As his description of the Nocturnal Council unfolds, his persistent allusions to Plato's *Republic* in the passage on the "young tyrant" are now developed. The virtuous, quasi-tyrannical philosophers, ruling with their "young associates" on the acropolis, are defined by their comprehension of the forms.

Tyrants, Philosopher-Rulers, and Forms

As in Book 4, the Athenian's vision of the virtuous philosopher with tyrannical power becomes closely aligned with the rule of Callipolis' philosopher-kings. By means of Socratic questioning, we have arrived at a position where the rule of philosopher-kings seems both inevitable and desirable. We can now see the truth of Aristotle's verdict on the *Laws* (*Pol.* 1265a): the Athenian gradually—only at the very end, as we now understand—brings things around to the educational system of Callipolis.[39] If the true saviors of the city have to understand the "one thing" to which everything in the city must look, then, the Athenian asks, "Is there any more accurate view or sight of anything, in any way, than being able to look to a single form from many diverse particulars?" (965c). When Kleinias responds with a mealy "perhaps," the Athenian very firmly insists: "Not perhaps, but really (*ontôs*)." This is the clearest "path" to knowledge (965c). The Athenian only rarely corrects and reproves his interlocutors in such a confrontational way. Looking at particulars through a philosophical lens—indeed, through the lens of the "forms"—is "really," despite what others may think, the best way to gain understanding. History, religious belief, practical experience, wide travel, a cynical outlook: none of these supposed methods of arriving at the truth can compare with a dialectical approach to

---

39. On the similarity of the education system for philosophers in both works, see the account offered by Schöpsdau 2011: 582–83.

the greatest questions.[40] That approach, the Athenian insists, leads to a reconsideration of the forms.

The Athenian introduces this topic by way of an allusion to the Socratic discussion of the cardinal virtues. He emphasizes that the "guardians" will have to "see precisely" (*akribôs idein*) what is "the same" in courage, moderation, justice, and prudence—that is, why these virtues are all called by the one name "virtue" (965c–d). Is virtue one, or a whole, or even both of these at once—or something again different? If these Socratic questions about virtue prove to be "elusive" (*diaphugontos hêmas*, 965d7), he says, then the city will never be "adequately sorted" (*hikanôs hexein*, 965d8) with respect to virtue. The philosophers of the Nocturnal Council will not be stuck in Socratic *aporia*; they will have to have answers to Socrates' characteristic "What is X?" questions.

The inference that the Athenian is alluding to the forms, as they were known in the *Republic*, is virtually inescapable: the forms, that is, not only of the four cardinal virtues, but also of the beautiful and the good (966a). Consider Cherniss's interpretation: "Since there is no reason to doubt that Plato wrote the *Laws*, there is no reason to suspect that he was unaware of the implications of the phraseology that he had hitherto used in connection with the doctrine of ideas; and, since he puts such emphasis upon the phraseology and the formulae here, he must have done so purposely and purposely refrained from making the implications explicit as he had done in the *Republic*."[41] Yes: that is correct. On the other hand, while Cherniss is also correct to say that the Athenian is not inclined to draw out any philosophical implications from his reference to the forms, he does clarify their ethical and political implications.

The consequences of the Athenian's allusions to the forms are far-reaching. Even the best efforts to establish a republican, mixed regime of law and self-government will inevitably be self-destructive without philosophical guidance. The Magnesian regime of law is doomed to wander in respect of its chief goal, unless it is saved by philosophers, not only at the foundation, but

---

40. See Schöpsdau 2011: 581 for a helpful description of "dialectic" as the art of seeing a single "form" in diverse particulars, comparing *Phaedr.* 265d3, *Rep.* 537c, *Soph.* 253d–e, and *Phil.* 16d–17a.

41. Cherniss 1953: 377. Strauss 1975: 184 agrees: "We are then forced to conclude that the ideas retain in the *Laws*, if in a properly subdued or muted manner, the status which they occupy, say, in the *Republic*." Schöpsdau 2011: 592 holds that the idea of the Good underlies the Athenian's search for the "one," arguing that virtually all interpreters have seen references to the "forms" in this discussion. On this controversy, see further Klosko 1988: 76; Stalley 1983: 135–36.

thenceforward, virtually on a daily basis. Note, however, that the Athenian himself allows these Socratic questions to stand as questions; he does not now provide any adequate responses to his own questions. Like Socrates in the *Republic*, who also resists explaining the Form of the Good, the Athenian simply emphasizes that, whatever his own possible limitations, the city's future philosophers must grasp these issues precisely. As the Athenian points out, in fact, even if they themselves cannot confidently answer these questions, "We will contrive" (*mêchanêsometha*) some other way in which philosophical understanding will come to exist in the city—presumably, via the Nocturnal Council (965e). Otherwise, they will have to face the possibility of abandoning their entire project.[42] "Not at all!" Kleinias exclaims: but how could someone "contrive" it (*mêchanôito*, 965e)? The Athenian responds: "Let's not yet discuss how we might contrive it (*mêchanêsaimetha*)"; rather, let us discuss whether it is necessary (966a). As we will soon gather, Kleinias is convinced that it is necessary.

The characters' repeated references to "contriving" are notable: they are reflected in the final lines of the dialogue, in a direct allusion to this passage. After the Athenian explains that the philosophers of the Nocturnal Council will be like men they have never before seen, Megillus exclaims to Kleinias: "Based on all that we have just said, either we must give up the idea of founding the city, or we must not let the stranger go, but by prayers and every contrivance (*mêchanais pasais*) we must make him a partner in founding the city" (969c). The Dorians are firmly convinced that the Athenian either has the requisite philosophical knowledge or can construct a philosophical council with that knowledge. The Athenian is revealed to be, in their conception at least, the savior of the city. The philosophical understanding that he or the "future philosophers" possess is essential to saving the city.

In their repetition of the vocabulary of "contrivance," these statements also echo the beginning of Book 4. While founding the city, the Athenian had said that if a powerful individual tramples the laws, then the city will have "no contrivance of salvation" (*ouk esti sôtêrias mêchanê*, 714a). On the other hand, he had also insisted that we should imitate "by every contrivance" (*pasêi mêchanêi*) the age of Kronos (713e7), i.e., by instituting a regime of law. By contrast with this foundation of the regime of law, however, the interlocutors agree at the very end of the dialogue that all "contrivances" should be geared toward installing the rule of *nous*, without which the city will inevitably fail.

---

42. For this interpretation of 965e4–5, see England 1921 2: 628, with *Laws* 770c–e.

What is necessary is not to establish laws as the "contrivance" that will restrain powerful individuals, but rather to find those individuals who can win clarity on the city's paramount goal, and to "contrive" to install them as "knowers," as "leaders," and as "saviors" on the acropolis.[43]

The Singular Freedom and Virtue of Philosophers

By means of the preceding discussion, the Athenian has convinced Kleinias that the ability to know the forms, and moreover to provide a demonstration (*endeixis*) in argument (*tên de endeixin tôi logôi*, 966b), is central to the Nocturnal Council's leadership of the city. Kleinias has come to believe that anything less than such knowledge amounts to a habit or disposition (*hexis*) that suits a slave (966b). Kleinias is unable to discern the implications of his remark. We had previously understood that all citizens, including magistrates, are "slaves" of the law. Now we are given a new and different account of the distinction between free and slave. Ordinary citizens are slaves because of their ignorance of the greatest things.[44] By contrast, only the philosopher is truly free.

Building on these implications, the Athenian repeats, not for the last time, that those who will be the *real* guardians of the laws (*tous ontôs phulakas . . . tôn nomôn*) must really know (*dei . . . ontôs eidenai*) the truth about serious matters, and "be adequate (*hikanous*) to interpret them in speech and to follow them in deed, judging according to nature what comes to be both well and badly" (966b). This passage adds several important dimensions to the Athenian's presentation of the Nocturnal Council. First, it confirms that the philosophers of the Nocturnal Council constitute the genuine guardians of the city, based on their knowledge of the city's true aims. Second, these philosophers judge nobility and its opposite according to the nature of things, not according to law or divine command. Third, they are competent to judge everything in the city, including its laws, according to the standards of nature: nature is the measure, and the philosophers do the measuring for humanity. Fourth, and finally, they are "adequate," both to know the truth and to abide by it.

---

43. Against the current tide of opinion in favor of a rule-bound, integrated Nocturnal Council, see, again, Brisson 2005: 109–16 and Brunt 1993: 250–51, who recognize that the Nocturnal Council represents the rule of *nous*. I differ with Brisson, however, when he argues that "through this College, the city becomes aware that it is an integral part of a universe that is not abandoned to chance, a universe which, because of the order it reflects, provides the city with the model it must follow if it wishes to achieve virtue" (111).

44. Cf. Cherry 2013: 55.

This final implication of the Athenian's description is especially significant. The philosophers' comprehension of the forms of justice, moderation, beauty, goodness, and courage is not powerless in relation to their character and behavior. On the contrary, their knowledge is expressed in "following in deed" their grasp of these ideas (*tois ergois sunakolouthein*, 966b7). Virtue is knowledge, after all, because the truly knowledgeable are ruled by their knowledge.[45] The truly knowledgeable philosophers are not corruptible like the rest of humanity. Contrast Kleinias' inference—which is strongly encouraged by the Athenian—that the prudent man must, upon hearing the Athenian's sermon on scary archaic justice (715e–716b), consider how to become one of "the followers of the god (*tôn sunakolouthêsontôn . . . tôi theôi*)" (716b). Once again, readers are invited to notice the verbal echo in these passages. Ordinary citizens, in the best case, "follow" the city's god, as described by the Athenian in the general prelude and again in Book 10. By contrast with these ordinary citizens, the philosophers live lives in which the god's role is dramatically reduced; the god is at most an object of study, not a source of ethical guidance. The philosophers' character is based on their own understanding of nature, which they "follow" in practice.

The Athenian's particular language also invites us to contrast these lines with his earlier speech on the weakness of mortal nature (874e–875d). He had said: "There is no human being whose nature is adequate (*phusis . . . hikanê*) both to know what benefits human beings in civic life, and, on the basis of this knowledge, always to be able and willing to do what is best" (875a). On the contrary, such human beings are now said to exist. The philosophers of the Nocturnal Council are not beleaguered by the ordinary defects of mortal nature, which are repeatedly said to undermine any exercise of political power that is not held strictly accountable by the law. By contrast, other cities, "where the guardians (*phulakes*) are not adequate (*hikanoi*) in word or deed (*logôi ergôi*), with an adequate understanding of virtue (*aretês peri gignôskontes hikanôs*)" will tend to fail miserably (964c). The philosophers of

---

45. On virtue and knowledge, see L.S. Pangle 2014 and compare the treatment of Brisson 2001: 173, who reaches a similar conclusion about the equivalence of virtue and knowledge by different means. By contrast with my own interpretation, however, Brisson finds the order in which virtue consists to be homologous in the individual soul, the city, and the cosmos as a whole; the homology itself, he argues, depends on the providential divinity who rationally governs the universe. *Contra* Brisson, it is possible to adopt a teleological view of human ethical and political life without a correspondingly teleological view of the cosmos; such at least is the Athenian's own approach.

the Nocturnal Council are "adequate in word and deed" and therefore different from both Magnesia's ordinary citizens and from all other political leaders.

Hence, they need not be—should not be—constrained by law. Rather, the philosophers possess the ultimate title to rule the city: wisdom. Recall the Athenian's statement: that "if" a human being were ever born, who was "by divine favor" adequate by nature (*phusei hikanos*) to know and to rule, then he would not "need to be ruled by any law" (875c). Now, at last, the Athenian is saying that such human beings, with an "adequate" nature, do in fact exist. They should not be ruled by law: "For no law or order (*oute nomos oute taxis oudemia*) is stronger than knowledge (*epistêmês*), nor is it right for *nous* to be a subordinate or a slave, but rather to be ruler over all things (*pantôn archonta*), if it is true and really free according to nature; but now it doesn't exist anywhere or in any way, except to a slight extent (*nun de ou gar estin oudamou oudamôs, all' ê kata brachu*)" (875c–d, tr. Pangle 1980, modified).[46] Philosophical knowledge gives the Nocturnal Council a title to rule Magnesia.[47]

Reimagining Divinity among the Philosophers

What, then, is the role of the gods in the lives of these philosophers? In short: they are the objects of philosophical study. The guardians will strive to understand—to whatever extent human beings are capable—the gods' power, specifically by working to "grasp every proof that there is about the gods" (*to pasan pistin labein tôn ousôn peri theôn*, 966c). Philosophical study of the gods yields nothing more (and nothing less) than a rational and articulate grasp of all (existing or possible) "proofs"—that is, arguments or means of persuasion, such as those found in the law courts of Athens—about the existence of the gods and their nature.[48] Without this understanding, no citizen will ever be

---

46. As Lewis 2009a: 654 (cf. Lewis 1998: 14) points out, the "slight extent" likely refers to the Nocturnal Council; but Lewis's integrationist interpretation differs from my own. (For further discussion of this passage, see the section "Rule of Law, Rule of *Nous*" in chapter 4).

47. The philosophers of the Nocturnal Council correspond to the "prudent men" of the sixth title to rule, according to which the wise lead the ignorant. This is the title that the Athenian had installed in Book 4, except that now the intermediary of a law-code is not only unnecessary but also unjust. The philosophers have the right to rule.

48. The philosophers do not have knowledge of the gods; their understanding, like the Athenian's, must remain provisional; cf. Cherry 2013: 57; Lewis 2010: 42–44; Lewis 2012: 24.

among those "approved with respect to virtue," that is, considered genuinely virtuous (966d).

This statement is a reflection upon, and a criticism of, the regime of law. If we understand the statement literally, then all ordinary citizens will fail to count as genuinely virtuous. Verbally echoing his statements about the philosophers as followers of their own rational understanding, the Athenian says that "most citizens" merely "follow the speech of the laws" (*têi phêmêi . . . tôn nomôn sunakolouthousin*, 966c; cf. earlier: 716b, "followers of the god"). They can be forgiven for doing so (966c). Through lacking ability, they embody nothing more than a shadow of virtue. Even Kleinias agrees (966d), though, once again, apparently without recognizing the far-reaching consequences of his agreement. If virtue is knowledge, then most Magnesians will lack harmony in their souls: they will embody the greatest ignorance (689a–b). Magnesia is anything but a community of the virtuous.

In the midst of making these statements, the Athenian also takes pains to indicate that the philosophers of the Nocturnal Council will not be impious. In that respect they differ considerably—supposedly—from those earlier philosophers (967c7: *tous philosophountas*) who subscribed to the theses on materialism and motion discussed in Book 10. Indeed, the Athenian now maintains that being "firmly pious" (*bebaiôs theossebê*, 967d4) depends on grasping, above all, the theses he had advanced in the first argument of Book 10: that soul rules body and that *nous* is found in the stars. He omits mention of the second and third arguments—the fundamental planks of the civil religion, according to which the gods take care of mortals, punish wrongdoers, and in both cases assure the victory of justice.[49] The Athenian focuses exclusively on the philosophical points discussed in the first argument of Book 10. (If you had thought that the Athenian held the second and third arguments to exemplify serious philosophy, then think again.)

Only a learned (cf. 967e), philosophical person, who can "give an account" of such matters (967e–968a), and who has also acquired the "ordinary virtues" (*dêmosiois aretais*), can be an "adequate ruler of the whole city" (*archôn . . . hikanos holês poleôs*, 968a). Like the philosophers of Callipolis, in fact, such a person must apply his philosophical understanding to the customs and lawful habits of the city (967e).

---

49. Strauss 1975: 184.

Legislating for the Nocturnal Council

Now the legislators can agree that this Nocturnal Council should become a guardian of the city "according to the law" (*kata nomon*, 968a7). Everything about the council, however, has suggested that its members will be anything but pious and lawful in a conventional sense. The Athenian keeps the idea of the "rule of law" alive precisely in order to pinpoint the paradoxes of establishing the rule of *nous* within the regime of law. The best that the rule of law can do is, paradoxically, to establish a philosophical council that is, in its intellectual substance and virtuous character, entitled to be above the law.[50] This paradox will not be the final ambiguity that besets Plato's last, longest, and greatest reflection on the regime of law.

The Athenian immediately makes manifest the difficulty of encompassing the council within the regime of law. Kleinias is excited to establish the council, in the belief that "the god is nearly leading us" in this direction (968b). Earlier, Kleinias had said, more accurately, that it was "the argument (*ho logos*, 962c9)" that was leading them to the Nocturnal Council. In either case, it is of course the Athenian himself who is, as always, leading his interlocutors onward. The Athenian's reply makes clear the central difficulty: "Legislation is not yet possible about such matters [as those concerning the council] until it has been organized, and then it is necessary for masters of what they must become masters of to do the legislating; but the preparation for such things, if done right, would already amount to schooling by long association" (968c3–7).[51]

This obscure and widely contested statement is, as Cherniss points out, *intended* to be puzzling: Kleinias responds to it with a baffled request for clarification (968c).[52] In the course of clarifying the point, the Athenian says that the legislators must compile a roster of those who are fit for guardianship by nature, by age, by their capacity for learning, and by their character and customs. It worth reminding readers that the oral flow of this conversation— between the Athenian and the elderly Dorians—has left the Dorians entirely lost. The Athenian's meaning is, indeed, far from perspicuous unless readers conduct a patient reconstruction of his views throughout the dialogue. The Dorians can be forgiven for wondering: Does the Athenian mean, literally, but

---

50. Cf. Strauss 1975: 181: "The obscurity is due to the impossibility of assigning to the wise as wise their proper place and status in a politically viable form." He is referring to the composition of the council and its relation to the ordinary magistrates.

51. Tr. Cherniss 1953: 373, modified. For extended discussion, see Lewis 1998: 11–14.

52. Cherniss 1953: 373.

paradoxically, that only future members of the Nocturnal Council who have had the requisite philosophical education will be able to develop a "roster" of candidates in the first place? Is it old men who are supposed to become philosophers in their old age, so as to assume the role of the elderly judges and rulers in the Nocturnal Council? If we are meant to imagine choosing younger men for the roster, however, then will the council have older men who are somehow already embodiments of *nous*?[53]

Beyond these difficulties, the Athenian points to the additional difficulties of discovering, second, what should be learned, and third, when and for how long the various studies should continue. "It is vain," he says, "to set these matters down in writing, for it would not be clear to the students themselves that they had learned anything at the appropriate time, until knowledge of the subject in question somehow arose within the soul of each one" (968d–e). Whatever the Athenian has in mind here, he certainly intends to indicate that an adequate knowledge of the council's philosophical education does not yet exist.[54] He may also be indicating that the council itself will have to legislate, not only for its own education, but also with regard to its own powers. These matters are not a secret, he says, but they cannot be outlined in advance (*aprorrēta*), because prescribing them beforehand would not clarify the matters under discussion (968e). The Athenian's obscure statements seem to imply that the Nocturnal Council can only be a law unto itself. At all events, no ordinary lawgiver can reasonably or justly give laws to the Nocturnal Council. Moreover, the Athenian is at pains to indicate that the powers and education of members of the Nocturnal Council lie outside the framework of Magnesia's existing law-code.

Is the Nocturnal Council a Practical Ideal?

The Athenian leaves open the question of whether the three old men will succeed in installing "knowers" on their city's acropolis. In imagining philosophers with a full and complete understanding of the forms, philosophers who can give a wholly adequate account of these matters in argument (cf. 966b), the Athenian is suggesting that these philosophers are (only) about as likely to

---

53. Schöpsdau 2011: 581 imagines that the Athenian will help the Magnesians make the transition to the establishment of the Nocturnal Council, heroically struggling (584) to make sense of the training of the young from the beginnings of the city onward.

54. Brisson 2001: 176 proposes to find the program of study in the *Epinomis*, but this later work, almost certainly not by Plato himself, obscures more than it clarifies the final pages of the *Laws*. Pierris 1998: 124–26 also takes this approach.

exist as the philosophers of Plato's Callipolis. Both Socrates and the Athenian are shown constructing a hypothetical body of "knowers" who resemble gods. These philosophers are individuals who can only be imagined, as though in dreams. Like the philosophers of the *Republic*, those of the Nocturnal Council are seriously intended, yes—as hypothetical embodiments of *nous*, whose existence is called upon to provide a regulative ideal for the regime of law, and a critical basis for reflecting on that regime. Conversely, the Athenian's interlocutors are, like Glaucon in the *Republic*, anxious to see this philosophical body come into existence for the sake of the city, even though both the Athenian and Socrates remain highly tentative.

Intriguingly, if the philosophers of the Nocturnal Council were to exist as the Athenian describes them, then their subordination to law would be a vast injustice—an injustice against the very "soul" of the city, against the philosophers who constitute the city itself. The Athenian's philosophical "knowers" have a right to rule, by virtue of the sixth title to rule. To deny them that entitlement would again constitute a vast injustice—not to mention an act of great imprudence. As the Athenian argued in Book 9, genuinely free and liberated *nous* should not be constrained by law, must less held accountable to ordinary citizens. For all these reasons it would be inappropriate to say, with Morrow for example, that the council's members "are always subject to the numerous checks that Plato's law provides."[55] For this characterization to be appropriate, the philosophers would have to lack the god-like character the Athenian ascribes to them. On the other hand, if the god-like human beings actually described by the Athenian were subject to those numerous checks, then the city would fail to respect their standing as individuals with souls governed by *nous*. The integrationist position is burdened by the insupportable cost of downplaying the Athenian's dramatic, if not hyperbolic, presentation of the Nocturnal Council.

From the perspective of certain Platonic dialogues, to be sure, it is impossible for human beings to offer fully satisfying answers to Socrates' characteristic "What is X?" questions. In Plato's *Apology*, Socrates is the wisest of human beings precisely because he is aware that he lacks knowledge of the "greatest things." If Socratic wisdom is humanity's ultimate philosophical achievement, then the philosophers of *Republic* and *Laws* are impossibilities, full stop, because they are imagined to know precisely these "greatest things." If knowledge of the greatest things is impossible for human beings, then both

---

55. Morrow 1960: 513.

Socrates (in the *Republic*) and the Athenian should be understood to be not only imagining an impossible ideal, but also actively calling attention to the impossibility of that ideal. In that case, the philosophers' "abandonment" of the city that needs them as an anchor and savior implies that the city itself will necessarily fail. If the city is unable to depend on philosophers to comprehend the forms in a fully articulate way, in argument (966a–b), then it will necessarily be slavish (966b) and liable to suffer what ordinary cities suffer (964c6–d1). The city's inability to cultivate virtue in citizens implies that it should be abandoned (770d–e). These dire consequences would follow even in a city ruled by philosophers, if those philosophers were "merely" capable of achieving Socratic *aporia*.

Kleinias and Megillus are as convinced as ever that the city needs political philosophers. They are in no position to resist the momentum of this final section, which suggests that philosophers alone can save the city. Readers, too, may have been "rooting" for the city all along; they may *want* these philosophers to appear at the end, like a *deus ex machina*, to save the city. No doubt they (as well-informed readers of Plato) have been wondering all along whether philosophers will appear at the dialogue's highly anticipated conclusion. Now they understand that those philosophers must be established as rulers on the Acropolis, on pain of the city's eventual failure. The dilemma is that without philosophical knowledge (understood in a highly demanding sense) the city will face catastrophe, but it may be that philosophical knowledge is unavailable to human beings. This dilemma carries with it implications for the Athenian Stranger's own project and in particular for his "truest tragedy."

Even if readers may harbor doubts based on "Socratic wisdom," though, the Athenian Stranger does not rule out the possibility that fully knowledgeable philosophers will exist—unless, *contra* his *ipsissima verba*, we somehow infer their impossibility from his exalted description of them. He does not subscribe to the view that philosophical wisdom consists precisely in awareness of one's own ignorance of the greatest things. He wishes to keep alive, at least in thought, the possibility of fully knowledgeable philosophers. As in Book 9 (875c–d), he gives that possibility just enough credibility that it will linger in the minds of readers as an open question. The question is meaningful only because the philosophers of the Nocturnal Council are a "live" enough option that they matter. They cannot be dismissed out of hand, as though they are clearly irrelevant.[56] Whether these philosophers will ever exist or not, and

---

56. They would become irrelevant, however, if we could easily dismiss them: for example, if we were asked to imagine that they would grow wings and conduct aerial surveillance on

whether they would want to rule if they were to exist (a related question that the Athenian Stranger does not raise), they remain relevant enough to form a legitimate foundation of criticism of the regime of law, from the perspective of a hypothetical, barely possible regime of *nous*. They "nag" readers with the possibility that humanity could achieve something higher and better—and that, without doing so, it will persist in its patterns of self-destruction and madness.

Perhaps, after all, the Athenian does not bother to reconcile the position of these philosophers with the city's law code because they are not meant to coexist with other, ordinary citizens within a practical, republican regime. If they were meant to coexist with the city, almost like Supreme Court justices, then why did the Athenian refuse to explain that point? Why did he leave their status hanging in the air at the very end? A better interpretation is that the Nocturnal Council is left standing, without explanation, as both a nettlesome question and as a source of criticism of the regime of law, and therefore of worry or anxiety for all those who would advocate for such a regime.[57]

Conclusion: *The Dialogue Ends in Perplexity*

The Athenian drops a bombshell in his final utterance in the work. In vocabulary that echoes his foundation of the regime of law, he says that the city should be handed over to the Nocturnal Council. Readers—and particularly those who would seamlessly integrate the council into the city's legal framework—have shown too little appreciation of the placement of the Athenian's culminating statement about the council. Why would the Athenian conclude the dialogue by implicitly posing questions about the relationship between *nous* and *nomos*? Is *nous* after all intended to displace *nomos* as the foundation of the city's well-being? Why would the Athenian not only fail to resolve the issue but also sow in his readers a number of potentially unsettling doubts? Why suggest, ominously, in the final movement, that Magnesia is doomed unless the interlocutors somehow "contrive," almost hoping against hope, to produce rare philosophical knowledge in the city (965e)?

Magnesia's citizens. Imagined in this way, they would have no hold on us as readers, no claim on our attention. Laks 2001: 114, to some extent at least, recognizes the importance of what I have called the "stalking horse" embodied by the best regime, by speaking of a "legislative utopia"—which is, in his view, internal to the *Laws* itself rather than derived from a comparison with the *Republic*—which "hovers" over the second-best city as an ideal.

57. For varying interpretations, see Ausland 2002 (the dialogue is "studiously ambiguous" on this question); and Kamtekar 1997: 251–52 ("the *Laws* in a sense establishes the possibility of philosophical rule and a good society").

The Athenian's final statement is a surprising conclusion—except that it is hardly a conclusion at all. Rather, it functions as a question, as though this long text itself were aporetic. While the Athenian's rhetoric strongly suggests that the three old men are always reaching the "end," his idea that the city should be handed over to the Nocturnal Council is (to speak charitably) undeveloped. This lack of development is striking, precisely because the details of the law code are so highly developed in every particular, in the eleven and one-half books that precede the discussion of the Nocturnal Council.[58] Readers are invited, even forced, to explore the aforementioned questions for themselves, and in particular to wonder about the worth of *nomos* in the absence of philosophers (or even in their presence).

As they ponder these questions, readers will understand, at least, that the final pages of the dialogue raise to consciousness a critique of all that has preceded. The achievements of the Nocturnal Council's philosophers reflect poorly on nonphilosophical citizens and Magnesia's regime of law. The Nocturnal Council is a hypothetical construct, unlikely to exist, but just possible; it cannot be ignored. It is useful in helping readers think through the limitations of the city's regime of law, when seen from a decidedly philosophical perspective.

This interpretation of the Nocturnal Council corresponds to a vision of the entire dialogue as an educational tool for readers. The dialogue is not intended to bring forward any realizable political regime, or even a political ideal to which lawgivers should aspire. Taken as a whole, the dialogue is intended to educate readers in the limited possibility of political improvement, even when well-intentioned philosophers intervene at the founding. The limitations of politics remain noteworthy even if the regime of law still has important benefits to offer ordinary citizens.

Appendix: The Composition of the Nocturnal Council

The composition of the Nocturnal Council is a complex issue.[59] In two separate (and, to some extent, divergent) passages, the Athenian says that the

---

58. This literary pattern, however, in which a long work concludes with a presumably flourishing regime crashing down at the end, can also be seen in at least one other significant work of the period, with which Plato was surely familiar: Xenophon's *Cyropaedia*. In that text, of course, it is only in the very final chapter that Cyrus' regime comes crashing down after his death.

59. Useful treatments include Brisson 2001: 165–70; Klosko 2006: 236–37; Morrow 1960: 500–515; Piérart 1974: 210–28 (which includes a useful discussion of the "observers").

Nocturnal Council is made up of the oldest ten Guardians of the Laws, the Supervisor of Education and his predecessors, all those who have won the prize of excellence (above all, the Auditors: 946b[60]), the "observers," and younger associates between thirty and forty years of age (951d–e, 961a–b).[61] The Athenian's descriptions of the Nocturnal Council's "full members" (i.e., not the younger associates) suggest that they will "save the city" because they have received an advanced philosophical education. Consider, for example, that the council's core members will have "adequate knowledge of virtue" (964c–d). They are likened to *nous* and think about the most important things in an exceptional way (965a). The Athenian alludes to the language of "forms" when he describes their knowledge (965c). Apart from the "younger associates," there is no room in the Nocturnal Council for nonphilosophers.[62]

The implications of the Athenian's presentation of the council are consequential. After working through the dialogue consecutively, readers may find it surprising that all the aforementioned magistrates turn out to be philosophers. It is only in retrospect that readers will see that, after all, the Athenian has made good on his sporadic indications that there will be separate educational tracks and distinct types of citizens, despite all appearances to the contrary. If readers wondered, understandably, how practical, nonphilosophical citizens could carry out the tasks assigned to the Supervisor of Education or the Guardians of the Laws, or why the Auditors were called "divine" or said to be the best citizens, then the Athenian has resolved the puzzles.[63] The Athenian

---

60. This is an inference: see Morrow 1960: 503.

61. At 964b8–9, the Athenian refers to the members of the Nocturnal Council as the "interpreters, the teachers, the lawgivers, the guardians of the others." With England 1921 2: 624, and against Schöpsdau 2011: 593–94, I take this description to refer to the general functions of the Nocturnal Council, and not to the specific office of the "Interpreters" (759d–e), because the word "interpreters" runs in parallel with other substantives that signify descriptions of functions, rather than particular offices.

62. *Contra* Bobonich 2002: 392.

63. Readers may wonder how to account for the Athenian's suggestion that Kleinias himself should be one of the first Guardians of the Laws (753a) if all the Guardians of the Laws are people of significant philosophical ability. Does the Athenian's suggestion imply, somehow, that Kleinias would be an appropriate member of this body, or that the Guardians of the Laws are somehow deficient in the ways that Kleinias is deficient? I think not. Kleinias is a Guardian of the Laws only while the city is being established—that is, only as a necessity of the transitional period: the Athenian makes his suggestion while discussing the "first" Guardians of the Laws (752e1), not those chosen according to the normal procedure once "a certain time has passed" (753b3, tr. Pangle 1980). For a discussion of the different methods of election of the Guardians of the Laws, both transitional and regular, see Morrow 1960: 204–6, 218. In this

offers few details as to how the system would work in practice; he does not draw attention to that question.

Why did the Athenian wait so long to introduce the Nocturnal Council? Why didn't he raise these issues in Book 6, when he first described the Guardians of the Laws and the Supervisor of Education? Tentatively, we may speculate that at that stage of the discussion the Athenian had not yet convinced Kleinias and Megillus—perhaps he had not convinced the dialogue's readers, either—that philosophy was essential to the city's good governance. The Athenian created the illusion that a regime of law is self-sufficient: that practical political men and women, raised well and in accordance with his laws, could govern the city successfully. He thereby gave the regime of law its due, by illustrating its capacities, and by fostering hope on its behalf, before suggesting that, appearances to the contrary, this regime has significant, even decisive, limitations.

Over the course of the next six books, he began to raise questions about that prospect. He gradually gave hints that things were other than they appeared. Apart from the indications of a two-tiered educational system, and a distinct pool of candidates for the city's high magistracies, he also showed that these magistrates had duties that require philosophical insight. He later developed that notion by discussing the Socratic paradox and demanding that judicial magistrates (for example, in the city's homicide courts) implement that paradox in actual judicial practice. Finally, he explained that certain magistrates would be needed to articulate and defend the city's theological beliefs. In other words, he impressed upon Kleinias and Megillus—and the dialogue's readers—that the regime of law, no matter how sound and well established, requires philosophy to "save" it. The regime of law is nothing without philosophy. Philosophy must rule the city by means of law.

Does the Athenian suggest that his arrangements are practicable? How, for example, is an educational system with different tracks supposed to be developed? Will the citizens know about it—since the Athenian keeps matters so obscure? How will the Athenian bring it about that only philosophical students or philosophers are chosen as the thirty-seven Guardians of the Laws, given the elections' openness to all candidates? The Athenian does not explicitly address these questions, because, I believe, he wants to keep the issue of philosophical rule in the background—to obscure it from the

---

transitional period, the selection of the members of the Nocturnal Council will work differently; see the discussion that follows, along with Schopsdau 2011: 584–85, *contra* England 1921 2: 636.

elderly Dorians. Many scholars have ignored those questions, but in doing so, they ignore issues that any respectable interpretation of the dialogue has to address.[64]

Although they have not always linked all these indications together, scholars such as Morrow, Schöpsdau, Brisson, and Bobonich have shown that there is a "backdoor" method by which education and recruitment are possible.[65] Their arguments can be strengthened considerably if we link them to the indications we explored in earlier chapters (see especially chapter 8, "Developing the Citizens' *Thumos* in Elections and Courts"). As Morrow has recognized, the Nocturnal Council's younger associates are the key to envisaging the process of recruitment in a practical way.[66] These younger associates are considered worthy of membership by virtue of their "nature and upbringing" (961b).[67] Having traced the Athenian's differential educational plans throughout the work, we can now see that this reference to "up-bringing" strongly suggests that the younger associates will have received a superior education prior to their selection for the Nocturnal Council. From early childhood onward, and somehow in connection with their families (751c; cf. 650b), they have shown themselves worthy of special training. They (or at least certain of them) have shone, since then, in every dimension of their education and civic activity. Once nominated by one of its full members, the candidate is then reviewed by the Nocturnal Council as a whole, unbeknownst to the candidate himself and to the other citizens; the Nocturnal Council then accepts or rejects the nomination (952a–b, 961a–b). If the candidate is approved, then as a younger associate he is to undertake the philosophical studies outlined by the full members "with all seriousness" (*pasêi spoudêi*, 952c). He can take advantage of these studies, not because of his "previous general education," but rather because he has received a superior education all along.[68]

The Athenian appears to return to the education of these younger associates in an obscure passage at the end (968d). How will the Nocturnal

---

64. It is inadequate to refer, with Bobonich 2002: 394, for example, to the "previous general education," instead of trying to explain how a system of educational tracking might work.

65. Cf. Brisson 2005: 112, who is right to speak of a "vast hidden process of selecting political élites"—although his method of working out this process differs from my own.

66. Morrow 1960: 508–9, followed by Schöpsdau 2011: 576–606, esp. 584–85.

67. Morrow 1960: 508–9.

68. The quoted phrase comes from Bobonich 2002: 394.

Council be established? Only, the Athenian says, through "teaching and much intercourse" (968c6–7), a phrase that recalls the free doctor. Pressed as to his meaning, the Athenian says that a list (*katalogos*) will have to be drawn up, of those who would be suitable (*epitêdeioi*) to guard the city "in age, ability to learn, and disposition of character and habits" (968c–d). If we were forced to imagine this description in practice, then the Athenian may have in mind a transitional period in which he himself teaches promising young people, who then become philosophers in their maturity and who finally provide a philosophical education to younger prospects.[69]

As plausible as this reconstruction may be, though, it leaves out of account the need, in the future, beyond any transitional phase, to renew these lists of promising young people continually, perhaps even from early childhood onward, in order to educate them with a view to their one day becoming younger associates themselves.[70] It is in this passage that the Athenian, briefly and obscurely, calls to mind the qualities of the "young tyrant" (and his counterparts in Plato's *Republic*)—a philosophically promising young man whose rule under the supervision of the true legislator has been suppressed by the regime of law (709e–710a). Now the Athenian has finally returned to the legislator and the promising young man. He is making provisions to educate that prospective philosopher under the supervision of the philosophically trained "true legislators" of the Nocturnal Council. While the general education of the citizens from childhood onward has been described (809e–810c, 817e–818e), the Athenian has not previously laid out the "more precise" education appropriate for prospective philosophers (809e, 818a). Instead, he has consistently deferred the discussion of this other, more sophisticated curriculum, on the grounds that it is impossible to legislate for them in advance (cf. 968e, 818e). Even to legislate about these matters, never mind precisely or not, is impossible to do in advance; but the Athenian now prepares (969a) to offer his opinions on this education. This willingness does not suggest any interest in joining the colony itself, but it does suggest that the Athenian is prepared to expound his own views on a philosophical educational system. The passage implies, therefore, that the city's educational system is missing an account of its most crucial component—the educational "track" by which philosophers

---

69. Cf. Cherniss 1953: 373–74 and Schopsdau 2011: 584–85.

70. Morrow 1960: 508 also takes the catalogue of persons fit to receive a philosophical education at 968d to refer in general to the younger associates of the Nocturnal Council, not to any "list" useful only in a transitional period.

are trained—and that the Athenian now intends, in a conversation beyond the dialogue, to make up that deficiency.[71]

These younger associates must leave the council at least by age forty. Why shouldn't they become permanent members of the council? If they return to take up civilian duties, then can we be sure of their election to high office?[72] Not necessarily. The Athenian says, however, that, as for those of them who maintain a good reputation (*tous d' eudokimountas*), the other citizens will "gaze admiringly at them and watch over them with special care" (. . . *apoblepontas eis autous diapherontôs te têrountas*, 952a–b); they will be honored if they do well and greatly dishonored if they turn out "worse than the majority" (*cheirous tôn pollôn*, 952a–b).[73] If they fail at lesser duties, not to mention greater ones, either because they turn out to lack ability or commit crimes because they are "bent by the weight" of their offices (945b5–8), then the Auditors can remove them from office. On the whole, however, they constitute a group of younger citizens set apart from the other citizens, usually because they deserve greater honor. They have already received a superior education from childhood onward; they will then have received a more advanced philosophical education in the Nocturnal Council itself; and they will return to life in the city with a special pedigree. Scholars have understandably seen links between the *cursus honorum* of the *Laws* and that of the *Republic*, as well as similarities in their educational systems.[74]

---

71. Strauss 1975: 185.

72. Morrow 1960: 508.

73. At 836a the Athenian uses nearly the same expression (. . . *mê apoblepein allose, têrein d' aei* . . . , 836a4–5) to describe the magistrates' keeping a watchful eye over the young, so as to limit their desires. Here the point is that the entire city will watch the younger associates in a special, honorific way (*diapherontôs*) that differs from the magistrates' ordinary surveillance. The Greek verb *apoblepô* carries with it connotations of gazing longingly or admiringly, or of training one's sights and attention on someone or something in a special way, because it is the best thing, the *telos*, or the "North Star" that provides guidance. In the *Laws* itself, see, for example, 626a (the Cretan lawgiver legislated by training his sights on military victory as the city's highest goal, cf. 705d); 628d (some legislators incorrectly train their sights on external war); 686d (the Athenian—ironically—"gazes with admiration" at the wondrous armies of the early Greeks); 707d (we are legislating by looking toward the virtue of the regime); 757c (proportional equality); 811b (which model should the Supervisor of Education look to in deciding what to teach the young?); 811c (the answer to the preceding question: look to the present speeches); 836a (the magistrates specially keep watch over the character of the young, working to limit their desires, a passage that foreshadows the present one); 897d (we cannot look directly at the sun, but rather must look at an image of the motion of intelligence).

74. Morrow 1960: 508–9; Schöpsdau 2011: 583–85. These similarities further support the idea that the younger associates have the philosophical natures described by Socrates in Plato's *Republic*.

While their electoral success is not guaranteed, their political "profiles" would be outstanding, both because of their prestige and education and because of the city's careful and honorific watchfulness over them. These factors, combined with the influence of the top magistrates, makes their success likely. If we reflect again on the elaborate electoral procedures outlined by the Athenian, then we can imagine what a potential rival, who has not enjoyed these advantages, might think when he confronts a competitor with this type of *curriculum vitae*.[75] These details are added, I believe, to give the picture a certain plausibility; they do not imply that the author is firmly settled on realizing this model in practice. The major focus of the text's conclusion remains the god-like members of the Nocturnal Council and their divine knowledge.

---

75. Perhaps the magistrates will use *dokimasia* in their favor. We know little of the *dokimasia* procedure in the *Laws*, and in particular, the Athenian does not specify which magistrates supervise the scrutiny of prospective Guardians of the Laws; cf. 765b, 767c–d, 766b–c. Morrow 1960: 218 speculates, quite reasonably, that the Guardians of the Laws themselves would conduct this scrutiny, at least once the city's institutions were functioning in a normal way. See Morrow (1960: 217–18n.156) for an illuminating explanation of the twofold process by which the same officials both elect and scrutinize the new Supervisor of Education. At all events, as Bobonich 2002: 393 has argued, following Morrow, "The younger associate members of the Nocturnal Council will come to fill many offices of the state."

12
The "Truest Tragedy" in Plato's Laws

AT 817B, THE Athenian offers the following response to hypothetical tragic
poets who inquire about Magnesia's attitude toward them:

> O best of strangers, we ourselves are, to the best of our ability, poets of
> a tragedy that is as beautiful and excellent as possible; at any rate, our
> entire *politeia* is framed as a *mimêsis* of the most beautiful and best life.
> We, at least, say that just *that* is really the truest tragedy. (817b)

This passage raises a number of central interpretive issues and "will take us
close to the core of the *Laws* as a whole."[1] Why, for example, is the representation of Magnesia's way of life said to be a tragedy? Why doesn't the Athenian
simply dismiss the tragic poets from the city, as in *Republic* Book 10, where
Socrates explains that Callipolis will admit only hymns to the gods and
encomia to good men (607a)? What *is* a tragedy, anyway? And in what sense
is the Athenian's tragedy supposed to be the "truest" tragedy?

The Conventional Interpretation: The Legislator
as Rival of the Tragic Poets

The Athenian's comment is located in a discussion that distinguishes between
"serious" and "comic" pedagogy. At 810e, encouraged to dare to legislate
in a countercultural way, the Athenian points out that Greece's traditional
educators—the poets—are divided into two groups, the serious and the
comic. He proposes that the text of the *Laws* itself should guide Magnesia's

---

1. Laks 2010: 217–18.

Tragedy, Philosophy, and Political Education in Plato's Laws. Ryan K. Balot, Oxford University Press.
© Ryan K. Balot 2024. DOI: 10.1093/oso/9780197647226.003.0012

educators when they sift through existing poetry and other writings in order to find suitable pedagogical material (811d–e). Throughout the dialogue, indeed, the Athenian proposes that his own sayings and writings rival, and even prove superior to, those of the traditional poets.[2] Serious writers and teachers will encourage their charges to develop a harmonious spirit and to exhibit courage and moderation. By contrast, comic poets focus on what is shameful or base and thereby encourage disorderly motion and a cowardly spirit (816d–817a). Apparently, then, the Athenian himself—in the day's speeches and in his own writings—is the best authority, certainly better than ordinary poets, when it comes to "serious" matters such as the appropriate cultivation of human souls.

The Athenian's rivalry with the poets provides the basis of what I call the "conventional" or "optimistic" interpretation. Tragedy is the appropriately serious genre that will teach Magnesia's citizens how to become virtuous and why happiness can be won through the cultivation of virtue. Consider Sauvé Meyer: "If tragedy is the genre that pronounces on serious subjects, then the truest tragedy is the composition whose pronouncements on these subjects are most correct. In Plato's view, the true tragedian is not the poet who encourages the human propensity to lament our misfortunes, but the legislator who teaches us that the only misfortune that can befall a person is to fail to achieve virtue."[3] Equally anti-tragic is Mouze's reading: even though human weakness will always make punishment necessary, the gods will bring it about that, ultimately, justice is meted out to lawbreakers. Either in this life or the next, criminals will be punished, and the just will be rewarded with happiness.[4] Although Magnesia's laws will occasionally be broken, then, a just social and ethical order will eventually be reestablished through the rewards and punishments granted by attentive gods.[5]

---

2. Cf., for example, Prauscello 2014: 105–51, Folch 2015; with Levin 2010, 2014.

3. Sauvé-Meyer 2011: 402. As Lutz 2012: 112 says, "The city described by the Athenian Stranger claims that the best life is one of harmony and happiness. Accordingly, this city would discourage poetry that ennobles conflicts, suffering, lamentation, and tears, for such poetry would make people softer and more susceptible to excessive fears and hopes."

4. Cf. Mouze 1998: 93.

5. When the Athenian refers to actual tragedies ("serious tragedies" at 838c4), he points out (tendentiously and incorrectly) that Thyestes, Oedipus, and Macareus all inflicted upon themselves the just penalty of death for their crimes (838c). The Athenian himself reinterprets well-known existing tragedies—against the grain—apparently in light of the optimistic interpretation. (It is usually overlooked that these supposed criminals inflict penalties on themselves; the gods play no direct role.)

These scholars share the belief that the Athenian is "redefining" tragedy for his own purposes.[6] His "serious" teachings, though, are true and therefore superior to those embodied in conventional tragedies. This interpretation depends on the use of tragedy in a nontheatrical sense, such as the one excavated by Halliwell. Halliwell singles out Plato as the author who first began to use tragedy in a nontheatrical sense, so as to be able to refer, for example, to the "whole tragedy and comedy of life" (*Philebus* 50b).[7] He argues that Plato regards "tragedy" as emblematic of a particular world view: "a mentality that finds the organization of the world—governed by divine powers capable of ruthless destructiveness, and limited by the inevitability of a death that negates everything worth having—to be fundamentally hostile to human needs and values and irreconcilable with a positive moral significance."[8] Halliwell concludes that Plato sought to overthrow this conventionally "tragic" world view and to replace it with one (here called the "truest tragedy") based on truths rather than illusions and, in particular, one based on a conception of the cosmos as rationally ordered and ruled by providential gods.

Halliwell's interpretation reveals the fundamental premise of the optimistic interpretation. The cosmos is a rationally ordered whole; the gods are providential stewards of humanity; the good human life is possible for those who correctly cultivate virtue; the good life may even be inevitable because of the gods' attentive care for justice.[9] How, though, we might wonder, could such a "moral theodicy," as Kuhn has labeled it, legitimately be called

---

6. Under his supposed redefinition, "any ethical treatise would count as a tragedy" (Sauvé Meyer 2011: 399).

7. Laks 2010: 220 recognizes that the "nontheatrical" sense of tragedy is one of the key points in the discussion. See Halliwell 2002.

8. Halliwell 2002: 109. On these themes, one might compare the critique of poetry found in Plato's *Republic*, where Socrates targets tragedy, and Homer the tragedian (cf. 607a). He argues that tragedy miseducates its audiences by magnifying the importance of life, death, and material goods, and hence, by nourishing the irrational part of the soul. See Halliwell 2002; Laks 2010: 220–22, 225.

9. Generally speaking, these unstated premises become clear when we attend to different scholars' statements about the theology of Book 10. Laks 2010: 230 holds, for example, that the content of the law finds "its ultimate basis in the ultimate order of things as expressed by cosmic law." His interpretation of the "truest tragedy" passage is colored by the belief that in Book 10 "Plato gives us the final version of his kinetics" and that Book 10 represents an "argument based on physical theory to establish the rationality of the universe" (cf. Laks 2000: 289 and 290, respectively; cf. 260–61, 291: "the theodicy of Book X"). The idea that Book 10 represents a theodicy is familiar in a wide range of literature on the dialogue: cf., for example, Bobonich 2002: 108–9; Mouze 1998: 93–95.

"tragic"?[10] And, more broadly, was the Athenian offering a theodicy in the first place? Whatever our answers, it is essential to interpret the "truest tragedy" passage in connection with the Athenian's theology.[11]

As a first step, we can say that the conventional reading corresponds to the interpretation that Kleinias and Megillus, along with the ordinary citizens of Magnesia, would be most likely to accept. According to their understanding, the "truest" tragic doctrine—as opposed to the defective doctrines of traditional Greek tragedies—maintains that the gods reward the just and punish the unjust, so as to remedy any "disproportion"[12] between the virtuous life and the happy life. That high-minded idea appears on the surface of Book 7 and corresponds to the equally ambitious religious teachings on the surface of Book 10. If this view is correct, then the Athenian was engaged in the project, supposedly characteristic of moral philosophers, of making the world "safe for well-disposed people."[13]

If we doubt the gods' justice and providence, however, then we will seek another, deeper interpretation beneath the surface of the Athenian's pregnant remark. The Athenian himself may reward the just and punish the unjust by means of the city's legal system; but, as we have seen in the discussion of Book 10, the gods will not fulfill ordinary citizens' immature hopes and longings. Can we find an interpretation of this rich passage that squares with our reading of Book 10?

Toward a Tragic Interpretation, Part I

Fundamental to any such interpretation is to recall that the Athenian is speaking at two different levels—one directed at Magnesia's ordinary citizens, and another directed at a more philosophical audience, whether inside or outside the text. The conventional reading reassures ordinary Magnesians that the world is rational, providential, and just: that "good Magnesians" will flourish now and in the afterlife. By contrast, a genuinely tragic interpretation acknowledges, with the Athenian, that the world is devoid of

---

10. Kuhn 1941: 22.

11. For the importance of not dismissing this passage as simply metaphorical, see Laks 2010: 219. Reflecting on a similarly pregnant passage in *Republic* Book 7, Kuhn 1942: 82 notes that many interpreters limit themselves to its meaning in a strictly local context and urges the importance of recognizing "that here, as in other parts of Plato's works, two levels of meaning are joined."

12. The term comes from Kuhn 1941, 1942.

13. Williams 1996: 52.

divine providence. Human progress and the achievement of justice depend on human agency. The fullest realization of human nature and human flourishing is possible only for a few. Others require a civil religion even to live decently.

Laks has recognized that "tragedy" involves the ideas of irreconcilable conflict and a frustration of human purposes. Noting the Athenian's statement that "true law" brings the drama to completion, he asks about the significance of *nomos*, and relatedly of punishment, for the Athenian's presentation of the "truest tragedy." Laks maintains that a decidedly political response to this question is desirable. The point is not so much that just gods will punish wrongdoers as that "punishment is inevitable because *the legislator must necessarily have recourse to it*" (Laks 2010: 230, emphasis original). According to Laks, "violence of whatever kind or degree is incompatible with the very concept of the 'constitution' (*politeia*)."[14] The dialogue exposes the contradiction between the lawgiver's need to use violence instead of rational persuasion. This contradiction speaks to the unavoidable, "tragic" conflict between reason and pleasure, which afflicts all human beings, even philosophers.[15]

This discussion has the merit of taking the Athenian at his word: his own project of legislation is a *tragic* project. Laks is correct, moreover, to search for the tragic in irreconcilable conflict and the frustration of human (i.e., the legislator's) purposes. Laks refuses, however, to reconsider the dialogue's supposed "theodicy." If the Athenian offers a theodicy in Book 10, though, then the conflict between reason and passion, however irreconcilable and intrinsic to humanity, does not demonstrate the existence of tragedy. Nor does the mere existence of laws that issue commands or use violence. Those conflicts can, at least potentially, be redeemed at a cosmic level by just gods.[16] Just gods

---

14. Laks 2010: 231, citing *Laws* 8.832c2–7.

15. Pangle 1980: 460 interprets the Athenian's statement in a similar way: "The city, man's political existence, his longing for justice and political nobility and civic friendship, necessarily point beyond what is possible in civic life. Politics is animated by longings it can never satisfy, and these longings too are natural to man. Man's nature is not harmonious in any straightforward way; the body and the soul, the parts of the soul, exist in a complex tension." As I suggest in the text, I believe that this interpretation has much to be said for it, particularly because Pangle 1976 clearly does not interpret Book 10 as a theodicy. Pangle does not, however, systematically develop his illuminating reflections in his interpretive essay. Waugh 2001: 30 argues: "*The polis needs not only philosophy, but also narrative discourse, and the power that such discourse holds over its audience—as Plato well knows—can equal or overcome that of philosophy. This is the tragedy of the Laws*" (italics original). This statement, too, largely on target, remains undeveloped.

16. "At least potentially," because Laks himself holds that the theology of Book 10 provides a metaphysical underpinning for the work: see above at note 9.

can offer reconciliation and a relief from frustration, at least in the afterlife. Divine remedies of this sort negate tragedy, at a different level, by rendering human suffering or frustration intelligible. As Kuhn (1941, 1942) saw, the Athenian's supposed theodicy eliminates the possibility of tragedy.

Compare St. Augustine's treatment of human suffering and conflict in *The City of God*. St. Augustine would agree with Laks that the human being is irreconcilably at odds with itself and that law and punishment are necessary to life on earth. He would add, however, that because of the providential framework in which the human "puppet" finds himself, his internal conflict should be no cause for alarm or (long-term) pessimism, much less tragedy.[17] Divine providence makes humanity immune to tragedy. On the one hand, our mortal difficulties—such as the ungovernable penis that Augustine dwells on—constitute a just punishment for the sins of Adam and Eve, which left an indelible stain on humanity. On the other hand, human limitations, conflicts, and frustrations could become tragic only if viewed from within the misguided framework of those "heretics" who fail to understand God's providential and rational plan for humanity (cf. Augustine, *DCD*, 11.22). If human life and the material world, as well as law, political authority, and punishment, and even the things that we conventionally consider "misfortunes" or "disasters," such as the sack of Rome—if all those things are intelligible against the backdrop of divine providence, if they are redeemed by divine justice, then there may be (time-bound) suffering and frustration, true, but there is no tragedy.

The lack of reconciliation and the frustration of human purposes are important elements of tragedy. It is essential to tragedy, however, that any human conflicts and necessities remain unredeemed. Tragedy arises specifically because human beings are held responsible, however unintelligibly, for their innate psychological conflicts or for necessities imposed on them by the gods, in the manner of Sophocles' Ajax or Oedipus. Sophocles' Oedipus strove to avoid his fate, but he still paid the penalty for his deeds; and there was no redemption after all. His suffering is a brute and unintelligible fact that cannot be explained or justified by reference to a providential cosmos or theology. Within the tragic universe, his greatness lay in his acceptance of responsibility in monstrous and incomprehensible circumstances. Sophocles' Ajax, similarly, incurred deep shame because he took responsibility for the

---

17. For an example of humanity's irreconcilable conflict with itself, see Augustine's telling comments on our turbulent emotions and our lack of control of the sexual passions at *DCD* 13.13, 14.12, and throughout.

disgraceful slaughter of flocks, which he carried out according to Athena's plan. Ajax killed himself and did not go to heaven, after receiving an apology from Athena. His suicide was the end of his story, except that other human characters, such as Teucer, Tecmessa, and Odysseus, were then left to make sense of this senseless situation. In both cases, these characters' sense of self was vulnerable to attack for reasons beyond their control, in utterly inexplicable, not to mention unjust, ways.[18] Their cases "show," within the tragic framework, that human beings do not possess the free, independent agency by which they may choose their life-courses or fates. It is not the mere existence of irreconcilable conflict, however inevitable, that makes for tragedy, but rather an evident lack of justice at a cosmic level.

Owing to the Athenian's efforts, Kleinias and the Magnesians will cling to a belief in providential, attentive gods. To the extent that they are deistic, their anxieties will be calmed. They can rest content with St. Augustine's perspective. Just, reasonable, and caring gods would not hold Oedipus or Ajax responsible. Their providential care would redeem the suffering brought about by humanity's universal psychological dissonance. Just gods make the world safe for well-disposed people, even if those people necessarily experience internal conflicts between reason and passion. From within the framework of Magnesia's civil religion, rewards and punishments will be allocated justly in the afterlife (e.g., 903c–d, 904e–905c). The gods own all mortal things and are our best and most attentive caretakers (902b–c). Even if we suffer unjustly in this life, that suffering will be noted by attentive gods, who will see to it that justice is eventually done. According to the Athenian, the gods are fully virtuous and care for all things as their own (900d). Despite the conflict between reason and passion or the need for legislative imperatives, then, Kleinias and the Magnesians will not interpret the world as a tragic home for humanity. Magnesia's civil religion insulates them from this experience. The conventional interpretation expresses the world view of ordinary Magnesians.

Kuhn's treatment is superior to that of Laks because it places theodicy at the center. To repeat: How can a "moral theodicy," he asks, legitimately be called "tragic"?[19] If the universe is a divinely ordered cosmos, in which the gods assign rewards and penalties fairly, and if Plato's theodicy is compellingly established, then why would the Athenian say that his vision of the

---

18. These ideas form the central arguments of Williams 1993.

19. This is the thrust of the argument of Kuhn 1941: 22–23. This essay, along with its companion, Kuhn 1942, offers a deep and searching examination of Plato's relationship with Greek tragedy, particularly on the subject of theodicy.

finest human regime or life is a tragedy? For, as Kuhn (1941: 22) recognizes, the key to the tragic experiences of Antigone, Ajax, and Oedipus is that "there is no reconciliation in the minds of these sufferers." There is no justice, no redemption, no way to render their circumstances intelligible. Their suffering and their "perplexity at the apparent disproportion of the moral order" (23) are intimately linked.[20]

Because of the Athenian's civil religion, Kleinias, Megillus, and the Magnesians remained undisturbed by these quandaries. Hence, Kuhn correctly distinguishes them from the characters of other Platonic dialogues. Invoking Hegel, Kuhn argues that we see in the Platonic dialogues (apart from the *Laws*) "the development of the consciousness of freedom" (Kuhn 1942: 59). Individuals in Plato's dialogues are given the choice (and assigned the correlative responsibility) to behave virtuously, and thereby to flourish as human beings, or the opposite. The Socratic discussions help to make them aware of their freedom in this crucial respect. While the Socratic dialogues consistently confront individuals with the choice of lives (Kuhn cites *Rep.* 578c as an example), this question—along with Socrates—is absent from the *Laws*. Like Cephalus, Kuhn argues, the old men of the *Laws* "have travelled well beyond the parting of the roads. They have already made their choice."[21] Through its gymnastic, military, and religious education, Magnesia is "a device to induce the right choice in the minds of the citizens"; that is, let us say, to make that choice for them.[22] It is this implication of Kuhn's discussion, in particular, that requires further elaboration in relation to the "truest tragedy."

Three Perspectives on Virtue and Happiness

Readers of Greek tragedy and Plato have before them three possible ways of addressing the possible disjunction, whether real or apparent, between virtue and happiness. The first is the perspective of tragic heroes such as Ajax, Antigone, and Oedipus. They accept responsibility for things (including

---

20. It is important that, according to Kuhn, Plato always maintained that virtue leads to happiness, that there is no "disproportion" between virtue and happiness (Kuhn 1941: 25–26; 1942: 51; Laks 2010: 228). Plato thereby negated the "tragic potentiality in life" (Kuhn 1941: 26; 1942: 51). Hence, although my account adapts certain lines of thinking from Kuhn, Kuhn would not accept my interpretation of the "truest tragedy."

21. Kuhn 1942: 71. Although Kuhn does not specifically address the point, this comment surely refers only to the elderly Dorians, and not to the Athenian himself.

22. Kuhn 1942: 71. On the Athenian's shielding of the Dorians from their own ignorance, see also Zuckert 2009: 62, 65–66.

both events and themselves) that are beyond their control. The gods provide no redemption for them, no reconciliation of the conflicts they confront. They do not expect to be happy; they may even take pride in their unhappiness. The second is represented by the philosophical life, embodied not only by Socrates but also by the Athenian. As the fulfillment of our human nature, the virtuous life is the flourishing, or happy, life. In this life philosophical individuals are both fully responsible for their choice of the good life and immune to misfortune. As we saw in our discussion of Book 10, the Athenian himself is motivated by this understanding of the philosophical life. He would fit straightforwardly into the other Platonic dialogues; the success of his own life does not depend on providential gods.

The final perspective is that of Kleinias, Megillus, and the Magnesians— the life of ordinary citizens who live according to Magnesia's civil religion. Although these characters are not philosophers, their religious beliefs shield them from the suffering of Oedipus, Ajax, and Antigone. Admittedly, they may, per Laks, experience suffering in life, because they are not ruled by reason. Their passions may drive them to break the law. They may find themselves punished or humiliated. As Kuhn points out, however, their ultimate choice is already made for them. They do not live in perplexity. They will believe that they are fully responsible for themselves. More important, their anxieties will be allayed, because the gods (supposedly) guarantee rewards for the just and punishment for the unjust. Their lives will be anti-tragic. The Athenian renders the world safe and hospitable for them.

We can now see why the conventional, metaphorical interpretation of the "truest tragedy" passage applies most clearly to Kleinias and other ordinary citizens. In the minds of Kleinias and Megillus, as well as the future citizens of Magnesia, tragedy will remain a serious theatrical genre that, at least in Magnesia, teaches the citizens important lessons that correspond to the legislator's teachings. The ethical and eschatological outlook that St. Augustine created for himself and his readers is similar to the one created by the Athenian for Kleinias and Megillus. The conflicts that human beings experience—between reason and passion, for example—will take on a cosmic significance in light of a broader narrative about humanity's place in the world.[23] The Athenian argues, for the sake of Kleinias and Megillus, that any

---

23. Compare T. Pangle 1980: 482, who argues that "tragic religiosity" depends on a belief in divine compassion and recognition for human suffering, which "makes political life less confident and less independent, and renders men prey to fanatic hopes and fears."

apparent misfortune or seemingly inexplicable disaster or even apparent in-justice is, in the end, explicable in light of the gods' providence.

Toward a Tragic Interpretation, Part II

Although Kleinias, Megillus, and the Magnesians remain undisturbed, they lack understanding of their lives. They fail to lead examined lives. As Kuhn (1942: 73) points out, Socrates does a great service to his interlocutors by inducing in them a consciousness of their own ignorance. We find the exact opposite in the Athenian's poetry, incantations, and religious mythmaking. He leads his citizens to self-certainty. Does the Athenian, after all, do the Magnesians a disservice by shielding them from their own ignorance—even by instilling a religious certainty that prevents them from experiencing even the merest iota of perplexity?

Such is the quandary of the Athenian's political project. Since he cannot openly discuss the choice of lives in the usual Socratic spirit, Kleinias, Megillus, and the Magnesians will remain ignorantly immersed in the city's conventions, even if those conventions are based on a correct theory of human nature and flourishing. Correspondingly, these ordinary citizens are not—contrary to the Athenian's proclamation in Book 10—responsible for their own characters or for their own lives. They are ignorant of the fateful choice between good and evil with which virtually all other Platonic characters are confronted.

In the natural course of things, then, the ordinary Magnesians fail to achieve a flourishing condition, because they fail to develop rationally or-dered souls. Their failure is no fault of their own: it is the fault of nature itself, which endows human beings unequally with the capacity to flourish. They are unjustly held responsible, so to speak, for their own unhappiness, because of this limitation. They are "held responsible" in the only meaningful way possible—that is, not in the sense that they are punished for their condition by gods or others, but in the sense that they lack the happiness of rational self-rule. Through no fault of their own choosing, but rather only through the limitations of their own natural constitutions, they are unable to embrace the life of *nous*, of virtue and self-knowledge, for its own sake. Why should the Athenian refuse to call their frustrations and failures "tragic"? Even though they themselves do not experience tragic suffering, their conflicts, frustrations, and limitations are never justified or explained. They are brute facts of a nature that turns out to be, in their cases, the very opposite of prov-idential or caring.

Against the background of our treatment of Book 10, the tragedy of the Magnesian regime lies in the necessary ignorance of the ordinary citizens for whom it is created. The key is not the inevitable need for punishment or the citizens' inevitable psychological dissonance. The real source of the Magnesians' tragedy is their need to be fed a rich soup of religious mythology in order even to approximate, however distantly, the philosopher's own grasp of the true relationship between virtue and happiness. The majority of human beings, like Kleinias and Megillus, live in a world of *muthos* and falsehood.[24] They cannot digest the truth, truly spoken. They cannot subscribe to the idea that justice is intrinsically good, that virtue is, all by itself, sufficient to enable human beings to flourish. They must be taught the truth indirectly, even ruled indirectly. Their necessary, unchosen ignorance makes their lives tragic. The best civic (i.e., nonphilosophical) lives are tragic because of the necessary pervasiveness of *muthos*. Far from admiring ordinary citizens' level of understanding, the Athenian is pointing out to the reader that the Magnesians' lives will be tragic precisely because they are unable to fulfill the teleological purposes defined for them by human nature. They fail to live lives of rational self-governance, or to embrace rational eudaimonism as a self-sufficient conception of their flourishing condition. They are thereby diminished as human beings. The gods provide no providential care or redemption, either in this life or the afterlife.[25]

If the art of politics is designed to care for souls (650b), then politics will inevitably fail to make sense if the Dorians can order their souls only by sacrificing the leadership of *nous*, that is, only by alienating their self-governance to another. Both the Dorians and the Athenian are, in this way, embroiled in the tragedy of politics, although only the Athenian can see this point and regret its senselessness.[26] Even so, these reflections may still contain a note of optimism. Magnesia's citizens are unable to live independent,

---

24. With this interpretation we can see the truth of Zuckert's judgment: the Athenian "describes his work as serious poetry or tragedy perhaps because it incorporates an understanding of the incompletely rational character of political, if not human life" (Zuckert 2009: 107). Human irrationality is expressed both in the need for violence and constraint to limit the passions and in the need for religious myths that underwrite the nonphilosophical appreciation of virtue.

25. In particular, neither the gods nor nature equip most human beings to achieve human flourishing as the Athenian understands it; cf. Lutz 2012: 156–57 for discussion.

26. These points may be summarized by saying that history takes back with one hand what theory promises with the other. While the Athenian often argues that history—i.e., what has always already happened with goats, symposia, and cities—can be transcended through the application of human rationality, it turns out that Magnesia itself cannot escape from the forces of passion, eros, and self-interest that tend to undermine peace and the achievement of justice.

free, and self-knowing lives, lives that are characterized by dignity and by an honest confrontation with the truth. Nonetheless, the Athenian judges that "the majority" will be better off if they subscribe to his civil religion, because their ordinary lives will, in any event, be free from the militarism with which they began.

In the *Cratylus*, Socrates offers an interesting and relevant etymology of the name "Pan" (408c).[27] Having explained that Pan is the dual-natured son of Hermes, whose name is supposedly related to "speech," Socrates argues that speech can be both true and false: "its true part is smooth and divine and dwells above among the gods, whereas its false part dwells below among the majority of human beings (*tois pollois tôn anthrôpôn*) and is rough and goat-like (*tragikon*); for here most stories (*muthoi*) and false things (*ta pseudê*) are found, in the tragic life" (*peri ton tragikon bion*, *Cratylus* 408c, tr. Reeve 1997, modified). Without explaining what he means, Socrates says that the tragic life of the majority of human beings, as opposed to gods, is the realm of stories (*muthoi*) and false things (*ta pseudê*). For most human beings, there is no human life apart from tragedy, because they have no access to the truth, which is "divine." This is the nontheatrical sense of the "tragic life" operative in the "truest tragedy" passage.[28]

The Athenian's Role in the Truest Tragedy

The Athenian reconciles Kleinias and the Magnesians to their existence by making that existence intelligible against a large cosmic backdrop. He enables them to live peacefully with one another and to live a better life than they could have lived on their own. The Athenian, and the city's future philosophers, will occupy the role of the *daimones* delegated by Kronos to govern human beings, who are incapable of self-government: they are demigods (*daimones*), that is, members of "a more god-like, superior species" (*genous theioterou te kai ameinonos*, 713c–d).[29] The conventional interpretation is an exercise in unpacking the *muthos* offered by the philosopher to ordinary citizens in order to help them make sense of the world, and hence to live as well as they can,

---

27. Adduced in this context by Halliwell 2002.

28. This statement holds true even if certain Greek tragedies—or trilogies and tetralogies, such as the *Oresteia*—seem optimistic about the heroes, the gods, and the possibility of achieving justice.

29. Cf. Pangle 1980: 485: the Athenian's reference to Athena's words to Telemachus suggests that "the philosopher thus dares to hint that he is the avatar of divinity."

based on the civil religion that he provides for them. His activity as a philosopher is to that extent philanthropic. The gods that he envisions are projections of his own philosophical care for his fellow human beings—an expression of his concern for others, which is staged in the action of the dialogue itself.

What are we to make of the Athenian's own position within the "truest tragedy"? He invites readers to ask this question because his reference to the "truest tragedy" is not only a comment on Magnesia and its regime, but also a comment on himself and his own political project. St. Augustine would hardly call his own project "tragic," but the Athenian designates *his* project that way. The civil religion obviously provides him with no consolation. Kuhn would say that the Athenian embraces rational eudaimonism and is therefore immune to tragedy; Pangle, too, views the Athenian's philosophical perspective as anti-tragic.[30] Is the situation more complicated, however, in part because the Athenian knows, like Socrates, that he does not possess a complete grasp of the truth about the cosmos and humanity's place in it? Does he see himself, even so, as invested in or tied to the political project he has initiated?

This question is raised by an earlier section in Book 7. In the midst of talking, as usual, about songs and dances and their impact on character, the Athenian compares himself to a shipwright. Like a shipbuilder who lays down keels, he remarks:

> I seem to myself to be doing the same thing, trying to separate the shapes of lives according to the character of souls, in truth to lay down their keels, and to examine correctly by which device (*poiai mêchanêi*) and through whichever means (*tisin pote tropois*) we will best convey our life through this voyage of existence. The concerns of human beings are not worth taking very seriously, yet it is necessary to take them seriously (*spoudazein*); and this is unfortunate (*ouk eutuches*). But since we are here, if we might somehow do this in a fitting way, then perhaps it would be well-measured (*summetron*) for us. (803a–b)

Although the Athenian works hard to legislate appropriately for Magnesia, this reflection hardly provides a ringing endorsement of the engaged political life.

---

30. In his comment on this passage, Pangle 1980: 485 argues that the Athenian "reveals that he possesses a strength of soul" that is rooted "in a resigned joy that comes from his knowledge and his contemplation of eternity." Pangle also characterizes the Athenian's outlook as "untragic" (483) and argues that "the city cannot share the untragic perspective of the philosopher" (490).

The Athenian himself, in fact, draws attention to the inscrutability of his statement (803b). Kleinias agrees that it is inscrutable. At first glance, though, the Athenian's explanation is even more mysterious than his initial statement. In language that foreshadows that of 817b, he says that he believes it necessary to take seriously that which is serious—and that the god is "by nature" worth taking very seriously, whereas the human being is merely a "plaything" (*paignion*) of the god, and "this is truly the best thing about him" (803c). Human beings should spend their time dancing and singing in honor of the gods, which is genuinely serious, rather than making war, which people currently consider the most serious of human activities. The Athenian concludes by characterizing human beings as "being mostly puppets (*thaumata*), but sharing in some little bits of truth" (804b). When Megillus protests that the Athenian is "belittling" (*diaphaulizeis*) humanity in every way (804c), the Athenian asks his forbearance, on the grounds that he spoke as he did while "looking away toward the god" and feeling the emotions to which his contemplation of the god might understandably give rise (804b). The Athenian then indulges Megillus by allowing that they should consider the human race to be "not lowly" (*mê phaulon*), but rather "worthy of a certain degree of serious attention" (*spoudês de tinos axion*)—"if you like (*ei soi philon*)" (804b–c).

This pregnant passage foreshadows the Athenian's comments on the "truest tragedy," in part through its emphasis on what is "serious" and what is not. In the later passage, the Athenian describes himself as a tragic poet, a poet preoccupied with what is "serious," and suggests that the tragedy he has composed, which is embodied in the *Laws* itself, is a representation of the life that is most beautiful and best. Yet, having read the earlier passage, we will be aware that the finest human lives that he has (seriously) described are unworthy of serious attention. The Athenian is constrained by a certain "necessity" (cf. *anankaion*, 803b) to take human affairs seriously, even though his larger philosophical vision reveals to him that what he is taking seriously (specifically, he says, the care of others' souls) is unworthy of "great seriousness." He is accordingly forced, for reasons that he does not yet explain, to behave in ways that he himself does not fully endorse—a situation that he considers "unfortunate."[31] Even though he remains clear-eyed and articulate about his

---

31. He feels—at least temporarily—that the work he is now laboring to undertake is essentially meaningless or worthless: the point is related to the question of whether the human wonder or puppet (*thauma*, 644d7) has been created (*sunestêkos*, 644d9, which is from the same root as *sunestêke* at 817b4, quoted above) as the "gods' plaything" or "for some serious purpose" (644d8–9). Cf. Benardete's suggestion, along the same lines, that "for the Stranger, the truest tragedy is that political life is too serious for it to be a life of play" (Benardete

condition, he cannot choose to avoid a path that diverts him from the highest life that he can imagine for himself. He is somehow trapped. As he points out, this condition is an "unfortunate" (*ouk eutuches*) one; but intriguingly, he was under no compulsion, at least in the ordinary sense, to discuss these matters with the Dorians in the first place.[32] What are we to make of his critique of political engagement, then, in light of his decision to engage in this legislative conversation?

While one might initially be repelled by the Athenian's statement, as though it were excessively self-important or self-pitying, it is also possible to interpret his statement more charitably. He recognizes that there are things in the cosmos more important than human beings—like mathematics, or the stars and planets, or the search for truth altogether, including the truth about the gods. He wants to spend his life taking those (serious) things seriously; he is, in reality, far less self-important than Kleinias, Megillus, and most people, who complain that he fails to take the human being seriously. Compared to the serious things he has in mind, the intolerably long stretches of legislative detail, in which the *Laws* abounds—such as how often a freedman ought to visit the hearth of his former owner (915a) or what penalty should befall a slave who keeps as his own something that he finds on the road (914b)— might well seem trivial, or even unworthy of serious time and thought.[33]

Kleinias and Megillus cannot accept this view of the gods or humanity. They live on a completely different plane, fully at home within the Athenian's

2000: 222–23)—which means, if I am not mistaken, that the Stranger's tragedy consists in being taken away from "play" (i.e., philosophy or the search for truth, which is "divine") and forced to turn to what is "serious" (i.e., the trivialities of human affairs, including war, and including laying down detailed rules that will govern farms, markets, and daily life).

32. Kurke 2013: 135–38, manages to construe this passage in an optimistic way, finding in it a "radical deconstruction" of the concepts of seriousness and play. While the Athenian does reorder the categories of seriousness and play, here and elsewhere in the dialogue, Kurke arrives at this strained account of the passage only through ignoring the Athenian's all-important introduction of the section at 803b and his condescending concession to Megillus ("if that is important to you," 804b–c).

33. One reason, in fact, for the traditional—even ancient—reaction that the *Laws* is a "frigid" (Lucian, *Icaromenippus*, 24) and forbidding (cf. Aristotle, *Pol.* 1265a) text is precisely the level of legislative detail that Plato forces on the reader. In setting the reader the challenge of wading through so much detail, Plato was not, I imagine, laying out a blueprint for political reform just before his death, for the sake of real lawgivers sent out by the Academy (Morrow 1960: 3–10). Instead, he was intentionally juxtaposing passages with seemingly needless details and passages that reflect on the profoundest human questions, with a view to causing his readers to experience the frustrations, boredom, and triviality that the Athenian remarks upon in this all-important passage. Cf. Laks 2000: 267, who helpfully comments on this type of juxtaposition without, however, analyzing it in this way or in connection with this passage.

religious and cosmic vision, in which they are the galaxy's celebrities.[34] They resist any hint that divine redemption is impossible. Yet the Athenian implies that, in actuality, the gods are remote from human affairs; they are not providential. Why would they care for human justice, if they are so far removed from our banalities? It is the Athenian who cares for human justice, by re-entering the Cave and legislating for the new foundation. Why would he do so? The reason, I propose, is that his own flourishing condition is constituted by his active embodiment of all the virtues he discusses—*nous*, moderation, justice, and courage. The Athenian himself self-consciously discerns the eudaimonistic significance of his own life. His own flourishing as a human being is constituted, at least in part, by his active, philanthropic care for others. He does not need the gods' redemption.

We might conclude that the Athenian is "constrained" to take human affairs seriously, because only by doing so can he achieve the best and most flourishing condition of which he is capable, as a human being. Nonetheless, the Athenian is forced to accept responsibility for his fellow human beings, while also knowing that he is unaware of the most important ethical and political truths that would enable him to do so effectively.[35] His imitation of the god—to which he frequently refers, and which he considers his highest aspiration—forces him, not only to seek the truth, but also to become the attentive supervisor of his fellow human beings, despite his awareness of his own ignorance.[36] Yet if the Athenian does not possess a firm grasp of ethical and psychological truths, not to mention theological ones, then he is in danger of leading the Dorians and the future Magnesians astray: that is why he often refers to the courage required to found a city. The tragic situation often sets the stage for individuals to be compelled to harm others—and to

---

34. In his commentary, Pangle 1980: 490 suggests that the Athenian hopes that a "new tragic sense . . . will penetrate the regime. . . . Although they will be told that the founders did not proceed 'without some inspiration from the gods' (811c; cf. 682e, 722c), they will not be led to believe that god's voice was heard in the conversation, or that the regime is the object of very special divine solicitude."

35. He is tentative in his presentation of his most important ideas, e.g., theological speculations: cf. Lewis 2012: 24; 2010: 42–44.

36. In saying that the Athenian is "forced" to take responsibility for his fellow human beings, I intend to evoke the "necessity" of 803b4–5 discussed just above. He is "forced" to do this because, in order to lead a good life, he is forced to "imitate the god," which means, in his view, trying to order his soul in a rational way, with *nous* as the "leader," as he often says, and in such a way as to exhibit the virtues that he attributes to the gods, such as justice, wisdom, and care (as a human being, he will also exhibit courage, a virtue not appropriate to the gods). Cherry 2013: 57 also notices the Athenian's dilemma.

accept responsibility for that—for reasons that are beyond their control. Such is the Athenian's own tragedy.

What is more, the Athenian convinces Kleinias and Megillus—and, as he indicates, he must convince them—that his word is law, in a quite literal sense. Based on the image of the puppet, he says, it will be clearer "that the individual, absorbing a true account[37] of these cords in himself, must live in accordance with this account, and that the city, taking the account either from a god or from a man who knows these things (*toutou tou gnontos tauta*), must set it up as law and thereby regulate both its own relations and its relations with other cities" (645b). Imitating the god, the Athenian is, in this analogy at least, "this man who knows these things," even though he is aware that he does not grasp the truth of human psychology. He also suggests, without quite saying, that the psychological "account" based on the puppet image is "true" (*alêthê*), even though he had just called this image "the *muthos* about our being puppets (*peri thaumatôn hôs ontôn hêmôn ho muthos*)" (645b). Although the Athenian persistently refers to his own epistemological limitations, the Dorians ignore his tentativeness and the qualified, provisional character of his claims.[38] They firmly attach themselves to him in the conviction that he grasps the truth. Strikingly, because of his strenuous efforts to convince them, they can hardly be blamed for doing so. Equally, because he is forced to take on this role in relation to them, we can hardly blame him, either.[39]

The "Truest Tragedy": An Astronomical Perspective

Is it merely coincidental that the Athenian moves on, just after the "truest tragedy" passage, to discuss the city's gods, blasphemy, astronomy, and mathematical education? That he emphasizes, right away, the difference between ordinary citizens and those with a more advanced education? That he begins to discuss several of the most nontrivial subjects of philosophy—mathematics, astronomy, and theology—after mentioning the tragic triviality of human

---

37. Grammatically speaking, "true" is a predicate adjective in this phrase, which should mean that the individual "takes this account to be true" and lives on its basis—a more literal translation that distances the Athenian, once again, from committing himself to the truth of his own puppet image. The "puppet" image at 803e suggests that the Athenian's later reflection on the "divine puppet" of 644d is negative and pessimistic—a pessimistic interpretation that Laks 2000: 277 surprisingly resists, on the grounds that the puppet is "astonishing in its capacity for harmony in spite of its being controlled by disparate elements."

38. Cf. Lewis 2009b: 88–89.

39. For further reflections along these lines, see Balot 2014b: 80–83.

affairs? We will see that the immediately subsequent discussions of astronomy and mathematics sharpen the Athenian's distinction between ordinary citizens and philosophers. While ordinary citizens are encouraged to defer to the Athenian's authority, philosophers, by contrast, benefit humanity by thinking independently and even "impiously" about topics such as planetary motion.

Immediately after making his difficult, self-reflexive remarks on tragedy, the Athenian describes the three subjects that free men will be required to learn, beyond the choral arts: numerical calculation; measurements of length, surface, and volume; and astronomy. After a lengthy discussion of mathematics (817e–820e), the Athenian turns to cosmology and astronomy. These subjects necessarily involve reflection on theology, since the sun, the moon, and the other stars are gods (820e–822d). These discussions should be read together, not only because they address subjects that all free men should comprehend, but also because the heavenly motions (e.g., the circular motion of the planets: 822a) can be described in the language of mathematics.[40]

The significance of the astronomical section is, on the face of it, straightforward. The Athenian points out that the Greeks currently consider it impious to investigate the gods and the cosmos and to seek their causes (821a).[41] As he indicates both here and later in the dialogue (819a, 966e–967e), philosophers interested in astronomical phenomena were often associated with atheism, because they brought forward materialistic explanations of astronomical phenomena.[42] Even so, he argues, if we examine such matters carefully, then we will recognize that the great gods, the sun, the moon, and the other stars are not random "wanderers," as the Greeks now believe (821b–c). Instead, each of them always moves along the same circular path, even if it seems to follow many diverse paths (822a). Recognizing this truth will enable the Greeks to

40. Cf. Morrow 1960: 482–83, for a discussion of the impact of the mathematical theories of Eudoxus of Cnidus on the interpretation and mathematical explanation of the heavenly bodies. The Athenian refers to the difficulty of these mathematical accounts, and the precision required to understand them, in his later arguments that the heavenly bodies are governed by *nous* (967b). At this level, at least, an understanding of astronomy is unavailable to most ordinary citizens, who will have only a basic grasp of the preliminary mathematical studies (cf. 818a). For further reflections on Eudoxus' contribution, see Knorr 1975: 273–85.

41. Does it ever dawn on Kleinias and Megillus that the Athenian is, by this definition, unquestionably impious in the eyes of the Greeks? He shows himself, both here and in Book 10, to have explored these questions in great detail. This question reveals, yet again, that the elderly Dorians relate to the Athenian as to a god. It is as though they fail to grasp that his understanding of the arguments for both a *nous*-governed cosmos and a materialistic cosmos has come about through human work and striving.

42. Cf. Schöpsdau 2003: 623.

avoid blaspheming when they speak or sing about the gods. The standard interpretation of this passage is as follows: "Ordinary Greek theological beliefs are thus radically in error and it is a central task of Magnesia's educational program to give the citizens sufficient mathematical and astronomical training to enable them to revise their beliefs intelligently in accordance with the truth. This recognition of the order of the stars plays an essential role in the arguments in Book 10 that the universe is ordered by intelligent gods who exercise supervision over it and over human affairs."[43]

A careful reading of the text, however, upends this standard interpretation and points toward the "truest tragedy." First, as Bobonich argues, citizens are supposed to "recognize" the order of the stars, but their sensory observations lead in the opposite direction. Kleinias declares emphatically that he has "often seen the morning star and the evening star and other stars, never moving along the same course, but wandering everywhere" (821c). The Athenian merely asserts that this conventional view is incorrect (822a). Even as he confirms the "appearance" of wandering, which is known to the senses, he gives no reason for profoundly changing ordinary opinion in his development of the city's astronomical doctrines. Understandably, he concludes this discussion in a tentative way: the lawgivers should teach citizens his new doctrines about circularity and order, yes, but only if they demonstrate that heavenly bodies do in fact operate according to these principles (822c). Kleinias agrees. Eventually, despite this important qualification, the Athenian's account of the heavenly bodies is transformed into a dogma in the minds, at least, of the Dorians and many modern scholars.

Supposedly, then, an adequate proof (or at least explanation) of these points will be delivered in Book 10. As we saw in examining Book 10, however, no adequate proof is forthcoming. Early on, without discussion, Kleinias rejects the atheists' view and proclaims his belief in the order and beauty of the seasons, the earth, the sun, and so on (886a). Obviously, his belief contradicts his earlier statement, based on his senses, that the heavenly bodies are wanderers (821c). At the relevant moment in the first argument of Book 10, the Athenian inquires into the motions of *nous* (897d). He emphasizes the impossibility of using the senses for this purpose: it would be like looking directly at the sun (897d). We cannot know *nous* adequately with our own eyes (897d–e). He also declines to offer any mathematical proof in support of his claim. Instead, referring only to beautiful images such as a sphere turned on

---

43. Bobonich 2002: 108.

a lathe (898b), they agree that intelligence must revolve in an orderly circular motion. On that basis, they conclude that soul manages and supervises the heavens—a conclusion that confirms Kleinias' stated belief at the beginning of Book 10, but contradicts the evidence of his senses.

Even if the Athenian has (mathematical) reasons of his own for believing in the heavens' order, beauty, and regularity, this belief can never be more than an article of faith for Kleinias and the Magnesians. Their belief that *nous* controls the heavens is never confirmed by what they see; much less is it confirmed mathematically, or in any more intellectually substantial way. It is "confirmed" only by the Athenian's image of the sphere turned on a lathe (898b). Interestingly, and in parallel, the Athenian returns to this point in Book 12, when he says that certain early natural philosophers were led astray by *their* sensory observations. Observation by means of the human senses (in particular, the eyes) leads to the view that the heavens are "full of stones, earth, and many other bodies without soul" (967c, cf. 966e). Since he cannot confirm his account on the basis of observation, and since he has not offered a mathematical proof for his assertions, he has certainly not confirmed these points for Kleinias or the Magnesians, or perhaps even himself.[44] The Athenian distinguishes carefully between his capacity to "clarify" (*dēloun*, 821e) the matter to the Dorians and the "demonstration" (cf. *deixômen, deichthentôn,* 822c) of such matters that, as they agree (822c), the Athenian has not given.[45]

As with all their revised ethical, political, and psychological beliefs, Kleinias and the ordinary citizens accept these astronomical points on authority alone. It is impossible to follow Bobonich in describing their unqualified deference to authority as giving "the citizens sufficient mathematical and astronomical training to enable them to revise their beliefs intelligently in accordance with the truth." Readers arrive once again at the "truest tragedy" of Kleinias and the ordinary Magnesians, who are led, as Kuhn had suggested, to an entrenched and contented dependence on the Athenian's authority in the important matter of the city's religion.

---

44. In fact, the Athenian says in Book 12 that now it is "the real belief," "the current dogma" (*to nun ontôs dedogmenon*, 967b, as opposed to the Greeks' previous "dogma," *to dogma*, 822), that if they were soulless, then heavenly bodies would never have "used such amazing calculations, so accurately" (967b). Even his own belief is simply that—a belief, if not a "dogma," albeit one that may (or may not) be based on rational inferences and mathematical calculations or arguments.

45. The same distinction is also evoked in other mathematical contexts in the Platonic dialogues, where Socrates does not rest content with likely arguments and typically demands a high standard of "proof": see Knorr 1975: 75–78.

The Athenian's Own Astronomical Views?

At least possibly, the Athenian's own view of heavenly motion is more substantial. To see why, we have to recognize that heavenly bodies can possess "souls" without our attaching any particular theological significance to that idea. Characters in several interconnected Platonic dialogues—including *Timaeus, Statesman,* and *Laws*—propose, as Menn has argued, that an incorporeal "soul" acts as a "mediator between body and *nous*."[46] For Menn, this view enabled them to explain more precisely how *nous*, as the virtue of reason in souls, "is also a cause in a different way from the other forms, that operating from within the souls in which it is present, it also imparts motion to the bodies in which it is not itself present, and so imposes order on the pattern in which the different parts of matter (or different regions of space) participate in the different forms." As Menn explains, the point is that prior to Plato thinkers such as Anaxagoras had to assume that *nous* operated directly on matter; the use of soul as a mediator was a quasi-scientific refinement of the model. Hence, the Athenian's repudiation of materialism, and his endorsement of the idea that the heavens are intentionally ordered, might amount to the quasi-scientific claim that the heavenly bodies move in rationally ordered ways, along paths that can be understood by (human or divine) intelligence—for example, mathematically.

The Athenian might hold such views without believing in his theory's supposed ethical and political implications, including implications about the divine punishment of wrongdoers. If that is correct, then the Athenian can be seen both to be drawn to scientific investigation as part of his philosophical work, in a spirit of openness and discovery, on the one hand, and, on the other, to be willing to use the rational principles of astronomical motion to provide legitimacy, in the minds of the Dorians, for the ethics and politics embodied in his law code.[47] The task of philosophy is not only to make discoveries and provide instruction, but also to foster a religious carapace that renders intelligible the ordinary citizens' lives and in particular their

---

46. See Menn 1995: 34, 46 for this quotation and the next quoted passage.

47. In making this suggestion, I would stress that the Platonic dialogues do not provide a clear and consistent picture of astronomical motion. See Gregory 2000: 112: "It would seem then that on cosmological grounds we can separate two groups of works, the *Timaeus, Philebus, Laws* and *Epinomis* as advocating regular and stable celestial motion, the *Phaedo, Republic,* and *Politicus* as not." We should also keep in mind that, as Hackforth 1936: 7 has argued, "Soul in its own nature is ethically neutral: the good soul owes its goodness to *nous*, the bad soul its badness to its lack of *nous*."

experiences of suffering. These reflections help to make sense of this passage in connection with the "truest tragedy" and with the Athenian's proposed course of mathematical study.

Mathematics: Necessity, Incommensurability, and Shame

Just after concluding his discussion of the choral art (817e), the Athenian explores mathematical education, moving from numbers to measurements of length, surface, and volume, to incommensurable magnitudes. While he does not provide any significant detail, he emphasizes the distinction between the many (for whom it is "shameful" not to know the things called "necessary," but for whom it is also impossible to pursue these subjects to the point of "precise accuracy") and the few (who will advance to a "precise" understanding of these subjects; 818a). One must know something about these matters, the Athenian asserts, to become a god-like human being, obviously one of the rare few, who might exercise supervision over other human beings (818c). This differentiation among human beings is the critical background for the Athenian's presentation of mathematical education. Why does he focus, surprisingly, on "necessity" to such an extent in his discussion of mathematics?

Arguably, at least, the Athenian focuses on "necessity"—the necessity (according to nature: 818d) against which not even the gods will fight (818a–e)—because he wants to emphasize the existence of external principles, i.e., mathematical principles, to which even the gods must be responsive. In his view (*dokô*), the Athenian explains, the divine necessities are "those which someone (*tis*) must 'do' (*praxas*) and learn in every way," if he intends to become god-like and supervise human beings (818b–c).[48] The Athenian himself is a "divine man," as are the future rulers of Magnesia; all these philosophers will grasp, he indicates, that the conventional dogma about the heavenly bodies is misguided (822a). The Athenian now elaborates upon the divine man's education in understanding the divine necessities. As many scholars have seen, he is laying out the educational scheme appropriate to members of the Nocturnal Council (818c–d)—the few, that is, who will benefit from a "precise" and rigorous education, whose identity the Athenian will explain

---

48. We will shortly consider the Athenian's unusual expression—i.e., to "do" (*praxas*) the necessities—in connection with a later passage that recalls it.

"at the end" (818a), i.e., in Book 12.[49] Those and only those who can master the divine necessities—the mathematical principles, comprehensible to natural philosophy, according to which the cosmos is governed—are entitled to rule the city.[50] The Athenian reveals, moreover, that those who grasp these principles have authority over the gods of the civil religion, who must conform to these necessities.

Intriguingly, in language that echoes this passage, the Athenian later contrasts the materialists who believe that "all *pragmata* arise through necessities (*anankais*)" with those who believe that all *pragmata* arise "through the thoughts of a will that intends to bring about good things" (*dianoiais boulêseôs agathôn peri teloumenôn*, 967a).[51] In Book 7, the Athenian is stating clearly that the world, including the heavenly bodies, behaves according to "necessity." The "divine necessities" can be described mathematically and must be understood by whoever, presumably a highly intelligent human being, can master these and other difficult subjects. Even if the Athenian uses the concept of "soul" in order to make an intervention in scientific debates, the "gods" do not explain anything. What is "divine" in the cosmos is rationality, pure and simple.[52] The heavenly bodies, the "gods" studied in the astronomical education, follow their orbits not because they choose to do so, as the Athenian suggests later [cf. the planets' use of "amazing calculations" (*thaumastois logismois*), 967b, and their *boulêsis*, 967a], but rather because not even gods can defy the reasoned conclusions of *logismos* (calculation), which is the object of study in precisely this passage (817e).[53] Mathematics, a pure activity of

---

49. E.g., Morrow 1960.

50. Cf. Pangle 1980: 493.

51. As Benardete 2000: 225 has observed, the Athenian's use of *praxas* (818b–c) is unusual and likely refers to geometrical construction, to "doing" geometry. At *Republic* 527a, Socrates says that the same language of "doing" geometry is characteristic of geometers, even though geometry exists not for the sake of action, but for the sake of knowledge. The verbal link between *praxas* and *pragmata* at 967a invites us to wonder who it is, precisely, who is "doing" the necessities. Certainly, the geometer, such as the Athenian himself, does the necessities, in the sense that he comprehends astronomy in a mathematical way. Perhaps the gods, too, must "do and learn [these necessities] in every way," if they want to "become" (*genoito*) gods; at all events, they cannot fight against necessity.

52. Cf. Hackforth 1936: 8.

53. Lutz 2012: 113–14 emphasizes the importance of necessity in this passage: "By teaching young people that the whole cosmos is subject to necessity, these lessons may help to persuade potential statesmen that they cannot rely on the gods to solve each and every problem for the city." Pangle 1980: 490 has linked this idea to the preceding discussion of tragedy: the Athenian hopes to inspire in the citizens a "new tragic sense" in which they "will have access to the perplexities the founders confronted, the aspirations they had to abandon or qualify, and

rationality (whether human or otherwise), is the key to understanding the cosmos, since even the gods must obey mathematical order. Most human beings cannot progress very far in their understanding of mathematics. They are still caught in the position of mistaking the civil religion for the truth about the cosmos. They cannot recognize the implications of mathematical necessity for the Athenian's double-layered presentation of heavenly motion, which is mathematical for those who understand it, and which involves, for everyone else, ambitious mythological claims about the gods' care for humanity and their capacity to intervene in human time.[54]

Conclusion: *The Athenian, the Elderly Dorians, and the Magnesians*

The Athenian's discussion of mathematics and astronomy should be read in connection both with the "truest tragedy" passage and with related passages in Book 12, where he finally, albeit vaguely, unveils his presentation of the Nocturnal Council. In the remainder of the discussion of mathematics, the Athenian emphasizes the shame he has experienced, both on his own behalf and on that of the Greeks as a whole, because of their ignorance of incommensurability (819d–e, 820b–c).[55] His discussion does not lay out entirely clearly how the study of these subjects is connected to his distinction between "the many," with their limited mathematical understanding, and "the few," with their more precise and developed education, and he defers consideration of these points till the end (cf. 818a, 818d–e, 820c–e). What is clear, however,

---

the alternatives they rejected. They will understand the achievements and disappointments to be the result not of unfathomable divine will, but of human reason struggling with natural necessities." See further Pangle 1980: 492–94, on mathematical necessities and the absence of references to divine will, as well as on the god-like character of those who can master "necessities" and thereby justify their title to rule the city.

54. Again, the distinction between mathematical "proof" and "likelihood" or "likely stories" is crucial in this context: while certain features of heavenly motion can be understood according to apodeictic mathematical reasoning, the Platonic characters, such as Timaeus and the Athenian Stranger, who speculate about the gods' providential care for human beings, speak in the language of *muthos* and likelihood: cf. Balot 2014b.

55. Our best reconstructions suggest that the relation of commensurables to incommensurables was a subject of contentious debate and enthusiastic inquiry during Plato's lifetime (consider, for example, the mathematical discussions of Theodorus and Theaetetus in Plato's *Theaetetus*), and that these discussions were, like Plato himself, closely associated in particular with Pythagoreanism. An excellent discussion of the impact of the discovery of incommensurability on Pythagorean theory and beyond can be found in Knorr 1975: 36–49; the same work also details Plato's own engagement with incommensurability throughout his dialogues.

is that what is worthy of a human being is to grapple with mathematics and thus with cosmology, ethics, and politics, at a speculative, philosophical level. The "serious" pursuits of the human *thauma* are not the human *pragmata* (803b3–4), which are "unworthy of great seriousness" and even "wretched" (cf. 803b, 804b), but rather the peaceful activities of *scholê*, perhaps the geometrical *pragmata*, which lead us to investigate and understand, altogether, the governing principles of the cosmos (cf. 803b–804b, with its many verbal echoes).

Because of their limitations, intellectual and otherwise, the Dorians will always live a life of shame, a "wretched" life, in which they fail to appreciate what they are missing. Kleinias will always be *phaulos*, as will Megillus. That is why they require a simple and readily explicable outlook on the gods and the cosmos. The Athenian's account of mathematics and astronomy therefore confirms our interpretation of the "truest tragedy."

The Athenian's position contrasts with that of the elderly Dorians in an interesting way. He has, to be sure, progressed much farther than they ever could in the understanding of mathematics, astronomy, ethics, and politics. He is, however, aware, as they are not, that his supposedly newfound (cf. 819d–e) grasp of incommensurable magnitudes is simply one movement in a long, slow, and never-ending process of discovery, refinement, and transformation. He is unwilling to settle for the dogma that he has delivered to the city. Instead, he continually seeks to improve his own understanding, in the recognition that all hypotheses and scientific understandings must remain provisional, because new developments will always threaten to overthrow previous accounts of cosmology and so on.

The result is that, even in the case of the best human being, to be human is to live a swinish life (cf. 819d–e); the necessity against which he cannot fight is, therefore, to investigate (cf. *skopounta*, 820c5) questions within the framework of graceful and worthy leisure. The Athenian will continue to feel ashamed about all the mathematics that he doesn't know, instead of complacently accepting that he has arrived at a worthy dogma about either mathematics or the cosmos. In the Athenian's presentation, the only relevant distinction among human beings is that between self-knowing swine and oblivious swine. The Athenian's own qualifiedly swinish life involves the additional risk of taking on, of necessity, responsibilities for which he knows he is not suited—namely, the care of the human herd (818b–c). That is what we see him "risking," once again, in the section on the city's astronomical education. He has left just enough of his own greatness visible that he may yet successfully "hunt" new friends by the end of Book 7 (cf. 823b).

References

Abolafia, Jacob. 2015. "Solar Theology and Civil Religion in Plato's *Laws*." *Polis* 32:369–92.

Adomenas, Mantas. 2001. "Self-reference, Textuality, and the Status of the Political Project in Plato's *Laws*." *Oxford Studies in Ancient Philosophy* 21:29–59.

Allen, Danielle S. 2000. *The World of Prometheus: The Politics of Punishing in Democratic Athens*. Princeton: Princeton University Press.

Annas, Julia. 2017. *Virtue and Law in Plato and Beyond*. Oxford: Oxford University Press.

Atack, Carol. 2020. "An Origin for Political Culture? *Laws* 3 as Political Thought and Intellectual History." *Polis* 37 (3): 468–84.

Ausland, Hayden. 2002. "La 'seconde navigation' dans la philosophie politique de Platon." *Revue Française d'Histoire des Ideés Politiques* 16 (2): 275–93.

Austin, Emily A. 2013. "Corpses, Self-Defense, and Immortality: Callicles' Fear of Death in the Gorgias." *Ancient Philosophy* 33: 1–20.

Balcer, J.M. 1977. "The Athenian Episkopos and the Achaemenid 'King's Eye.'" *American Journal of Philology* 98 (3): 252–63.

Ballingall, Robert A. 2017. "The Reverent City: Plato's Laws and the Politics of Ethical Authority." PhD diss., University of Toronto.

Ballingall, Robert A. 2023. *Plato's Reverent City: The Laws and the Politics of Authority*. Cham, Switzerland: Palgrave Macmillan.

Balot, Ryan K. 2001a. "Aristotle's Critique of Phaleas: Justice, Equality, and *Pleonexia*." *Hermes* 129 (1): 32–44.

Balot, Ryan K. 2001b. *Greed and Injustice in Classical Athens*. Princeton, NJ: Princeton University Press.

Balot, Ryan K. 2006. *Greek Political Thought*. Oxford: Blackwell.

Balot, Ryan K. 2009a. "The Freedom to Rule: Athenian Imperialism and Democratic Masculinity." In *Reflections on Empire: Ancient Lessons for Global Politics*, edited by Toivo Koivukoski and David Tabachnack, 54–68. Toronto: University of Toronto Press.

Balot, Ryan K. 2009b. "The Virtue Politics of Democratic Athens." In *The Cambridge Companion to Ancient Greek Political Thought*, edited by Stephen Salkever, 271–300. Cambridge, UK: Cambridge University Press.

Balot, Ryan K. 2013. "Democracy and Political Philosophy: Influences, Tensions, Rapprochement." In *The Greek Polis and the Invention of Democracy: A Politico-Cultural Transformation and Its Interpretations*, edited by Johann P. Arnason, Kurt A. Raaflaub, and Peter Wagner, 181–204. Oxford: Blackwell.

Balot, Ryan K. 2014a. *Courage in the Democratic Polis: Ideology and Critique in Classical Athens*. New York: Oxford University Press.

Balot, Ryan K. 2014b. "Politics, Philosophy, and Likelihood in Three Platonic Dialogues." In *Probabilities, Hypotheticals, and Counterfactuals in Ancient Greek Thought*, edited by Victoria Wohl, 65–83. Cambridge, UK: Cambridge University Press.

Balot, Ryan K. 2017. "Was Thucydides a Political Philosopher?" In *The Oxford Handbook of Thucydides*, edited by Ryan K. Balot, Sara Forsdyke, and Edith Foster, 319–38. New York: Oxford University Press.

Balot, Ryan K. 2020a. "An Odd Episode in Platonic Interpretation: Changing the Law in Plato's *Laws*." In *Ethics in Ancient Greek Literature: Aspects of Ethical Reasoning from Homer to Aristotle and Beyond; Studies in Honour of Ioannis N. Perysinakis*, edited by Maria Liatsi, 61–79. Berlin: de Gruyter.

Balot, Ryan K. 2020b. "*Polis* and *Cosmos* in Plato's *Laws*." In "Democracy and Its Rivals: Plato's *Statesman* and *Laws*." Special issue. *Polis: The Journal for Ancient Greek and Roman Political Thought* 37:516–33.

Balot, Ryan K. 2021. "Epilogue: Identity, Politics, Power: From Classical Antiquity to the 21st Century." *Polis: The Journal for Ancient Greek and Roman Political Thought* 38:127–33.

Balot, Ryan K. 2024(a). "Corrupting the Youth in Plato's *Menexenus*." In *The Athenian Funeral Oration*, edited by David M. Pritchard, 221–40. Cambridge, UK: Cambridge University Press.

Balot, Ryan K. 2024(b). "Freedom, *Pleonexia*, and Persuasion in Plato's *Gorgias*." In *The Cambridge Companion to Plato's Gorgias*, edited by J. Clerk Shaw, 172–92. Cambridge, UK: Cambridge University Press.

Balot, Ryan K., and Daniel Schillinger. Forthcoming. "Paradoxes of Honour and Fame: The Case of the Ancient Greek Hero." In *A Cultural History of Fame in Antiquity*, edited by Charles W. Hedrick Jr. London: Bloomsbury Academic.

Barker, Ernest. (1918) 2010. *Greek Political Theory: Plato and His Predecessors*. London: Routledge.

Bartels, Myrthe L. 2017. *Plato's Pragmatic Project: A Reading of Plato's Laws*. Hermes Einzelschriften 111. Stuttgart: Franz Steiner Verlag.

Beiner, Ronald. 2010. *Civil Religion: A Dialogue in the History of Political Philosophy*. Cambridge, UK: Cambridge University Press.

Belfiore, E. 1986. "Wine and the Catharsis of Emotions in Plato's *Laws*." *Classical Quarterly* 36 (2): 421–37.

Benardete, Seth. 2000. *Plato's "Laws": The Discovery of Being*. Chicago: University of Chicago Press.

Berlin, Isaiah. 1990. *The Crooked Timber of Humanity: Chapters in the History of Ideas*. Edited by Henry Hardy. Princeton, NJ: Princeton University Press.

Betegh, Gábor. 2016. "Archelaus on Cosmogony and the Origins of Social Institutions." *Oxford Studies in Ancient Philosophy* 51:1–40.

Bloom, Allan. 1968. *The Republic of Plato*. Translated with an Interpretive Essay. New York: Basic Books.

Bobonich, Christopher. 1991. "Persuasion, Compulsion, and Freedom in Plato's *Laws*." *Classical Quarterly* 41:365–88.

Bobonich, Christopher. 1996. "Reading the *Laws*." In *Form and Argument in Late Plato*, edited by Christopher Gill and Mary Margaret McCabe, 249–82. Oxford: Oxford University Press.

Bobonich, Christopher. 2002. *Plato's Utopia Recast: His Later Ethics and Politics*. New York: Oxford University Press.

Bobonich, Christopher, ed. 2010. *Plato's "Laws": A Critical Guide*. Cambridge, UK: Cambridge University Press.

Bobonich, Chris, and Katherine Meadows. "Plato on Utopia." 2020. *The Stanford Encyclopedia of Philosophy* (Winter 2020 ed.), Edward N. Zalta (ed.). https://plato.stanford.edu/archives/win2020/entries/plato-utopia/.

Boegehold, A. L. 1996. "Resistance to Change in the Law of Athens." In *Demokratia: A Conversation on Democracies, Ancient and Modern*, edited by Josiah Ober and Charles Hedrick, 203–14. Princeton, NJ: Princeton University Press.

Bravo, Francisco. 2003. "Le Platon des *Lois* est-il hédoniste?" In Scolnicov and Brisson 2003: 103–15.

Brill, Sara. 2013. "'A Soul Superlatively Natural': Psychic Excess in *Laws* 10." In Recco and Sanday 2013: 189–214.

Brisson, Luc. 1998. "Vernunft, Natur und Gesetz im Zehnten Buch von Platons *Gesetzen*." In Havlíček and Karfík 1998: 182–200.

Brisson, Luc. 2001. "Le Collège de Veille (nukterinòs súllogos)." In Lisi 2001b: 161–77.

Brisson, Luc. 2003. "Les *agronómoi* dans les *Lois* de Platon et leur possible lien avec le *nukterinòs súllogos*." In Scolnicov and Brisson 2003: 221–26.

Brisson, Luc. 2005. "Ethics and Politics in Plato's *Laws*." *Oxford Studies in Ancient Philosophy* 28:93–121.

Brisson, Luc. 2011. "Plato's Laws: A Critical Guide." Review of Christopher Bobonich (ed.), *Plato's "Laws": A Critical Guide*. Cambridge, UK: Cambridge University Press, 2009. *Notre Dame Philosophical Review*, October 17, 2011. https://ndpr.nd.edu/reviews/plato-s-laws-a-critical-guide-2/.

Brisson, Luc. 2019. "Polis as *Kosmos* in Plato's *Laws*." In *Cosmos in the Ancient World*, edited by Philip Sidney Horky, 122–41. Cambridge, UK: Cambridge University Press.

Brisson, Luc. 2020. "Plato's Political Writings: A Utopia?" *Polis* 37:399–420.

Brisson, Luc, and Jean-François Pradeau. 2020. *Lois*. In *Platon: Oeuvres Complètes*, edited by Luc Brisson, 679–1008. Revised edition. Paris: Éditions Flammarion.

Brown, Eric. 2000. "Justice and Compulsion for Plato's Philosopher-Rulers." *Ancient Philosophy* 20:1–17.

Brunt, P. A. 1993. "The Model City of Plato's *Laws*." In *Studies in Greek History and Thought*, 245–81. Oxford: Clarendon Press.

Burnet, J., ed. 2011. *Platonis Opera*. Vol. 5. Oxford: Oxford University Press. First published 1907.

Bury, R. G., trans. 1967–1968. *Plato. Plato in Twelve Volumes*. Vols. 10 and 11. Cambridge, MA: Harvard University Press.

Canevaro, Mirko. 2017. "The Rule of Law as the Measure of Political Legitimacy in the Greek City States." *Hague Journal on the Rule of Law* 9:211–36.

Cherniss, H. 1953. "Review of G. Müller, *Studien zu platonischen Nomoi*." *Gnomon* 25 (6): 367–79.

Cherry, Kevin M. 2013. "Politics and Philosophy in Aristotle's Critique of Plato's *Laws*." In *Natural Right and Political Philosophy: Essays in Honor of Catherine Zuckert and Michael Zuckert*, edited by Ann Ward and Lee Ward, 50–66. Notre Dame, IN: University of Notre Dame Press.

Clark, Randall Baldwin. 2003. *The Law Most Beautiful and Best: Medical Argument and Magical Rhetoric in Plato's Laws*. Lanham, MD: Lexington Books.

Cleary, John J. 2001. "The Role of Theology in Plato's *Laws*." In Lisi 2001b: 125–40.

Cohen, David. 1993. "Law, Autonomy, and Political Community in Plato's *Laws*." *Classical Philology* 88 (4):301–17.

Cooper, John M. 1997. *Plato: Complete Works*. Indianapolis, IN: Hackett.

Cooper, John M. 1999a. "Plato's *Statesman* and Politics." In *Reason and Emotion: Essays on Ancient Moral Psychology and Ethical Theory*, 165–91. Princeton, NJ: Princeton University Press.

Cooper, John M. 1999b. "Plato's Theory of Human Motivation." In Cooper, *Reason and Emotion*, 118–37..

Cusher, Brent Edwin. 2014. "How Does Law Rule? Plato on Habit, Political Education, and Legislation." *Journal of Politics* 76 (4): 1032–44.

de Nicolay, René. 2021. "The Birth of Unlawful Freedom in Plato's *Laws* 3." *Polis* 38:494–511.

des Places, Édouard, and Auguste Diès. 1951–1956. *Platon: Les Lois*. 4 Vols. Paris: Les Belles Lettres.

Dodds, E. R. 1951. *The Greeks and the Irrational*. Berkeley: University of California Press.

England, E. B. 1921. *The Laws of Plato*. 2 vols. Manchester, UK: University of Manchester Press.

Farrar, Cynthia. 2013. "Putting History in Its Place: Plato, Thucydides and the Athenian *Politeia*." In *"Politeia" in Greek and Roman Philosophy*, edited by Verity Harte and Melissa Lane, 32–56. Cambridge, UK: Cambridge University Press.

Ferrari, G. R. F. 1997. "Strauss's Plato." *Arion: A Journal of Humanities and the Classics* 5 (2): 36–65.

Flores, Samuel Ortencio. 2022. "Philosopher-Strangers: *Xenia* and Panhellenism in Plato's *Laws*." *Polis* 39:237–60.

Folch, Marcus. 2015. *The City and the Stage: Performance, Genre, and Gender in Plato's "Laws."* New York: Oxford University Press.

Fossheim, H. J. 2013. "The *Prooimia*, Types of Motivation, and Moral Psychology." In Horn 2013: 87–104.

Frede, D. 2010. "Puppets on Strings: Moral Psychology in *Laws* Books 1 and 2." In Bobonich 2010: 108–26.

Friedland, Eli. 2020. *The Spartan Drama of Plato's* Laws. Lanham, MD: Lexington Books.

Gagarin, Michael. 2020. "Storytelling about the Lawgiver in the Athenian Orators." *Cahiers des études anciennes* 47:33–44.

Gerson, Lloyd. 2003. "*Akrasia* and the Divided Soul in Plato's *Laws*." In Scolnicov and Brisson 2003: 149–54.

Geuss, Raymond. 2005. "Thucydides, Nietzsche, and Williams." In *Outside Ethics*, 219–233. Princeton: Princeton University Press.

Geuss, Raymond. 2008. *Philosophy and Real Politics*. Princeton: Princeton University Press.

Gregory, A. 2000. *Plato's Philosophy of Science*. London: Duckworth.

Griffith, Tom, trans. 2016. *Plato: Laws*. Edited by Malcolm Schofield. Cambridge, UK: Cambridge University Press.

Grube, G. M. A., trans. 1997. "Republic." In Cooper 1997, 971–1223. Revised by C. D. C. Reeve.

Hackforth, R. 1936. "Plato's Theism." *Classical Quarterly* 30 (1): 4–9.

Halliwell, Stephen. 2002. *The Aesthetics of Mimesis: Ancient Texts and Modern Problems*. Princeton, NJ: Princeton University Press.

Halper, E. C. 2003. "Soul, Soul's Motions, and Virtue." In Scolnicov and Brisson 2003: 257–67.

Havlíček, A. and P. Karfík, eds. 1998. *The "Republic" and the "Laws" of Plato: Proceedings of the First Symposium Platonicum Pragense*. Prague: Oikoumene.

Hitz, Zena. 2010. "Degenerate Regimes in Plato's *Republic*." In *The Cambridge Critical Guide to Plato's Republic*, edited by Mark McPherran, 103–31. Cambridge, UK: Cambridge University Press.

Hobbs, Angela. 2000. *Plato and the Hero: Courage, Manliness, and the Impersonal Good*. Cambridge, UK: Cambridge University Press.

Horn, Christoph, ed. 2013. *Platon: Gesetze/Nomoi*. Berlin: Akademie Verlag.

Immerwahr, H. 1973. "Pathology of Power and the Speeches of Thucydides." In *The Speeches in Thucydides*, edited by P. A. Stadter, 16–31. Chapel Hill: University of North Carolina Press.

Irwin, Terence. 2010. "Morality as Law and Morality in the *Laws*." In Bobonich 2010: 92–107.

Johnstone, Steven. 1999. *Disputes and Democracy: The Consequences of Litigation in Ancient Athens*. Austin: University of Texas Press.

Jouët-Pastré, E. 2001. "Le Jeu de l'Écriture du Phèdre aux Lois." In Lisi 2001b: 33–40.

Kahn, Charles. 2004. "From *Republic* to *Laws*: A Discussion of Christopher Bobonich, *Plato's Utopia Recast*." *Oxford Studies in Ancient Philosophy* 26:337–62.

Kamtekar, Rachana. 1997. "Philosophical Rule from the *Republic* to the *Laws*: Commentary on Schofield." Proceedings of the Boston Area Colloquium in Ancient Philosophy 13:242–52.

Kamtekar, Rachana. 2005. "The Profession of Friendship: Callicles, Democratic Politics, and Rhetorical Education in Plato's *Gorgias*." *Ancient Philosophy* 25, no. 2 (Fall): 319–39.

Kamtekar, Rachana. 2010. "Psychology and the Inculcation of Virtue in Plato's *Laws*." In Bobonich 2010.

Klosko, George. 1988. "The Nocturnal Council in Plato's *Laws*." *Political Studies* 36:74–88.

Klosko, George. 2006. *The Development of Plato's Political Theory*. 2nd ed. New York: Oxford University Press.

Klosko, George. 2008. "Knowledge and Law in Plato's *Laws*." *Political Studies* 56 (2): 456–74.

Klosko, George. 2011. "Knowledge and Law in the *Laws*: A Response to Xavier Marques." *Political Studies* 59:204–8.

Knorr, Wilbur Richard. 1975. *The Evolution of the Euclidean Elements*. Dordrecht: D. Reidel.

Kochin, Michael S. 2002. *Gender and Rhetoric in Plato's Political Thought*. Cambridge, UK: Cambridge University Press.

Kraut, Richard. 2010. "Ordinary Virtue from the *Phaedo* to the *Laws*." In Bobonich 2010: 51–70.

Kuhn, Helmut. 1941. "The True Tragedy: On the Relationship between Greek Tragedy and Plato, I." *Harvard Studies in Classical Philology* 52:1–40.

Kuhn, Helmut. 1942. "The True Tragedy: On the Relationship between Greek Tragedy and Plato, II." *Harvard Studies in Classical Philology* 53:37–88.

Kurke, Leslie. 2013. "Imagining Chorality: Wonder, Plato's Puppets, and Moving Statues." In *Performance and Culture in Plato's "Laws"*, edited by Anastasia-Erasmia Peponi, 123–70. Cambridge, UK: Cambridge University Press.

Laks, André. 1990. "Legislation and Demiurgy: On the Relationship between Plato's 'Republic' and 'Laws.'" *Classical Antiquity* 9 (2): 209–29.

Laks, André. 1991. "L'utopie Législative de Platon." *Revue Philosophique de la France et de l'Étranger* 18 (4): 417–28.

Laks, André. 2000. "The *Laws*." In *The Cambridge History of Greek and Roman Political Thought*, edited by C. Rowe and M. Schofield, 258–92. New York: Cambridge University Press.

Laks, André. 2001. "In What Sense Is the City of the Laws a Second-Best One?" In Lisi 2001b: 107–14.

Laks, André. 2005. *Médiation et coercition: Pour une lecture des Lois de Platon.* Villeneuve d'Ascq, France: Presses universitaires du Septentrion.

Laks, André. 2010. "Plato's 'Truest Tragedy': *Laws*, Book 7, 817a–d." In Bobonich 2010: 217–31.

Laks, André. 2012. "Temporalité et utopie: Remarques herméneutiques sur la question de la possibilité des cités platonicienne." In *Utopia, Ancient and Modern: Contributions to the History of a Political Dream*, edited by F. Lisi, 19–37. Sankt Augustin, Germany: Academia Verlag.

Laks, André. 2013. "Private Matters in Plato's *Laws*." In Horn 2013: 165–88.

Laks, André. 2022. *Plato's Second Republic: An Essay on the Laws.* Princeton, NJ: Princeton University Press.

Landauer, Matthew. 2022. "Drinking Parties Correctly Ordered: Plato on Mass Participation and the Necessity of Rule." *Journal of Politics* 84 (4) (October): 2011–2022.

Lane, Melissa. 2011. "Persuasion et force dans la politique platonicienne." In *Aglaïa: Autour de Platon: Mélanges offerts à Monique Dixsaut*, edited by A. Brancacci, D. El Murr, and D. P. Taormina, 133–66. Paris: Vrin.

Lanni, Adriaan. 2012. "Publicity and the Courts of Classical Athens." *Yale Journal of Law and the Humanities* 24: 119–35.

Larivée, Annie. 2003a. "Du vin pour le Collège de veille? Mise en lumière d'un lien occulté entre le Choeur de Dionysos et le *nukterinòs sullogos* dans les *Lois* de Platon." *Phronesis* 48 (1): 29–53.

Larivée, Annie. 2003b. "L'incarnation legislative du soin de l'âme dans les *Lois*: Un heritage socratique." In Scolnicov and Brisson 2003: 98–102.

Levin, Susan B. 2010. "Politics and Medicine: Plato's Final Word Part II: A Rivalry Dissolved: The Restoration of Medicine's *Technê* Status in the Laws." *Polis* 27 (2): 193–221.

Levin, Susan B. 2014. *Plato's Rivalry with Medicine: A Struggle and Its Dissolution.* Oxford: Oxford University Press.

Lewis, V. Bradley. 1998. "The Nocturnal Council and Platonic Political Philosophy." *History of Political Thought* 19 (1): 1–20.

Lewis, V. Bradley. 2009a. "Higher Law and the Rule of Law: The Platonic Origin of an Ideal." *Pepperdine Law Review* 36:631–59.

Lewis, V. Bradley. 2009b. "'Reason Striving to Become Law': Nature and Law in Plato's *Laws*." *American Journal of Jurisprudence* 54:67–91.

Lewis, V. Bradley. 2010. "Gods for the City and Beyond: Civil Religion in Plato's *Laws*." In *Civil Religion in Political Thought: Its Perennial Questions and Enduring Relevance in North America*, edited by Ronald Weed and John von Heyking, 19–46. Washington, DC: Catholic University of America Press.

Lewis, V. Bradley. 2012. "The Limits of Reform: Punishment and Reason in Plato's Second-Best City." In *The Philosophy of Punishment and the History of Political Thought*, edited by Peter Koritansky, 10–32. Columbia: University of Missouri Press.

Lisi, Francisco L. 1998. "Die Stellung der *Nomoi* in Platons Staatslehre: Erwägungen zur Beziehung zwischen *Nomoi* und *Politeia*." In Havlíček and Karfík 1998: 89–105.

Lisi, Francisco L. 2001a. "Contemporary Readings of Plato's *Laws*." In *Plato's "Laws" and Its Historical Significance*, edited by Francisco L. Lisi, 11–24. Sankt Augustin, Germany: Academia Verlag.

Lisi, Francisco L., ed. 2001b. *Plato's "Laws" and Its Historical Significance*. Sankt Augustin, Germany: Academia Verlag.

Lisi, Francisco L. 2004. "Héros, dieux, et philosophes." *Revue des Études Anciennes* 106 (1): 5–22.

Lutz, Mark. 2012. *Divine Law and Political Philosophy in Plato's Laws*. DeKalb: Northern Illinois University Press.

Lutz, Mark. 2015. "The Argument and the Action of Plato's *Laws*." In *Brill's Companion to Leo Strauss's Writings on Classical Political Thought*, edited by Timothy W. Burns, 424–40. Leiden: Brill.

MacIntyre, Alasdair. 1984. *After Virtue: A Study in Moral Theory*. Notre Dame, IN: University of Notre Dame Press.

Mansfield, Harvey C., trans. 1998. *Niccolò Machiavelli: The Prince*. 2nd ed. Chicago: University of Chicago Press.

Mara, Gerald M. 2008. *The Civic Conversations of Thucydides and Plato: Classical Political Philosophy and the Limits of Democracy*. Albany: State University of New York Press.

Marquez, Xavier. 2011. "Knowledge and Law in Plato's *Statesman* and *Laws*: A Response to Klosko." *Political Studies* 59:188–203.

Masters, Roger D. 1984. "Human Nature and Political Theory: Can Biology Contribute to the Study of Politics?" *Politics and the Life Sciences* 2 (2): 120–50.

Mayhew, R. 2008. *Plato: Laws 10*. Oxford: Oxford University Press.

Mayhew, R. 2010. "The Theology of the *Laws*." In Bobonich 2010: 197–216.

Meilaender, Peter C. 2008. "Review of C. J. Rowe, *Plato and the Art of Philosophical Writing*. Cambridge/New York: Cambridge University Press, 2007." *Bryn Mawr Classical Review* https://bmcr.brynmawr.edu/2008/2008.12.22/.

Melzer, Arthur M. 2014. *Philosophy between the Lines: The Lost History of Esoteric Writing*. Chicago: University of Chicago Press.

Menn, S. P. 1995. *Plato on God as Nous*. Carbondale: Southern Illinois University Press.

Millender, E. G. 2002. "*Nomos Despotés*: Spartan Obedience and Athenian Lawfulness in Fifth-Century Thought." In *Oikistes: Studies in Constitutions, Colonies, and Military Power in the Ancient World Offered in Honor of A. J. Graham*, edited by Vanessa B. Gorman and Eric W. Robinson, 33–59. Leiden: Brill.

Minowitz, Peter. 2009. *Straussophobia: Defending Leo Strauss against Shadia Drury and Other Accusers*. Lanham, MD: Rowman and Littlefield.

Mohr, Richard D. 1985. *Platonic Cosmology*. Philosophia Antiqua, vol. 42. Leiden: Brill.

Morrow, Glenn. 1939. *Plato's Law of Slavery in Its Relation to Greek Law*. Urbana: University of Illinois Press.

Morrow, Glenn. 1954. "The Demiurge in Politics: The *Timaeus* and the *Laws*." *Proceedings of the American Philosophical Association* 27:5–23.

Morrow, Glenn. 1960. *Plato's Cretan City: A Historical Interpretation of the "Laws"*. Princeton, NJ: Princeton University Press.

Mouze, L. 1998. "La dernière tragédie de Platon." *Revue de Philosophie Ancienne* 16 (2): 79–101.

Nagy, Gregory. 1983. "Poet and Tyrant: *Theognidea* 39–52, 1081–1082b." *Classical Antiquity* 2 (1): 82–91.

Nails, Debra, and Holger Thesleff. 2003. "Early Academic Editing: Plato's *Laws*." In Scolnicov and Brisson 2003: 14–29.

Neschke-Hentschke, A. 2001. "Loi de la nature, loi de la cite: Le fondement transcendant de l'ordre politique dans les *Lois* de Platon et chez John Locke." In Lisi 2001b: 255–73.

Nightingale, Andrea W. 1996. "Plato on the Origins of Evil: The Statesman Myth Reconsidered." *Ancient Philosophy* 16 (1): 65–91.

Nightingale, Andrea W. 1999a. "Historiography and Cosmology in Plato's *Laws*." *Ancient Philosophy* 19 (2): 299–325.

Nightingale, Andrea W. 1999b. "Plato's Lawcode in Context: Rule by Written Law in Athens and Magnesia." *Classical Quarterly* 49 (1): 100–122.

Nussbaum, Martha C. 1980. "Shame, Separateness, and Political Unity: Aristotle's Criticism of Plato." In *Essays on Aristotle's Ethics*, edited by Amélie Oksenberg Rorty, 395–435. Berkeley: University of California Press.

Ober, Josiah. 1989. *Mass and Elite in Democratic Athens: Rhetoric, Ideology, and the Power of the People*. Princeton, NJ: Princeton University Press.

Ober, Josiah. 1998. *Political Dissent in Democratic Athens: Intellectual Critics of Popular Rule*. Princeton, NJ: Princeton University Press.

Ober, Josiah. 2005a. "The Athenian Debate over Civic Education." In *Athenian Legacies: Essays on the Politics of Going on Together*, 28–56. Princeton, NJ: Princeton University Press.

Ober, Josiah. 2005b. *Athenian Legacies: Essays on the Politics of Going on Together*. Princeton, NJ: Princeton University Press.

O'Meara, Dominic J. 2017. *Cosmology and Politics in Plato's Later Works*. Cambridge, UK: Cambridge University Press.

Pangle, Thomas L. 1976. "The Political Psychology of Religion in Plato's *Laws*." *American Political Science Review* 70 (4): 1059–77.

Pangle, Thomas L., trans. 1980. *The "Laws" of Plato*. Chicago: University of Chicago Press.

Pangle, Lorraine Smith. 2014. *Virtue Is Knowledge: The Moral Foundations of Socratic Political Philosophy*. Chicago: University of Chicago Press.

Papadis, Dimetris. 1998. "Regent und Gesetz in Platons Dialogen *Politeia* und *Nomoi*." In Havlíček and Karfík 1998: 106–16.

Parens, Joshua. 1995. *Metaphysics as Rhetoric: Alfarabi's Summary of Plato's "Laws"*. Albany: State University of New York Press.

Parry, Richard D. 2003. "The Cause of Motion in *Laws* X and of Disorderly Motion in *Timaeus*." In Scolnicov and Brisson, 268–75.

Peponi, Anastasia-Erasmia, ed. 2013. *Performance and Culture in Plato's Laws*. Cambridge, UK: Cambridge University Press.

Pesic, Peter. 2003. *Abel's Proof: An Essay on the Sources and Meaning of Mathematical Unsolvability*. Cambridge, MA: MIT Press.

Piérart, M. 1974. *Platon et la cité grecque: théorie et réalité dans la Constitution des 'Lois'*. Brussels: Palais des Académies.

Pierris, A. L. 1998. "The Metaphysics of Politics in the *Politeia*, *Politikos*, and *Nomoi* Dialogue Group." In Havlíček and Karfík 1998: 117–45.

Popper, Karl. 2011. *The Open Society and Its Enemies*. Routledge Classics. London and New York: Routledge.

Pradeau, J.-F. 1998. "L'Exégète Ennuyé: Une Introduction à la Lecture des *Lois* de Platon." In Havlíček and Karfík 1998: 154–81.

Prauscello, Lucia. 2014. *Performing Citizenship in Plato's Laws*. Cambridge, UK: Cambridge University Press.

Raaflaub, Kurt A. 2004. *The Discovery of Freedom in Ancient Greece*. Chicago: University of Chicago Press.

Rabieh, Linda R. 2020. "Gender, Education, and Enlightened Politics in Plato's *Laws*." *American Political Science Review* 114 (3): 911–22.

Recco, Gregory, and Eric Sanday, eds. 2013. *Plato's* Laws: *Force and Truth in Politics*. Bloomington: Indiana University Press.

Redfield, James. 1985. "Herodotus the Tourist." *Classical Philology* 80:97–118.

Reeve, C.D.C. 1997. trans. "Cratylus." In Cooper, 101–56.

Reid, Jeremy. 2020. "The Offices of Magnesia." *Polis* 37 (3): 567–89.

Roberts, Jean. 1987. "Plato on the Causes of Wrongdoing in the *Laws*." *Ancient Philosophy* 7:23–37.

Roochnik, David. 2013. "The 'Serious Play' of Book 7 of Plato's *Laws*." In Recco and Sanday 2013: 144–53.

Rowe, C. J. 2003. "Socrates, the Laws, and the *Laws*." In Scolnicov and Brisson 2003: 87–97.

Rowe, C. J. 2007. *Plato and the Art of Philosophical Writing*. Cambridge, UK: Cambridge University Press.

Rowe, C. J. 2010. "The Relationship of the *Laws* to Other Dialogues: A Proposal." In Bobonich 2010: 29–50.

Russell, Frank S. 2000. *Information Gathering in Classical Greece*. Ann Arbor: University of Michigan Press.

Rusten, Jeffrey. 2015. "*Kinesis* in the Preface to Thucydides." In *Kinesis: The Ancient Depiction of Gesture, Motion, and Emotion*, edited by Christina Clark, Edith Foster, and Judith P. Hallett, 27–40. Ann Arbor: University of Michigan Press.

Rutenber, Culbert Gerow. 1946. *The Doctrine of the Imitation of God in Plato*. New York: King's Crown Press.

Sagar, Rahul, and Andrew Sabl, eds. 2018. *Realism in Political Theory*. London: Routledge.

Salem, Eric. 2013. "The Long and Winding Road: Impediments to Inquiry in Book 1 of the *Laws*." In Recco and Sanday: 48–59.

Salkever, Stephen G. 2002. "The Deliberative Model of Democracy and Aristotle's Ethics of Natural Questions." In *Aristotle and Modern Politics: The Persistence of Political Philosophy*, edited by Aristide Tessitore, 342–74. Notre Dame, IN: University of Notre Dame Press.

Sallis, John. 2013. "On Beginning after the Beginning." In Recco and Sanday 2013: 72–80.

Samaras, Thanassis. 2002. *Plato on Democracy*. New York: Peter Lang.

Santas, G. 2003. "Justice and Gender in the *Laws* and in the *Republic*." In Scolnicov and Brisson 2003: 237–42.

Sassi, Maria Michela. 2008. "The Self, the Soul, and the Individual in the City of the *Laws*." *Oxford Studies in Ancient Philosophy* 35:125–48.

Saunders, Trevor J. 1973. "Penology and Eschatology in Plato's *Timaeus* and *Laws*." *Classical Quarterly* 23 (2): 232–44.

Saunders, Trevor J. 1991. *Plato's Penal Code: Tradition, Controversy, and Reform in Greek Penology*. Oxford: Oxford University Press.

Saunders, Trevor J. 2001. "*Epieikeia*: Plato and the Controversial Virtue of the Greeks." In Lisi 2001b: 65–93.

Sauvé Meyer, Susan. 2003. "The Moral Dangers of Labour and Commerce in Plato's *Laws*." In Scolnicov and Brisson 2003: 207–14.

Sauvé Meyer, Susan. 2011. "Legislation as a Tragedy: On Plato's *Laws* VII, 817b-d." In *Plato and the Poets*, edited by Pierre Destrée and Fritz-Gregor Hermann, 387–402. Leiden: Brill.

Sauvé Meyer, Susan, ed. 2015. *Plato: Laws 1 and 2*. Clarendon Plato Series. Oxford: Oxford University Press.

Sauvé Meyer, Susan. 2021. "Civic Freedom in Plato's *Laws*." *Polis* 38:512–34.

Schlosser, Joel Alden. 2023. "'What Really Happened': Varieties of Realism in Thucydides' *History*." In *The Cambridge Companion to Thucydides*, edited by P. Low, 301–16. Cambridge: Cambridge University Press.

Schofield, Malcolm. 1978. Review of Leo Strauss, *The Argument and the Action of Plato's "Laws"*, 1975. *Classical Review* 28 (1): 170.

Schofield, Malcolm. 1999. "The Disappearing Philosopher King." In *Saving the City: Philosopher Kings and Other Classical Paradigms*, 28–45. London: Routledge.

Schofield, Malcolm. 2003. "Religion and Philosophy in the *Laws*." In Scolnicov and Brisson 2003, 1–13.

Schofield, Malcolm. 2006. *Plato: Political Philosophy*. Oxford: Oxford University Press.

Schofield, Malcolm. 2010. "The *Laws'* Two Projects." In Bobonich 2010: 12–28.

Schofield, Malcolm. 2012. "Injury, Injustice, and the Involuntary in the *Laws*." In *Virtue and Happiness: Essays in Honour of Julia Annas*, edited by Rachana Kamtekar, 103–14. Supplementary Volume. *Oxford Studies in Ancient Philosophy*.

Schofield, Malcolm. 2013. "Friendship and Justice in the *Laws*." In *The Platonic Art of Philosophy*, edited by George Boys-Stones, Dimitri El Murr, and Christopher Gill, 283–97. Cambridge, UK: Cambridge University Press.

Schofield, Malcolm. 2016. "Plato's Marionette." *Rhizomata* 4 (2): 128–53.

Schofield, Malcolm. 2021. "Plato, Xenophon, and the Laws of Lycurgus." *Polis* 38:450–72.

Schöpsdau, Klaus. 2003. *Platon: Nomoi (Gesetze) Buch IV–VII*. Göttingen: Vandenhoeck and Ruprecht.

Schöpsdau, Klaus. 2011. *Platon: Nomoi (Gesetze) Buch VIII–XII*. Göttingen: Vandenhoeck and Ruprecht.

Scolnicov, Samuel. 2003. "Pleasure and Responsibility in Plato's *Laws*." In Scolnicov and Brisson 2003: 122–27.

Scolnicov, Samuel, and Luc Brisson, eds. 2003. *Plato's "Laws": From Theory into Practice*. Sankt Augustin, Germany: Academia Verlag.

Sedley, David. 1999. "The Ideal of Godlikeness." In *Plato 2: Ethics, Politics, Religion and the Soul*, edited by Gail Fine, 309–28. Oxford: Oxford University Press.

Sedley, David. 2013. "The Atheist Underground." In *"Politeia" in Greek and Roman Philosophy*, edited by Verity Harte and Melissa Lane, 329–48. Cambridge, UK: Cambridge University Press.

Shaw, J. Clerk. 2015. *Plato's Anti-hedonism and the Protagoras*. Cambridge, UK: Cambridge University Press.

Stalley, R. F. 1983. *An Introduction to Plato's* Laws. Indianapolis, IN: Hackett.

Stalley, R. F. 1994. "Persuasion in Plato's *Laws*." *History of Political Thought* 15 (2): 157–77.

Strauss, Leo. 1964a. "On Plato's *Republic*." In *The City and Man*, 50–138. Chicago: University of Chicago Press.

Strauss, Leo. 1964b. *The City and Man*. Chicago: University of Chicago Press.

Strauss, Leo. 1975. *The Argument and the Action of Plato's "Laws"*. Chicago: University of Chicago Press.

Strauss, Leo. 1987. "Plato." In *History of Political Philosophy*, edited by Leo Strauss and Joseph Cropsey, 3rd ed., 33–89. Chicago: University of Chicago Press.

Strauss, Leo. 1988. "What Is Political Philosophy?" In *What Is Political Philosophy? And Other Studies*, 9–55. Chicago: University of Chicago Press. (Original work published in 1959, The Free Press, Glencoe, IL).

Strauss, Leo. 2004. "The Place of the Doctrine of Providence According to Maimonides." *Review of Metaphysics* 57 (3): 537–49.

Teegarden, David. 2013. *Death to Tyrants! Ancient Greek Democracy and the Struggle against Tyranny*. Princeton, NJ: Princeton University Press.

Thompson, Michael. 2008. *Life and Action: Elementary Structures of Practice and Practical Thought*. Cambridge, MA: Harvard University Press.

Tong, Zhichao. 2020. "The Imperative of Competition: Epistemic Democracy in the International Context." PhD diss., University of Toronto.

Vince, J. H., trans. 1986. *Demosthenes: Orations XXI–XXVI*. Loeb Classical Library 299. Cambridge, MA: Harvard University Press.

Waldron, Jeremy. 1995. "What Plato Would Allow." *Nomos* 37:138–78.

Waugh, Joanne. 2001. "Oral Preambles and Written Laws: The Dialogic Character of the *Laws* and Lawfulness." In Lisi 2001b: 27–31.

Weiss, Rosalyn. 2006. *The Socratic Paradox and Its Enemies*. Chicago: University of Chicago Press.

Wilburn, Joshua. 2013. "Moral Education and the Spirited Part of the Soul in Plato's *Laws*." *Oxford Studies in Ancient Philosophy* 45:63–102.

Williams, Bernard. 1981. "Internal and External Reasons." In *Moral Luck: Philosophical Papers 1973–1980*, 101–13. Cambridge, UK: Cambridge University Press.

Williams, Bernard. 1993. *Shame and Necessity*. Berkeley: University of California Press.

Williams, Bernard. 1996. "The *Women of Trachis*: Fictions, Pessimism, Ethics." In *The Greeks and Us: Essays in Honor of Arthur W. H. Adkins*, edited by Robert B. Louden and Paul Schollmeier, 43–53. Chicago: University of Chicago Press.

Wu, Tim. 2020. "What Really Saved the Republic from Trump?" *New York Times*, December 10, 2020.

Zuckert, Catherine H. 2009. *Plato's Philosophers: The Coherence of the Dialogues*. Chicago: University of Chicago Press.

Zuckert, Catherine H. 2013. "On the Implications of Human Mortality: Legislation, Education, and Philosophy in Book 9 of Plato's *Laws*." In Recco and Sanday 2013: 169–88.

Zuckert, Michael. 2013. "It Is Difficult for a City with Good Laws to Come into Existence: On Book 4." In Recco and Sanday 2013: 86–104.

Subject Index

For the benefit of digital users, indexed terms that span two pages (e.g., 52–53) may, on occasion, appear on only one of those pages.

Index Locorum

For the benefit of digital users, indexed terms that span two pages (e.g., 52–53) may, on occasion, appear on only one of those pages.